# DICKENS STUDIES ANNUAL
## Essays on Victorian Fiction

# DICKENS STUDIES ANNUAL
## Essays on Victorian Fiction

EDITORS

Stanley Friedman
Edward Guiliano
Michael Timko

# DICKENS STUDIES ANNUAL

## Essays on Victorian Fiction

VOLUME
26

*Edited by*
Stanley Friedman, Edward Guiliano, and Michael Timko

AMS PRESS
NEW YORK

DICKENS STUDIES ANNUAL
ISSN 0084-9812

**COPYRIGHT** © 1998 by AMS Press, Inc.
*Dickens Studies Annual: Essays on Victorian Fiction* is published in cooperation with Queens College and the Graduate Center, CUNY.

**International Standard Book Number**
**Series: 0-404-18520-7**
**Vol. 26:0-404-18546-0**

*Dickens Studies Annual: Essays on Victorian Fiction* welcomes essay and monograph-length contributions on Dickens as well as other Victorian novelists and on the history of aesthetics of Victorian fiction. All manuscripts should be double-spaced, including notes, which should be grouped at the end of the submission, and should be prepared according to the format used in this journal, which follows *The MLA Manual of Style*. An editorial decision can usually be reached more quickly if two copies are submitted. The preferred editions for citations from Dickens's works are the Clarendon and the Norton Critical when available, otherwise the Oxford Illustrated or the Penguin.

Please send submissions to the Editors, *Dickens Studies Annual,* Room 1522, Graduate School and University Center, City University of New York, 33 West 42nd Street, New York, N.Y, 10036; please send subscription inquiries to AMS Press, Inc., 56 East 13th Street, New York, N.Y. 10003.

Manufactured in the United States of America

All AMS books are printed on acid-free paper that meets the guidelines for performance and durability of the Committee on Production Guidelines for Book Longevity of the Council on Library Resources.

# Contents

# List of Illustrations

# Preface

In preparing this annual volume, we have been helped by many persons. We are grateful to our editorial and advisory boards for their suggestions, and we especially thank the scholars and critics who have generously read and evaluated submissions, for we believe that outside assessments of articles allow *Dickens Studies Annual* to remain receptive to extremely different topics and a wide variety of approaches. In addition, we greatly appreciate the comprehensive review essay provided by Professor Joseph W. Childers.

For various kinds of assistance, we are indebted to the following administrators: President Frances Degen Horowitz, Provost Geoffrey Marshall, and PhD Program in English Executive Officer William P. Kelly, all of The Graduate School and University Center, CUNY; President Allen Lee Sessoms, Provost John A. Thorpe, Dean Raymond F. Erickson, and Department of English Chair Steven F. Kruger, all of Queens College, CUNY; and President Matthew Schure, New York Institute of Technology.

We thank Gabriel Hornstein, President of AMS Press, for his consistent belief in the importance of our enterprise, and we commend our editor at AMS Press, Jack Hopper, for his exemplary efficiency and good humor. Finally, we acknowledge with gratitude the work of our editorial assistant for *Dickens Studies Annual,* Anne Kincaid, who cheerfully performed many of the tasks needed to keep our vessel on course.

# Notes on Contributors

BARBARA J. BLACK is an Associate Professor of English at Skidmore College. Her work has appeared in such journals as *Victorian Poetry, Nineteenth-Century Contexts,* and *In-between: Essays and Studies in Literary Criticism.* Her book, *On Exhibit: Victorians and Their Museums,* is forthcoming from the University Press of Virginia.

JOEL J. BRATTIN is Associate Professor of English at Worcester Polytechnic Institute. He is on the editorial boards of *Nineteenth-Century Prose* and the California Carlyle edition, is a contributing editor for *UniVibes,* and is an advisory editor for the *Charles Dickens* volume in the Oxford Author Companions series. He is editing *Our Mutual Friend* for the Everyman Dickens series, and creating a Dickens CD-ROM for Primary Source Media.

TIMOTHY L. CARENS received his PhD from the Department of English at New York University. He is currently working on a book entitlted "Imperial Plots: Civilizing Missions in Victorian Domestic Narratives."

JOSEPH W. CHILDERS is Associate Professor of English at the University of California, Riverside. He is the author of *Novel Possibilities: Fiction and the Formation of Early Victorian Culture* (1995) and is co-editor of *The Columbia Dictionary of Modern Literary and Cultural Criticism* (1995).

STEPHEN HAKE is currently the scholar in residence at the Rivendell Study Center (Penn State) in Le Raysville, Pennsylvania. For many years he taught English literature at Sun Yat-Sen University in Kaohsiung, Taiwan. He is seeking to develop alternatives to institutional higher education.

MARK M. HENNELLY, JR. is Chair of the English Department at California State University, Sacramento, and has written numerous essays on Victorian fiction. His most recent work appears in *The Thomas Hardy Year Book (Tess), Nineteenth-Century Contexts* (Little Dorritt), *Journal of Evolutionary Psychology* (*Oliver Twist*), and *Dickens Quarterly* (*Our Mutual Friend*).

PAUL A. KRAN is a doctoral candidate in the Program in Comparative Literature at Rutgers University. He is currently completing a dissertation on representations of the figure of Salomé in fin-de-siècle literature, opera, and visual art.

JOSEPH LITVAK is Professor of English at Bowdoin College. He is the author of *Strange Gourmets: Sophistication, Theory, and the Novel* (1997) and *Caught in the Act: Theatricality in the Nineteenth-Century English Novel* (1992).

TERESA MANGUM is an Associate Professor of English at the University of Iowa. Her first book, *Married, Middlebrow, and Militant: Sarah Grand the New Woman Novel*, is forthcoming from the University of Michigan Press. Her current work examines Victorian representations of aging.

JEROME MECKIER is Professor of English at the University of Kentucky and a former president of the Dickens Society. He has written two books on Dickens—*Hidden Rivalries in Victorian Fiction: Dickens, Realism, and Revaluation* (1987) and *Innocent Abroad: Charles Dickens's American Engagements* (1990)—and numerous articles, including contributions to volumes one and twenty-one of *Dickens Studies Annual*.

KATHLEEN SELL is an Assistant Professor of English at Riverside City College, California, and is completing her dissertation on gender and narrative voice in the nineteenth-century novel at Claremont Graduate University.

JON SURGAL is completing a book to be called "The Dickens Orphans." His peculiar fascination with orphans extends to his work in television, from the CBS serial adaptation of Lucy Maud Montgomery's *Emily of New Moon*, on which he served as story editor, to the NBC series *Muggsy*, which he created.

LISA SURRIDGE is an Assistant Professor of English at the University of Victoria, Canada. She has published articles on theatricality in the works of Charlotte Brontë and Geraldine Jewsbury; and on the representation of domestic violence in novels by the Brontës, Wilkie Collins, and Charles Dickens. She is co-editor with Richard Nemesvari of M. E. Braddon's sensation novel *Aurora Floyd*, forthcoming from Broadview Press.

JEREMY TAMBLING is Professor in Comparative Literature in the University of Hong Kong. He is author of *Dickens, Violence, and the Modern State* (1995) and edited the Penguin edition of *David Copperfield*. His most recent book is *Opera and the Culture of Fascism* (1996). Currently, he is working on Henry James.

VALERIE WAINWRIGHT, a tenured lecturer at the Faculty of Letters and Philosophy of the University of Florence, has written essays on Defoe and Gaskell as well as on historical subjects. At present she is completing a study of the ways in which issues involving notions of character, identity, and morality are explored in the nineteenth-century English novel.

ANNA WILSON has published three novels—*Cactus, Altogether Elsewhere,* and *Hatching Stones.* She has recently completed a study of feminist interventions in the public sphere, *Persuasive Fictions and Perceived Changes: Feminist Narrative and Critical Myth.* She currently teaches American literature, women's studies, and lesbian and gay studies at Bowdoin College.

# Courtly Wild Men and Carnivalesque Pig Women in Dickens and Hardy

## Mark M. Hennelly, Jr.

> The emphasis, in the Realist novel, on human reason can be tied to the absence or suppression of the play spirit in so many fictional worlds: excessive rationalization undermines the spontaneity and freedom inherent in the playful exchange of human desire (170).—Nancy Morrow, *Dreadful Games: The Play of Desire in the Nineteenth Century Novel*

> Renaissance grotesque imagery, directly related to folk carnival culture, as we find it in Rabelais, Cervantes, and Shakespeare, influenced the entire realistic literature of the following centuries. Realism of grand style, in Stendhal, Balzac, Hugo, and Dickens, for instance, was always linked directly or indirectly with the Renaissance tradition (52).—Mikhail Bakhtin, *Rabelais and His World*

The value of seeing Dickensian play scenes in the comparative context of play motifs flourishing throughout nineteenth-century fiction becomes unpredictably clear upon reviewing James Ivory's 1986 film version of E. M. Forster's *A Room With a View* because it provides a pictorial reprise of the literary playfulness that Dickens typifies, transforms, and transcends. The specific sequence which best clarifies this play significance begins with Lucy Honeychurch, her mother, and her financé Mr. Cecil Vyse surprising the naked George Emerson, Lucy's brother Freddy, and the Reverend Mr. Beebe as they play water soccer and other aquatic games in a local swimming hole, their carnivalesque "Garden of Eden." In the film, this unexpectedly ribald recognition scene provocatively dissolves into Lucy's piano playing, followed by the portentous lawn-tennis match; and then the sequence is climaxed by Lucy's momentous decision to call off her wedding with the pedantic Vyse because he "wouldn't play tennis with Freddy" (259; ch. 17).[1] Though himself "painfully bewildered" by Lucy's unreasonable reasoning, Cecil's response sustains her rejection of him by revealing, again, that his unplayful

1

posturing indeed places a symbolic vise on all around him (thereby proving
his own moral vice): "I never do play tennis . . . I could never play. I don't
understand a word you say" (259; ch. 17). On the tennis court, this killjoy's
play would surely result in a love match; in the love court, Lucy awards his
unplayful discourse with the same low score.[2]

Reflected in Lucy's eagerly laughing rather than demurely lowered eyes is
the view that the playful skinnydipping becomes an epiphany for her just as
we will see the Wild Man's mating display become one for Dickens' Mrs.
Nickleby. For Lucy, it "had been a call to the blood and to the relaxed will,
a passing benediction whose influence did not pass, a holiness, a spell, a
momentary chalice of youth" (204; ch. 12). In fact, her approving view of
all the playfully exposed flesh is related to the carnivalesque tradition so dear
to Dickens, and here it immediately prepares for the courtship foreplay latent
in the piano playing and the tennis match. During the first of these scenes,
Lucy "played from memory the music of the enchanted garden" from Gluck's
*Armide* as George, her true love, listens unobserved and while the serpent
Cecil, displaying his "discontent, called out: 'Now play us the other garden—the one in *Parsifal.*' " At his provoking suggestion, flustered Lucy
"played a few bars of the Flower Maidens' song very badly" (235–36; ch.
15). Significant here is the fact that, as in so many nineteenth-century novels,
playing music echoes the old romance and carnivalesque motif of the *music of
the flesh,* and in this scene more particularly, the music echoes the sublimated
amatory differences between the carnal delights of George and Gluck's Re-
naud in his garden and the chaste devotion of Cecil and Wagner's Parsifal,
the Pure Fool, in his *hortus conclusus.*

The erotic nuances of this scene subsequently give way to the tennis court
and its more energetic suggestions of a love game and courting ritual just like
"The Fives Court" we will discuss in *Nickleby*. Never realizing "that it may
be an act of kindness in a bad player to make up a fourth," Cecil refuses to
play, while the chivalric (and carnal) George, much like his patron saint,
aggressively assumes the "service" position and "surprised" his fair Lucy
"by his anxiety to win." Indeed, George "wanted to live now, to win at
tennis, to stand for all he was worth in the sun." It is, of course, playfully
ironic that, as Cecil reads blissfully from Miss Lavish's fictional re-creation
of that momentous afternoon in Florence when George first kissed Lucy, his
"metacommentary" so closely counterpoints the game that it prompts Lucy
to "miss her stroke." Thereupon, after besting Lucy in the match, George
courteously "jumped over the net and sat at her feet" (238–39; ch. 15), and
they "merrily" engage in thinly-disguised and displaced verbal love play
over their tennis play.

The more one views Ivory's film or reads Forster's retrospective novel
with an eye toward such play motifs, the more one sees that, as in Dickens'

own pivotal window scenes, the central scopic metaphor itself is often made manifest in terms of liminal or threshold play: "One could play a new game with the view" (238; ch. 15). In short, what one ultimately sees in *A Room With a View* is a review of the centrality of play in nineteenth-century culture—a centrality perhaps finally due to the fact that at its most tolerantly self-critical moments the culture exhibited what Morse Peckham calls "the gratification of the orientative drive" toward "continuous transvaluation" (365, 367), that is, toward a kaleidoscopic vision which flexibly views life's values as pluralistic and heterogeneous like Dickens' favorite game "called Yes and No" (*Christmas Books* 55).[3] There is play in life; and so satisfaction, if not survival, demands play from us. From a different angle, the folklorist Thomas Burns discovers this same eye-opening vision dramatized in the nineteenth-century board game, "The Checkered Game of Life," whose popularity in a minor way also provides a context for the enormous popularity of Dickens' spectacular *theatri mundi*.[4] Significant counterpointing between backgammon and Harthouse's courting and thus the more subtle interplay between various epistemological views and emotional gambits occur, for example, in this fairly characteristic interlude from *Hard Times,* where Dickens plays a three-ring-circus "game with the view" (including the reader's) not unlike Forster's:

> "I cannot bear to see you so, Sir." said Mrs. Sparsit. "Try a hand at backgammon, Sir, as you used to do when I had the honour of living under your roof." "I haven't played backgammon, ma'am," said Mr. Bounderby, "since that time." "No, Sir," said Mrs. Sparsit, soothingly, "I am aware that you have not. I remember that Miss Gradgrind [by this time Louisa is the unfortunate *Mrs. Bounderby*] takes no interest in the game. But I shall be happy, Sir, if you will condescend."
>
> They played near a window, opening on the garden. It was a fine night; not moonlight, but sultry and fragrant. Louisa and Mr. Harthouse strolled out into the garden, where their voices could be heard in the stillness, though not what they said. Mrs. Sparsit, from her place at the backgammon board, was constantly straining her eyes to pierce the shadows without.     (187–88; bk. 8, ch. II)

The imaginative diversity and inventiveness of such recurring passages in Dickens suggest that he is much more than just a barometer of the climate of literary play in the nineteenth-century. To mix metaphors, he is even more than a bellwether for the large flock of other literary players. In a meaningful sense, Dickens stands far above the rest, even Lewis Carroll, not only because of the ways he reinvigorates traditional play motifs but also because of the way he reinterprets (one could almost say reinvents) them, especially those of the folkloric variety. Consequently, in order to appreciate his play achievements more fully, we need to compare and contrast the play in other nineteenth-century novels with that in Dickens' *Nicholas Nickleby* (1838–39) and then explore the pertinent change of emphasis in Hardy's *Jude the Obscure* (1895) since, unexpectedly, Hardy seems the heir apparent of Dickens' play strategies. This task should help clarify Dickens' often unconventional appropriation of familiar play conventions. It should also, then, further develop the kind of critical mentality and even imagination best suited to participating actively in Dickens' primary play world. Toward this end, an initial word is in order regarding the relevant differences between the play approaches of Nancy Morrow and of Mikhail Bakhtin.

Though Morrow devotes half a chapter to *Jude* (105–17), she does not even include a treatment of Dickens in her *Dreadful Games: The Play of Desire in the Nineteenth-Century Novel,* and we can only assume this is because she does not see Dickens' famous concern with ''the romantic side of familiar things'' as falling within her focus on the Realist tradition (and not because she doesn't see Dickens as playful).[5] I should add here that since Morrow is primarily concerned with *metaphors* rather than *acts* of play, it may be that the innumerable play acts in his novels seem to make Dickens too obvious (and thus unsubtle) a master of play. At any rate, even though Michael R. Booth has noted ''the urban and topographical realism'' (104) of *Nickleby,* Morrow's equation of Realism with Reason presumably disqualifies the (Romantic?) Inimitable, as the citation from *Dreadful Games* at the opening of the essay implies. Dickens would heartily agree with all but the first part of Morrow's equation since his brand of grotesque realism repeatedly subverts and so enlarges the boundaries of the Real. And Morrow's exclusion of him from her great (albeit basically tragic and ultimately existential) tradition of Realism seriously limits the scope of her study.

Since for Morrow nineteenth-century realistic novels essentially ''fear'' play, they displace ludic values onto often ambiguous metaphors rather than openly and actively celebrating the performative play impulse: ''What appears, in so many nineteenth-century novels, to be an antipathy toward play, is, in fact, a fear of the way that game playing distorts the nature of both virtue and vice, making these opposites almost indistinguishable' (172–73). Thus for Morrow, games in the Realist tradition are not only *dreadful games;* they are also subtle, often macabre masks: ''the games characters play in realist fiction ultimately disguise, rather than reveal, their essential identities'' (174). Dickens acknowledges this same sense of play in an 1855 entry in his *Book of Memoranda,* where he outlines a presumably autobiographical story that anticipates Meredith's ''most contagious game: / HIDING THE SKELE-TON'' (st.17) in *Modern Love:* ''A misplaced and mismarried man. Always, as it were, playing hide and seek with the world and never finding what Fortune seems to have hidden when he was born'' (entry 49).[6] Since this notion of the ludic does imply the play *delusions* so symptomatic, for example, of ''the games of the prison children'' (I: 7, 69) in *Little Dorrit,* it should

clearly fit Morrow's bill here. Still, the risible and often ribald games significantly performed in the open forecourt of novels by tricksters, clowns, and
fools like Sam Wellers, Dick Swiveller, and Sloppy would not qualify for
Morrow's play standards. Thus, her limited approach excludes itself from
helping us understand many of the most entertaining (and enlightening) players and play motifs in Dickens.

Bakhtin, though, spins a completely different play story, for his *carnivalesque* view of play contends that archetypal players are realistic paradoxically because they *are* metaphorical. In other words, players wearing
carnivalesque masks reveal rather than conceal themselves. These players are
empirically vital, living reincarnations of the traditions of the folk or common
people, and their play presence is especially visible in a "festive square" or
city "court" like the crucial Cursitor Court in *Bleak House:*

> it is precisely here, of course, that the masks of the clown and the fool (trans-
> formed in various ways) come to the aid of the novelist. These masks are not
> invented: they are rooted deep in the folk. They are linked with the folk through
> the fool's time-honored privilege not to participate in life, and by the time-
> honored bluntness of the fool's language; they are linked as well with the
> chronotype of the public square and with the trappings of the theater. All of
> this is of the highest importance for the novel.     (*Dialogic Imagination* 161)

Such a description is thus also of the highest importance for understanding
Dickens' "masks of the clown and the fool" and may even recall what
Fred Kaplan dubs his "usual Grimaldi reflex" when the Inimitable leaped or
bounded onto a theatrical stage with a kind of buck-and-wing flourish and
echoed his clownish hero by crying "Here we are!" (191, 126). Further,
carnivalesque forms are also relevantly participational because "carnival
does not know footlights, in the sense that it does not acknowledge any
distinction between actors and spectators." In fact, like so many Victorian
novels, "Carnival is not a spectacle seen by the people; they live in it, and
everyone participates because its very idea embraces all the people" (*Rabelais
and His World* 7).

In his account of Rabelais, which is extremely relevant to a novel like *The
Old Curiosity Shop,* Bakhtin finds "the concept of grotesque realism" (18),
as illustrated particularly by billingsgate, bodily organs, banquet liberties, and
boisterous buffoonery, to be central to any understanding of the carnivalesque.[7] But Bakhtin contends that previous studies have misrepresented
carnivalesque and grotesque realism because (like Morrow) they "particularly
stress the element of alienation" (47) rather than more properly understanding
that "in the system of grotesque imagery death and renewal are inseparable
in life as a whole, and life as a whole can inspire fear least of all." In the
memorable idiom of Sam Weller, "Wotever is, is right, as the young nobleman

sveetly remarked wen they put him down in the pension list 'cos his mother's uncle vife's grandfather vunce lit the king's pipe with a portable tinder box" (714; ch. 51). Consequently, the carnivalesque "grotesque (and in painting, also, as in Holbein's or Dürer's 'dance of death') is a more or less funny monstrosity,'' and "the theme of death as renewal, the combination of death and birth, and the pictures of gay death play an important part in the system of grotesque imagery" (50–51). As I have argued in "The *Danse Macabre* Motif in Dickens," this is exactly the point of his repeated imagery of "playing at leap-frog with the tombstones" (*Pickwick* (400; ch. 29), and again for Bakhtin this sense of the carnivalesque is realistic precisely because it is playful: "In reality, it is life itself, but shaped according to a certain pattern of play" (7). Thus, "the character of a popular-festive comic performance" is literal, unabashed joy; but its very unsubtlety is itself subtle: "it is gay and free play, but it is also full of deep meaning" (207).

In a passage which particularly suggests the carnivalesque atmosphere of *The Old Curiosity Shop,* Bakhtin, like Dickens, finds the carnivalesque to be a highly subversive "pangenre":

> A boundless world of humorous forms and manifestations opposed the official and serious tone of medieval ecclesiastical and feudal culture. In spite of their variety, folk festivities of the carnival type, the comic rites and cults, the clowns and fools, giants, dwarfs, and jugglers, the vast and manifold literature of parody—all these forms have one style in common: they belong to one culture of folk carnival humor.     (*Rabelais and His World* 4)

And yet again such traditional play also holds out the promise of a new golden age because carnivalesque laughter "was linked with the procreating act, with birth, renewal, fertility, abundance. Laughter was also related to food and drink and the people's earthly immortality, and finally it was related to the future of things to come and was to clear the way for them" (95). Consequently, it celebrated a "victory over fear" (91), and its dialogue between fear and festivity, which Bakhtin discovers as the pulse of the medieval culture, anticipates the same heartbeat in Dickens' Victorian culture:

> As opposed to laughter, medieval seriousness was infused with elements of fear, weakness, humility, submission, falsehood, hypocrisy. . . . Seriousness had an official tone and was treated like all that is official. It oppressed, frightened, bound, lied, and wore the mask of hypocrisy.     (*Rabelais and His World* 94)

Further, Bakhtin significantly argues that, as "the state encroached upon festive life" in the seventeenth and eighteenth centuries, carnivalesque play was driven deeper and deeper underground into grotesque forms, or sometimes "these festivities were brought into the home and became part of the family's private life'' (33), which so often occurs in the hallowed playgrounds of Dickensian homes like the Micawbers'.

It goes without saying that Bakhtin's approach is much closer to the spirit of the present study than is Morrow's because it highlights the importance of folk traditions as primarily revealed in immediate play performances rather than in displacing metaphors and because Bakhtin finds re-creation rather than alienation at the heart of carnivalesque play—and not in spite of the fact but *because* of the fact that play is so closely linked with death. At any rate, bearing in mind the opposed approaches of both Morrow and Bakhtin, we are better able to compare and contrast the play motifs in different nineteenth-century novels with those in Dickens in *Nicholas Nickleby*.

Toward this purpose, one could distinguish between the play motifs in romance fiction like Scott's *Ivanhoe* (1819) and those in more realistic works like *Jude the Obscure* (1895) and then argue that in novels informed by the traditions of both romance and realism (as most novels are), the play differs according to the degree to which a work is romantic or realistic. Personally, though, I find little help in such narrow genre distinctions. If we briefly consider the play in *Ivanhoe*, for instance, ''the knightly games'' (111; ch. 8) at the Ashby tournament certainly appear more stylized and rule-bound than the ''Remembrance Games'' (320; bk. 11; ch. VI) in *Jude*, yet the romance's own internal play structure reveals that they are also more formal than the rustic games of Scott's merry outlaws in the forest, which difference seems to be one of his significant criticisms of the artificial laws of chivalry. Even though Scott's romance often reads like a contest between the personi-fied court cards in a playing deck or between the chess figures of a live chess board, still the literal games do reinforce and clarify the metaphoric games of love and war, much like ''the Christmas games'' in *Sir Gawain and the Green Knight*. Further, a faithful retainer like the ''playfellow, Wamba the Jester''—the traditional ''knave or fool'' (131; ch. 10)—seems a prototype of Sam Weller, even though his more stereotyped literary role is restricted by its historical placement in the ''merry England'' of the romance's first sen-tence. In other words, Sam's role is displaced by time, and hence it appears much more ''warious.''Innovatively then, Dickens further modifies the tradi-tional character and thereby creatively individualizes Sam's play. Finally, the language of play in *Ivanhoe* loses—and yet still achieves—significant connotative value because the reader is explicitly advised that French ''is not only the natural language of the chase, but that of love and war, in which ladies should be won, and enemies defied'' (78; ch. 5). Such semantic demy-thologizing of play metaphors and etymology tends to sacrifice the reader's semiotic discovery of the original freshness in the ''martial game'' (99; ch. 7) of the tournament being played for the ''peculiar honour of naming the Queen of Love and Beauty'' (110–11; ch. 8). Still, the point of the knightly

Ivanhoe's complaining when he lies wounded at Torquilstone that "I must lie here like a bedridden monk, . . . while the game that gives me freedom or death is played out by the hand of others!" (313; ch. 29) seems as psychologically relevant as similar metaphors in more "realistic" fiction, for example, like the gambling and sporting tropes in Thackeray's *Henry Esmond*. In sum, play in romance fiction (like that in realist fiction) is not susceptible to predictable type-casting.

Rather than comparing and contrasting realistic with romance play or even acts with metaphors of play, one might more profitably argue that nineteenth-century literary play motifs rebound between the *courtly* tradition inherited from the Provençal troubadour poets and the *carnivalesque* tradition of *Bartholmew Fair*. The first form, as Laura Kendrick has documented in *The Game of Love: Troubadour Wordplay,* seems primarily verbal, witty, and restricted to interior play courts, while the latter appears to be more emotional, physical if not gymnastic, and performed upon outside playgrounds. In actual literary practice, though, (as with the realistic and romance traditions) there are very few pure forms, and the dance is just one form that bounds through both play boundaries.[8] Moreover, both the court and carnival are significantly concerned with what *Nicholas Nickleby* calls premarital and extramarital "connubialities" or foreplay and mating rituals. Many of the witty puns in the troubador courtly game of love celebrate the carnal—Kendrick argues that even the essential "*salio* (to leap)," as we will also see in Wild-Man games, is often metaphoric "for the word *fotre* (fuck)" (49)—just as the etymology and practice of the carnivalesque emphasize the *carnal.* On the other hand, open-air ring dances, sometimes performed during the seasons of the carnival and fair, display as much graceful art as grotesque nature. As Bakhtin suggests, however, it is clear that the carnivalesque is significantly displaced and diluted in a novel of (courtly) manners like Austen's *Emma.* Moreover, there is much more courtly restraint (though not necessarily more verbal wit) in Austen's primarily interior world than in the essentially carnivalesque spirit capering through Dickens' village greens, street games, and even iconoclastically in some of his indoor arenas like that housing the madcap pugilistic contest between Nicholas and Squeers in *Nickleby.* Still, I ultimately question Bakhtin's belief that the novel of courtly manners represents an abject freezing of carnivalesque waters because the conventions of both traditions seem to me to be different tides of the same archetypal play current. And as we are now ready to observe in comparing composite examples of these two play spirits, Dickens braves their common current with more hope than any other nineteenth-century novelist. In other words, since Dickensian play itself toys with dogmatically binary distinctions, no reductive approach can adequately frame the more dialogic, if not finally indeterminate, field of his differential play.

As a comparative example of significant play motifs in Dickens, I would like to discuss *Nicholas Nickleby,* especially chapter 41 where Mrs. Nickleby's "amorous neighbor," much like *Jude*'s Arabella, courts her after his own curious fashion. What we find here, I think, is that the different play motifs coordinate and integrate attitudes toward nature, nurture, home, death, art, self, and especially love. Moreover, this playful episode proves how Dickens, like Hardy, typically both serves and subverts established literary traditions. Finally, an awareness of traditional courtly and carnivalesque play tropes and of Dickens' adaptation of them further demonstrates just how uniquely rewarding an extended reading of a single episode from his novels can be.

The very first paragraph of the text characteristically sets the stage for this later wooing scene by introducing the courtship and marriage of the older Nicklebys, who both "had wedded an old flame out of mere attachment" rather than for monetary gain. And play imagery relevantly reinforces the fact that in their early married years Cupid remained more important than *cupiditas*: "thus two people who cannot afford to play cards for money, sometimes sit down to a quiet game for love." The next paragraph diagnoses the evolution of their "life-matrimonial" by suggestively comparing it to "a sparring match" in which the "two principles . . . chivalrously set to, for the mere pleasure of the buffeting." Another play metaphor then records the transformation of the Nicklebys to "the adventurous pair of the Fives' Court" (1; 1), a reference to the game of Fives which resembles handball, is played in a closed-in court, and features competitors alternately smashing the ball with their fists and palms. Fives' Court is also a reference to the famous site of benefit boxing matches.[9] For Dickens, such an allusion becomes almost a metaphysically playful conceit, which for him (and Hardy) always seems to present both martial and marital connotations, just as tennis courts and courting rituals can again both involve love matches between athletic and amorous adversaries. Later, Mrs. Nickleby's lack of "a previous acquaintance with the etymology of the word" *smifligate* (349; ch. 27) causes her some difficulty in understanding Mr. Pyke's coinage of that neologism; but a brief discussion of the play etymology of the word *court* should help us understand that, indeed like both Hardy and the good Mrs. Nickleby, Dickens also relevantly "communicate[s] a great many precepts applicable to the state of courtship" (358; ch. 28).

In Dickens, the common movement through an enclosed space, often a circle and just as often signalled by the word *court* or one of its cognates, coordinates common play activities like sports, family nurturing, interpersonal love, institutional law-giving, and even creative art. In other words, the legal court, the royal court, the neighborhood courtyard, the art of courtly love, and the love of courtly art all refreshingly (or distressingly) appear in the context of some play court. Joseph Strutt's immensely popular *The Sports and Pastimes of the People of England* (1801), which Dickens owned and which provides a wonderful introduction to his play themes besides itself prefiguring modern play theory, quotes the *Romance of Three Kings' Sons and the King of Sicily* to illustrate some of "the principles of courtly behaviour" and their relation to different play *courts*:

> He every day was provyd in dauncying and in songs that the ladies coulde think were convenable for a nobleman to conne: but in every thinge he passed all them that were there. The king for to assaie him, made justes and turnies; and no man did so well as he, in runnyng, playing at the pame [a form of tennis], shotyng, and castyng of the barre, ne found he his miaster.          (xx–xxi).[10]

Johan Huizinga's discussion of the *"Cours d'amour"* in his chapter on "Play and Poetry" in *Homo Ludens* is further relevant here because it suggests "that the love-court was a poetic *playing* at *justice*" (215), which helps to place, for example, "Bardle against Pickwick" beginning on Valentine's Day, as much as Chaucer's *The Court of Love* or Carroll's trial of the Knave of Hearts (one of the court and courting cards), in their proper play context. But Dickens plays wonderfully fast and loose with this context and these connections, relating the court homophonically, if not always etymologically, to other privileged terms like *courtesy, courage,* and *care* (beside *circus*), all of which he likens to the French *coeur,* that most Dickensian of all Dickensian terms—the heart.[11] For example, in the moments before David Copperfield begins courting Dora's heart, her father Mr. Spenlow "launched into a general eulogium on the Commons" Court. He first emphasizes the chess-like precision and game-like security of this play space: "It was the most conveniently organized place in the world. It was the complete idea of snugness. It lay in a nutshell." Further, he ironically anticipates David's courting of his daughter when he notes the prescribed tactics in divorce and restitution cases: "You made a little game of it, among a family group, and you played it out at leisure." Thus, he ultimately and unintentionally provides a running series of puns on different notions of *court,* whether ludic, legal, or loving:

> the Ecclesiastical Delegates were the advocates without any business who had looked on at the round game when it was playing in both courts, and seen the cards shuffled, and cut, and played, and had talked to all the players about it, and now came fresh, as judges, to settle the matter to the satisfaction of everybody.          (388–89; ch. 26).

In *Nicholas Nickleby,* this concept of the play court relates to

> those ancient laws of chivalry, which not only made it proper and lawful for all good knights to hear the praise of the ladies to whom they were devoted, but rendered it incumbent upon them to roam about the world, and knock on

the head all such matter-of-fact and unpoetical characters, as declined to exalt,
above all the earth, damsels whom they had never chanced to look upon or
hear of—as if that were any excuse!                                    (190; ch. 16).

The narrator's facetious tone here in describing these formal, chivalric games
of love and war, which are so prominent in novels like *Ivanhoe* and *Henry
Esmond,* is not, however, always so flippant. Pluck is emphatically satiric
when he remarks that "formalities, formalities, must not be neglected in
civilized life" (343; ch. 27); but the narrator's identical assertion regarding
Mr. Kenwigs muffling door knockers to preserve quiet for his wife's birthing,
though whimsical, is open to various ironic readings: "There are certain polite
forms and ceremonies which must be observed in civilised life, or mankind
relapse into their original barbarism" (459; ch. 36). The pertinent point here,
I think, is that as it continues the critique of customs and forms begun in
*Pickwick, Nickleby* suggests that certain civilized (and often courtly) formalities and shibboleths prove less valuable than our original "wild" condition
because they become less humane than the primitive play, as we will see,
celebrated in the related Wild Man and carnivalesque traditions. On the other
hand, Dickens' dramatization of "the state of courtship" in *Nickleby,* unlike
Hardy's in *Jude,* implies that sometimes courtly play *can* still humanistically
bridge a culture's ritualistic origins and its present institutionalized state of
decline. Thus, even though Nicholas tells Madeline Bray's father Walter that
"I will not trouble her with such forms" (as receipts upon payment) during
what is actually their clandestine courting, the self-centered patriarch ironically rejoins, "we'll have as many forms as we can" (606; ch. 46).

At any rate, the various play dimensions of courtship enjoy central roles in
*Nickleby,* with the almost archetypal model for such roles being the courtship
dramatized in Chapter 41. We should note, though, others like the instance
of the "black monk" who trespasses through a liminal "small postern in the
wall of the sisters' orchard" in the interpolated romance tale, "The Five
Sisters of York." He argues against the sisters wasting their time "by means
of idle toys" and allowing "the policy of courts" to tempt them from their
"peaceful homes to scenes of revelry." Indeed, some such courtly temptations
even arrive on "jaded *coursers*" (57–66; ch. 6, emphasis added). Smike,
who plays Nicholas's "squire," himself sometimes seems "an accomplished
courtier" (375; ch. 29), especially in contrast to the many mock "courtesies"
of Ralph with his "hard, horny hand" (336; ch. 26). At Mr. Lillyvick and
Miss Petowker's wedding, which all the attending Crummles' players "make
. . . rather theatrical," one performing bridesmaid admits that she also "would
rather court the yoke than shun it," which seems to cue Mr. Folair's joke
abut the courting "noose" and then the groom's unplayfully angry retort that
such carnivalesque ribaldry "aimed a blow at the whole framework of society." Folair sheepishly replies that he did not mean to suggest "that you were

caught and trapped'' (like Jude and Sue) by courting, but Lillyvick remains indignant: ''Noose! As if one was caught, trapped into the married state, pinned by the leg, instead of going into it of one's own accord and glorying in the act!'' (323–28; ch. 25). Finally, ''the whole courtship'' of Matilda Price and John Browdie, on the one hand, and its parodic counterpart, that of Nicholas and Fanny Squeers, on the other, are metonymically disclosed when Tildy decides that the two couples must ''have a game at cards.'' Thus, ''they sat down to play speculation'' by trading partners ''two against two,'' whereupon Tildy, who ''was of a playful turn'' anyway, discloses to Nicholas and her two jealous opponents, ''I should like to have you for a partner always.'' Then with an affecting pout, she amends the proverb lucky at cards, unlucky at love to ''You'll have a bad wife, though, if you always win at cards.'' Subsequently, the two courtships proceed like foiling ''cut-and-thrust counts in melodramatic performances'' (104–13; ch. 9).

Thus, the various courtly relationships between play and love circulate throughout the entire novel, but the thematic courting is centered in chapters 39, 40, and especially 41. In fact, the two preceding chapters provide a clarifying play context for the garden courting episode and thereby illustrate how Dickens often varies and reinforces certain central play motifs in successive, thematically interdependent chapters. For instance, chapter 39 celebrates the London honeymoon of none other than Mr. and Mrs. (Tildy) Browdie, when they are accompanied by none other than that ''queer bridesmaid'' and unsuccessful speculation player, Miss Fanny Squeers. In the hymeneal chant of the Yorkshire groom, ''Here be a weddin' party—broide and broidesmaid, and the groom—if a mun dean't joy himsel noo, when ought he, hey?'' (39:503). And it should be noted here that, besides their amorous play, the ''connubialities'' of these newlyweds involve their cooperative gulling of Squeers and release of Smike. Tildy is invariably ''skittish and full o' tricks'' (546; ch. 42), and her husband even more emphatically plays ritual Wild Man or Trickster as he assumes ''a very odd and excitable state'' and feigns temporary insanity: ''snapping his fingers, and dancing scraps of uncouth country dances''(507). And later when he explains such a pious fraud to Nicholas, his accompanying behavior complements his ritualistic fooling as he engages in ''flirtations with eatables'' and rushes ''to play such a knife and fork'' game at their carnivalesque feast of fools: ''He chuckled, roared, half-suffocated himself by laughing large pieces of beef into his windpipe'' (542–43; ch. 42).

In the next chapter, Nicholas's misadventure with Miss Cecilia Bobster presents a comedy of courtly errors (which never becomes a tragedy like Jude's) when he storms his castle of love, only to find it is the wrong castle—and what is worse, the wrong love. Much of the moralizing about barriers in love and much of the hysterical (in both senses of the word) melodrama involving *interruptus* seem to parody similar motifs in *The Romance of the*

*Rose* and its version of garden courting. In this context, the final chapter of this deranged and disarranging courting triptych may clear up the lover's delusions here, just as the narrator of *The Romance of the Rose* suggests about his "games of Love": "I tell you that he who will hear the end of the dream can learn a great deal about the games of Love. . . . The truth, which is hidden, will be quite open to you when you hear me explain the dream, for it doesn't contain a lying word" (Lorris 59). At any rate, Nicholas's dreamy "romance" spoofs the courtly belief that the "sweet face" of the beloved represents "a glimpse of some better world" or Golden Age and that "Mystery and disappointment are not absolutely indispensible to the growth of love, but they are very often, its powerful auxiliaries." Such sentiments seem especially suspicious, as this revel playfully reveals, when the name of the damsel in distress can only be remembered because it rhymes with "lobster," when the courtly lover is "angry with the young lady for being so easily won," and (again) especially when "*it was the wrong lady*" (519–26, Dickens' emphasis).

These first two chapters, though, are mere preludes to Dickens' most significant commentary on courting rituals, which occurs in chapter 41 (528–40) when Mrs. Nickleby's "amorous neighbor" courts her both from the other side and even from atop the liminal garden wall of her *hortus conclusus*. In order to comprehend fully the foreplay of this "very wild" (533) man, we must first understand the pedigree of his courting, its folk antecedents in primitive "wild man" rituals, and its later adaptations in medieval "wild man games." The most plausible literary source for wild man lore as for so many of Dickens's traditional play motifs is again his personal copy of Joseph Strutt's *Sports and Pastimes of the People of England*. Strutt even includes an illustrated "representation of this facetious spirit" of the "Wild Man or Woodwose or Wodehouse, a character very common and popular in pageants of former times" (299, illustration top facing 298). And he pertinently associates the Wild Man with a playful ballad, "The mad, merry pranks of Robin Good Fellow," with the vegetative figure of the *Green Man,* and with firework displays including those names "Ears of Corn," "air-balloons," and "Chinese Fires" (298–99). Dickens' own Wild Man is similarly a "facetious spirit" who causes "a large cucumber" to "shoot up in the air with the velocity of a sky-rocket," who awaits the arrival of "a balloon," and who is preoccupied with "the young Prince of China" (Dickens often invokes the Orient when referencing the orientation of play).

Like Hardy's acquaintance with the St. George mummers play in *Return of the Native* and with the skimmington mockeries in *The Mayor of Casterbridge* (both of which traditions are related to Wild Man mythology), Dickens' most immediate knowledge of the Wild Man tradition, however, probably comes from his own direct experience with popular, carnivalesque pageants.

This experience is reflected in the Crummles troup's production of "The Indian Savage and the Maiden," which ludicrously prefigures the Wild Man's later garden courting by including amorous "thumps in the chest," the ecstatic dance, and especially a "botanical curiosity resembling a small pickled cabbage" (289; ch. 23). In fact, as practiced and later played (287–88; ch. 30) by Mr. Folair and the Infant Phenomenon, this farcical mating ritual is clearly a development of traditional Wild Man motifs and thus a fitting prelude to their more nonsensical and more stately recreation in the garden:

> the savage jumped for joy; then the maiden jumped for rapture at the sweet smell of the pickled cabbage. Then the savage and the maiden danced violently together, and, finally, the savage dropped down on one knee, and the maiden stood on one leg upon his other knee; thus concluding the ballet, and leaving the spectators in a state of pleasing uncertainty, whether she would ultimately marry the savage, or return to her friends.          (289; ch. 23)[12]

What is particularly interesting here and what occurs relevantly throughout Dickens, as it also does in Rabelais (Bakhtin's denial notwithstanding), is the illustrated fact that the carnivalesque and the courtly are not finally opposing forms. Repressed elements of the carnivalesque, like the Wild Man's play, inevitably return displaced in the courtly tradition until Dickens releases their pent-up energies. Similarly, "the language of the court," which is punned upon throughout *Gargantua and Pantagruel,* invariably collapses under pressure from the carnivalesque as Panurge's boasting suggests when Friar John appears to doubt his priapic powers: "Thou seemest in some measure to mistrust the readiness of my Paternity, in the practising of my Placket-Racket within the Aphrodisian Tennis-Court at all times fitting, as if the stiff God of Gardens were not favourable to me" (434; bk. III, ch. 27).

Richard Bernheimer's *Wild Men in the Middle Ages,* particularly his lengthy chapter on the "Erotic Connotations" of the Wild Man, clarifies the pertinent heritage of this figure and its relationship to courting rituals. Bernheimer repeatedly finds links between the Wild Man motifs and the world of play not only because "his uncouth dance" is the Wild Man's characteristic action but also because "playing with the wild man" became an expression often used for participating in Wild Man rituals (53, 55). In fact, the name of one such ritual itself is *ludus de homine salvatico,* and another is *magnus ludus de homine salvatico.* In the graphic arts, the Wild Man often relevantly appears as "aged without abandoning his playfulness" and is even known as "Master of the Playing Cards" (47) in connection with floral and animal forms naturally associated with him and designating different card suits—Dickens' Wild Man even searches for a complementary "Queen of Diamonds" (648; ch. 49). Bernheimer goes so far as to insist that in connection with the Wild Man "everything is treated as a game or a joke"

(159), just as Bakhtin insists with the carnivalesque tradition, even though, unaccountably, he only touches upon the Wild Man's role in the carnivalesque, 391–93). Bernheimer likewise discusses the "theatrical embodiment" of the Wild Man as "Herlekin" by relevantly associating him with the traditions of the Fool and Clown, which are also linked to Jude: "The final outcome of this development may be anticipated: the sartorial tradition of the wild man and his demonic relatives and associates was inherited by the Harlequin of the modern stage, who is no other than the funny devil Herlekin acclimatized to a baroque environment" (83–84).[13]

The Wild Man is further relevantly characterized by wild, unpredictable movements, especially bounding leaps and jumps, by his old age and his uncut, straggly black hair, and by his loud bellowing, though he plays a *senex erotus* as frequently as a *senex irratus*. In the primitive Wild Man rituals, this outlawed free spirit often "appears spontaneously, roaring and snorting" (52–53); then he is dragged away by the authorities, and his merits are tried before a court, which is followed by his imprisonment, or even actual or symbolic execution. Often in the rituals "the female figure with her ring" helps to tame or capture the Wild Man through his love for her. Thus, his figurative significance is sometimes associated with death and rebirth and sometimes with the related transformative power of love. In this latter capacity, the ritual provides a fertility function "presenting human love in terms of the erotic behavior of the wild man," whose fecundity symbolizes if not engenders the creative impulses of the entire community. Thus, his "mock ceremonies were allowed to be held in imitation of the corresponding human events or as magical substitutions for them if they failed to materialize" (175). In this synecdochic sense, the Wild Man's play personifies a sacred marriage between the most healthy energies of primitive, pastoral-agrarian, and more civilized cultures, and his ritualistic drama is ultimately displaced into medieval romance forms like *Sir Orpheo,* where the power of love conquers the power of death. Eventually, though, the Wild Man is "regarded as funny or pathetic rather than awe-inspiring," and so his tamed processual play and domesticated processional pageantry both grow more acceptable to ecclesiastical and civil authorities (50).

Still, the Wild Man's related abilities "to treat agricultural labor as a game" (160) and to promote natural human foreplay and fertility link his mythology with "the ancient traditions about the good life of the uncivilized" and "the hallowed, never forgotten ideals of the Golden Age" (175), as Dickens himself realized in pieces like "Arcadian London" and "The Noble Savage."[14] In the imagery of the "so-called 'Feer tapestry'," which is "the last word in amorous wild-man iconography," Bernheimer relevantly finds that "the finest consummation of love is reserved to those who abandon the safety of human habitation and have the courage to retire into the woods; and that only by thus cutting the ties that link us with humanity can we hope to preserve those values of absolute loyalty and faithfulness which are in jeopardy whenever the pressure of the multitude prevails.'' The point is that the more emphasis there is on lawful or official versions of love, the more rigidly courtly and less flexibly carnivalesque or playful love seems to be; the more it also tends to become not just desacralized and denaturalized, but also dehumanized. The Wild Man's playful traditions (much like the unicorn's upon which he frequently rides) consequently attempt to naturalize, sacralize, and ultimately rehumanize both the literary art of courtly love and the libidinal act of carnal love: ''The more a marriage rose above the level of crudity, the more insistent must have been the desire to escape from continuous communal supervision into the freedom and intimacy of nature'' (160–63, figures 43–44).

Such Wild Man play motifs are prevalent throughout Dickens, but are especially personified in Hugh in *Barnaby Rudge,* Quilp in *The Old Curiosity Shop,* and the ''wild'' neighbor here in *Nicholas Nickleby.* In fact, even before her gracefully gross courtly lover bellows his mating call and begins his Wild Man foreplay, Mrs. Nickleby prefigures the paradoxes of the Wild Man when she characteristically indulges in a ''curious association of ideas'' for the benefit of her young daughter Kate. As they stroll by the garden wall secretly separating them from the Wild Man, Mrs. Nickleby recalls her husband saying that pigs ''always put him in mind of very little babies, only the pigs had much fairer complexions; and he had a horror of little babies, too, because he couldn't very well afford any increase to his family, and had a natural dislike to the subject.'' Such reflections may recall the ''pig-faced lady'' (646; ch. 49) often exhibited at fairs that Mrs. Nickleby identifies at a later reappearance of her Wild Man—in this sense they may include Ursula the pig woman from Dickens' beloved *Bartholomew Fair* who, like the Wild Man, is also associated with bears. Such reflections even seem to anticipate tiny Alice's remark in the ''Pig and Pepper'' chapter of her *Adventures* that the little creature she carries ''would have made a dreadfully ugly child: but it makes a rather handsome pig'' (87; ch. 6). That is, on the one hand, they suggest our beastly nature if not the beast-with-two-backs that spawned us. On the other, they prefigure the tricks of Hardy's pig woman Arabella and suggest a carnivalesque subversion of conventional values by stressing that fair and foul are near of kin and even perhaps, like the puns of Yeats's Crazy Jane, that nothing can be sole or whole that has not been rent. More particularly here, they may give Kate some pause about her own begetting and even her father's love for her, especially since she is so intent at this point on asking about her mother's ''suitor.'' Thus, the various relationships between suckling pigs and nursing babies clearly capture some of the ultimately comforting (after being initially confusing) paradoxes of the blessedly bestial Wild Man. In this sense, they also prefigure his immediate and tumultuous intrusion into that traditionally figurative virginity belt, the enclosed garden, which invasive action gives both Mrs. Nickleby "and her daughter a violent start."

Significantly, even though "a kind of bellow" from an "unseen bellower" suddenly seems "to come from the very foundation of the garden wall," after her first surprise, Mrs. Nickleby remains remarkably calm and repeatedly advises Kate not to "be flurried" because the mating call is only "designed to attract our attention." Mrs. Nickleby's composure at such simian foreplay is especially noteworthy here given both her own flair for a dramatic "gush of supposes" (640; ch. 49) and her paradoxically *yeabynay,* if not sympathetically carnivalesque notions about courtly and other civilized codes of conduct: "she had not an atom of pride or formality about her, still she was a great stickler for dignity and ceremonies" (582; ch. 45). Thus, it almost seems as if she demurely accepts her role in the taming of the Wild Man ritual. As if recognizing that this is a truly natural and hence renewing ceremony, she also intuits that she must play her part in the ritual for the instruction of young Kate as much as for the mutual salvation of the Wild Man and indeed her entire community. The pivotal major figure himself characteristically appears to rise from the lower depths, what Bakhtin terms the "carnivalesque grotesque," the "foundation" or elemental world of primitive origins and ultimate destinations. And as personified in his repeated act of climbing to the top of (and over) the liminal garden wall, the mounting Wild Man is traditionally associated with transcending "the courtly technique of amorous delay" (Bernheimer 149). Even the ladder which he ascends, descends, and ascends again is sometimes a play prop in Wild Man liturgy (Bernheimer 128).

Further, the Wild Man's characteristic satyr romp, appropriately identified later in the text as a "species of savage dance" (649; ch. 49), is clearly announced when "a shouting and scuffling noise, as of an elderly gentleman whooping, and kicking his legs on loose gravel with great violence, was heard." Then ensues the aforementioned cucumber fireworks as prelude to an even more earthy and grotesquely carnivalesque mating display:

> a fine vegetable marrow, of unusually large dimensions, was seen to whirl aloft, and come toppling down; then several cucumbers shot up together; and finally the air was darkened by a shower of onions, turnip-radishes, and other small vegetables, which fell rolling and scattering and bumping about in all directions.

As Kate grows "quite terrified" by such vegetable pyrotechnics and priapic vitality, the comically cosmic explosion of mast, elemental fodder much like the "tripe" image in Rabelais (Bakhtin, *Rabelais* 162–64, 221–22, 224–25), gradually gives way to the beastial-beatific vision itself: "the old black velvet cap" suspensefully "followed by a very large head, an old face in which were a pair of the most extraordinary grey eyes: very wild, very wide open, and rolling in their sockets with a dull languishing leering look, most ugly to

behold.'' At this juncture, we might note that Dickens revealed to Mary Boyle
in 1858 that he considered himself to be a kind of Wild Man: ''I am a man
full of passion and energy, and my own wild way that I must go is often—at
the best—wild enough'' (Kaplan 412). And as he disclosed in an 1855 letter
to Maria Beadnell (by now Mrs. Henry Winter), he always considered their
youthful love a form of profound play: ''I have never blamed you at all but
I have believed until now that you never had the stake in that serious game
which I had'' (*Selected Letters* 112). In other words, passionate energy and
playful love both conflate even in Dickens' personal Wild Man associations.

At any rate, by this time Kate Nickleby is horrified to the point of nearly
pinching her mother's ''arm black and blue'' so that the more experienced
grand dame must admonish her daughter with the real purport of the whole
experience: ''how can you be so foolish? I'm ashamed of you. How do you
suppose you are ever to get through life, if you're such a coward as this?''
In turn, she then confronts their playful ravisher with rhetoric that makes
clear the relationships between the floral precincts and the female person:
''How dare you look into this garden? . . . This is private property, sir; you
ought to know that'' (later he even climbs down her chimney!). But perhaps
as surprising as Mrs. Nickleby's personal transformation into a kind of mother
goddess here is the Wild Man's own subsequent poetic wooing when he
crowns her ''Queen of my soul'' and compares them both ''to the bees . . . -
when the honey season is over,'' again echoing traditional Wild Man verses
(Bernheimer 149). Indeed, when he proclaims the garden to be ''a sacred and
enchanted spot,'' he explicitly identifies it as the holy court or liminal precinct
of ritualistic love play. Characteristically comparing Mrs. Nickleby to Venus,
he insists that ''the most divine charms'' both of this playful place and
implicitly of her own sweet person can even ''force the fruit and vegetables
into premature existence.'' Thus, his typical Wild Man trope discovers correspondences between play, agriculture, and love, as Mrs. Nickleby herself
metamorphoses into a primal earth mother or Venus Geneatrix. In this context,
one might consider Arabella to be a ''wild woman'' (Bernheimer 156–58),
but she finally proves too cynical (or too modern?) for this traditional role
since Hardy typically denies the truly transformative power of folkloric play
in late Victorian culture.[15] At any rate, after devising many similar conceits,
the Wild Man concludes his natural art of courtly love with a valentine flourish
of nonsense and sensibility:

> I am not a youth, ma'am as you see; and although beings like you can never
> grow old, I venture to presume that we are fitted for each other. . . . If you bless
> me with your hand and heart, you can apply to the Lord Chancellor or call out
> the military if necessary—sending my toothpick to the commander-in-chief will
> be sufficient—and so clear the house of them before the ceremony is performed.
> After that, love bliss and rapture; rapture love and bliss. Be mine, be mine!

At the same time that this playful demiurge seems so clearly linked with Wild Man mythology, however, we are pointedly told that his Plutonian "black velvet cap" hides "a perfectly bald head," which conversely subverts the traditionally hirsute pate and person of the Wild Man. It appears, then, as if Dickens is primarily concerned with humanizing the figure by emphasizing the "funny or pathetic" qualities of the Wild Man over his "awe-inspiring" ones. For example, Mrs. Nickleby humorously begs Frank Cheeryble and Tim Linkinwater: "don't hurt a hair of his head, I beg. On no account hurt a hair of his head" (646; ch. 49) when this bald, indomitable figure playfully slides down her chimney. Further, Mrs. Nickleby's comment to Kate that he is "quite the counterpart of your grand-papa" also renders him more familiar or familial than ferocious at the same time that it uncannily demonstrates the relevant universality of his redemptive play energy. When he is yanked down below his wall stage like a Punch hand puppet, he again seems to be more of a tumbling merry-andrew than Orphic miracle man, though once more the Wild Man's imprisonment by "the keeper," just one of the many "persecutors of this unfortunate gentleman" (647; ch. 49), is usually a traditional episode in the ritual. And here the keeper's remarking of his prisoner that "Nothing will prevent his making love" again reinforces the priapic powers of this playful primate. Moreover, his guard's feeling that "it was a blessing he went mad" and that "He's a deal pleasanter without his senses than with 'em" also ironically demonstrates the redemptive value of dying to the wasteful logic of the civilized intellect and gamely embracing the loving nonsense of the natural instincts and imagination, which Wild-Man rituals, like the related mythology of the Natural Fool, often dramatically suggest.

And yet the repressive keeper himself certainly does not comprehend his prisoner's value, and Mrs. Nickleby must go to some lengths to instruct Kate that the Wild Man's play may be more sane or at least more humbly honest than his jailer's proud pretense.[16] Already "with perfect seriousness" and courteous sympathy, Mrs. Nickleby has confided to the Wild Man that "It's a very painful thing to have to reject [your] proposals," and the overall tone of her rejection of his suit and yet affirmation of his noble savagery is remarkably different from any of her other speeches in the novel, almost as if she has momentarily absorbed his spirit of profound playfulness by virtue of his traditional contagious magic.[17] Thus, she appropriately concludes the courting ritual by debating the Wild Man's "infirmities of nature" with her daughter, thereby recalling the court's typical judgments in the older Wild Man ceremonies. And her climactic defense of his courtly "method" and playful "madness" not only validates the universality of Wild Man lore but also relevantly celebrates her own renewed selfhood as she grows ever young under his aegis, younger even than any "chit of a girl" whom the Wild Man *could* have courted—present filial company clearly not excepted:

He may be a little odd and flightly, perhaps, many of us are that; but downright mad! and express himself as he does, respectfully, and in quite poetical language, and making offers with so much thought, and care, and prudence—not as if he ran into the streets, and went down upon his knees to the first chit of a girl he met, as a madman would! No, no, Kate there's a great deal too much method in *his* madness; depend upon that, my dear.

Somewhat unexpectedly, I think, the nineteenth-century novelist whose play motifs most closely resemble those in Dickens is Thomas Hardy. Both writers are powerfully and comparably influenced by the "folk carnival culture" and "grotesque imagery" that Bakhtin above finds rooted in "the Renaissance tradition."[18] An unsigned review of Hardy's *The Trumpet Major* appearing in the November 20, 1880, issue of *Athenaeum*, linked his art with Dickens': "Mr. Hardy seems to be in the way to do for rural life what Dickens did for that of the town. Like the elder novelist, he finds his characters entirely in the middle or lower middle class. With the 'nobility and gentry' he has nothing to do" (Cox 70). Still, even though Hardy's ashes lie next to Dickens' in the Poets' Corner of Westminster Abbey, these two giants of Victorian fiction are not frequently discussed in the same breath. As a youth Hardy sought out Dickens' recognition in a Hungerford Market coffee-shop but feared actually speaking to the celebrated writer (Evelyn Hardy 333). In 1849 Hardy attended a school that he quipped was "somewhat on the Squeers model" from *Nickleby* (Millgate 45), and in 1863 he even listened to a Dickens "Reading" in the Hanover Square Rooms. Hardy's singular appreciation of Dickens, in fact, employs one of the Inimitable's own favorite play metaphors: "It has been the peculiarity & the marvel of this man's power that he has invested his puppets with a charm that has enabled him to dispense with nature" (*The Literary Notebooks of Thomas Hardy* I:164, 363). And yet when answering questions for "Charles Dickens: Some Personal Recollections and Opinions," a 1912 retrospect which appeared in the *Bookman*, the younger novelist felt that his own " 'literary efforts did not owe much to [Dickens's] influence'." Still, he pointedly concludes the interview with "No doubt they owed something unconsciously, since everybody's did in those days" (*Literary Notebooks* I: 363). Whether "unconsciously" inherited from Dickens or whether influenced by a common folk tradition, though, Hardy's play motifs do significantly recall Dickens' own—at least up to a point.

To understand clearly the significant similarities between Hardyesque and Dickensian play we need to consider *Jude the Obscure*, which at first glance might appear to be his least playful work.[19] Like all of Hardy's fiction, the world of *Jude* seems controlled by something like the "caprice of the weather-god" (75; bk. II; ch. 3). This is the cosmic principle of unpredictable playfulness that appears to govern at least the human world with a kind of "unnatural" or *inhumane* selection. More memorably caricatured in Hardy's poetry, this tormenting Trickster variously becomes the "Spinner of the Years" in "The Convergence of the Twain," the smirking "Spirit of Irony" in " 'And There Was a Great Calm,' " and most famously, perhaps, the desultory gamester "dicing Time" who "for gladness casts a moan" in "Hap." Such improvidentially Providential playfulness sports with the earth like a "tainted ball" in "God-Forgotten" so that as the *Götterdammerung* approaches in "The Darkling Thrush," the ancient harmony of the spheres runs dissonant, its natural score misplaying on "strings of broken lyres."

In *Jude*, the old rustic world of fruitful play has likewise been soured by dispassionate modernity. For instance, on the very first page of the novel, the epigraphic letter of the law in Phillotson's textbooks tends to "kill," or at least stifle, his "cottage piano" because, almost like Forster's Mr.Vyse, "he had never acquired any skill in playing" (1, 9; ch. II). This ironic prelude sets the stage for the theme Hardy really seems most interested in—the complete failure of contemporary love play, which is illustrated in the significant differences between the "social ritual" (I: 9, 51) of modern marriage, especially in deritualized urban centers, and the "old custom" (I: 8, 46) of peasant courting and love-making in the rural countryside. Mrs. Edlin becomes the choric cricket from the ancient hearth chirping about the courting past as she advises Sue, "Why when I and my poor man were married we thought no more o't than of a game o dibs!" (V: 4, 227). Or as she later reprises her remembrance of carnivalesque play things past for Phillotson: "I don't know what the times be coming to! Matrimony have growed to be that serious in these days. . . . In my time we took it more careless. . . . When I and my poor man were jined in it we kept up the junketing all the week, and drunk the parish dry" (291–92; bk. 5; ch. V).

Many of these ideas are relevant to Dickens' play themes. For example, Jude even recognizes the fact that "those legal fellows have been playing at" (V: 2, 209) contriving his formal divorce from Arabella, just as Dickens ridicules the chicanery of the love court in Bardell vs. Pickwick, the difference being that Dickens takes much more playful relish in exposing the dirty tricks involved in legal foul play. As an original charter member of Walter Besant's Rabelais Club (Besant, *Autobiography* 240–42), Hardy's, like Dickens' depiction of tavern life echoes much of the carnivalesque tradition as, for instance, when Jude rubs shoulders in the Christminster pub with various strolling players: "two ladies who sported moral characters of various depths of shade, according to their company, nicknamed 'Bower o' Bliss' and 'Freckles'; some horsey men 'in the know' of betting circles; a travelling actor from the theatre" and other "devil-may-care" curiosities including a man who trains "bull-pups" for blood sport besides several "racing gents" (96–97; bk. 7; ch. II). This particular evening Jude ludicrously wagers that he can "rehearse" the Nicene Creed and then the Apostles Creed "in the Latin tongue," and his eventual pathetic performance becomes a carnivalesque example of "drinking theologically" (Bakhtin: *Rabelais* 216–17) as much as it is a sacred slanging match, drinking bout, and memory game. In other words, it is the same kind of play performance that Dickens might stage at the Jolly Sandboys or Three Jolly Fellowship Porters, though the intimations of classical tragedy are more insistent here than in Dickens, who more often features what Bakhtin calls the "gay carnivalesque." Later in *Jude* appears the even more "curious and interesting group of itinerants, who frequented the numerous fairs and markets held up and down Wessex." These include "a shooting-gallery proprietor and the ladies who loaded the guns, a pair of boxing masters," "a swing-boat owner, and a 'test-your-strength' man" (197; bk. 6; ch. IV). All these carnivalesque gamesters support Phillotson's cause at the "public meeting" arranged to debate whether the schoolmaster should lose his position because he had helped his wife Sue to move in illicitly with Jude, thereby "condoning her adultery." Hardy devotes a paragraph to a lively but indirect description of the "general scuffle" instigated by this playful "phalanx of supporters." Dickens likewise revels in such scenarios, but presumably would also have made much more of the mock heroic potential of the pitched battle as he does in the Squeers-Nicholas melee in *Nickleby*. Such a "farcical yet melancholy event" (196–97; bk. 6; ch. IV) would have remained primarily farcical in Dickens because playful social spectacles in his fiction (except for the two historical novels) are usually comic, while acts of individual or interpersonal play gradually do grow melancholic and macabre, especially from Esther burying her doll baby in *Bleak House* onward.[20]

Though Hardy is more sexually open in his novels than Dickens could be, the Inimitable clearly would also have delighted in Arabella's playful ruse of the "cochin's egg," that is, the previously mentioned "old custom" of a farm "maiden" hatching an egg in the warm, "safe place" between her generous breasts. For the pig woman, this custom suggestively becomes an even more primitive courting ritual licensing direct foreplay. Arabella's "strategy" here is to tempt the over-matched Jude to locate her warm nest and crack her "egg-shell" of "a very rare sort," one, in fact, significantly protected by "a piece of pig's bladder" (46–47; bk. 8; ch. I). Arabella's ensuing challenge, "You must find me first!" prompts a game of sexual hide-and-seek, which ends, presumably, with the couple in bed together and the poor cochin's egg very much the worse for wear. When she later recalls this seduction scene, however, Arabella consciously perverts its healthy bawdiness by tricking Jude back to her father's house and keeping him drunk until he remarries her. Still, Morrow seems to me to be clearly inaccurate when she concludes her discussion of *Jude* with a complete rejection of its carnivalesque appeal: "Throughout Hardy's novel, images of games and play mark the degradation of the human heart and imagination" (116). And Dickens, I think, would have been as fascinated by the open sexual play of the first scene as we know he was by the playfully frank ribaldry of Rabelais,[21] and just as probably he would have rejected the opportunity to undercut such play ironically in a later scene since even with the somber Clennam in *Little Dorrit,* his most Judelike hero, Dickens invariably celebrates the enduring spirit of renewal in traditional, folk play motifs like the "Wallflower" game.[22]

To be sure, though, Dickens would have been equally delighted with the interpolated "strange tale of a most immoral case . . . in a church out by Gaymede," which occurs while workers are painting the ten commandments and drinking at the same time. "Putting their rum-bottle and rummers upon the Communion table," they fall asleep but then awaken to envision "a terrible thunderstorm a-raging, and they seemed to see in the gloom a dark figure, with very thin legs and a curious voot, a-standing on the ladder, and finishing the work." Next Sunday morning, "when the people came and service began, all saw that the Ten Commandments wez painted with the 'Nots' left out" (5:6,239). This inset-piece is much in keeping with the interpolated tale of Gabriel Grub and his meeting with the goblins leap-frogging tombstones in *Pickwick,* except that the diablerie in this tale is more clearly carnivalesque than in Gabriel Grub's "Christmas games" and their fairly conventional morality. And yet what Bakhtin calls the traditional *Nemo* game's "free carnivalesque play with official negations and prohibitions" (*Rabelais* 414) does occur in even darker form in the shadowy figure of Nemo in *Bleak House.* And Rabelais, Dickens, and Hardy all curiously link bounding limbs with ritualistic liminal boundaries, particularly feet, feasting, and playful misrule like that practiced by the limber limbs at Sleary's Circus in *Hard Times.*

For our purposes, however, the major instance of Hardy's ironic play again occurs at the end of *Jude* in "The Remembrance games" (320–25; bk. 11; ch. VI) section, which counterpoints the ancient (and barely *remembered*), renewing function of ritualistic play with the decline and death of Jude so that the festive memorials read more like "the funeral games" (31; bk. 6; ch. I) from the *Iliad* that Jude had earlier boasted of translating. Thus, this section also ironically teases the reader into playing memory games with different past moments in the text, besides with the implied contrasts between the epic heroism of Achilles who, together with his entire Greek culture, was tested by love play and the obscure heroism of Jude and his culture's being trapped between the courting customs of two generations. In other words, play serves a distinctly structural function in Hardy all the while it deconstructs structuralism. This section of *Jude,* in fact, contrasts the carnivalesque "horse-play" enjoyed during the water sports and the dancing shared under "the joyous throb of a waltz" with the absurdist "smile of some sort upon the marble features of Jude" as his own isolated dance of death is terminating. In Dickens, the boisterous play of Dick Swiveller, the "Liverer," comparably counter-points the bells knelling the death of Nell in *The Old Curiosity Shop;* in Hardy, though, play does not ring so triumphantly when "the bells struck out joyously." Rather, Arabella's unpredictable, half-guilty compassion, compli-cated by her final lie to Mrs. Edlin and the memory of Sue's "staid, worn" life with a man "she can't stomach," both seem to make Jude's existential demise a sardonic and entropic example of endgame.

Addressing the characters more exclusively, we hear other echoes of Dick-ensian play motifs. For instance, the first appearance of Little Father Time is cued and clarified by a play image, as so often occurs with character introduc-tions in Dickens. Here this improbable personification of "Age masquerading as Juvenility" rides the coach with an unfamiliar kitten which "indulges in playful antics." But the lack of sympathetic responsiveness from this "soli-tary boy" (unlike his "fellow-passengers," who laugh at the kitten's play) seems to say that "All laughing comes from misapprehension. Rightly looked at there is no laughable thing under the sun." Thus, if even his kitten familiar appears to be a bound prisoner of "its too circumscribed play," the boy, "like an enslaved and dwarfed Divinity" is "doubly" (V: 3,218) a victim of his own completely censored and limited play spirit. Phillotson, too, seems a dupe of unattainable play since, though he earnestly strives to keep his kittenish Sue free from "the treachery of living on with a husband and playing him false" (IV: 4, 183), he still eventually concurs with those who believe "that Sue had played him false" (IV: 6, 195).

Sue Brideshead's own connections with play are much more subtle and help to reveal her invariably mixed motivations. On the one hand, Sue is something of "a tomboy" since as a little girl she mastered male sports and would "hit in and steer down the long slide on yonder pond," while the astonished boys would "cheer her." On the other hand, Sue engaged in aesthetics as well as athletics when she unexpectedly entertains literary visions from Scott and Poe, having, like Jude, "the same trick as a child of seeming to see things in the air" (II: 6, 90). Perhaps it was from such romance sources that Sue imbibed her dual courtly love roles of playing coquette if not courte-san one moment and virginal queen the next. As Elizabeth Grosz describes such a playfully deluded and deluding "narcissistic woman," "she always remains one step beyond her lover's grasp, always slightly out of reach, as lack sustaining his desire" (131). When Sue was eighteen and "formed a friendly intimacy with an undergraduate at Christminster," her sexual reserve caused him to warn that she "might play that game once too often" (III: 4, 117). Later the narrator judges similarly: "A Nemesis attends the woman who plays the game of elusiveness too often" (V: 1, 215). Related to this game is what Sue calls her (and Jude's) "sort of trick" (IV: 2, 167) of pretending to meet as kissing cousins so that they can disguise or at least displace their attraction as lovers. This "tantalizing, capricious little woman" still later "played the thoughtful nurse for half-an-hour" (IV: 6, 200) for Phillotson, once again revealing her typical rhythms of attractive desire and repugnant withdrawal, much like Estella's in *Great Expectations*. Such rhythms characterize the alternating movements of the mating dance of Jude's checkered cousin whose "intellect played like lambent lightning over the conventions and formalities" (VI: 3, 272).

In another playful dance step, Arabella's own opening mating dance with Jude playfully parallels Sue's since when the "pig-breeder's" daughter first meets Jude, "they walked in parallel lines, one on each bank of the stream, towards the small plank bridge" (I: 6, 33) in Marygreen, just as when his Shelleyean cousin first encounters Jude in Christminster, the two proceed on opposite sides of the street as "they walked on in parallel lines" (II: 4, 81) toward a common meeting spot. And just as Sue bounds over conventional boundary lines, so too Arabella's play suggests a kind of ritualized release or liberation as she uniquely initiates foreplay by throwing a pig's "piece of flesh" (I: 6, 32) or Rabelaisian codpiece at Jude and concludes it with that "curious and original manoeuvre" she practices throughout the novel—the playful creation of fetching dimples as if "by magic" (34). In fact and also ironically like Estella, Arabella characteristically looks at courting as sporting, or better a kind of sporting business if not blood sport, since "she like[s] to set herself to catch him the right way" (36). In this sense she recalls Chaucer's Monk "that loved venerye" since the pun on *venery* suggests both the game of the chase and the game of love. "In a physical sense," then, as Jude later admits to her, Arabella remains "the stronger" in both Darwinian games of Natural and Sexual Selection: "You could push me over like a ninepin"(VI: 9, 311). Thus, throughout the text, Arabella can repeatedly utter "the low and triumphant laugh of a careless woman who sees she is winning her game (I: 7, 39).

From the very beginning, Jude himself, much like, say, the prematurely sententious Ivanhoe, or Henry Esmond, or Adam Bede, or Will Ladislaw, or Arthur Clennam, appears to mime a "young harlican" (I: 1, 11) as he plays the scarecrow for Farmer Troutham. Jude's self-parodic play, which is later projected onto the anachronistic Little Father Time, ironically marks the merry green fields where "echoes of songs from the ancient harvest days" still seem to ring and where carnivalesque "energy, gaiety, horseplay" characterize the "love-matches that had populated the adjoining hamlet" and "had been made up there between reaping and carrying" (I: 2, 13). It is not much later than this that Jude sends his request for textbooks in Phillotson's piano, as he suffers under the "grand delusion!" that some magical "law of transmutation" (I: 4, 26–27) exists which will allow him to reduce all ancient babble to Wessex English. After receiving the texts and discovering that no such lexical philosopher's stone survives, however, Jude acknowledges "the shabby trick played him by the dead languages" (I: 5, 27), as Hardy character-istically resorts to the play of differences to convey significant, ironic truths in his text.

Turning then from learning to love, Jude's passive courting of Arabella teaches him "that he should assert mere sportiveness on his part as his reason in seeking her" precisely because his playful princess of the pigs is "quite antipathetic to that side of him which had been occupied with literary study and the magnificent Christminster dream" (I: 6, 35). Conversely, Arabella's own sense of "courting in such a business-like" (I: 7, 37) manner is antipa-thetic to the idealism of courtly lover Jude, and thus he proves no match (in either sense) for this venal Venus, and so finds himself gamely but tragically "entrapped" (I: 11, 56) in a hopeless marriage. It is consequently appropriate that he and Sue both commiserate with the equally tricked rabbit in its "trap [which is] dragged about by the writhing animal" (IV: 2, 169). During the Great Wessex Agricultural Show, Jude and Sue can even love "playfully" as if they have momentarily "returned to Greek joyousness" (V: 5,235). The actual frustrating fragility or delirium of such playful *jouissance,* like that of George Eliot's Hetty and Arthur in *Adam Bede* or Dickens's Little Emily and David Copperfield, however, is revealed when they approach no closer to Christminster than hawking "Christminster cakes" or toy "windows, and towers, and pinnacles!" (V: 7,247). Thus, immediately after Jude finally re-lates the novel's epigraph to their own tragic inconsistency: "'Sue, Sue! we are acting by the letter; and 'the letter killeth'!'" the frustrated wish of his significant subjunctive mood adopts a play metaphor which poignantly typifies his own ultimate, obscure entrapment by universal blood sport: "Where is your scorn of convention gone? I *would* have died game!" VI: 8, 308–09) Hardy's emphasis).

In conclusion, we should stress that the relative frequency and significance of play acts and metaphors in Hardy almost approximates their proportionate numbers and values in Dickens. What is more, Hardy similarly hearkens back to a simpler rural existence on the village green when the joys of play seemed immediately available to human culture, just as they also do in the retrospec-tive *A Room With a View.* Thus, both Hardy and Dickens emphasize the ritualistic pedigree of play and rely more on carnivalesque and popular festive motifs than any other nineteenth-century British novelists. Historically closer to folk traditions and not depressed by *fin de siècle* decadence and Modern-ism's encroaching epistemological crisis, however, Dickens seems much more fertile and versatile in invoking play tropes. Hardy, on the other hand, almost exclusively reduces such tropes to the overlapping practices of sexual foreplay and blood sport. Recovering and then adapting more primitive play forms could still ultimately redeem humanity for Dickens, while for Hardy, choric hymns to residual or ritual forms of primitive folk play only ironically chant its haunting absence in his dispassionate, dis*court*eous, and deritualized waste land.

# NOTES

1. Richard Schickel relevantly opens his review of the film version of *A Room With A View*:

Scandalous! Miss Honeychurch likes to play Beethoven on the pianoforte. This is not a composer with whom respectable young Edwardian women are supposed to be emotionally involved. And, indeed, playing him makes her feel 'peevish,' or perhaps guilty of allowing this expression of her passionate inner nature to burst out. (80)

In his next paragraph, Schickel points out that Lucy's tennis playing similarly reveals her passionate nature in the film. In the novel Lucy plays Gluck, not Beethoven.

2. See Babcock's pertinent discussion of the "double system of signification." For example,

The influence of carnival themes, forms, and symbols and the related Renaissance concepts of the wisdom of folly and the philosophy of serious play on eighteenth and nineteenth-century literature is considerable. Although carnival recedes into the background, it never disappears entirely from the novel. Rather this semiotic is formalized; carnival becomes an aesthetic means to serve aesthetic aims—a counterpoint to the serious message and essentially metonymic structure of the novel, contributing to the forms of ironic possibilities (930).

3. Unless otherwise noted, all citations to Dickens' works refer to the *Oxford Illustrated Dickens* edition. For accounts of window imagery in Dickens, see Greenstein's three essays.
4. For a discussion of this game, see Burns.
5. In discussing play motifs in "serious" literature, we are, of course, only scratching the surface of nineteenth-century cultural play, which is evident in the so-called "sporting" magazines and novels like *Bell's Life in London* and Robert Smith Surtee's *Jorrock's Jaunts and Jollities* (1838), in play and sporting scenes in the art world (see Wood ch. 22), and in the philosophy of a thinker like Nietzsche (see Hyland 82–83). This play milieu influenced Dickens' novels, and his own play motifs further influenced this milieu.
6. In a related play trope echoing his "friend the Boots" in a recent Christmas story, Dickens reflected upon himself to Mary Boyle: "when you come to think what a game you've been up to ever since you was in your cradle, and what a poor

sort of chap you are, and how it's always yesterday with you or else tomorrow, and never today, that's where it is'' (Kaplan 339–40).

7. See my ''Carnivalesque 'Unlawful Games' in *The Old Curiosity Shop*.''
8. See Bakhtin's discussion of ''court festivals'' and ''court masquerades'' which tend to represent fusions of both traditions (*Rabelais and His World* 102–03).
9. See Chaney for a further discussion of this reference. She writes, for example, that ''Dickens's familiarity with pugilism and the various aspects of its mystique—its jargon, its personalities, and its importance to all classes, finds expression in most of his novels'' (87). See also Huizinga's treatment of the playful 'love-courts'' (125).
10. Iona and Peter Opie relevantly judge Strutt's book ''a remarkable undertaking that embodies considerable research, and can scarcely be faulted in what it says, only in what it does not say, for it allows small space to the 'sports of children' '' (vii).
11. See Jaeger's relevant discussion of the relationships between ''courtier'' and *curalis* (14–16), and Michell's treatment of the relationships between city court and the harmony of the spheres (42–46). Sicher's account of ''the organization of space'' (22) in *Hard Times* is also relevant here.
12. In fact, Marcus writes of those later performers in the garden, Mrs. Nickleby and her sylvan suitor:

In these two unique brings, in their styles, their trains of association, their unshakable belief that the articulation of their mutual solitude are public discourse, Dickens anticipated the Victorian phenomenon of nonsense literature—a literature in which the imaginations of childhood and insanity consort  (110).

And Ganz writes of the same scene that ''Dickens' ecstasy in the free play of the imagination upon the inconsistencies of human behaviour culminates in the vegetable-throwing courtship of Mrs. Nickleby'' (148). We might finally note here apropos of Wild Man motifs that in *Hard Times,* Mr. E. W. B. Childers is

so justly celebrated for his daring vaulting act as the Wild Huntsman of the North American Prairies; in which popular performance, a diminutive boy with an old face, who now accompanied him, assisted as his infant son: being carried upside down over his father's shoulder, by one foot, and held by the crown of his head, heels upwards, in the palm of his father's hand, according to the violent paternal manner in which wild huntsmen may be observed to fondle their offspring.					(I: 6, 29–30)

13. Consequently, it seems to me that a discussion of the Wild Man would further enhance Eigner's fine study of the Harlequin figure.
14. In fact, in the ''Arcadian London'' chapter of *The Uncommercial Traveller,* which wistfully limns the rustic attractions of the deserted metropolis during the autumn holiday season, Dickens repeatedly details such Wild Man motifs. During this ''Golden Age revived'' (166), for example, he senses ''reviving within me that latent wildness of the original savage'' (159). He also finds repeated links between

love and play, seeing London as now the very "abode of Love" (165), where "there is nothing to do but love," which is illustrated in marathon street dances and even in "a neighboring billiard-room" (166–67). In the related satire "The Noble Savage" from *Reprinted Pieces,* Dickens again draws upon Wild Man motifs: animals, death, demonology, dancing, agriculture, courting, "pantomime" rituals, persecution, and final evaluative judgments. But his protestations of wanting "to abhore, detest, abominate, and abjure" the "howling, whistling, clucking, stamping, jumping, tearing savage" (*The Booklovers Edition of the Works of Charles Dickens* 226–27) finally seem much too much and eventually reveal the piece as an ironic, if not allegorical, satire on the modern vices of savage nobles.

15. For a more recent account of the Wild Woman "archetype," see Estes.
16. This certainly is not true, however, of the miserly Arthur Gride, a mock wild man who later courts Madeline Bray.
17. If Kaplan is correct in arguing that Mrs. Nickleby presents an amalgam of Dickens' equally troublesome mother and wife (119, 222), then her temporary, playful graciousness and gracefulness can be attributed to her fictional ability to give her Wild Man, Dickens, his "deserved" due for once.
18. For an account of Hardy and the carnivalesque, see my "The 'Original Tess': Pre-Texts, *Tess,* Fess, Tesserae, Carnivalesque." Wotton has briefly treated Hardy in terms of Bakhtin and Rabelais (61–64), while Fishler has discussed Hardy's (carnivalesque) pun on *spirits* in *Jude.* Firor remains the standard though much outdated study of folklore in Hardy.
19. In *Far From the Madding Crowd* (1874), for example, the central importance and folkloric contexts of Bathsheba's "childish game" (31:191) of sending an anonymous valentine to Boldwood, which pleads "Marry Me," or Troy's role as a Trickster (the title of chapter 34 even labels him "A Trickster") might suggest that this early work is Hardy's most playful piece. But, again, all his novels rely heavily on folkloric play motifs.
20. *A Tale of Two Cities* proves an exception to this rule since its social spectacles, like the "wine game," are more horrifying than farcical. The "No-Popery Dance" functions similarly in *Barnaby Rudge.* For a discussion of these motifs, see my "Playing at Leap-Frog with the Tombstones" (227,233).
21. For a discussion of Dickens' interest in Rabelais, see my "Carnivalesque 'Unlawful Games' in *The Old Curiosity Shop.*"
22. For a discussion of this motif, see my "The 'Games of the Prison Children' in *Little Dorrit.*"

# WORKS CITED

Babcock, Barbara. "The Novel and the Carnival World: An Essay in Memory of Joe Doherty." *Modern Language Notes* 89(1974): 911–37.

Bakhtin, Mikhail Mikhailovich. *The Dialogic Imagination: Four Essays*. Ed. Michael Holquist. Trans. Caryl Emerson and Michael Holquist. Austin and London: U of Texas P, 1981.

————. *Rabelais and His World*. Trans. Helene Iswolsky. Forward Krystyna Pomorska. Cambridge and London: M.I.T. Press, 1968.

Bernheimer, Richard. *Wild Men in the Middle Ages: A Study in Art, Sentiment, and Demonology*. Cambridge: Harvard UP, 1952.

Besant, Walter. *The Autobiography of Sir Walter Besant*. London: Hutchinson, 1902.

Booth, Michael R. "Melodrama and the Working Class." *Dramatic Dickens*. Ed. Carol Hanbery MacKay. New York: St. Martin's, 1989. 97–109.

Burns, Thomas A. "*The Game of Life:* Idealism, Reality and Fantasy in the Nineteenth and Twentieth-Century Versions of a Milton Bradley Game." *The Canadian Review of American Studies* 9(1978): 50–83.

Carroll, Lewis. *The Annotated Alice: Alice's Adventures in Wonderland and Through the Looking Glass*. New York: Herder and Herder, 1972.

Chaney, Lois E. "The Fives' Court." *The Dickensian* 81(1985): 86–87.

Cox, R. G. (ed.). *Thomas Hardy: The Critical Heritage*. London: Routledge, 1970.

Dickens, Charles. *Charles Dickens' Book of Memoranda*. Intro. and annot. Fred Kaplan. New York: New York Public Library, 1981.

————. *The Oxford Illustrated Dickens*. 21 vols. London: Oxford UP, 1951–1959.

————. *Selected Letters of Charles Dickens*. Ed. and arran. by David Paroissien. Boston: Twayne, 1985.

————. *The Works of Charles Dickens*. Booklovers Edition. 30 vols. Managing Ed. John H. Clifford. New York: The University Society, 1908.

Eigner, Edwin M. *The Dickens Pantomime*. Berkeley: U of California P, 1989.

Estes, Clarissa P. *Women Who Run with Wolves: Myths & Stories of the Wild Woman Archetype*. New York: Ballantine, 1994.

Firor, Ruth A. *Folkways in Thomas Hardy*. Philadelphia: U of Philadelphia P, 1931.

Fischler, Alexander. "Gin and Spirits: The Letter's Edge in Hardy's *Jude the Obscure*." *Journal of English and Germanic Philology* 84(1985): 515–33.

Forster, E.M. *A Room With a View*. New York: Knopf, 1953.

Ganz, Margaret. "*Nicholas Nickleby:* : The Victories of Humor." *Mosaic* 9(1976): 131–48.

Greenstein, Michael. "Between Curtain and Caul: *David Copperfield*'s Shining Transparencies." *Dickens Quarterly* 5(1988): 75–81.

———. Lenticular Curiosity and *The Old Curiosity Shop*." *Dickens Quarterly* 4(1987): 187–94.

———. "Magic Casements and Victorian Transparencies: Post-Romantic Modes of Perception." *Dickens Studies Annual* (1985): 267–86.

Grosz, Elizabeth. *Jacques Lacan: A Feminist Introduction*. London and New York: Routledge, 1990.

Hardy, Evelyn. *Thomas Hardy: A Critical Biography*. New York: Russell & Russell, 1970.

Hardy, Thomas. *Far from the Madding Crowd*. Ed. Carl J. Weber. New York: Holt, 1959.

———. *Jude the Obscure*. Ed. and intro. Irving Howe. Boston: Riverside, 1965.

———. *The Literary Notebooks of Thomas Hardy*. Vol. 1. Ed. Lennart A Bjork. New York: New York UP, 1985.

———. *Selected Poems of Thomas Hardy*. Ed. John Crowe Ransome. New York: Collier, 1960.

Hennelly, Mark, M., Jr. "Carnivalesque 'Unlawful Games' in *The Old Curiosity Shop*." *Dickens Studies Annual* 22(1993): 67–117.

———. "The 'Games of the Prison Children' in *Little Dorrit*." *Nineteenth-Century Contexts* 20 (1997): 187–213.

———. " 'Playing at Leap-Frog with the Tombstones': The *Danse Macabre* Motif in Dickens." *Essays in Literature* 22(1995): 227–43.

———. "The 'Original Tess': Pre-Texts, *Tess,* Fess,Tesserae, Carnivalesque." *The Thomas Hardy Year Book* 24 (1997): 17–59.

Huizina, Johan. *Homo Ludens: A Study of the Play Element in Culture*. Boston: Beacon, 1955.

Hyland, Drew. *The Question of Play*. Lanham, Maryland: UP of America, 1984.

Jaeger, C. Stephen. *The Origins of Courtliness: Civilizing Trends and the Formation of Courtly Ideals—939–1210*. Philadelphia: U of Pennsylvania P, 1985.

Lorris, Guillaume de and Jean de Meun. *The Romance of the Rose*. Trans. Charles Dahlberg. Hanover and London: UP of New England, 1983.

Kaplan, Fred. *Dickens: A Biography*. New York: William Morrow and Co., 1988.

Kendrick, Laura. *The Game of Love: Troubadour Wordplay*. Berkeley: U of California P, 1988.

Marcus, Steven. *Dickens: from* Pickwick *to* Dombey. New York: Clarion Books, 1968.

Meredith, George. "Modern Love." *The Pre-Raphaelites And Their Circle.* Ed. Cecil Y. Lang. *Boston: Riverside, 1968. 299–319.*

Michell, John. *The Dimensions of Paradise: The Proportions and Symbolic Numbers of Ancient Cosmology.* London: Thames and Hudson, 1988.

Millgate, Michael. *Thomas Hardy: A Biography.* New York: Random House, 1982.

Morrow, Nancy. *Dreadful Games: The Play of Desire in the Nineteenth-Century Novel.* Kent, Ohio: Kent State UP, 1988.

Opie, Peter and Iona. *Children's Games in Street and Playground.* Oxford: Oxford UP, 1969.

Peckman, Morse. *Beyond the Tragic Vision.* New York: George Braziller, 1962.

Rabelais, François. *The Works of Mr. Francis Rabelais Doctor in Physick. Containing Five Books of the Lives, Heroic Deeds and Sayings of Gargantua and His Sonne Pantagruel.* 1653 [Trans. Sir Thomas Urquhart]. Illust. W. Heath Robinson. 2 vols. London: Navarre Society, n.d.

Schickel, Richard. *"A Room With a View." Time* 10 (Mar.1986): 80.

Scott, Sir Walter. *Ivanhoe.* Intro. Delancey Ferguson. New York: Collier, 1962.

Sicher, Efraim. "Acts of Enclosure: The Moral Landscape of Dickens' *Hard Times*." *Dickens Studies Annual* 22(1993): 195–216.

Strutt, Joseph. *The Sports and Pastimes of the People of England.* 1801. Rpt. 1903. Detroit: Singing Tree Press, 1968.

Wood, Christopher. *Victorian Panorama: Paintings of Victorian Life.* London: Faber, 1976.

Wotton, George. *Thomas Hardy, Towards A Materialist Criticism.* Totowa, New Jersey: Barnes & Noble, 1985.

# Bad Scene: *Oliver Twist* and the Pathology of Entertainment

## Joseph Litvak

As Goldblum's father, Judd Hirsch overplays as ripely as
Goldblum underplays, shuffling across the screen like an
old man making his way to the bathroom, and doing lovable-
cranky, clogged-artery Jewish shtick.

James Wolcott, reviewing *Independence Day*
in *The New Yorker*

As almost every commentator on *Oliver Twist* (1837) will tell you, the most
famous scene in the novel is the one in which Oliver says he wants some
more—more of the thin gruel on which he and the other workhouse boys are
expected to survive. Yet no one ever explains *why* this is the most famous
scene—more famous than far more sensational scenes, like the murder of
Nancy or the accidental suicide of Sikes. The scene's fame no doubt owes
something to Lionel Bart's musical version of the novel, in which Oliver's
demand not only provokes the indignation of the authorities, but ostentatiously
serves as the cue for the show's title song as well. I want to suggest, however,
that the scene derives considerable emblematic force from its status as a
*scene about food*—more precisely, from its conjunction of the scenic with
the alimentary, a conjunction to which, if it were not for the notoriously
unappetizing nature of the food in question, the term "entertainment," as
distinguished from the term "spectacle," would seem especially well suited.

And yet, the term may be more appropriate than we think. For "entertainment," in Dickens, is not always cause for celebration. To be sure, entertainment, signifying both the agreeable diversion and the hospitable feeding of
others, and finding perhaps its ideal (not to say mandatory) expression in the
festivities known as Christmas, seems a distinctly Dickensian value, almost
a distinctly Dickensian invention.[1] All the more striking, then, that the term
so often undergoes a kind of sarcastic deformation in Dickens' writing. Think,

33

for instance, of the parasitic tenacity with which it attaches itself to a charming host like Pecksniff. Or consider the following example from *Oliver Twist* itself, where just before Oliver asks for more, the narrator characterizes the workhouse as "a regular place of public entertainment for the poorer classes; a tavern where there was nothing to pay; a public breakfast, dinner, tea, and supper all the year round; a brick and mortar elysium, where it was all play and no work."[2]

Such sarcasm hardly seems out of place in a novel about legally enforced starvation, a novel where the food that does get served, even when it is not repulsively insipid or grotesquely meager, is never glorious. But the bitter taste of "entertainment" in *Oliver Twist,* as in other texts by Dickens, may betoken a broader concern on Dickens' part about what we might call entertainment's performativity, its practical effects.

"It is the custom on the stage, in all good murderous melodramas," Dickens writes at the beginning of chapter 17, in an often-cited passage from *Oliver Twist,* "to present the tragic and the comic scenes, in as regular alternation, as the layers of red and white in a side of streaky bacon" (168). If this analogy evinces Dickens' well-known insistence on the affinity between the novel and the theater, the bacon metaphor embedded within it signals an almost equally unsurprising construction of the popular entertainer's relation toward his audience—a relation, at once as abstract as that between producer and consumer, and as intimate as that between host and guest, in which entertainment functions, familiarly, as the control and gratification of certain collective *appetites.*

But what if we take the bacon more literally, and ask what it's doing in a novel whose shamelessly entertaining villain does not just happen to be Jewish? You don't have to be Jewish yourself for the phrase "adding insult to injury" to cross your mind. Nor do you have to keep kosher—the Jewish villain flagrantly does not—for the term "good murderous melodramas" (speaking of insult and injury) not to go down so easily. Are these exemplary works murderous merely because they represent murder, or do they themselves have a murderous potential, a capacity for violence directed, say, at their spectators, even the non-Jewish ones? And might this violence have something to do with the violence necessary to produce, from a pig, a side of streaky bacon in the first place? In the world of entertainment according to Dickens, who's eating what—or whom?

These questions might be dismissed as melodramatic in their own right, except that, in his preface to *Oliver Twist,* Dickens himself, playing up the book's aversively strong taste, promoting its brutally carnivorous realism over a finicky scenic decorum, simultaneously works to keep the former within the limits of the latter. Of the novel's detractors, who have objected to its unglamorized representation of criminal low life, Dickens, again at his most disgustedly sarcastic, writes, or bites:

There are people of so refined and delicate a nature, that they cannot bear the
contemplation of such horrors. Not that they turn instinctively from crime; but
that criminal characters, to suit them, must be, like their meat, in delicate
disguise. A Massaroni in green velvet is an enchanting creature; but a Sikes in
fustian is insupportable. A Mrs. Massaroni, being a lady in short petticoats and
a fancy dress, is a thing to imitate in tableaux and have in lithograph on pretty
songs; but a Nancy, being a creature in a cotton gown and cheap shawl, is not
to be thought of. It is wonderful how Virtue turns from dirty stockings; and
how Vice, married to ribbons and a little gay attire, changes her name, as
wedded ladies do, and becomes Romance.                                    (35)

No self-respecting author, Dickens goes on to assert, "ever has descended to
the taste of this fastidious class" (36). This class, of course, is also a gender.
But while these misogynistic lines would seem to establish a clear hierarchy
of honestly virile "meat" over hypocritically feminine "disguise," they en-
tangle themselves in a bit of cross-dressing, in which the role of Vice's
husband is assumed by "ribbons and a little gay attire." This local cross-
dressing, moreover, points to Dickens' own continuing investment in a general
theatricality. For though he explicitly places himself in the truth-telling tradition of writers such as Fielding and Defoe, who "brought upon the scene the
very scum and refuse of the land" (35), his language, reversing the procedure,
brings upon the very scum and refuse of the land the scene.

   That is, Dickens' claim to have beefed up what would otherwise have
amounted to the mere *spectacle* of crime never gets outside the spectacular
frame of reference; as Horkheimer and Adorno say of the culture industry in
general, "the diner must be satisfied with the menu."[3] The superiority of
Nancy and Sikes to their prettified counterparts, for instance, registers as
a difference of *costumes,* a difference between "green velvet" and "short
petticoats," on the one hand, and "fustian" and "cheap shawl[s]," on the
other. Aggressively though Dickens gestures beyond the visual toward the
greater authenticity of the gustatory, or the *dis*gustatory, those appeals, as
their gestural form virtually guarantees, only reinforce the reign of visuality.
"It was my attempt," Dickens elaborates, "to dim the false glitter surrounding [crime], by showing it in its unattractive and repulsive truth. . . . I
painted it in all its fallen and degraded aspect" (36). Where genteel hypocrisy
insists that its meat appear "in delicate disguise," Dickens, showing the
repulsive, presenting the repulsive as show, offers not meat in some unadulter-
ated form, but rather *painted* meat, meat in *in*delicate disguise. Any way you
slice it, what you get is still spectacle.

   "As opposed to what?," you may ask. My point here is not to reveal the
"failure" of Dickens' attempt to transcend spectacle. On the contrary, I would
argue that he makes no such attempt. But he appears or pretends to make it,
and the question of why he does so returns us to the question of entertainment—to the question of the relationship, in Dickens, between entertainment

and spectacle. In the preface to *Oliver Twist,* Dickens, defending the novel against those who would denounce its "bad, depraved, vicious taste,"[4] presents himself not as an entertainer, but as a messenger of "stern truth" (35), humbly doing "a service to society" (34). As a shrewd showman, however, he understands quite well the entertainment-value of what he refers to elsewhere as the "attraction of repulsion."[5] Playing the earnest public servant, he can enjoy at the same time a less respectable, and more profitable, identification with the fat boy in *Pickwick Papers,* who "wants to make your flesh creep."[6] With one eye on his hungry orphan asking for more gruel, Dickens keeps the other on his better-fed reader, who, having flesh enough for creeping to occur, hungers for just that sensation. And what better way to make this reader's flesh creep than by *displaying* flesh, producing a novel that resembles not a side of streaky bacon itself, but rather an immense butcher-shop window, attractively-repulsively featuring, along with the meat of thieves and prostitutes, such items as "beef-faced boys" (140), lots of fat men, and, last but not least, somewhere between bacon and pastrami, that "vile"(155) old pork-eating Jewish ham, the more-than-ripely overplaying Fagin?[7]

But why last if not least? Dickens himself has little to say about Fagin in the preface, concentrating on Sikes and Nancy as the novel's privileged embodiments of "scum and refuse"; but it is Fagin, after all, or, rather, before all, whom the book charges most heavily, most saliently, most allegorically, with the function of representing repulsiveness, who constitutes its prime cut of bad meat. Who, aside from Dickens, could forget a passage like the following?:

> The mud lay thick upon the stones, and a black mist hung over the streets; the rain fell sluggishly down, and everything felt cold and clammy to the touch. It seemed just the night when it befitted such a being as the Jew to be abroad. As he glided stealthily along, creeping beneath the shelter of the walls and doorways, the hideous old man seemed like some loathsome reptile, engendered in the slime and darkness through which he moved: crawling forth, by night, in search of some rich offal for a meal.                    (186)

Describing Fagin, in Gail Turley Houston's words, both "as an offal-seeking mouth, and as feces," figuring "the Jew" as excremental food in search of excremental food, this passage about creeping flesh may well make one's flesh creep, though not, I suspect, in the way that Dickens has in mind.[8] It is not a uniquely twentieth-century response, or an inordinately "refined" one, anyway, to think that the passage's excrementally bad taste, which it lays on as thick as the mud upon the stones, is the taste not of "the Jew," but of its own anti-Semitism.[9]

As we shall see, too, there is more where that came from. At this point, however, I want to argue that Dickens "forgets" Fagin for the same reason that he only *pretends* to transcend spectacle—a reason other than feeling guilty about Jew-bashing, which won't register until later in his career, through the character of Riah in *Our Mutual Friend.* We tend to think of spectacle as what one critic has called "a subversive anti-culture," as the vaguely exotic repressed that must always return to disrupt the surprisingly precarious structures of Victorian orthodoxy.[10] Like other Jewish characters in Victorian fiction, Fagin is closely associated with spectacle and theater. But his power to attract by repelling—his power to *engross*—doesn't simply arise from his status as "Dickens's deftest showman of a villain."[11] Doing Jewish shtick, doing his routine, he does something more than routine; chewing the scenery, he would chew his way through to the scenery's other side. In his loathsomely reptilian fashion, he brings out the larger cultural fantasy to which the pleonasm, "Jewish shtick"—unless fleshed out metonymically, as in the epigraph to this paper, where Jewish shtick becomes *clogged-artery* Jewish shtick—can only allude etymologically: the fantasy that, just as the Yiddish *shtik,* literally meaning "piece," as in "piece of meat," reminds us how close a bit is to a bite,[12] so the theatrical Jew, like an old man making his way to the bathroom (to invoke my epigraph once again), will lead his spectators from the scene proper to a scene *im*proper, a place of "slime and darkness," of "scum and refuse," where the differences between sex and death, enjoyment and disgust, evacuation and consumption, muscle and organ, meat and meat-eater, all collapse.

This fantasy of transgression, of moving from the scene to the *ob*scene, is the fantasy that a mediated, sanitized, at best pseudosubversive *spectacle* will turn into a thrillingly carnal, authentically subversive *entertainment.* It may seem twisted—to cite the title of the novel's latest cinematic adaptation—to implicate entertainment, with all its blandly feel-good connotations, in the obscene; but sometimes, one kind of tastelessness or unsavoriness—like that of gruel—has curious affinities with an apparently antithetical kind of tastelessness or unsavoriness—like that of offal. This spin on entertainment is no more (or less) twisted, at any rate, than the murderous rhetoric—the promise of being scared out of your skin, blown away, and so forth—with which every summer blockbuster, nowadays, entices its mass audience; no more (or less) perverse, for that matter, than Dickens' own designs upon both readerly and characterly flesh, whose attractive and repulsive confusion the word *entertainment,* meaning "to hold mutually," itself implies.

In a fascinating recent study of Dickens' lifelong obsession with cannibalism, Harry Stone discusses, among a wide range of other texts from the Dickens corpus, two essays, collected in *The Uncommercial Traveller,* in which Dickens' cannibal imagination finds itself irresistibly drawn to the Paris morgue.[13] For my own purposes, the value of these essays lies in their representation of the morgue as a grisly, gristly theater in which what gets staged is not just cannibalism, but entertainment *as* cannibalism. And though, as my terms suggest, the essays, written more than twenty years after *Oliver Twist*, remain inside the framework of spectacular visuality, they go further than either the preface to the novel or, as we shall see, the novel itself, in elaborating the fantasy of entertainment—both a promise and threat—always on the verge of *exceeding* that framework.

In the first of these essays, entitled, "Some Recollections of Mortality," Dickens finds himself part of a "ravenous" (189) crowd gathered in front of "the obscene little Morgue" (188), waiting to see the corpse of an old man killed by a falling stone. As the crowd grows restless—it includes "a pretty young mother, pretending to bite the forefinger of her baby boy" (190)—the Custodian, clearly a canny impresario, addresses it:

> Patient, patience! We make his toilette, gentlemen. He will be exposed presently. It is necessary to proceed according to rule. His toilette is not made all at a blow. He will be exposed in good time, gentlemen, in good time. . . . Entertain yourselves in the meanwhile with other curiosities. Fortunately, the Museum is not empty today.                                                                  (191)

Insofar as the word "entertain" itself encrypts, as I have noted, an image of fleshly undifferentiation, the sarcasm hovering over the Custodian's "entertain yourself," like the sarcasm that seems to attend almost every other Dickensian use of "entertainment" as well, loses some of its bite. Or rather, its mordancy may repeat, even as it would deny, the oral aggression to which entertainment regularly invites us. Instead of constituting a macabre parody of entertainment, that is, the scene at the obscene little morgue may simply constitute its definitive manifestation.

Precisely *as* a scene, of course—"His toilette is not made all at a blow"—it keeps the ravenous crowd at a distance, imposing, and interposing, a certain mimetic prophylaxis. But if the young mother merely "*pretends* to bite the forefinger of her baby boy," merely *hints at* at the reversible relation between consuming spectator and consumed spectacle, that playful soupçon, as though unable to resist literalizing itself, gives way, a few pages later, to a more in-your-face image of the edible infant. Describing the corpse of a baby whose mother is indeed suspected of murdering it, Dickens writes:

> It had been opened, and neatly sewn up, and regarded from that point of view, it looked like a stuffed creature. It rested on a clean white cloth, with a surgical instrument or so at hand, and regarded from that point of view, it looked as if the cloth were "laid," and the Giant were coming to dinner.                              (196)

In all good murderous melodramas, as in a side of streaky bacon, the tragic and the comic alternate; in this dead-baby joke, this bit of sick humor or morbid farce, the tragic and the comic are so thoroughly interlarded, as in a well-marbled piece of meat or a juicy roast chicken, that you don't know whether to laugh or to gag—or to jump back, lest the "stuffed creature," "with a surgical instrument or so at hand," suddenly grab one of those instruments and aim it at your throat.

Meanwhile, back at the morgue, where the *plat du jour* is dead old man rather than dead baby, Dickens more subtly, though no less ghoulishly, turns his hungry eye on the other spectators, proleptically abolishing (even while affirming) the distance between them and the corpse, reading their indifference to it as their nondifference from it.

> The uncommercial interest, sated at a glance [at the old man], directed itself upon the striving crowd on either side and behind. . . . The differences of expression were not many. There was a little pity, but not much, and that mostly with a selfish touch in it—as who would say, "Shall I, poor I, look like that, when the time comes!". . . . There was a wolfish stare at the object. . . . And there was a much more general, purposeless, vacant staring at it—like looking at wax-work, without a catalogue, and not knowing what to make of it. But all these expressions concurred in possessing the one underlying expression of *looking at something that could not return a look.*   (192; Dickens' emphasis)

*"Looking at something that could not return a look"*: this formula ought to proclaim the triumph of life over death; but in rendering that formula as empty as so much "vacant staring," in reducing most of his fellow spectators to so many of the living dead, Dickens does not just deliver a banal indictment of the stupefied body-in-entertainment. Even more "wolfish" than the stare that it takes in, his own not-so-easily "sated" gaze implicitly leaves itself open to being ingested in turn by the next entertainment-starved tragicomic ironist. Like Miss Havisham decomposing herself into her wedding cake, Dickens flirts with the possibility of being swallowed in his own right.

Flirting—that is, *just* flirting—Dickens keeps his act clean, if not kosher. But while the diner must still be satisfied with the menu, this menu rather generously specifies the content of the obscenity that it advertises—an obscenity linked here not with an old man on his way to the bathroom, but with an old man on the way to his toilette. Not that this obscenity can only take the latter form, or that it fails to travel well outside of Paris: just as the fantasy of entertainment, which promises/threatens such obscenity, extends beyond this short piece, into Dickens' novels, so, as my references to contemporary show business suggest, does it extend beyond Dickens and Victorian culture.

Both inside and outside Dickens, moreover, that fantasy, while Jewishly inflected in ways that I will indicate, does not batten exclusively on Jewish bodies. Sometimes, as the old man in the morgue goes to show, the entertaining body is racially unmarked, unlike that of Fagin or other, more recent, virtuosos of Jewish shtick. At other times, a less determinately racialized body will suffice, as in the case of Sampson and Sally Brass, who are banished at the end of *The Old Curiosity Shop* to "the obscene hiding-places of London," where they go, Fagin-like, "in search of refuse food or disregarded offal," and in whom at least one critic has discerned " 'Jewish' characteristics."[14] Or consider the following passage from the second morgue-centered essay, called "Travelling Abroad":

> This time, I was forced into the same dread place, to see a large dark man whose disfigurement by water was in a frightful manner comic, and whose expression was that of a prize-fighter who had closed his eyelids under a heavy blow, but was going immediately to open them, shake his head, and "come up smiling." Oh what this large dark man cost me in that bright city!          (65)

Recounting the cost, Dickens tells of how, when he tries to "freshen himself with a dip in the great floating bath on the river" (58), instead of washing that man right out of his hair, he imagines getting him in his mouth:

> I made haste to participate in the water part of the entertainments, and was in the full enjoyment of a delightful bath, when all in a moment I was seized with an unreasonable idea that the large dark body was floating straight at me.

> I was out of the river, and dressing instantly. In the shock I had taken some water into my mouth, and it turned me sick, for I fancied that the contamination of the creature was in it.          (65)

Nor does "the water part of the entertainments" end at the bath: like a bad meal, the fantasized taste of the dark man keeps coming back, as when, "[t]hat very day, at dinner, some morsel on my plate looked like a piece of him, and I was glad to get up and go out" (66). Swallowing the other, it seems, is worse than being swallowed by him. "[I]n a frightful manner comic," the large dark man makes Dickens sick because, in his "disfigurement," he indeed figures all too well "the contamination of the creature"—the creature being Dickens himself, whose obvious taste for dark comedy intimates that you are what you eat.

Fagin is not one of Victorian fiction's many dark-skinned Jews—applying a different racial cliché, Dickens makes him a redhead—but, like his frightfully comic confrère, he has an uncanny ability to mimic the author, around whom the water part of the entertainments, or "the great floating bath" of entertainment itself, where bodies would refreshingly commingle, thickens, as a result of that mimicry, into "slime and darkness," rather like the "social paste" in which Dickens, in a letter to John Forster, reports getting mixed up with "the jews of Houndsditch."[15] Much as Fagin refuses to be part of any Jewish community, his shtick sticks, both like meat to the ribs and like mud slung at an authorial portrait. When we first encounter him, he resembles not only greasy meat, but his very creator, who, as we have seen, makes such a show of bringing home the bacon:

> In a frying-pan, . . . some sausages were cooking; and standing over them, with a toasting-fork in his hand, was a very old shrivelled Jew, whose villanous-looking and repulsive face was obscured by a quantity of matted red hair. He was dressed in a greasy flannel gown, with his throat bare; and seemed to be dividing his attention between the frying-pan and a clothes-horse, over which a great number of silk handkerchiefs were hanging.                      (105)

"Dressed in a greasy flannel gown," the diabolical Fagin, this passage invites us to imagine, could—or should—end up in the frying-pan himself. As Robert Tracy has pointed out, Dickens, "who would have known that his own name was a euphemism for the devil," puts a lot of himself into his villainous Jew.[16] Indeed, so intense and enduring was the identification that, as Dickens approached the platform to give the last public reading in which he impersonated Fagin, he announced, "I shall tear myself to pieces."[17] Yet the spectacular sparagmos that would in effect end Dickens' life is already anticipated—anxiously anticipated—in the novel itself, where the meat-purveying author projects himself, via Fagin, into what is cooking. In his most archly droll vein, Dickens writes of the "liberal exercise of the Jew's toasting-fork on the heads and shoulders of the affectionate youths" (105) in his gang; but then, cannibalism, we know, works both ways: "the Dodger snatched up the toasting-fork, and made a pass at the merry old gentleman's waistcoat; which, if it had taken effect, would have let a little more merriment out, than could have been easily replaced" (135).

As early as *Oliver Twist,* then, Dickensian entertainment implies the author's transformation into a *corps morcelé.* But not just into any *corps morcelé:* the body that gets carved up here belongs to a Jew-devil. "What right have they to butcher me?" (472), asks Fagin, the night before he is led to the scaffold. One answer, apparently so self-evident as to go without saying in the narrative, is that he must be punished precisely for pointing a toasting-fork—and later, a knife (108)—at Christian children. As Deborah Heller has observed, Dickens uses Fagin to update the medieval stereotype of the Jew "as subhuman monster, as poisoner, as kidnapper, mutilator, murderer of innocent Christian children, on whom, perhaps, he cannibalistically feeds in observance of alien rituals."[18] Butchering the butcher, Fagin's executioners would avenge his crime against Christianity.

As I've been trying to suggest, however, this revenge smacks of overkill, not to say of bad faith. For the novel figures the Jew's body as virtually butchered from its first appearance, and this fantasy of cutting up and eating the Jew keeps repeating itself all the way to the end, from the Dodger's "ma[king] a pass" at Fagin with the toasting-fork, to the image of Fagin crawling forth in search of rich offal, to that of an angry crowd, "snarling with their teeth," and—itself hungry for rich offal—swearing "they'd tear his heart out" (445).[19]

It may be for just such confusions, though—more than for any specific violence against Christian children—that the Jew gets punished. I've emphasized, of course, that the fantasy of entertainment, with its scenarios of mutual cannibalism, plays out the confusion latent in the word *entertainment* itself. So what makes Fagin's confusions different from all other confusions? Why is it that, as soon as desiring the Jew becomes desiring *like* the Jew, it's curtains for Mr. Entertainment?

And curtains it is. In other words, not just Fagin's death by hanging, which he trenchantly misrepresents as an act of butchery, but the entire sequence of events from his trial to the execution itself, gets framed emphatically as a *spectacle*. The novel's penultimate chapter, titled "Fagin's Last Night Alive," makes a point of underlining its theatrical circumscription of the Jew's now intolerably entertaining body: "Those dreadful walls of Newgate . . . never held so dread a spectacle as that" (470); "Everything told of life and animation, but one dark cluster of objects in the center of all—the black stage, the cross-beam, the rope, and all the hideous apparatus of death" (475). If the life/death opposition holds up better here than in "Some Recollections of Mortality," this is because the opposition is undergirded by the elaborate "apparatus" of spectacle itself, which, putting death on stage, puts it at a distance, so that, when Mr. Brownlow takes Oliver to see Fagin in his prison cell, he can reply confidently to the guard who warns, "It's not a sight for children, sir": "It is not indeed, my friend . . . but . . . as this child has seen him in the full career of his success and villainy, I think it as well—even at the cost of some pain and fear—that he should see him now" (471). No child abuser himself, Brownlow, subjecting Oliver to what's good for him, knows that, as a "sight," the painful and frightening encounter with Fagin will be its own best cure.

But what exactly does this salutarily dread spectacle consist of? Or rather, what does it seek to contain? Dickens describes Fagin in his cell: "His red hair hung down upon his bloodless face; his beard was torn, and twisted into knots; his eyes shone with a terrible light; his unwashed flesh crackled with the fever that burnt him up" (470). "Twisted into knots," Fagin's beard seems to have Oliver inscribed within it, rehearsing, at the level of the name, the capture that, at the level of the plot, has itself already taken place twice, most insidiously through Fagin's power as an entertainer:

> . . . the old man would tell them stories of robberies he had committed in his younger days: mixed up with so much that was droll and curious, that Oliver

could not help laughing heartily, and showing that he was amused in spite of all his better feelings.

In short, the wily old Jew had the boy in his toils.          (185)

Etymologically knotted together with that oddly dirty word, *toilette,* the *toils* in which a "mixed[-]up" Oliver twists evoke the horrifying possibility that, in seducing Christian children, the Jewish entertainer will turn them, vampirically, into obscene little replicas of himself. Indeed, what's most modern about Fagin's atrocity is precisely that he enacts it through the medium of entertainment, prefiguring, in this regard, the myth of a (Jewish) "Hollywood cultural elite" undermining the values of (Christian) America by preying on its children.[20] That this modernized version of the blood libel often colludes with, or hides behind, a more permissible homophobia is not exactly irrelevant to *Oliver Twist,* either—though most criticism, and even as self-consciously hip a reinterpretation as the recent film, *Twisted,* shown in 1996 at Gay and Lesbian Film Festivals in New York and Boston, seems unable to conceptualize Fagin as Jewish and pederastic at once.[21] Suffering from no such inhibition, the novel itself luridly suggests how Fagin's "liberal exercise" of Jewish showbiz savvy might twist or pervert its helplessly laughing little victim, "instilling into his soul the poison which [Fagin] hoped would blacken it" (184), implanting in Oliver the same perverse sexuality—the sexuality *of* the same—as the villain's.

Oliver's surname, of course, may hint that he already has tendencies that way—just as his aptly termed Christian name, insofar as it has liver in it, already tastes like rich Jewish offal. Yet, with its implicit Faginization of the protagonist, Oliver's name may also hint at the ultimate effect of the villain's Jewish-homosexual agenda—at a Jewish perversion *beyond* homosexuality. For if Oliver's name incorporates the "in-sa-ti-a-ble" (136) Fagin—Tracy points out that "to twist" means "to eat heartily" as well as "to hang"—[22] or if (what may come to the same thing) Oliver's name signals that Fagin has already incorporated Oliver, it would emblematize the extreme consequence of Fagin's cannibalistic recruitment: the mixing-up or kinky twisting-together of bodies and characters to such an extent that the difference between eater and eaten disappears, and that entertainment becomes not just cannibalism but *self*-cannibalism, or, if you prefer, *autophagia,* a word that seems to have swallowed up Fagin itself.[23]

As performed by Fagin, then, "You are what you eat" becomes "*You* are what you eat": the confusion of bodies results in the image of a body turned inward and feverishly feeding upon itself. Appropriately enough, the Cruikshank illustration accompanying Dickens' account of Fagin's last night alive (fig. 1) shows him *biting his fingernails,* as Fagin has indeed been caught doing, several chapters earlier: "His right hand was raised to his lips, and as,

Figure 1. George Cruikshank, Fagin in the condemned cell

absorbed in thought, he bit his long black nails, he disclosed among his toothless gums a few such fangs as should have been a dog's or rat's'' (417). Yet, as my reading of the novel's title suggests, this autophagic motif is not limited to the character who, rich refuse himself, goes in search of rich refuse. Rather, the villain's most villainous deed is to compound the confusion by liberally contaminating other characters, causing a small epidemic of self-devouring involution.

If Fagin infected only the boys in his gang, the damage, though sensational, would be minor. But it reaches beyond the usual list of innocent victims. As everyone knows, the novel's menu of perversions includes, in addition to pederasty, the always-good-for-a-laugh autoeroticism personified by the character whom Dickens habitually refers to as "Master Bates." Between self-love and the novel's equally overt theme of self-murder, however, there stretches a perverse continuum of self-eating, on which we find, alongside Fagin, not only Oliver and his workhouse companions, driven by hunger to "sucking their fingers most assiduously, with the view of catching up any stray splashes of gruel that might have been cast thereon" (56), but grown-up figures as well, like—to take a melodramatic example—Oliver's evil half-brother, Monks, "whose lips are often discoloured and disfigured with the marks of teeth" and who "sometimes even bites his hands and covers them with wounds" (413); or—to take a more purely "comic" example—the lovable-cranky Mr. Grimwig, whose wig is grim because he's always threatening to eat his head.

However tonally and thematically disparate, these instances of autophagia point to the persistence in the novel of a certain generalized obscenity: they bespeak what we might call, almost paradoxically, the obscenity of everyday life. But while these miscellaneous symptoms therefore seem to take us far from the world of entertainment, "entertainment" is never far from them. For "to entertain" means not only "to amuse" and "to provide with food," but also "to hold in the mind," "to consider"—as Fagin himself, for that matter, seems to be doing while "absorbed in thought"—and Dickens in fact often uses "entertain" in this third, relatively abstract sense to comment on the various self-consuming pathologies that proliferate in the narrative. Of Grimwig's compulsively repeated offer to eat his own head, for example, Dickens writes: "Mr. Grimwig's head was such a particularly large one, that the most sanguine man alive could hardly entertain a hope of being able to get through it at a sitting" (147).

And then there's this passage, almost as bizarre in its own way, about Bill Sikes's dog, which we first see "licking a large, fresh cut on one side of his mouth" (152), and growling at his master, who, wielding a poker and brandishing a large knife, snarls, "Come here, you born devil! Come here! D'ye hear?":

> The dog no doubt heard; because Mr. Sikes spoke in the very harshest key of a very harsh voice; but, appearing to entertain some unaccountable objection to having his throat cut, he remained where he was, and growled more fiercely than before: at the same time grasping the end of the poker between his teeth, and biting at it like a wild beast. (153)

Refusing to be entertained, we might read this joke about the dog entertaining an objection as a harsh reminder of how entertainment would make wild beasts of us all, reducing even our acts of consciousness to so many stupid pet tricks. Or we might say, so many indeed: so many as to be *too* many. We should at least entertain the possibility that Fagin hangs not because his practice of entertainment might turn everyone into a dog like himself, but because it might turn everyone and his dog into an entertainer.

Dickens may find the prospect of an entertainment at once privatized and ubiquitous—like, say, television—as distasteful as the experience of getting stuck in the "social paste" formed by "the jews of Houndsditch." Should the canine (rat-like, reptilian) Jewish villain continue to spread his plague, should he diffuse it widely enough for it to become *mass* entertainment, his obscenity might prove truly repulsive, replacing the consumer who wants some more with a consumer who has had enough already. Dickens may have killed himself by playing Fagin, but he isn't about to commit *professional* suicide by allowing his readers to get fed up. Neither starving us nor clogging our arteries with too much rich food, he takes care to *thin out* his Jewish entertainer by making a spectacle of him. Even wilier, in short, than "the wily old Jew" himself, he keeps us in his toils by keeping us coming back for less.[24]

# NOTES

1. See Paul Schlicke, *Dickens and Popular Entertainment,* for a reading of Dickens' relation to entertainment as essentially affirmative.
2. *Oliver Twist,* ed. Peter Fairclough (Harmondsworth: Penguin, 1985), 55. Subsequent references to the novel will be to this edition, and will be included parenthetically in the text.
3. *Dialectic of Enlightenment,* 139.
4. This phrase, attributed to Lord Melbourne, is cited in Wills, "Love in the Lower Depths," 60.
5. See, for example, "The City of the Absent," in *The Uncommercial Traveller and Reprinted Pieces Etc.* (London: Oxford UP, 1968), 234. Subsequent references to this volume will be included parenthetically in the text.
6. *The Pickwick Papers,* 180.
7. See Audrey Jaffe, "Spectacular Sympathy: Visuality and Ideology in Dickens's *A Christmas Carol,*" 264 (note 9), on how "Dickens . . . drew on forms of representation widely present in everyday life, ones influenced perhaps most significantly by the use of plate glass." I am indebted more generally to Jaffe's account of the *distance* peculiar to spectacle.
8. *Consuming Fictions: Gender, Class, and Hunger in Dickens's Novels,* 32.

9. It is well known that at least one contemporary Jewish reader, Eliza Davis, to whose husband Dickens had sold his London residence, took Dickens to task for the "great wrong" against the Jews that the character of Fagin represents. On the Dickens-Davis correspondence, and its consequences, see, for example, Stone, "Dickens and the Jews," 242–46; and Kaplan, *Dickens: A Biography*, 472–73.

10. Nina Auerbach, *Private Theatricals: The Lives of the Victorians*, 16.

11. Auerbach, 40.

12. More explicitly theatrical, the related German *Stück* can mean "play" as well as "morsel." It also has the force of "commodity" or "piece of work," underscoring the anticapitalist tendencies of certain anti-Semitisms. I am concerned here primarily with Fagin's role as precursor of the *entertainment* industry (or of *show* business); but he is also a precursor of the entertainment *industry* (or of show *business*).

13. *The Night Side of Dickens: Cannibalism, Passion, Necessity.*

14. *The Old Curiosity Shop*, 566. On the "Jewishness" of the Brasses, see Lane, "Dickens' Archetypal Jew," 97.

15. Letter to Forster, August 19 (?), 1840. *The Pilgrim Edition of the Letters of Charles Dickens*, 118.

16. " 'The Old Story' and Inside Stories: Modish Fiction and Fictional Modes in *Oliver Twist*," 21.

17. Cited in Collins, ed., *Charles Dickens: The Public Readings*, 471.

18. "The Outcast as Villain and Victim: Jews in Dickens's *Oliver Twist* and *Our Mutual Friend*," 49.

19. In a discussion of the image of a Jewish Jack the Ripper, Gilman, in *The Jew's Body*, writes: "This image of the Jack [*sic*] as the *shochet* [the ritual butcher] rested on a long association in the Western imagination between Jews and the mutilated, diseased, different-looking genitalia" (119). Giving the genitalia a gender, Gilman goes on to relate their "mutilation" to "the Jewish mark of sexual difference—circumcision" (119). The fantasy of butchering the butcher is inseparable from a fantasy about the Jewish male body.

20. From Bob Dole's radio address of July 27, 1996: "And to those in places like Hollywood and New York City who have the ability to influence our children, I would just ask that you look in the mirror every day before you go to work and ask yourself if what you will do that day will send the false and deadly message to America's youth that drugs are harmless fun." Cited in Seelye, "Dole Focuses on Terrorism and Drugs in a Radio Talk," 14.

21. Criticism has various ways of (and motives for) sustaining the cultural project we might call the desexualization of the Jewish man. See, for example, Heller's "failure": "A contrary view of Fagin as pederast—for which I fail to see any convincing evidence—is presented by Garry Wills . . . " (134). Indeed, for Wills himself, the pederastic Fagin can only be "contrary" to, rather than dialectically bound up with, the Jewish Fagin: "The popular anti-Semitism [Dickens] assumed in his audience, and shared with it, in the 1830s was one of the 'covers' for the pederastic story he was telling" (64).

22. Tracy, 2.

23. Houston discusses "Grimwig's autophagic refrain," 35. For another instance of Dickensian autophagia—where the metaphor of self-eating is used not by Dickens but about him—consider this posthumous appraisal by R. H. Hutton: "We well remember the mode in which he used to read, 'The golden ripple on the wall ... [etc.]' It was precisely the pathos of the Adelphi Theatre, and made the most painful impression of pathos feasting upon itself." Cited in Collins, "Dickens' Public Readings: The Performer and the Novelist," 124.

24. A version of this essay was presented at the conference on "Victorian Spectacle," sponsored by the The Dickens Project at the University of California at Santa Cruz in August, 1996. I am grateful to Hilary Schor and Helena Michie for inviting me to speak at this conference, and to members of the audience for their stimulating comments during the discussion period. I also wish to thank Sheila Emerson and William Keach for their astute readings. As always, Lee Edelman's help, and the example of his work, have been invaluable.

# WORKS CITED

Auerbach, Nina. *Private Theatricals: The Lives of the Victorians.* Cambridge: Harvard UP, 1990.

Collins, Philip, ed. *Charles Dickens: The Public Readings.* Oxford: Oxford UP, 1975.

———. "Dickens' Public Readings: The Performer and the Novelist." *Studies in the Novel* 1 (1969): 118–32.

Dickens, Charles. *The Pilgrim Edition of the Letters of Charles Dickens.* Ed. Madeline House and Graham Storey, assoc. ed. Kathleen Tillotson. Oxford: Oxford UP, 1969.

———. *The Old Curiosity Shop.* Ed. Paul Schlicke. London: J. M. Dent, 1995.

———. *Oliver Twist.* Ed. Peter Fairclough. Harmondsworth: Penguin, 1985.

———. *The Pickwick Papers.* Ed. Robert L. Patten. Harmondsworth: Penguin, 1974.

———. *The Uncommercial Traveller and Reprinted Pieces Etc.* London: Oxford UP, 1968.

Gilman, Sander. *The Jew's Body.* New York: Routledge, 1991.

Heller, Deborah. "The Outcast as Villain and Victim: Jews in Dickens's *Oliver Twist* and *Our Mutual Friend.*" *Jewish Presences in English Literature.* Eds. Derek Cohen and Deborah Heller. Montreal and Kingston: McGill-Queen's UP, 1990.

Horkheimer, Max, and Theodor W. Adorno. *Dialectic of Enlightenment.* Trans. John Cumming. New York: Continuum, 1993.

Houston, Gail Turley. *Consuming Fictions: Gender, Class, and Hunger in Dickens's Novels.* Carbondale: Southern Illinois UP, 1994.

Jaffe, Audrey. "Spectacular Sympathy: Visuality and Ideology in Dickens's *A Christmas Carol.*" *PMLA* 109 (March 1994): 254–65.

Kaplan, Fred. *Dickens: A Biography.* New York: William Morrow: 1988.

Lane, Jr., Lauriat. "Dickens's Archetypal Jew." *PMLA* 73 (1958): 94–100.

Schlicke, Paul. *Dickens and Popular Entertainment.* London: Allen and Unwin, 1985.

Seelye, Katharine Q. "Dole Focuses on Terrorism and Drugs in a Radio Talk." *The New York Times* 28 July 1996:14.

Stone, Harry. "Dickens and the Jews." *Victorian Studies* 2 (1959): 223–53.

———. *The Night Side of Dickens: Cannibalism, Passion, Necessity.* Columbus: Ohio State UP, 1994.

Tracy, Robert. " 'The Old Story' and Inside Stories: Modish Fiction and Fictional Modes in *Oliver Twist.*" *Dickens Studies Annual* 17 (1988):1–33.

Wills, Garry. "Love in the Lower Depths." *New York Review of Books* 26 October 1989:60–67.

Wolcott, James. "Reborn on the Fourth of July." *The New Yorker* 15 July 1996:80–81.

# The Parable of the Spoons and Ladles: Sibling and Crypto-Sibling Typology in *Martin Chuzzlewit*

*Jon Surgal*

The pictorial wrappers for the monthly numbers in which *Martin Chuzzlewit* first appeared were adorned with this legend:

The
Life And Adventures
Of
Martin
Chuzzlewit
His Relatives, Friends, and Enemies.
Comprising
All His Wills And His Ways:
With An Historical Record Of What He Did,
And What He Didn't:
Showing, Moreover,
Who Inherited The Family Plate,
Who Came In For The Silver Spoons,
And Who For The Wooden Ladles.
The Whole Forming A Complete Key To The
House Of Chuzzlewit.
Edited by Boz.
With Illustrations By "Phiz."[1]

Exhaustive as it may seem, there is nothing in this introductory compendium to establish which of the novel's two Martin Chuzzlewits is the eponymous one. The ambiguity is very probably deliberate. I believe that Dickens is offering the two Martins as complementary representations of the same figure,

51

the Redeemable Chuzzlewit. Like Old Scrooge and the young Scrooge in the book Dickens composed concurrently with *Chuzzlewit,* Old Martin and Young Martin are versions of the same self: the older self is alienated and unsatisfyingly affluent, the younger one exiled and disempowered; the older self is forced to keep watch and forbear to interfere while the younger one endures hardship; and both selves are in the end reunited compatibly[2] and redeemed by means of suffering, revelation, and conversion. It is significant that between the Scrooges and between the Martins there is an age difference indicative of a missing generation. There is to be no symbolic rapprochement here between father and son: the young Scrooge must be as figuratively orphaned as the young Martin is literally so, and the elder figure functions not *in loco parentis* but as paraclete for his other self and hence as self-rescuer as well.

Granting, then, that each Martin has a claim to being the subject of the wrapper title, what are we to make of the reference to "His Wills," that first among items of which the book is said to be comprised? Evidently "His Wills" are of signal import: not only do they take precedence over "His Ways" (a phrase which suggests the character depiction for which Dickens was revered, as well as the geographical wanderings of both Martins and their more philosophical wanderings through the dark wood of error to the path of righteousness), they take precedence too over the "Historical Record Of What He Did, And What He Didn't," which is to say the plot itself. It is simple enough to define "His Wills" if reference is being made to the wills of Old Martin. His ostensible disinheriting of his grandson and his demonstrations of physical infirmity create among his relations the expectation of a revised Last Will, a new testament. Implicitly, perhaps, an ironic reference is being made to the biblical New Testament. The expectation of another will and the consequent scramble to court Old Martin's favor set in motion the whole plot of Pecksniff's scheming sycophancy: clearly the question of the old man having more than one will is a central concern. How, then, are we to interpret the pluralization of "Wills" if we ascribe these wills to Young Martin? Certainly he is, by dint of his obstinacy and selfishness, a willful fellow. Arguably, he may be said to exhibit "Wills" just as he may be said to exhibit "obstinacies" and "selfishnesses." Such locution, however, seems to me too awkward and arbitrary for prominent inclusion in a title, and I believe that there are other kinds of will altogether which, taken together with the exercise of willfulness, justify the plural form in this instance. Certainly there is will in the sense of wishing, which is so much at issue in terms of Martin's reckless offers of generosity, not to mention his own ambitions. Then too there is free will, that quality which enables Martin to transform himself, to accept his author's (if not his Author's) offer of grace. It is through his free will that Martin accepts education, and through free will that he earns his legacy, both material and spiritual, from his grandfather.

This, I think, provides an answer to the question of "Who Came In For The Silver Spoons." Born with a silver spoon in his mouth, Martin employs obstinate will by replacing the spoon with his foot and must then employ free will to learn the distinction between wishful will and creditable deed and win entitlement to his gleaming birthright. Who, then, may be said to have come in "For The Wooden Ladles"? Pecksniff comes in for something of a ladling at the hands of Old Martin, certainly, but in other respects his change of fortunes consists not so much of a disappointing inheritance but of punitive divestment: he loses his own money in the fraudulent Anglo-Bengalee Disinterested Loan and Life Assurance Company venture, he loses the complicitous loyalty of his daughters Cherry and Merry, and he loses the potentially profitable influence he supposes himself to have established over Old Martin. The bulk of the Wooden Ladles must be acknowledged as falling to a character whose motivations for malevolence are more complex than Pecksniff's and whose fate is more dreadful, this being the undutiful son of Old Martin's brother Anthony, the monstrous Jonas Chuzzlewit, whose luckless career counterpoints the fortunate fall and rise of Young Martin and who may be said to represent the alternative version of Chuzzlewit orphanhood.

Jonas inherits the family curse of solipsism in its most virulent form: it is in him a case of terminal selfishness. Jonas is consistently destructive in his graspingness and consistently brings down retributive destruction on himself. He receives his patrimony—and achieves his orphan status—after an attempted patricide, which he believes to have been successful, and this inheritance disappears, thanks to his intemperate pursuit of profit, down the Anglo-Bengalee oubliette. Destruction begets destruction as Jonas attempts to cut his losses by the murder of Tigg Montague, mastermind of the Anglo-Bengalee scam, and this act in turn leads to his own disgrace and suicide. But Jonas, when we first encounter him, is not yet (so far as we know) a criminal. He is presented, like Young Martin, as an unpleasant and selfish young member of the Chuzzlewit clan. He is, in fact, the only other male of the younger generation to bear the surname.[3] Like Martin, he is a candidate for the Silver Spoons, is an impediment to Tom Pinch, is flirted with by Pecksniff's daughters, is bilked by confidence men, is orphaned. In this novel, Dickens gives us for the first time—but by no means the last—a complementary pair of center-stage orphans subject to contrasting fates, the contrast in this case being employed to illustrate the distinction between redemption and damnation.

If, as I have argued elsewhere (Surgal 300), *Oliver Twist* may be read as an allegory and *The Old Curiosity Shop* as a hagiography, then Dickens may be considered to have offered us in *Martin Chuzzlewit* nothing less than a biblical parable.

## II

The novel opens with a genealogy tracing the Chuzzlewit family back to Adam and Eve. Facetious in tone, it purports to justify the self-importance of the Chuzzlewits as "not only pardonable but laudable, when the immense superiority of the house to the rest of mankind, in respect of this its ancient origin, is taken into account" (51), and Dickens concludes by grandly congratulating himself for having "proved the Chuzzlewits to have had an origin" (52). Obviously there is no distinction whatsoever in having an origin, and the unsavory lineage particular to the Chuzzlewits renders them "highly improving and acceptable acquaintance to all right-minded individuals" (52) not as paragons but as cautionary examples. The extended tongue-in-cheek conceit of the genealogy is an effect straight out of Fielding or Smollett, and Dickens clearly revels in it, but he is too accomplished a craftsman to defer raising the curtain on his drama by the length of a chapter for the sake of a stylistic exercise or a *soupçon* of backstory easily incorporated elsewhere in the narrative. The novel begins with the genesis of the Chuzzlewits because the Bible begins with the Book of Genesis. A biblical parable requires a biblical context, after all. And what biblical point of reference could be more appropriate to a family history cataloguing "the number and variety of humours and vices that have their root in selfishness" than Genesis? From Adam to Joseph, the first book of the Pentateuch is a chronicle of acquisitiveness and intra-familial competition unrelieved by anything but an occasional chorus of "begats."

Not only is selfishness ubiquitous in Genesis, it is more often than not associated with the maternal line, particularly in matters of inheritance, and Dickens probably found in this association some degree of corroboration for his intractable resentment of his mother. The first sin in the Bible is also the first legacy and is attributed to Eve's acquisitiveness. Another kind of acquisitiveness leads the daughters of Lot to seduce their father in order to "preserve seed" (Genesis 19:32 and 19:34) and secure his deoxyribonucleic legacy. Sarah persuades Abraham to cast out Hagar and Ishmael so that "the son of this bondswoman shall not be heir with my son" (Genesis 21:10). Rebecca dupes Isaac into bestowing his testamentary blessing on Jacob, her favorite. Laban—brother of Rebecca and father of Rachel, hence doubly identified with the maternal line—engages in a long-running swindling contest with Jacob over property rights to brides and dowries,[4] and Rachel steals Laban's household images by way of inheritance compensation. Two generations later, Tamar tricks her father-in-law Judah into impregnating her with male heirs.

If the frequent incidence of maternal culpability in Genesis influenced the composition of *Martin Chuzzlewit,* however, it did so by pointing out a road best left untaken. The novel is notable for the omission of those irresponsible mother figures so common in Dickens.[5] The omission serves to focus attention on the personal accountability and entitlement of Young Martin and Jonas, undiluted by any significant reference to their maternal lines. In this way the association of selfishness with the family name is given added emphasis. The competition for the family silver is reduced to a one-on-one contest between the two young Chuzzlewits.[6] And Dickens calls our attention at the outset to that aspect of Genesis which most explicitly illustrates this contest, the recurring theme of sibling rivalry. The theme is played out by Cain and Abel, by the sons of Noah, by Ishmael and Isaac, by Jacob and Esau, and by Joseph and his brothers. The twin sons of Tamar recapitulate the competition between Jacob and Esau to be first out of the womb, and the sons of Joseph—Manaseh and Ephraim—provide a variation on the competition between Jacob and Esau for the patriarch's dying blessing, which itself is a variation on the competition between Cain and Abel when they make their offerings to the Lord. God's preference for Abel over Cain is unexplained, while Isaac is deceived into granting his blessing to the younger of his sons and Jacob recapitulates his own selection by passing over his elder grandson to "set Ephraim before Manaseh" (Genesis 48:20).

The Book of Genesis is given, like the rest of the Old Testament, to a prevailing bias in favor of fathers, but it offers a consistent pattern of thwarted primogeniture. This may be taken to represent among other things a sublimation of hostility toward the father (and by extension the God of Creation) and its transference into a more acceptable hostility toward the figure of the older sibling. There is every reason to suspect that the same dynamic is at work in *Martin Chuzzlewit*. Filial hostility in the novel is never blessed by the author's sympathy, as it is on occasion in *Barnaby Rudge*. The parricide plotted by Jonas is without moral extenuation, since old Anthony—grasping and knavish as he may be—is not ungenerous with his son, particularly as regards information. "I," he explains, "when I have a business scheme in hand, tell Jonas what it is, and we discuss it openly" (176). Jonas is the partner of his father's schemes and the beneficiary of his will. His only legitimate grievance against Anthony is that the father has passed on to the son the Chuzzlewit curse of selfishness, and this in itself may be viewed as a twisted act of generosity. His contention that Anthony has no right to live so long is indefensible on its merits.[7] Dickens chides Anthony for his selfishness but lays no sin at his door sufficient to warrant murder by his son. Jonas forfeits the perquisites of primogeniture, then, by an attempt at unjustifiable parricide, and he is punished by the loss of those most tangible gifts from his father, fortune and life. As for Young Martin, no less resentful than Jonas by inclination, he is spared the potential taint of a father-son confrontation by entering the novel as an orphan, with the generational syndoche that shifts his resentment to Old Martin, who cannot be held to account for that most ambivalently valued of parental generosities, the gift of life.[8] The novel alternates its focus between the two Chuzzlewit heirs, the elder condemned by the author for acting out the sins of the Chuzzlewit fathers in their direst form, the younger rewarded for ultimately renouncing them.[9]

Clearly Young Martin and Jonas are brothers under the skin. The fraternal nature of their competition is suggested as early as Jonas' first appearance in the novel, when he is introduced as a rival for Old Martin's inheritance. Why then did Dickens cast the two young men as cousins? From a tactical standpoint, surely, it gave him the opportunity to contrast two versions of orphaning, one immaculate and the other steeped in sin. There was also, perhaps, a more personal motive. The distancing between Martin and Jonas is, after all, no isolated phenomenon: Dickens was routinely reluctant to confront the complexities of full-blooded sibling rivalry between his principal characters. Oliver and Monks are merely half-brothers, as are Edward and Hugh in *Barnaby Rudge*. Little Nell's brother Fred falls off a shelf in *The Old Curiosity Shop* and disappears from contention early on. By the time of *A Tale of Two Cities,* the rival twins Darnay and Carton are so far distanced as to be unrelated not only by blood but by nationality as well.

What prompted this circumspectness in the matter of siblings? The question leads us back to the Blacking Factory, and beyond. Warren's Blacking was not only Dickens' private trauma but his personal origin myth as well. Certain elements inevitably attendant on the trauma were denied a place in the myth. The myth casts Elizabeth Dickens as her son's betrayer and John Dickens as both abandoner and rescuer. It is at pains to deny any ill will toward sister Fanny, privileged and cosseted at the Royal Academy of Music while Charles endured the misery of his labor at 33 Hungerford Stairs. Watching her receiving a second prize for piano, a silver medal for good conduct and the personal congratulations of Princess Augusta, he tells us in his Autobiographical Fragment, "I could not bear to think of myself—beyond the reach of all such honourable emulation and success. The tears ran down my face. I felt as if my heart were rent. I prayed, when I went to bed that night, to be lifted out of the humiliation and neglect in which I was. I never had suffered so much before." And yet, he insists, "There was no envy in this" (Forster 1:31). The assertion is almost impossible to accept at face value. The passage it qualifies gives a portrait of envy in its most poignant aspect. Who indeed would not feel envy under such circumstances?

The refusal of Dickens to acknowledge his own envy is not at all unlike the refusal of Young Martin to acknowledge his obstinacy and selfishness.[10] Like Martin, he substitutes what he wishes to be true for what is true. Dickens clearly wished very hard to have been free from envy where his sister was concerned. What made this impossible was not simply the sudden differentiation between them but the complex similarity which had preceded it. They were the eldest child and the eldest son. They were the family showpieces, often performing public duets as children. Even in their divergence they shared a special status: they were the two non-residents of the Marshalsea, the exiles from the family exile. Sibling rivalry coexisted with a profound bond, and it was the bond Dickens chose to privilege in both his personal myth and his work. The rivalry he found difficult to acknowledge overtly. Throughout his career he was able to channel his ambivalent feelings for John Dickens into the creation of both good and bad fathers, but a sister who would willingly harm her brother was not to figure prominently in his work until *Great Expectations,* the novel which more than any other challenges the shibboleths of its author's personal myth.[11] Envious brothers turn up here and there, but Dickens so strongly disapproves of them and so thoroughly denies them any empathy that rather than acknowledging his own envy he seems to be reinforcing his denial of it. His relations with Fanny were sometimes strained—at one point he vowed never to forgive her for meddling in his courtship of Maria Beadnell, his first love—and yet, as Forster tells us, "Extreme enjoyment in witnessing the exercise of her talents, the utmost pride in every success obtained by them, he manifested always to a degree otherwise quite unusual with him" (1:31). The word *manifested* is well chosen: what Dickens showed was apparently a good deal less complicated than what he felt. Of all the tribulations associated with the Blacking Factory era, he "never suffered so much" as he did from having his own situation contrasted with that of his sister. And yet the obvious implication of this suffering, a perfectly understandable feeling of envy, was something he utterly refused to accept. His veneration for the relationship between brother and sister was as unequivocal as his hostility toward his mother. Indeed, it probably absorbed some of the gentle sentiments dislodged by that hostility, and in his work it became, as Peter Ackroyd puts it, "the paradigm for human relationships in general." And, as Ackroyd points out, "that loving sexless union of siblings is commemorated again and again in his novels" (28), nowhere more fulsomely than in the relationship between Tom Pinch and his sister Ruth. The brother-sister paradigm was a prominent feature of the world according to Dickens.[12] Where the paradigm is imperfect, it is usually the result of a brother's insufficient appreciation of a dutiful sister, as is the case with the brothers of Louisa Gradgrind, Amy Dorrit and Lizzie Hexam, brothers whose resentment and hostility are presented as irrational and indefensible and whose sisters endure their abuse with usually impenetrable forbearance. Mutual brother-sister competition is for the most part displaced or relegated to subtext.

There is another, more speculative source to be considered for Dickens' discomfort regarding sibling rivalry. He was two years old when his brother Alfred Allen was born and not yet three when the baby died of "water on the brain." "If the infant Charles had harboured resentful or even murderous

longings against the supplanter,'' Ackroyd reasons, ''how effectively they
had come home to roost! And how strong the guilt might have been'' (18).
Such guilt might well have been a factor in the adult Dickens' reluctance to
pit brother against brother. And the guilt could only have been reinforced and
enhanced eight years later when the birth of another brother, Alfred Lamert,
was followed by the death of an infant sister, Harriet, from smallpox in a
scenario easily construed by an imaginative ten-year-old as the displaced
consequence of his early feelings of resentment toward an older sister. Competition between brother and sister may have achieved its discomforting special
status for Dickens long before the shadow of the Marshalsea divided Fanny's
expectations from his own.

Whatever the etiology of his attitude toward sibling rivalry, Dickens developed in his work a divided approach to it. He distanced his protagonists from
it as a source of friction but indulged himself in it regularly and ruthlessly
as a craftsman. In his two most autobiographical works, no hero's sibling
escapes alive.

Given this highly charged fraternal ambivalence, it is little wonder that
Dickens chose to cast his first great contest between orphans as a competition
between cousins. And yet the choice is less evasive than it seems. In the
genealogy of Genesis, to which Dickens so imperatively draws our attention
by his imitation, the cousinly relationship is significantly identified with the
sibling relationship. Abraham and Sarah are not only husband and wife but
also half-siblings, which makes their son Isaac in effect his own cousin. This
in itself would suggest that Jacob and Esau, his children, are not only brothers
but cousins as well. The double relationship is, as it happens, doubly confirmed in that their mother Rebecca is the grand-daughter of their grandfather
Abraham's brother, which means in short that Isaac and his wife Rebecca are
related by blood in much the same way as Martin and Jonas. Not only are
their children cousins, they both marry cousins: Esau marries his paternal
cousin, the daughter of Ishmael, while Jacob marries his maternal cousins.
The sons of Jacob by Rachel and her sister Leah are all second cousins to
each other, and those who are the sons of Leah are first cousins to Joseph
and Benjamin, the sons of Rachel.

The identification of siblings with cousins provided Dickens with what was
for him a familial analogy ideal to his purposes. That this analogy was deliberate is suggested not only by his referring us to Genesis but also by the fact that
Jonas and Martin replicate the biblical pattern of cousins marrying cousins. In
the case of Jonas, such a marriage is necessarily ill-fated, mixing bad blood
with bad blood and compounding the family curse. Young Martin is more
fortunate in his choice. As his grandfather's ward, Mary Graham stands in
cousinly relation to him, but she brings fresh blood to their union, blood
which promises to dilute the cursed blood of the Chuzzlewits.

Martin's fortunate status is emblematized for us at the point of his first serious crisis in colors so vivid as to command our particular attention. Expelled from Pecksniff's house, he stops "to breakfast at a little road-side alehouse" and, Dickens tells us, "he looked at the highly-coloured scripture pieces on the walls, in little black frames like common shaving-glasses, and saw how the Wise Men (with a strong family likeness among them) worshipped in a pink manger; and how the Prodigal Son came home in red rags to a purple father, and already feasted in his imagination on a sea-green calf" (275). As Martin sets out on the road to redemption, then, he is vouchsafed a sign (which he is as yet incapable of recognizing) of the destiny that is his for the earning. Like shaving-glasses, the biblical scenes reflect a transformation. They suggest to us that Martin and his grandfather will achieve the getting of wisdom and celebrate in each other the birth of Christian forgiveness, that Martin himself is embarking on the journey of the Prodigal Son and will return, figuratively flayed and ragged, from across a green sea to a father figure who embraces him even while purple with anger at Pecksniff.[13]

At the very outset of his wanderings, then, Martin is cast in a parable. But this is a parable insufficient by its nature to accommodate the full scope of Dickens' narrative intentions. As befits a tale told by Jesus, it concerns itself with repentance, redemption and (implicitly) resurrection, with the Prodigal Son rejoiced over because he "was dead, and is alive again; and was lost, and is found" (Luke 15:32). The question of birthright, of Who Came In For The Silver Spoons, is somewhat fudged. Jesus tells us that "joy shall be in heaven over one sinner that repenteth, more than over ninety and nine just persons, which need no repentance" (Luke 15:7), but Dickens is dealing not so much with joy as with Flatware. When the Prodigal's elder brother cries foul over the fatted calf—"thou never gavest me a kid, that I might make merry with my friends" (Luke 15:29)—their father reassures him that he has not been dispossessed: "Son, thou art always with me, and all that I have is thine" (Luke 15:31). The New Testament, like Dickens, is given to privileging a paradigm of sibling amity, and the Prodigal Son parable does not fully sustain the winner-loser differentiation Dickens planned to make between Martin and Jonas, a differentiation as harsh as the one from which he himself had "never suffered so much."

To achieve his effect he turned to the less meliorative Testament for anticipatory versions of the parable more suitable to his purpose.

## III

The very first sentence of *Martin Chuzzlewit* culminates in a reference to Cain, and Dickens consistently employs images of Cain to describe Jonas

Chuzzlewit. Jonas himself associates his attempted patricide with fratricide when he tells Old Martin, "I've been as good a son as ever you were a brother" (454), and the punishment he undergoes in consequence of it is, like Cain's, greater than he can bear. "The weight of that which was stretched out, stiff and stark, in the awful chamber above-stairs," Dickens tells us, "so crushed and bore down Jonas that he bent beneath the load" (384). Confronting Tom Pinch, Young Martin's delegated representative,[14] in "a struggle for the path" (460),[15] Jonas impugns his cousin as "a vagabond member of my family," but Tom takes issue with the biblical reference: "Any comparison between you and him," he tells Jonas, "is immeasurably to your disadvantage" (458). Tom speaks here for Dickens. Each of the cousins will be "a fugitive and a vagabond" (Genesis 4:14), but only in the case of Jonas will this be the result of a homicide, and Dickens stresses the importance of this distinction from the outset in a significant revision of the scriptural text, describing Cain as "a murderer and a vagabond" (51). Jonas confirms Tom's judgment on him in attempting to inflict a Cain-like blow by proxy: "He flourished his stick over Tom's head; but in a moment it was spinning harmlessly in the air, and Jonas himself lay sprawling in the ditch. In the momentary struggle for the stick, Tom had brought it into violent contact with his opponent's forehead; and the blood welled out profusely from a deep cut on the temple" (459). Jonas receives the mark of Cain from his own stick. Small wonder, then, that the man he will murder, Tigg Montague, has a foreboding dream of "a strange man with a bloody smear upon his head" (728).

Jonas himself has a dream in which the death blow he will soon deal is associated with the rising of the sun, directing our attention toward the east of Eden. On his way to the murder, he looks back to see if his footsteps are "already moist and clogged with the red mire that stained the naked feet of Cain" (797). And like Cain he is denounced by that red mire, cursed from the earth by his victim's blood, unable to hide his crime: "He had hidden his secret in the wood; pressed and stamped it down into the bloody ground; and here it started up when least expected." As Cain is confronted with his crime and cursed by God, so Jonas is called to account and cursed by Old Martin when he appears in epiphany as *deus ex machina,* "an old man who had renewed his strength and vigour as by a miracle, to give it voice against him!" (859). Jonas finds the ground betraying him again—much as Cain, "a tiller of the ground" (Genesis 4:2), is twice betrayed by that ground, first when it produces an offering which displeases the Lord and again when it incriminates him—and once again his punishment is greater than he can bear: "Inch by inch the ground beneath him was sliding from his feet; faster and faster the encircling ruin contracted and contracted towards himself, its wicked centre, until it should close in and crush him" (861).

Jonas is depicted as Cain in his aspect of monster, irretrievably set apart, incapable of regeneration and reintegration. In *The Changes of Cain,* Ricardo

J. Quinones describes the tradition of "Monstrous Cain" (41) with particular reference to *Beowulf*'s Grendel and the Cain of the Corpus Christi plays. Like the blustery, vulgar, and grasping Corpus Christi Cains, Jonas represents what Quinones calls "the profane other, the other that is not only in our midst but within us as well, the *homo profanus,* overzealous in the pursuit of vulgarity" who "shows all the aggressiveness of . . . *homo economicus*" (55). Like Grendel, Jonas is a "dark doer of hateful deeds in the black nights" (*Beowulf* 6), a "terrible walker-alone," an "enemy of mankind" (*Beowulf* 4). Jonas is a monster not because he does evil but because he is irrevocably committed to evil, because he is unredeemable, hence unassimilable. That Old Martin should castigate Jonas for his crimes by calling him "monster" (860) is perhaps to be expected; more revealing is the fact that Mercy Pecksniff instinctively recognizes her husband-to-be for the monster he is even as she flirts with him, long before she has direct experience of his true monstrousness.[16] She calls him "a monster" (464) and "a perfectly hideous monster" (466), and six times within the span of two pages she taunts him by calling him "Griffin" (466–67). Dickens has already established the griffin as representative of misanthropy in Chapter 6,[17] and Jonas is thus identified as inhuman, grotesque, and socially alienated. He is also perforce associated with the griffin's role as guardian of hidden treasure.[18] This is something of a subtle irony, since Jonas hides his treasure where he himself cannot find it.[19] I think it significant that Jonas appears in his epiphany as "the Griffin" (466) in the scene directly following his altercation with Tom Pinch. The mark of Cain having been set on him, he is immediately recognizable as a monster, recognizable in fact as Monstrous Cain, a "fright of a Griffin with a patch over his eye" (467).

Jonas consummates the role of Cain with the murder of Tigg Montague. Tigg is a chameleon figure whose very name flip-flops during the course of the novel. He serves not precisely as an Abel figure but rather as a kind of all-purpose alter-ego. He makes his first appearance as Montague Tigg, the parasite of Old Martin's nephew Chevy Slyme, whom he claims as both an "adopted brother" (99) and a projection of himself—"I say we," he says, "meaning Chiv" (101)—and then, having divested himself of Slyme, he attempts unsuccessfully to graft himself to Young Martin, directing a pawnbroker to "deal with my friend as if he were myself" (282). Ultimately, after reinventing himself as Tigg Montague, he attaches himself to Jonas in a pas-de-deux of mutually assured destruction. So mutable is Tigg that in the end he becomes the victim of his victim.

Young Martin, on the other hand, is destined by Dickens to prevail. The Cain-Abel polarity, like the Prodigal-Unprodigal polarity, will not in itself suffice to define the competition between Jonas and his cousin. Indeed, Young Martin is himself in certain respects associated with Cain. There is, to begin with, his chosen profession. Cain is the first architect, after all: we are told in Genesis 4:17 that "he builded a city" east of Eden. Martin's plans to build a city in the American Eden come to little, but he creates his architectural masterwork, the rebuilding of the "ruined tower" of his grandfather's love (740), when like Cain he abandons Eden for points east.[20] Then too, there is Jonas' description of him as a vagabond, an uncharitable characterization to be sure, but an accurate one distinctly invoking Cain. And when Martin is bored to sleep by an opinionated American woman, he is subjected to "an imperfect dream that he had murdered a particular friend, and couldn't get rid of the body" (436). Yet Martin is clearly no Monstrous Cain. Rather he represents what Quinones calls "Regenerate Cain" (85), for whom Byron's revisionist version of Cain is the seminal figure. Dickens drops a broad hint when he has an American correspondent ask Martin "to favour me with any critical observations that have ever presented themselves to your reflective faculties, on 'Cain, a Mystery,' by the Right Honourable Lord Byron" (429). Martin has not yet formed any "critical observations" nor brought to bear any "reflective faculties" on the status he shares with Cain, that of rebel and *homo viator,* but he will eventually do so, transforming himself into a Regenerate Cain in the Byronic tradition: a quester, a questioner, a self-aware and sympathetic figure (though not as sympathetic as Dickens intended) with the potential for reintegration. The killing of Abel, always implicitly suicidal, is not necessarily irreversible in its literary applications. The "particular friend" Martin has murdered will turn out to be his better self, and he will restore this better self to life. His vagabondage will turn out to have been a pilgrimage in search of that self, and his architectural triumph will not only reunite Young Martin with Old Martin but also reintegrate Cain Martin with Abel Martin.

But if Martin represents *homo duplex* in the matter of the Cain and Abel duality, he does not play Abel to the Cain of Jonas. As between Nell and Quilp in *The Old Curiosity Shop,* the defining *scène à faire*—in this case the murder scene—is missing. (Pecksniff, swindled by Jonas, is more the family victim than Martin, but Pecksniff assumes the role of "good son" in a pinch-hit capacity, masquerading not as Abel but as his own namesake Seth, the son appointed to replace Abel.) If a sustaining biblical parallel is to be discerned in the relationship between Jonas and Martin, it must both accommodate and go beyond the rivalry of Cain and Abel. We may therefore discount such biblical references in the body of the novel as those to the golden calf (229) and the camel's eye (474). The extended association between Jonas and the prophet Jonah, from whom his name derives, also fails to address sufficiently the issue of sibling differentiation, but it does somewhat quirkily reinforce the notion of his monstrousness. Pecksniff plots "the casting overboard of Jonas" (452), and Jonas—like Martin, and like Tigg for that matter, a dreamer of prophetic dreams—plays the reluctant prophet when he attempts to take flight in disguise on the Antwerp packet. Compelled to disembark, he is in effect cast overboard. The syntactically idiosyncratic Mrs. Gamp, layer-out of old Anthony, wishes the packet "in Jonadge's belly" (699), and—since she is in the habit of calling Jonas "Jonagge"—she seems to get her wish when Jonas is shortly thereafter advised to "take particular care" of his digestion (715), a somewhat ironic adjuration since what sticks in his belly is that he is being blackmailed over the supposed terminal indigestion of the father he believes he has poisoned.[21] With her characteristic mangling of scriptural text, Mrs. Gamp manages not only to invoke the association between Jonas and Jonah, but also to "confound the prophet with the whale" (699), thus adding Leviathan (and its Hobbesian association with materialism) to the Griffin in the rogues gallery of Jonas' monstrous incarnations.

The derivation of Jonas' name is clearly significant, but—invoking as it does a biblical outcast without a mortal deuteragonist—it does not serve to define his relationship with Martin, whose own name carries some interesting, if more speculative, implications. A "martin" is a kind of swallow, by which Dickens may have meant to suggest the young man's flight and return. It is also a slang term for "dupe," by which sense Dickens may have meant to call attention to his penchant for deluding himself. In any case, such implications do not necessarily distinguish Martin from Jonas, who is also given to flight and return, as well as to self-delusion. Unique to the name Martin is its evocation of St. Martin of Tours, the first and best-known St. Martin, best remembered for sharing his cloak with a poor man, an act of generosity which earned him a revelation and redirected his destiny. Young Martin reproduces this process in Eden when, barely recovered from his own illness, he finds himself called upon to minister to a stricken Mark Tapley. He too is rewarded with a revelation: "he felt and knew the failing of his life, and saw distinctly what an ugly spot it was" (597). And from this revelation proceeds his resolve to rebuild his life.

But what of the parable of differentiation? What of the Silver Spoons and Wooden Ladles? Dickens intends for Young Martin both to come in for the family silver and to enjoy the use of it. He must, in other words, not only prevail but endure. And the Cain-Abel polarity will not permit this. Is there a subsequent biblical analogue which expands appropriately upon the drama of differentiation? There is, and the apple does not in this instance fall far from the tree of knowledge: we need not look beyond Genesis for a workable template. The drama of differentiation recurs in the story of Jacob and Esau, and, as Quinones notes, "the later story provides retrospective illumination and even foundation support for the Cain-Abel story" (24). Dickens requires the figure of Cain to establish the intrinsically evil and inevitably murderous nature of Jonas, but the narrative elements he uses to distinguish between Martin and Jonas are those which distinguish between Jacob and Esau.

Where Abel and Cain are differentiated solely by divine preference, Jacob and Esau are initially differentiated, like Martin and Jonas, by patriarchal selection. The drama of differentiation remains within the family, and the beneficiary of the selection process is granted the right to enjoy the secular perquisites of his selection, to prevail and endure.

Like Abel and Cain, Jacob and Esau are brothers, but they are also, like Martin and Jonas, cousins. By patterning the Martin-Jonas relationship in accordance with "the later story," Dickens is able to employ its "retrospective illumination" to invoke the strong suggestion of sibling rivalry without violating his sensibilities by actually depicting it.

Jacob and Esau provide a precedent for both rivals marrying within the family circle, and the transformation of Jacob into Israel, designated heir to the family estate,[22] is analogous to the transformation of Martin into a worthy legatee of his grandfather's name and possessions.

Finally, and most significantly, there is the matter of what Mark Tapley calls "earning credit." Jacob achieves his initial selection by bartering with Esau for his birthright and hoodwinking Isaac for his blessing. It may be argued that Esau puts himself out of contention for having "despised his birthright" (Genesis 25:34), much as Jonas forfeits redemption by his filial undutifulness. Yet Jacob's chicanery cannot be offered as evidence of moral superiority. He cannot be said to have earned credit by his actions, any more than the selfish and obstinate Martin can be said to have earned credit for his initial status as his grandfather's favorite. The selection of Jacob, like the selection of Martin, represents an offer of grace. Dickens would have us believe this to be prevenient grace, the opportunity to earn sanctifying grace by "coming out strong" from a purgative trial by suffering. Such a trial is undergone by both Jacob and Martin. In each case it involves expatriation, wandering in the wilderness, hard work and privation. "It's only a seasoning," as Mark Tapley puts it, "and we must all be seasoned, one way or another. That's religion, that is, you know" (448). Dickens is advancing a cosmology in which the seasoning of Martin, recapitulating the seasoning of Jacob, will earn him sanctifying grace and reintegration into his family as heir apparent to the patriarch.

And yet the redeemed Martin is uncomfortably similar in affect to the unreconstructed Martin. As Alexander Welsh observes, "Before his illness and near death in far-off Eden young Martin is insufferably selfish; that he is almost as insufferable in his converted state as in his unconverted state merely underlines the point: if ever a hero was saved arbitrarily, by grace, it is he" (121). Indeed, his "seasoning" sometimes seems to be justification after the fact for a predetermined salvation, an obligatory gesture on the part of Dickens to stress the role of volition. It is a gesture which is somewhat at odds with the comic tone of the novel, a tone not similarly violated by either the excessive sentiment lavished on Tom Pinch or the misanthropic excesses of Jonas.

Excess and comedy were native and compatible in Dickens. Conversion of the protagonist was a new variation in his repertoire. It rings true for Scrooge but falls flat with Martin. Conversion presupposes free will, and Martin's free will is compromised by the behind-the-scenes manipulations of his grandfather, whose predisposition toward him turns out to have been constant, whose resources turn out to have been consistently applied toward his "coming out strong." Even Mary Graham, for love of whom Young Martin makes his initial assertion of free will by rebelling against his grandfather, turns out to have been in fact preselected for him by Old Martin himself.

There is little question but that in *Martin Chuzzlewit* Dickens intended free will to play a major role in resolving the fates of his characters. We have the evidence of it when Old Martin underscores his condemnation of Pecksniff by reminding him that "he had not trapped him to do evil, but that he had done it of his own free will and agency" (889). Dickens had no conscious sympathy with the Calvinist tenet of predestination, and a defining element of Pecksniff's hypocrisy is his frequent assertion of his own election. The novel purports to deal with the "humours and vices that have their root in selfishness," and the assertion of self is predicated on the existence of free will. But the exercise of free will turns out to be an unreliable criterion in the differentiation between Martin and Jonas. Neither young man is completely a free agent. Where Martin benefits from the meliorative intercession and unstinting favor of his grandfather, Jonas suffers from a palpable predisposition toward evil.

Like most Victorian thinkers, Dickens did not consciously believe in original sin. He felt that moral transgression was for the most part attributable to environmental factors, that both the transgressors and their environments were susceptible to reform. Such was the conviction which would prompt him to undertake, with the backing of philanthropist Angela Burdett-Coutts, improvement of the Ragged Schools and the establishment of a home for "fallen women." Yet he was always tempted toward a deterministic view of crime, a bias which actually intensified over the course of his career and expressed itself almost irresistibly in regard to murder. Jonas is among those Dickens characters "whose often motiveless malignity," according to Alexander Welsh, "suggests that they are not really moral agents at all—that is, do not make moral choices." These characters do evil, like Cain himself, because it is their nature. "The Cain-like villains may be human enough," Welsh notes, "but are originally and irrevocably committed to evil, as if from spite. In the end, Dickens can think of no appropriate fate for them except extermination" (125–26).

Despite Dickens' intentions, then, the differentiation process seems to have been largely accomplished prior to any exercise of free will on the part of Martin or Jonas. It resembles in this sense the process of differentiation between Jacob and Esau as interpreted by St. Paul, who dismisses volition as a causative factor when he tells us that "the purpose of God according to election" is determined "not of works, but of him that calleth" (Romans 9:11). Reminding us that God predicts the outcome of their rivalry while Jacob and Esau are still in the womb, "neither having done any good or evil" (Romans 9:11), Paul argues thus:

> As it is written, Jacob have I loved, but Esau I have hated.[23]
> What shall we say then? Is there unrighteousness with God? God forbid.
> For he saith to Moses, I will have mercy on whom I will have mercy, and I will have compassion on whom I will have compassion.[24]
> So then it is not of him that willeth, nor of him that runneth, but of God that sheweth mercy.                                    (Romans 9:13–16)

Paul's didactic conclusions definitively establish the parabolical nature of the story. Commenting on the passage in the *Enchiridion,* Augustine reduces the argument to its essence: "He who said, 'I will have mercy on whom I will have mercy,' loved Jacob of His undeserved grace, and hated Esau of His deserved judgment" (113). It is, in the end, this same arbitrariness which Dickens brings to bear in differentiating between the Chuzzlewit orphans.

What shall we say then? Is there unrighteousness with Dickens? Rather let us say that the realist in Dickens recognized always that the world is a mean place and redemption an exceptional event. The monstrousness of Jonas, like the monstrousness of Cain, is native to some degree in each of us—it is a question not of original sin but of human imperfection—and, in the absence of some countervailing force, our monstrousness is more likely than not to lead us to corruption, free will or no free will. Such a countervailing force exists in Young Martin, but so off-putting is the young man's selfishness and obstinacy that Dickens cannot quite bring himself to trust to free will—even augmented by the flotation device of prevenient grace—to effect his rescue from his faults. Thus Martin is offered cooperating grace—something more akin to a life raft towed by an unseen ship—through which God, or in this case his stand-in, Old Martin, intervenes to collaborate with free will in effecting salvation.

The result of this collaboration is that Martin earns considerably less "credit" in our eyes than were he to struggle ashore under his own power. We do not accept him comfortably in the converted state as we do Scrooge, whose collaborators turn out to be the repressed voices of his own unconscious. And yet the compromising of *Martin Chuzzlewit* as a moral tract actually enhances its power as a parable of differentiation. The arbitrariness of salvation in the novel reveals to us a dangerous and uncertain world in which, as Primo Levi observed at Auschwitz, "there comes to light the existence of two particularly well differentiated categories among men—the saved and the drowned. Other pairs of opposites (the good and the bad, the wise and the foolish, the cowards and the courageous, the unlucky and the fortunate) are considerably less distinct, they seem less essential, and above all they allow for more numerous and complex intermediary gradations'' (87–88).[25] The polarity between the saved and the drowned is as absolute as it is arbitrary.

In the Blacking Factory, Dickens had the rare fortune to experience both drowning and salvation. Cast out like a ''small Cain,'' as he put it in the Autobiographical Fragment (Forster 1:23),[26] cast overboard like Jonas, he lost not only all hope but also all faith in an equitable universe. His subsequent rescue from the lower depths did more to confirm than confute his sense of arbitrary selection. He had learned that fate was unfair; now he found it to be capricious as well. His personal trauma of differentiation was in fact a double trauma, which left him with a permanent anxiety regarding entitlement and probably played a large part in motivating his chronic literary penchant for doubling, for examining alternative destinies. In *Martin Chuzzlewit,* he played the optimist by attempting to portray in Young Martin a version of his own rise to success and prominence through diligence and industry, through coming out strong from a purgative seasoning and a sea change, his most recent experience of these having occurred on his ill-fated American tour. Yet the realist in him remained convinced that chance alone distinguished between safe passage across a sea of troubles and being cast overboard: ''I know,'' he wrote in the Fragment, ''that, but for the mercy of God, I might easily have been, for any care that was taken of me, a little robber or vagabond'' (Forster 1:25).

Martin and Jonas recapitulate the helplessness of Dickens' abandonment to the mercy of that arbitrary and indecipherable Will which supersedes all other wills. Whether they are to be saved or drowned is ultimately beyond their control. In the end, Martin and Jonas are differentiated not so much by the personal and ethical distinctions between them as by the absoluteness of their polarity. For the Chuzzlewit orphans, there are no options besides salvation and drowning, no intermediary gradations. Their coexistence implies competition, and their competition implies a categorical resolution. To accommodate such a resolution, Dickens invoked the categorical distinctions of the Old Testament to illustrate his parable of entitlement to New Testament grace.

# NOTES

1. The working drafts for the wrapper title and some revealing speculation as to their chronology (suggesting, for example, that the Silver Spoons and Wooden Ladles were the last entries added to the compendium) are provided in *Dickens' Working Notes For His Novels,* edited by Harry Stone (16–45).

2. The reborn Scrooge exults in having become "as merry as a schoolboy" (*A Christmas Carol* 127).

3. I am discounting here the "grand-nephew of Mr Martin Chuzzlewit," who is identified as young but not specifically as a Chuzzlewit, and George Chuzzlewit, "a gay bachelor cousin, who claimed to be young but had been younger" (107–08).

4. The dowry issue also provides a spectacular illustration of hypocrisy, one of those significant "vices that have their root in selfishness." The most wholesale act of genocide perpetrated in Genesis (leaving aside the genocidal behavior of God Himself) is a grim parody of dowry dispute on behalf of Jacob's daughter Dinah. She is "defiled" by Shechem, prince of the city of Shalem (Genesis 34:2), who then petitions her brothers for permission to marry her. They agree to the marriage on condition that Shechem and the entire male population of his city be circumcised. The prince accepts this condition. There is a mass circumcision, and three days later, while all the men of Shalem are "sore" (Genesis 34:25), Dinah's brothers enter the city, slaughter them, despoil their possessions and take captive their women and children. The hypocrisy even of Pecksniff blanches by comparison.

5. The character most frequently associated with traditional maternal functions is the outrageous Mrs. Gamp, who performs professionally as both nurse and midwife while remaining so isolated from any sense of family connection that she speaks a language more or less unique to herself and maintains her closest relationship with an imaginary friend.

6. Pecksniff, despite his schemes and expectations, is shown to have never been in serious contention for a family legacy.

7. "Why don't you make over your property?" Jonas demands. "Buy an annuity cheap, and make your life interesting to yourself and everybody else that watches the speculation. But no, that wouldn't suit *you*. That would be natural conduct to your own son, and you like to be unnatural, and to keep him out of his rights. Why, I should be ashamed of myself if I was you, and glad to hide my head in the what-you-may-call-it," by which, Dickens tells us, he means "grave, or tomb, or sepulchre, or cemetery, or mausoleum, or other such word which the filial tenderness of Mr Jonas made him delicate of pronouncing" (362–63). It is worth noting in connection with the Silver Spoons that while thus addressing his father "Jonas shook his Brittania-metal teaspoon at him" (362).

8. So frequently does Dickens portray the torment of children that their very conception sometimes seems an act of parental hostility. One is reminded of the Delmore Schwartz story "In Dreams Begin Responsibilities," in which the narrator—displaced in time like Ebenezer Scrooge—witnesses his parents agreeing to marry and cries out, "Don't do it. It's not too late to change your minds, both of you. Nothing good will come of it, only remorse, hatred, scandal, and two children whose characters are monstrous" (6). For Dickens, the alternative to such an attempt at retroactive prevention often amounts to terminal punishment for parents—punishment, in the case of *Martin Chuzzlewit,* for precisely those consequences enumerated by Schwartz: remorse, hatred, scandal, and two undutiful children.

9. In the interest of transferring culpability for the sins of the fathers from Anthony to Jonas, Dickens goes so far as to invert their appearances, telling us "the son had so well profited by the precept and example of the father, that he looked a year or two the elder of the twain" (107).

10. "I have often heard," says Martin, "that [obstinacy and selfishness] have been, time out of mind, the failings of our family; and I believe there's some truth in it. But I can't say of my own knowledge. All I have to do, you know, is to be very thankful that they haven't descended to me, and to be very careful that I don't contract 'em" (150).

11. Fanny Dickens lends her name and her talent as a performer to the character of Fanny Dorrit, who brings a certain amount of sibling tension to *Little Dorrit,* but the tension here is between sisters, the provocation is all one-sided, and provoking Amy Dorrit is like striking a lucifer on the surface of a clear, still lake. Dickens gave the name Fanny to eleven of his characters, and the complexity of his feelings for his sister is suggested by the fact that these characters vary in nature from the martyred Fanny Dombey to the mean and misshapen Fanny Squeers.

12. The paradigm was in fact a feature of his household life, in that his most satisfactory male-female relationships were those he shared with his live-in sisters-in-law, Mary and Georgina.

13. An examination of Martin in the role of prodigal son has been made by Cynthia Sulfridge in an article titled "Dickens's Prodigal and the Myth of the Wandering Son."

14. In embarking for America, Martin commends Mary Graham to the protection of Tom on the grounds that "it will be a great consolation to you to have anybody, no matter how simple, with whom you can speak about ME" (298).

15. A struggle for the path is an ancient device for differentiating between two characters contending for the same position of favor—one thinks immediately of Oedipus—and Dickens uses it in chapter 17 of *Barnaby Rudge* to effect Barnaby's introduction to his father.

16. Her direct experience reaches its apotheosis when Jonas administers to her in quick succession a curse and a blow (528), both of which evoke association with the Cain story.

17. The griffin's misanthropy is established by reference to Dickens' beloved Tom Pinch. Dwelling lovingly on some of Tom's endearing mannerisms, Dickens tells us that "no cynic in the world, though in his hatred of men a very griffin, could have withstood these things in Thomas Pinch" (147).

18. Griffins were supposedly indigenous to the Rhipaean mountains. "They found gold in the mountains," according to Bulfinch, "and built their nests of it, for which reason their nests were very tempting to the hunters, and they did their best to keep vigilant guard over them. Their instinct led them to know where buried treasure lay, and they did their best to keep plunderers at a distance. The Arimaspians, among whom the Griffins flourished, were a one-eyed people of Scythia" (129). Thus even in the land of the one-eyed, the griffin is a monster and an alien, with every man's hand against him.

19. There is a further irony, which applies to both Jonas and his murder victim, in that the attempt to profit from life insurance results in the profitless forfeiture of life.

20. When Dickens began his novel, architecture was much in the public mind, associated with both progress and corruption. As Peter Ackroyd points out, "The rebuilding of the House of Commons after the fire seven years before, the construction of the great new railway stations, and the expansion of London itself, had combined to turn the architect into one of the most central and controversial figures of the period. Only two years before, in fact, Dickens's brother-in-law, Henry Austin, had written a pamphlet entitled *Thoughts on the Abuses of the Present System of Competition in Architecture*" (388).

21. The doctor who so advises Jonas takes advantage of the occasion to make slighting reference to the profession of apothecary, "which is a low thing; vulgar, sir; out of nature altogether" (715), thus attenuating the irony, since it is from an apothecary that Jonas has procured his poison.

22. The newly renamed Jacob is told by God that "the land which I gave Abraham and Isaac, to thee I will give it, and to thy seed after thee will I give the land" (Genesis 35:12).

23. Paul refers here to Malachi 1:2,3.

24. Paul refers here to Exodus 33:19.

25. The distinction drawn by Levi in this passage from *Survival in Auschwitz* would provide him with the title for his later book, *The Drowned and the Saved*.

26. Dickens specifically characterized himself as a small Cain "except that I had never done harm to anyone," which actually makes him out to have been more of a small Esau.

# WORKS CITED

Ackroyd, Peter. *Dickens*. New York: HarperCollins, 1990.

Augustine, St. *The Enchiridion on Faith, Hope, and Love*. Chicago: Gateway, 1961.

*Beowulf*. Tr. E. Talbot Donaldson. New York: Norton, 1975.

Bulfinch, Thomas. *Bulfinch's Mythology*. New York: Avenel, 1979.

Dickens, Charles. *A Christmas Carol*. In *The Christmas Books, Volume 1*. Harmondsworth: Penguin, 1985.

———. *Dickens' Working Notes for His Novels*. Ed. Harry Stone. Chicago: U of Chicago P, 1987.

———. *Martin Chuzzlewit*. Harmondsworth: Penguin, 1985.

Forster, John. *The Life of Charles Dickens*. 2 vols. London: J.M. Dent, 1966.

Levi, Primo. *Survival in Auschwitz (Se questo è un uomo)*. New York: Collier, 1993.

Quinones, Ricardo J. *The Changes of Cain*. Princeton: Princeton UP, 1991.

Schwartz, Delmore. *In Dreams Begin Responsibilities.* New York: New Directions, 1978.

Sulfridge, Cynthia. "Dickens's Prodigal and the Myth of the Wandering Son." In *Studies in the Novel,* vol. XI, no. 3:318–25.

Surgal, Jon. "Little Nell: The Monster with Two Heads." In *Victorian Literature and Culture,* 1991, vol. XIX: 293–314.

Welsh, Alexander. *The City of Dickens.* Cambridge: Harvard UP, 1986.

# "Let Me Pause Once More":
# Dickens' Manuscript Revisions in the
# Retrospective Chapters
# of *David Copperfield*

## *Joel J. Brattin*

*David Copperfield* is the favorite Dickens novel of many readers, as it was of Dickens himself: in his preface to the 1867 "Charles Dickens" edition, he admitted that "of all my books, I like this the best."[1] Copperfield himself narrates the book in the first person, and while Dickens used first person narrators subsequently in both *Bleak House* and *Great Expectations,* there is a special quality in David's narration that is absent from Esther's and Pip's. This quality derives, at least in part, from a unique element in the structure and narrative form of *David Copperfield*: the retrospective chapters.

In these four chapters, David Copperfield looks back over significant phases of his life—particularly, significant phases of his love life. The first of the four, chapter 18, titled "A Retrospect," treats young David's infatuation with Miss Shepherd and Miss Larkins, and also introduces Agnes in her role as David's "good angel." The second, chapter 43, "Another Retrospect," concerns David's wedding to Dora. The third, chapter 53, is also titled "Another Retrospect"; this one treats Dora's death—in Agnes's presence. The fourth and final retrospective, chapter 64, titled "A Last Retrospect," concludes the novel. This essay examines Dickens' holograph manuscript of these four chapters, probing what they reveal about David Copperfield as character and narrator.

The manuscript of *David Copperfield,* like the manuscripts of most of Dickens' novels, is now in the Forster Collection at the Victoria and Albert Museum, in South Kensington.[2] This highly-revised manuscript provides a fascinating and often overlooked opportunity to explore Dickens' creative process at the stage of composition when his creative energies were most highly engaged. The manuscript, with its complex webs of interlineations and deletions, offers powerful evidence of Dickens' preoccupation with the themes of love, memory, time, and reflection; his careful treatment of these themes in the retrospective chapters significantly shapes the novel as a whole, and plays a vital role in creating the distinctive—though elusive—tone of *David Copperfield.*

The first retrospective chapter, chapter 18, begins with David exclaiming:

> My school-days! The silent gliding on of my existence—
> unseen
> the ~~unnoticed~~, unfelt progress of my life—from childhood up to youth! Let me
> think, as I look back upon that flowing water, now a ~~dusty channel gone~~ dry
> channel overgrown with ~~weeds~~ leaves, whether there are any marks along its
> course, by which I can remember how it ran.                        (226/24)

Several of the features that will figure in future retrospects are already present in these revised sentences: the self-conscious attempt to examine the past ("Let me think"), the combination of exuberance ("My school-days!") with a kind of calmness, often associated with a water-metaphor ("silent gliding," "flowing water"), and the explicit treatment of memory ("by which I can remember"). All these elements are present in the first version of the paragraph. Dickens devotes most of his attentions in revision here to the adjustment of the "dry channel" metaphor. The point of the revisions seems to be to avoid presenting his present life too unattractively: a "dry channel" does not seem quite as dry as a "dusty" one, and a channel overgrown with "leaves" sounds at least marginally more pleasant than one overgrown with "weeds." The contrast between past and present is sharper, then, in the original manuscript version.

Agnes appears in all four retrospects. Appropriately, she is the first named character in the chapter; the phrase "Agnes says No but I say Yes" is an interlinear addition to the third paragraph of the manuscript (226–27/24). Characteristically, Agnes supports David here, telling him that the "giddy height" of "the first boy" in David's school is *not,* for him, "unattainable" (226).

The retrospect then treats David's early adventures in love. David asks himself "who is this that breaks upon me?"

> Shepherd
> This is Miss ~~Wilkins~~, whom I love.                        (227/24)

Dickens' adjustment of the name from Wilkins to Shepherd is an improvement for several reasons. Earlier in the novel, Dickens has already introduced two

Opening paragraph of chapter 18, "A Retrospect": "My school-days! The silent gliding on of my existence—the unseen, unfelt progress of my life. . . ." (see p. 74).

Detail from chapter 18: "This is Miss Shepherd, whom I love" (see p. 74).

The highly-revised opening paragraph of chapter 43, "Another Retrospect": "Once again, let me pause upon a memorable period of my life...." (see p. 78).

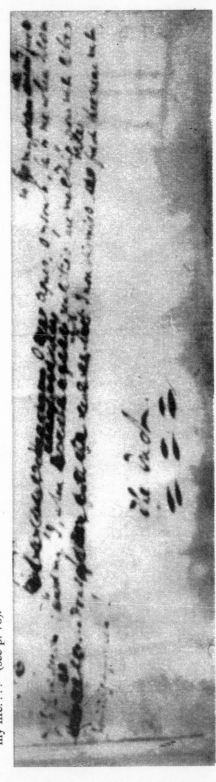

Conclusion of chapter 64, "A Last Retrospect": "O Agnes, O my soul..." (see p. 88).

characters who bear the name "Wilkins": Master Micawber, so named early
in chapter 12 (149), and Mr. Micawber, who signs his full name at the conclusion of chapter 17 (226), just before this first retrospect. Furthermore, the
name Shepherd affords an oblique reflection of David's lamb-like innocence.
Finally, Miss Shepherd stands in contrast to Agnes, whose name is cognate
with *agnus,* Latin for lamb.

Dickens presents David's infatuation for this Miss Shepherd comically, as
the revisions of the following passage show:

> iñ xxx secretly      twelve          I wonder
> Why do I xxx give Miss Shepherd Brazil nuts? for a present?
>              of affection
>   xxx xxx not expressive of xxx, they are
> They are difficult to pack into a parcel          (227/24)

That there are precisely "twelve" nuts, and that David gives them "secretly,"
contributes to the gentle absurdity of the situation. David's comment "I wonder" reminds us all the more strongly of David's adult presence as narrator,
looking back with amusement on his past. His awareness that the nuts are
"not expressive of affection," also expressed through interlineation, adds
another delicate comic touch.

David's infatuation with Miss Shepherd comes to an end in the next paragraph:

>        devotion of years a life     a life
> All is over. The love of years – it seems years     (227/24)

Dickens' adjustments in this passage work in two different directions: Dickens
heightens the absurdity of this brief and childish love-affair by twice revising
the already exaggerated "years" into "a life." In the same sentence, he tones
down the expression of David's feeling for Miss Shepherd from "love" (a
word Dickens takes very seriously) to "devotion," which picks up additional
comic and ironic resonances from the religious context in which it is placed:
David's "devotion" to Miss Shepherd began and ended in a cathedral.

Dickens lays the ground for David's future relationship with Agnes with
great care. David tells us

>      very dull
> I should be very miserable but that Agnes who is xx a sister to me  (228/25)

Here, Dickens has David tone down his perception of Agnes's importance,
in the direction of restraint: without the support of Agnes, David would, no
doubt, have been "miserable." But as David would probably have failed to
recognize this at the time, Dickens substitutes the word "dull."

In tiny handwriting at the very bottom of the page, Dickens begins a crucial passage about Agnes. David tells us that the girl he first knew at Mr. Wickfield's has grown up, and is no longer a child;

> Agnes ~~is such~~—my sweet ~~friend and~~ sister ~~whom I love~~ as I
> 26
> ~~thoughts~~ xx thoughts,
> call her in my ~~thoughts~~ my counsellor and friend ~~the good~~
>                        ^
>                                            come within ~~the~~
> the better angel of the lives of all who ~~know her quiet~~
> ~~influence~~ her                 ~~good~~ good          influence
> ~~excellence is now a woman of her~~ calm self-denying ~~nature~~—
>                                   ^                    ^
> is ~~a woman~~ quite a woman.                              (229/25-26)

The deletions and interlineations in this highly revised passage reveal a great deal about Dickens' conception of Agnes—and about what he wants to reveal about her and David at this point in the novel. At the bottom of page 25, Dickens deletes a reference to her as David's friend, preferring to establish the "sister" relationship more firmly; still more interestingly, he deletes a reference to David's "love" for her. At the top of the following manuscript page, he emphasizes David's idealization of her by revising "the good" to "the better angel." He also revises her "quiet excellence" twice, first to her "calm self-denying nature" and finally to her "calm good self-denying influence." The piling on of adjectives is a bit awkward, but Dickens is undoubtedly right to emphasize the importance of Agnes's "influence" on David. At the end of the sentence, Dickens deletes "a woman," and then adds "quite a woman." The subtle difference emphasizes the nicety of David's observations of Agnes.

In the latter half of this chapter, David falls into a passion for another woman, "the eldest Miss Larkins." After several paragraphs revealing the youthful follies of his thoughts, feelings, actions, and fantasies, David the narrator reflects, self-consciously:

> ~~no doubt~~      —I believe on looking back, I mean—
> I am a sensible fellow, I believe but this all this and modest I am sure;
>                ^                 ^
>
> but ~~I do~~ all this ~~at this time of my life~~ goes on notwithstanding.      (231/27)

The interlineation of "—I believe on looking back, I mean—" is typical of these retrospects: David is both narrator and character, and in the retrospective chapters, he negotiates very carefully between these two positions. The deleted phrase "at this time of my life" is another marker identifying David's childish behavior and fantasies—"all this"—as belonging to his youth. Dickens seems to have decided that the time during which "all this [went] on" would be clear enough with no marker, and omitted it.

Miss Larkins, at a dance, introduces David to Mr. Chestle, "a plain elderly gentleman," who is very friendly to him. With becoming modesty, Mr. Chestle says "I suppose you don't take much interest in hops; but I am a pretty large grower myself; and"

> like to        our
> "if you ever~come over to ~~that~~ neighborhood—neighborhood
>              our    we
> of Ashford—and take a run about ~~my~~ place, ~~I~~ shall be glad for you to stop as
> long as you like."                      (232/27)

David makes nothing of this conversation with an elderly man he takes to be "a friend of the family." Moreover, most readers are likely to make little of it. But by the end of the chapter, when we learn that Miss Larkins is to marry Mr. Chestle, the plural pronouns in his allusions to "our neighborhood" and "our place," as well as in his friendly statement that "we shall be glad" for a visit, all created by interlineations, take on a new and foreshadowing meaning.

David learns of Miss Larkins's engagement to Mr. Chestle from Agnes, who asks him if he knows who is to be married:

> "Not you, ~~is it Agnes~~ I suppose Agnes?"

>       raising her cheerful face from the music she is copying
> "Not me!" ~~Do~~~"Do you hear him Papa? The eldest Miss Larkins!"
>                                       (232/28)

Dickens' interlinear addition reveals Agnes with a characteristic expression, performing an action which also reveals her character: she is cheerfully working, copying a music manuscript which she will no doubt later play for the delight of her father and David.

The next retrospective chapter is 43, but another paragraph, from chapter 33, "Blissful," merits some discussion first. Chapter 33, treating David's young love for Dora Spenlow, concludes with a short paragraph that has a strongly retrospective flavor. Dickens writes this final paragraph on a page that follows page 22, and he (reasonably enough) writes "23" at the top of the page—but the paragraph is so short that he later superimposes "22 1/2" on the top:

> What an idle time! What an insubstantial, happy, foolish time! Of all the times
>                        so contradictory notable
> of mine that Time has in his grip, there is none ~~so contradictory~~~that~
> in one retrospection I can smile
> ~~I can laugh~~ at half so much, and think of half so tenderly.     (418/22$^{1}$/2)

The tone here is much like that of the first retrospect: a combination of enthusiasm, self-critical amusement, and tenderness. The word "retrospection," interlined here, is important, as is the revision of "I can laugh" to "I can smile." David the narrator finds his younger self amusing, but not quite ridiculous, and this retrospection invites the reader to share the same attitude.

Dickens seems to have found this retrospective paragraph of great importance, copying it verbatim into his working plan for the eleventh monthly installment. Except for these sentences, the number plan is almost empty of notes: on the right hand side, Dickens gives the title of the novel, and the numbers and titles of the three chapters the installment is to contain, with no notes for the other two chapters and just three fragmentary sentences about "Miss Mills" under the heading of "Chapter XXXIII / Blissful." On the left side, there are eight brief notations and queries, but the only entry of any substantial length is at the bottom of the page, where Dickens quotes his own manuscript:

> What an idle time! What an *i* unsubstantial, happy, foolish, time! Of all the times of mine, that *ha* Time has in his grip, there is none that in one retrospection I can smile at half so much, and think of half so tenderly!

The two deletions here, which may be the initial letters of the words "idle" or "insubstantial" and "has" or "have," are probably not true revisions but seem to be simple errors of haste in copying. The exclamation point at the end of the final sentence, which does not appear in the manuscript of the chapter itself, nor in the published text, may perhaps suggest how meaningful this retrospective passage was to its author.[3]

Chapter 43, "Another Retrospect," treats David's marriage to Dora Spenlow, and the language of the opening sentence is characteristic of all the retrospective chapters. In this case, Dickens revises the language extensively:

```
            Once again once again         to xxx      memorable
  Again∧  Let me once again once again let me pause∧upon a period
                        stand aside. xxx xxxx and xxx xxx xxx
     of my life. and Let me set myself again aside
  xxx xxx xxx xxx xxx I see                xxx accompanying
     the phantoms of those days go by me, with the shadow of    .
                       in
  myself among them dim procession.                    (534/23)
```

Again and again, Dickens writes "again"; again and once again, he deletes it. In the act of writing "let me pause," Dickens *does* pause, repeatedly, to look back at what he has experienced, and at what he has written, weighing and re-evaluating carefully. Dickens adds and deletes a phrase after "pause"; he then interlines the word "memorable" (without a caret), announcing the retrospective quality of this chapter, which, like all the others, focusses centrally on memory. The narrator announces his intention to "set [him]self again aside," or "stand aside," letting the world of the past take over and surrendering to "the phantoms of those days" for a time. The final two sentences of this paragraph appear in the first edition as a single sentence: "Let me stand aside, to see . . . ". As originally written, the short sentence "Let me stand aside" has greater power and impact; after all, we do not often see a narrator "stand aside" from his narration. But the published version has its virtues too, announcing more clearly *why* the narrator will stand aside: to allow the past to speak more directly.

In the next paragraph, David speaks of walking with Dora on a Common that is now "all in bloom,"

> bright
> a field of ~~burnished~~ gold,

perhaps an oblique reflection of the "Copper field" of Dickens' title (534/23). In this same paragraph Dickens develops the river image, begun in the first retrospective chapter: narrator David tells us that "the unseen heather lies in mounds"

> covering    In a breath, the
> and bunches underneath a ~~sheet~~ of snow.ʌ~~As the river and~~
> ~~As the~~ river that flows ~~for us~~ through our Sunday      ~~now~~
> the ?wanderings ~~it its ?face ?upon my face~~ walks ~~is glitters~~
> is sparkling        summer      is ~~ruffling ruffled the cold~~
> ~~sparkling~~ in the ~~summer~~ sun, ~~and now ?raffles in the ?winter~~
> ruffled by
> ~~wind ?raffling in~~ the winter wind.                    (534/23)

The extensive revisions here remind us that this is more than just a bit of pretty writing. This passage plays a role in the metaphorical scheme Dickens establishes: this river, which is the river of life and death, "flashes, darkens, and rolls away," "faster than ever river ran towards the sea" (534).

In the following paragraphs, the narrator speaks of attaining the age of 21, of "taming the stenographic mystery" and becoming a reporter, and of his success in taking to writing. Here is how the passage describing the latter appears in the manuscript:

> I ~~have~~ xxx have taken
> I have come out in another way,~~ besides~~ the xxxxxx
> with ~~fear and~~ fear and trembling, to authorship.
> ~~something and it has been published in a magazine~~
> I ~~have written~~ wrote      in secret, and sent it to a magazine,
> a little ~~piece~~ something ʌand it was published in the magazine.    (535/23)

The interlinear addition of "with fear and trembling" is significant, as is the interlinear detail about writing his "little piece" "in secret." The interlinear information in this passage is clearly autobiographical; one suspects that Dickens adds the personal details in order to make the passage more emotionally powerful and meaningful—for David Copperfield the narrator, for his readers, and for himself.

David tells of his engagement to Dora, describing it in terms that make it seem like a dream. Traddles congratulates him, and David says "we talk, and walk, and dine, and so on; but"

> thoroughly
> I don't believe it. ~~thoroughly~~ it. Nothing is ~~exactly~~ quite real.          (537/25)

Here, Dickens adjusts David's ability to believe and accept his position as a man engaged to Dora. He writes "I don't believe it," modifying the sentence first to "I don't believe it thoroughly" and then "I don't thoroughly believe it." The next sentence was evidently going to read "Nothing is exactly real," but becomes "Nothing is quite real." The modifiers "thoroughly" and "quite," both added to the manuscript, do not appear in the text as published in the first edition; by cutting the modifiers, Dickens provides an even stronger sense of unreality here.

Another unreal evening, the eve of his wedding, David hears a tapping at the door. He opens it to see "Dora's eyes and face"; her aunt

> Lavinia has dressed her in tomorrow's dress, bonnet and all,
> for me to see. ~~dear~~          my
>     and I take my little wife to ~~her~~ heart.          (538/25)

Traditionally, it is bad luck for the groom to see the bride in her wedding gown before the wedding day; Dickens' interlineation of "for me to see" emphasizes this, and the phrase serves as foreshadowing. Dickens interlines the adjective "dear" for Dora, but then deletes it; Dickens emphasizes Dora's diminutive stature, rather than David's attachment to her, here. This, too, foreshadows later problems in the relationship.

The ceremony itself is "all a more or less incoherent dream" (539), one element of which is the memory

> ~~one~~                    behind me
>     an xxx xxx ancient mariner
>        of a ~~boatman~~
>     strongly flavoring
> ~~flavoring~~ the church with Rum; ~~and breathing hard~~ stirring
> ~~my hair with balmy breezes of the same~~.          (539/26)

The "ancient mariner," reminiscent of Coleridge's mariner who "stoppeth" the narrator of "The Rime of the Ancient Mariner" while "The Bridegroom's doors are opened wide" (lines 2 and 5), does not detain David for long, but he does pose a threat, of sorts; Dickens undoubtedly intended to call up this image through his revision of "a boatman" to "an ancient mariner." Dickens originally had the mariner "breathing hard" on David, "stirring" his "hair with balmy breezes of" rum, but perhaps decided this was too much to inflict on poor enchanted David.

The ceremony concludes, and in the closing lines of the chapter, David remembers Dora waving goodbye, rushing back to Agnes,

> above all the others,
> And giving ~~her last~~ Agnes ₌her last kisses and farewells.        (541/27)

Agnes is always important in the retrospective chapters, and here Dickens' interlineation emphasizes her paramount position for Dora.

When David is alone with Dora at the end of the chapter, she asks him if he is happy now and is sure he does not repent. After this key question, Dickens writes

(Printer. White line here)

and then goes on to pen the last two sentences of the chapter:

> I have stood aside to see the phantoms of those days ~~gone~~ by me. They are
> ~~gone in fact~~ gone ~~like the realities~~ and
> xxx I resume the journey of my story.
> ₌~~with sorrow in a~~ xxx ~~sorrow in my heart that has~~        (541/27)

Dickens has David assert once more, as he asserted in the first sentence of the chapter, that he is standing "aside" for the phantoms of the past; in the original versions of the final sentence, Dickens' vision (and David's) is considerably darker, noting not only that the phantoms are gone, but that the "realities" too are "gone in fact," and that they have left a "sorrow" in David's "heart." Dickens altered these sentences not because they were untrue, nor because he feared spoiling any surprise in the plot, but because he wanted to avoid disturbing the delicate feeling that characterizes this retrospective chapter.

Chapter 53, also titled "Another Retrospect," treats Dora's death. This chapter, like the others, is strongly associated with memory. The predominant feeling here, unlike the others, is one of pain; David labors to present material that he cannot remember without distress. Dickens' difficulties with the opening sentences of this chapter reflect David's interior struggles:

```
                yet                                    there is
  I must L̶e̶t̶ m̶e̶ pause  once m̶o̶r̶e̶. I̶ c̶a̶n̶n̶o̶t̶ O m̶y̶ my child wife, i̶n̶
                     ^
                   again
  a figure in the f̶l̶u̶t̶t̶e̶r̶i̶n̶g̶ moving          quiet, xxx xxx xxx still,
  t̶h̶e̶ m̶o̶v̶i̶n̶g̶ crowd before my memory, t̶h̶a̶t̶ s̶t̶a̶n̶d̶s̶ s̶t̶i̶l̶l̶ . . .            (654/27)
                                    ^
```

As we have seen, Dickens revised the opening of chapter 43 extensively to
reach "Once again, let me pause . . . "; similarly, he revises the opening of
chapter 53, trying "Let me pause once more" and "Let me pause once again"
before the final formulation, "I must pause yet once again." Once more, the
act of retrospection involves "pausing," and here, where David must tell of
Dora's death, it seems even more difficult for him to force himself to narrate.
The second sentence of this chapter originally began "I cannot": presumably,
David was going to state still more explicitly how difficult a task this narration
is. Instead, the second sentence becomes an apostrophe to Dora, David's
"child wife," and a plea from that figure to "Stop and think of me."

There are relatively few places in Dickens' manuscripts where we can be
certain that any length of time passed between the original inscription of a
passage and Dickens' revision of that passage. Often, the form of a revision
makes it clear that revision must have occurred before a given sentence was
completed, but it is rare to have proof of the contrary situation: only in a
handful of cases do we have solid evidence establishing that significant time
elapsed between inscription and revision. Here, however, we have such evidence, provided by two different colors of ink. Dickens used blue-black ink
for the bulk of this chapter, but there are a few occasional revisions in an
entirely different ink that now appears brown in color. Here in this first
paragraph, Dickens added the words "quiet" and "still," as well as the
indecipherable deleted words between them, at some period of time after the
initial composition. That Dickens went back to this passage yet again, at a
still later time, is demonstrated by his addition of the word "and" between
"quiet" and "still," before the chapter was published (654, note 2).

The figure of Dora, "quiet" and "still," says to David's memory, "Stop
and think of me," and in the second paragraph, Dickens writes

```
  All else grows dim and r̶u̶n̶s̶ fades away.
  I̶ d̶o̶, a̶n̶d̶ i̶t̶ i̶s̶ a̶l̶l̶ b̶e̶f̶o̶r̶e̶ m̶e̶. Y̶e̶a̶r̶s̶ I am again with
  Dora in our l̶i̶t̶t̶l̶e̶ cottage.                                          (654/27)
```

Dickens' substitution of "All else grows dim and fades away" is an effective
replacement for the lackluster "it is all before me." Dickens seemed to have
felt that "I do" was redundant, and deleted it; interestingly, he restored the
phrase, but as a separate sentence, before publication (654, note 3).

Dickens divided this chapter into five sections: an introduction, a conclusion, and three intervening sections set apart by explicit time markers. The final paragraph of the introduction begins like this:

> xxx rest and pause
> O~~the~~ strange ~~stoppage~~ᴧin my life there seems to be.
> What a.                                                                    (655/27)

Here, Dickens tones down the emotion, emphasizing "rest" and "pause" once more, rather than the more abrupt shock of a "stoppage." Still, we have a series of brief "stoppages," or, better, pauses, as we linger on the "three times [that] come the freshest on [David's] mind" in our inexorable progress toward Dora's death (655).

The first time marker is "It is morning" (655). Dickens set this short section off by interlining the message "(Printer. White line here.)" (655/27). The introductory section and the "morning" section together take up the first manuscript page; the "evening" section begins at the top of the next page, as follows:

> 28
> (Printer. White line here.)
>         It is evening; and I sit in the same chair, by the same bed, with the same
> face turned . . .                                                       (655/28)

Here again, Dickens squeezes in his message to the printer, as an addition to the manuscript.

In this evening section, David admits to Dora that he is lonely downstairs without her. She asks if he really misses her:

> poor
> "Even ~~little~~ giddy ~~foolish me~~ stupid me?"                        (656/28)

Here, Dickens carefully balances sympathy and criticism, in the self-abnegating words Dora chooses. The word "little" may elicit sympathy, but "poor" does so even more explicitly; on the opposite pole, the rejected word "foolish" invites criticism, and the replacement, "stupid," directs judgment all the more strongly. The fact that Dora utters these words of sympathy and judgment of herself (or that David says that she did—or that Dickens says that David says that she did) complicates matters only slightly; however we read the speech, Dickens heightens both our sympathy and our judgment of Dora through his revisions.

David replies to her question with a rhetorical question of his own: "My heart, who is there upon earth that I could miss so much?" (656). Dora responds that she is "glad," and

"yet so sorry!" ~~And she laughed and cried upon my breast~~
             She
~~She crept~~ close to me, folding me in both her arms. ~~and~~
creeping
  laughs, and sobs    is
~~laughed and sobbed~~, and then ~~was qui~~ quiet and quite happy.  (656/28)

Dickens carefully adjusts Dora's emotional response to David, delaying
Dora's laughter and crying until she is embracing her husband. Dickens also
adjusts verb tense here, bringing the laughing and sobbing, as well as the
quieting, into the present tense for a more immediate impact.

 Just after this, Dora thinks of Agnes—probably in answer to David's rhetorical question, though neither David the character nor the first-time reader of
the novel is likely to recognize this. Dora sends Agnes her love, and asks
David to tell Agnes that she wants "very, very, much to see her" (656). After
this, when David mentions getting well, she says that she sometimes thinks
that this

"will never be!" ~~And you are very lonely downstairs~~.  (656/28)

Presumably Dora is thinking of Agnes as a future mate for David, but Dickens
does not allude to this quite so strongly here, preserving a delicacy in the
scene.

 The next section begins with "It is night" (656). Dickens' call for white
space here is clearly *not* interlined (656/28); evidently Dickens decided to
use the white space as a structural element at this time, and went back to add
the previous two messages for the printer. Dickens then writes

    my child-wife ~~the blossom is fading, and~~ xx xxx
~~I think~~ I know, now, that ~~the pretty blossom is fading~~
            ^
Do
  soon
~~Dora~~ will leave me ~~soon~~?  (656/28)
     ^

Dickens recasts what was originally a somewhat tentative statement about
Dora's impending death, turning it into a question. Still more revealing is
Dickens' revision of how that death is expressed: his first version is David's
metaphor, "the pretty blossom is fading." Rejecting that as too sentimental,
he deletes it and then replaces it with almost the same words, "the blossom
is fading." He also considers calling Dora by her name, and only at last does
he fall back on the old formulation, supposedly of Dora's choosing, "my
child-wife."

 In the following paragraphs, Dora gently suggests to David that perhaps
things are best as they are, and that she may not have been ready or "fit to
be a wife." David protests:

~~"As God is my witness~~ "We have been very ~~happy, Dora~~
happy, ~~Dora"~~ my sweet Dora."                    (657/29)

Dickens rejects David's pious interjection, which is too noisy and formal
even for a death-bed scene. Dickens also goes to some lengths to find an
epithet more affectionate than simply "Dora."

Dora says once again that perhaps it is "better as it is," and David rejoins

      dearest, dearest        so        seems
"Oh‸Dora, do not speak to me‸ Every word‸is a reproach!"     (657/29)

In this sentence, Dickens interlines the affectionate words "dearest, dearest,"
intending them to precede Dora's name, though they follow it in all published
texts including the Clarendon. David's feelings of guilt and self-pity are
stronger in the version of this speech as Dickens originally penned it: at first,
David omits the words of affection, silences Dora by commanding her not to
speak to him at all, and identifies her words as reproaches. Revision modifies
and softens this position: by interlining "dearest, dearest," David expresses
feeling for her; by adding "so," he allows her to speak; and by altering "is"
to "seems," he is less accusatory.

Near the end of this "night" section, Dora says

                            Hush, hush! Now, make me one
            poor                   ~~promised me to~~
"Oh how my ~~dear~~ boy cries! ~~I asked Agnes to make the~~
promise. I want to speak to Agnes.
~~put the Doady give me promise me one~~
~~room quite nice room in perfect order for you.~~     (657/29)

Dickens deletes the reference to Agnes's tidying up, substituting for it Dora's
crucial request for some conversation with Agnes. She repeats this request
again at the end of this same paragraph, and again Dickens' revisions are
revealing. Dora says "I want to speak"

                         speak xx to Agnes ~~and~~
"to Agnes by herself. I want to ~~speak to Agnes with my~~
~~whole heart tell her something~~ quite alone."     (657/29)

Dora is, of course, going to speak to Agnes "with [her] whole heart," but as
she would be unlikely to tell David this now, and particularly as Dickens
does not now want to reveal the substance of the conversation, he deletes this
reference, as well as the reference to Dora "tell[ing] her something."

The concluding portion of the chapter, which begins with "Agnes is downstairs," is also set off by a white line in the printed text; Dickens evidently

forgot about this structural device for a moment, or longer, and had to go back at some point to interline his usual direction to the printer (658/30).

While Agnes goes upstairs to speak with Dora, David meditates downstairs, alone. "Alone, that is to say, with Jip"—in a sentence which stands unrevised in the manuscript, but does not appear in the published text (658/30).[4] David asks himself the question prompted by Dora's comments upstairs: "Would it, indeed, have been better if we had loved each other as a boy and girl, and forgotten it?"

> reply!  be not too hard
> O heart, undisciplined heart, reply!ᴀSpeak not too
> with speak not too plainly be not too hard with
> plainly to me in this hour of trial!  (658/30)

Dickens asks, twice, that the narrator's "undisciplined heart" should "be not too hard with [him]," and twice deletes the request; he asks, twice, that it "speak not too plainly" to him "in this hour of trial," and twice deletes that as well. Dickens considered and reconsidered this passage, not just at the time of original inscription and revision, but at least twice subsequently, as he added the interlined word "reply," along with the preceeding comma, the following exclamation point, and the caret below, in brown ink, rather than in the blue of the rest of the passage. Furthermore, the first words of the sentence, "O heart," are not deleted in the manuscript, nor from the first set of extant proofs, yet the words are absent in the first published text (Clarendon 658, note 7).

This chapter concludes with not one, but two deaths: when Dora's dog Jip learns that he may never again go upstairs to see Dora, the dog lies down at David's feet and dies; when Agnes returns downstairs to tell David of Dora's death, David points to the dog. (I transcribe the manuscript of the remainder of the chapter.)

> "Agnes! See here!" Look, look, here!
> But what is this? That face, so full of pity and of
>     that awful mute appeal to me,
> grief, that rain of tears,ᴀthat solemn hand upraised to
> Heaven towards Heaven!—that awful dumb appeal to me
> "Agnes?" Is she dead? Speak to me!
> I drop with the word.  It is over.
>     Darkness comes before my eyes; and, for a time, all
> Dead. ᴧ
>                     my remembrance.  As I emerged
>     things are blotted out of my of remembrance xxx xxx emerged
> again upon realities, so let me make make
>     again upon reality so let me pass on to that from this xxx
>     xxx
>     xxx xxx to the course of my narrations.  (658/30)

In replacing "See here!" with the more urgent "Look, look, here!" Dickens must have inadvertently omitted the closing quotation marks. In the following paragraph, Dickens deletes the superfluous question "But what is this?" and moves "that awful dumb appeal to me" from the end of the sentence to the middle, altering the word "dumb" to "mute," which has fewer negative connotations. Dickens also took care to alter "to Heaven" to "towards Heaven," eliminating the awkward suggestion that Agnes was actually able to reach so far. Dickens omits the questions "Is she dead? Speak to me!" as well as the monosyllabic response "Dead" and the melodramatic "I drop with the word," in favor of the more restrained and realistic "It is over," which effectively echoes the earlier subdivisions of the chapter, "It is morning," "It is evening," and "It is night." After Dickens establishes that "for a time, all things are blotted out of [David's] remembrance," he considers adding another sentence, offering a transition from this retrospective treating a time of crisis to the regular "course of his narrations," where he once again "emerge[s]" "upon reality"—but no such transition is really needed, and Dickens deletes the sentence, deciding that the gap between this chapter and the next needed no explicit bridge. By deleting the last sentence, Dickens allows some of the tensions of this chapter to remain unresolved, creating a delicate suspense for his original serial readers, who had to wait a month before they could read the following chapter.

The final chapter of *David Copperfield* contains "A Last Retrospect," as the interlined chapter title tells us (748/42). Dickens extensively revised the initial sentence of chapter 64, just as he did the initial sentences of chapters 43 and 53:

> I look back, once more
> my written story ends. ~~Let me I have a backward glance upon ?myself my life~~
> And now, ~~once more~~ ˄It is xxx ~~one more~~ xx xxx xx—~~upon~~—for
> before I                                                          these
> the last time—~~upon and upon myself and~~ xx ~~past and~~ xx past ~~turn and~~ close the˄
> leaves. ~~on which I have dwelt so long~~.                        (748/42)

The complexity of the revisions offers an immediate clue to the importance of this final retrospective. Dickens tries and rejects the phrase "once more" repeatedly, just as he tried and rejected "once again" repeatedly for chapter 43, and substituted "once again" for "once more" in chapter 53. "Once more" finally stands in the second sentence, as an interlinear addition. Obviously, these retrospectives involve looking backward, and David as narrator is willing to look backward very explicitly; he is unwilling to call this creative act of memory and affection "a backward glance upon [his] life," deleting this phrase and substituting the more direct and less negative-sounding "I look back, once more." Dickens adds "—for the last time—" in order to emphasize the unique function of this particular retrospect. Dickens deletes two other suggestive passages: one, in which he specifies what he will look back upon, and another, where he alludes to the length of his whole retrospective autobiographical project. Though many words in the first passage are illegible, it is clear that David would be looking back "upon himself and" upon the "past," but this hardly needs saying, and Dickens omits the superfluity. Dickens also deletes the rather apologetic phrase "upon which I have dwelt so long," perhaps deciding that a false modesty here would be unbecoming.

The second short paragraph acknowledges the primacy of Agnes in David's life. In the third paragraph, David considers others who have figured in his life, asking

> What faces are the most distinct to me, in ~~all~~ the fleeting crowd?
> ~~What else do I see? Let me look for one last moment~~.    (748/42)

The original question, "What else do I see?" sounds impersonal; the interlined revision, specifying "faces," is warmer, and also allows for a type of hierarchy of values, as David will go on to say which are the faces that are "most distinct," including Peggotty, Aunt Betsey, and Mr. Dick. David's initial plea, "Let me look for one last moment," would be misplaced here; the last four printed pages surely represent more than a "last moment," even if this is to be David's final retrospect, so Dickens omits the phrase.

Dickens has David look back at several key characters, finally giving Traddles, for example, his due; part of how Dickens rewards Traddles for his generosity to Sophy's many sisters, "the girls," is by portraying, through interlinear addition and a passage added to the verso of the manuscript, the "crowd of them, running down to the door, and handing Traddles about to be kissed, until he is out of breath" (750/44 and verso).

Dickens revises the final paragraph of this retrospective, also the final paragraph of the novel, extensively. Here, David finally turns his full attention to Agnes:

>                  ~~this~~ thy
>           so S~~o~~ may xxx ~~that one~~ face
> ~~Kiss me my dear!~~ xxxx xxx O ~~Agnes~~ Agnes, O my soul,ₐbe by
>            so            xxx xxxx
> me when I close my life indeed; ~~and~~ may I, when ~~the world is~~
> xxx xxxx             these
> ~~fading~~ realities are melting from me like xxx xxxx shadows
>         which           still
> ~~of~~ xxx ~~find thee near me that~~ I now dismiss, ~~see~~ find thee
> near me pointing upward!    (751/44)

The one unrevised detail is the final one, alluding so closely to the penultimate retrospective treating Dora's death. This final paragraph originally opened with a surprisingly intimate detail, David's call for a kiss from Agnes, and though Dickens omits this, he steadily increases the intimacy of the language which positions Agnes's face, altering "that one face" (imagined at a distance) first to "this face" (positioned more closely) and finally to "thy face" (with the narrator now speaking intimately and directly to Agnes herself, rather than *of* her, to the reader). Dickens develops all mention of Agnes's face through interlineation; originally, David simply calls for her to "be by me," but adds the warm, personalizing detail of the face, just as he did in the third paragraph of this same chapter. In the next part of this sentence, alluding to David's eventual death, Dickens revises the expression "when the world is fading" to "when realities are melting," allowing the contrast between realities and "the shadows which I now dismiss." Dickens also alters "these shadows," which alludes more specifically to the shadows of the figures he recalls in this last retrospective, to "the shadows," referring more generally to all his memories together.[5] Dickens apparently began to write "find thee near me" after "when realities are melting from me like the [or these] shadows," deleting the phrase "find thee near me" in order to add "which I now dismiss." These four added words constitute David's farewell to his art, and his farewell to his creative memory, constituted through retrospection; only after this does he write of his hope that he may "still find [Agnes] near [him]," when he is as close to the end of his life as he is to the end of his autobiography.

The retrospective chapters are important in establishing the feeling and tone of *David Copperfield*. Treating milestones in the emotional development of David Copperfield, and milestones in his relationship with Agnes, these chapters emphasize some of the most vital themes of this novel: memory, affection, time, reflection, and love. Dickens' revisions in the manuscript show him carefully developing these themes, and compellingly focus our understanding and appreciation of David's understanding of himself, of Agnes, and of the other shadows and realities which surround him.

## NOTES

N. B. The compositor has in some cases not been able to reproduce exactly the positioning and spacing of the words in the manuscript.
The accompanying facsimiles (facing page 74) illustrate this difficulty.

1. *David Copperfield*, ed. Nina Burgis (Oxford: Clarendon P, 1981) 752. All subsequent references to the text of *David Copperfield* are to this edition.

2. I gratefully acknowledge Christopher Dickens and the Trustees of the Victoria and Albert Museum for their permission to quote from the manuscript. My citations from the manuscript give the number of the corresponding page in the Clarendon edition of the novel, followed by the number Dickens assigned his manuscript page.

3. The revision in the chapter, and the lack of substantial revision in the number plans, affords powerful proof that Dickens copied the passage from the manuscript into the plans (which he seems to have used as a memory aid in holding the various threads of the novel in his mind over the course of its composition), and not from the plans into the manuscript. Harry Stone correctly suggests that more usually, Dickens used the left side of the plans to deal "with overall matters of planning and decision making"; see Stone, ed. *Dickens' Working Notes for His Novels* (Chicago: U of Chicago P, 1987) xvi.

4. Burgis records this sentence as "Alone with Jip"; see 658, note 4.

5. Burgis claims that the word "the" is missing from the manuscript (751, note 1), but the word is present, altered from the interlined word "these."

# A Sisterhood of Rage and Beauty: Dickens' Rosa Dartle, Miss Wade, and Madame Defarge

*Barbara Black*

> But [Polly] was a good plain sample of a nature that is ever,
> in the mass, better, truer, higher, nobler, quicker to feel, and
> much more constant to retain, all tenderness and pity, self-
> denial and devotion, than the nature of men.
>
> —*Dombey and Son* (27)

Any discussion of Dickens and his female characters must confront the great faith he places upon women in his novels. His interest in the domestic sub-lime—that elevation of the home fundamental to the separate spheres of Victorian gender configuration—leads consequently to an apotheosis of women. As the genii of the hearth, women are ready moral agents able to resurrect and repair the many men of their lives—father, brother, em-ployer—who journey out into the world and are tainted by it. Dickens' belief in women's potential for good is evident in the characteristic statement above from *Dombey and Son*. Here Dickens describes women as "better, truer, higher, nobler, quicker to feel" than men. Dickensian women are virtuous in their capacity for service to others, in their "self-denial and devotion." It seems that Dickens' conceptions of femininity are hardly complex and offer little challenge to the critical commonplace of the Victorian angel in the house. For like his favorite child and favorite self, David, Dickens would wish for every man an Agnes as the reward for life's arduous peregrinations.

And yet alongside this feminine ideal lies an uneasy and unsettling connec-tion between women and violence in Dickens' novels. Dickens depicts men violating women, women who do violence to others, and women who violate and mutilate themselves. Explicit violence exists often in the novel's periph-ery, in fleeting suggestions concerning tertiary characters such as the woman

91

in the police station in *Our Mutual Friend* "who was banging herself with increased violence, and shrieking most terrifically for some other woman's liver" (67). An examination of female violence in the Dickens corpus, moreover, uncovers the rage that seethes beneath the surface of many of Dickens' most famous, mild heroines. Nascently violent, Florence Dombey represses the death-wishes she feels for her father; finally violated, she shuns her own breast branded by "the darkening mark of an angry hand" (680). In reading Little Dorrit's life, we come to understand the harsher implications of the equation above from *Dombey and Son*: For women, "devotion" and "self-denial" are synonymous. Amy's commitment to the ideal of service involves the affliction of unshod feet and the punishment of a malnutrition that verges on anorexia. Even Esther, whom many readers embrace as the genuine voice of a sincere discourse and who is saved from explicit violence by Hortense's function in the novel, speaks a language churning with rage:

> [H]ow often had I considered within myself that the deep traces of my illness, and the circumstances of my birth, were only new reasons why I should be busy, busy, busy. . . . So I went about the house, humming all the tunes I knew; and I sat working and working in a desperate manner, and I talked and talked, morning, noon, and night.          (612, 686)

The rhythms of this passage suggest that Esther's function as a "pattern" is *for her* far less congenial than it is compulsive, debilitating, and "desperate." Although Edmund Wilson contrasts Esther, whom he calls the "sweet and submissive illegitimate daughter" with Miss Wade, the "embittered and perverse illegitimate daughter" (53), Esther shares with Miss Wade a peculiarly female rage. Her dutiful housewifery, symptomatic of the pain she feels in her own mutilated face, maps out a radically different pattern: Out of victimization emerges the potential for rage.

From the extensive ranks of Dickens' violent women, then, I have chosen to discuss three particularly resonant female characters in the Dickens ouevre: Rosa Dartle, Miss Wade, and Madame Defarge. They are intriguing, in part, because relatively little has been written about them.[1] In *The Triumph of the Novel*, for example, Albert Guerard discounts the significance of Miss Wade for "she occupies relatively few pages" (41). And Nina Auerbach's treatment of *David Copperfield* in *Woman and the Demon*, despite its promising title, focuses on the angelic Agnes, locating the demonic as the exclusive property of the utterly masculine Steerforth. But these characters further intrigue because they defy standard categorizing of Dickens' women into groups such as "heroines," "old maids," "shrews," "adventuresses," and "new women."[2] I have joined Rosa, Miss Wade, and Madame Defarge in a sisterhood because they share two qualities: rage and beauty. As enraged yet beautiful women, Rosa, Miss Wade, and Madame Defarge are doubly passionate and thus doubly threatening to Dickens, his narrators, and his novels. Their rage cannot be dismissed as geriatric like that of Mr. F's aunt in *Little Dorrit* and Mrs. Sparsit in *Hard Times* nor defused through caricature like that of Mrs. Joe in *Great Expectations* or Miss Nipper in *Dombey and Son* nor contained as lower-class like that of Hortense or Molly in *Great Expectations*. Instead, time and again, their characters are centers of attraction—and distraction—for Dickens' imagination;[3] and, thus, they risk becoming the unruly presence in the text, the fissure in the narrative that escapes narratorial control.

This study has been inspired by something I have long known: Rosa has an unforgettable face. When I last taught *David Copperfield,* Rosa monopolized the class's final discussions, for students felt duly haunted by a suspicion that Dickens, although the master of wrap-up endings, had far from mastered her. In similar fashion, Michael Slater writes of Miss Wade: she is a "vital creation, who stays in the reader's mind long after the minor role she plays in the novel's intricate plot has been forgotten" (269). Time and again, readers seem to sense what too many scholars have often neglected: the narrative gaze's relentless pursuit of these enraged beauties and the questions that pursuit raises—questions of gender, body, and voice or narrative. Striking as both physical and textual presences in their novels, Rosa, Miss Wade, and Madame Defarge represent what Peter Brooks in *Body Work* calls the "semioticization of body" and "somatization of story" central to nineteenth-century realism (xii). In these characters the body, the word, as well as the psyche intersect; here Dickens anticipates Freud's attempts to read the psychic as it is inscribed upon the body. Somatic voices, marked and signifying bodies—such inscriptions expose not only the buried lives of imagined women but also the psychic traces of a male authorial imagination. As we read, we realize that we do not forget these characters because Dickens cannot. The undocile sisters of Freud's Dora, Rosa, Miss Wade, and Madame Defarge challenge the mid-Victorian ideal of female passionlessness and look forward instead to fin de siecle representations of women, to the late-Victorian fascination with female monsters and monstrous femininity, and to Freud's explorations into hysteria and into the connections between repression and expression. As Peter Gay argues in his recent revisionist portrait of the nineteenth century, *The Cultivation of Hatred,* rage and aggression for the Victorians wore a familiar and attractive face.[4]

While few readers will deny these characters their rage, some indeed overlook their beauty. For example, Slater contrasts the "beautiful and spirited" Estella and Bella with Madame Defarge whom he groups with Miss Havisham as the "two grim older women" (277); however, Defarge is the same age as Rosa, thirty years old, and only slightly older than Miss Wade, who is twenty-six. To underscore their attractiveness Dickens introduces these characters in voyeuristic moments. In fact, rarely do we encounter Rosa, Miss Wade, and

Madame Defarge without a voyeur present: Equipped with the feminine quality Laura Mulvey calls "to-be-looked-at-ness" (19), they function to be watched, and their scenes are intensely visual. For David, Rosa's mesmeric charm conjures up a sexual fantasy—"The air of wicked grace: of triumph, in which, strange to say, there was yet something feminine and alluring . . . worthy of a cruel Princess in a Legend" (563). And in presenting Madame Defarge, Dickens repeatedly foregrounds her body, detailing her clothes and what lies underneath: the knife in her girdle, the heart under her "rough robe," the loaded pistol "lying hidden in her bosom," and the sharpened dagger "lying hidden at her waist." Lingering over her robe, the narrator observes, "Carelessly worn, it was a becoming robe enough, in a certain weird way, and her dark hair looked rich under her coarse red cap" (391). Dickens' striking choice of the word "weird" here is much like Freud's *unheimlich* as indicative of something alluring yet frightening, familiar yet strange and indefinable.[5] Here the eroticism of the strange upholds Barthes's sense of narrative as striptease, especially in the succeeding lines when the narrator imaginatively unwraps Madame Defarge's clothes and lays bare her Amazonian, primal fleshliness, "bare-foot and bare-legged, on the brown seasand" (391). Such description gives the lie to Slater's insistence on the "virtual absence in Dickens' fiction of any descriptions of female beauty below neck-level" (359).

Rosa and Miss Wade enter their respective texts in the act of mesmerizing Dickens' narrators. Here the sheer abundance of detail indicates the narrators' fascination; the dilatory description suggests the narrators' erotic surge:

> There was a second lady in the dining-room, of a slight short figure, dark, and not agreeable to look at, but with some appearance of good looks too, who attracted my attention: perhaps because I had not expected to see her; perhaps because I found myself sitting opposite to her; perhaps because of something really remarkable in her. . . . She was a little dilapidated—like a house—with having been so long to let; yet had, as I have said, an appearance of good looks.                                                                  (251)

> The shadow in which she sat, falling like a gloomy veil over her forehead, accorded very well with the character of her beauty. One can hardly see the face, so still and scornful, set off by the arched dark eyebrows, and the folds of dark hair, without wondering what its expression would be if a change came over it. That it could soften or relent, appeared next to impossible. That it could deepen into anger or any extreme of defiance, and that it must change in that direction when it changed at all, would have been its peculiar impression upon most observers. . . . Although not an open face, there was no pretence in it. I am self-contained and self-reliant . . . this it said plainly. It said so in the proud eyes, in the lifted nostril, in the handsome, but compressed and even cruel mouth.                                                                                        (23)

Both introductions present the image of sexualized femininity, its seizure by the "phallic gaze,"[6] and the heightened pleasure afforded the gazer when beauty is linked with pain. Throughout *Little Dorrit*, the narrative focus seems unable to relinquish the erotics of pain as it gazes upon Miss Wade, who, as the self-tormentor, is a body in pain explicitly and, later, doubly so through Tattycoram's mirroring of her: "It was wonderful to see the fury of the contest in the girl, and the bodily struggle she made as if she were rent by the Demons of old" (25). In *David Copperfield*, Rosa Dartle's scar keeps the observer ever aware of the presence of pain; from it, David "could not dissociate the idea of pain" (367). In short, David cannot stop talking about Rosa's disfigurement:

> [A]nd [she] had a scar upon her lip. It was an old scar—I should rather call it, seam, for it was not discolored, and had healed years ago—which had once cut through her mouth, downward towards the chin, but was now barely visible across the table, except above and on her upper lip, the shape of which it had altered.     (251)

In her passion, a passion "killing her by inches" (673), in what David calls "an eagerness that seemed enough to consume her like a fire" (367), a rage that "might tear her within" (606), Rosa's scar becomes enlarged and swollen: "I saw her face grow sharper and paler, and the marks of the old wound lengthen out until it cut through the disfigured lip, and deep into the nether lip, and slanted down the face" (366). Rosa's scar is a grotesque erogenous zone that is simultaneously the site of her pain. And, although David finds the wound horrifying—"There was something positively awful to me in this"-(367)—the scar fascinates him—"I could not help glancing at the scar with a painful interest when we went in to tea" (253). As an image for the female genitalia, for a wounded sexuality or for a sexuality that is little else than pain, Rosa's scar attracts and repels male fascination. For David, Rosa seems "to pervade the whole house"; he is expectant of her approaching, crushing anatomy—"I heard her dress rustle . . . I saw her face pass. . . . she closed her thin hand on my arm like a spring, to keep me back" (366).

Such spectacular, specular bodies in pain lead to the gazer's eventual stupefaction.[7] This surprising turn is apparent from the start when, in introducing Rosa, David betrays his own nervousness about the indefinability yet certainty of her appeal. Now the dilatory expression of Rosa's introduction seems more like stammering when David confesses that the sight of her is both agreeable and disagreeable; she is "perhaps" this, "perhaps" that, "perhaps," most truthfully, "remarkable." So too is Mr. Meagles captivated yet confused by Miss Wade. We are told "Mr. Meagles stared at her under a sort of fascination" (319), surveying this "handsome young Englishwoman" with a "puzzled look" and confessing "that you were a mystery to all of us. . . . I don't know what you are'' (323)—a sentiment Clennam later echoes with ''I know nothing of her'' (523). The inscrutable and erotic most clearly merge in the details of Miss Wade's introduction: the shadow, the dark tresses, and especially Dickens' synecdochic use of the veil. When Dickens uses this motif again to describe Miss Wade's ''composure itself (as a veil will suggest the form it covers) [intimating] the unquenchable passion of her own nature'' (319), the narrative again turns striptease, energized by the erotics of concealment. Yet we have also confronted the incomprehensible femininity that threatens to disable the male gaze.

Rosa, Miss Wade, and Madame Defarge present an instability in the text because they are objects of the gaze that aspire to be themselves gazing subjects. Such a battle over the gaze ensues when, for example, David spends the night at Highgate only to find Rosa's likeness ''looking eagerly at [him] from above the chimney-piece'' in his room (255). Here her presence forces him to continue to look and submit to being looked at himself. Indeed, he is compelled to correct the painter's omission and to see the face as he must see it in life, with scar intact. Even in the darkness afforded by night and sleep, he knows that her gaze remains vigilant, chasing him in his dreams. As the novel progresses, David's chronic watching comes to resemble something more like hypnosis, and we wonder who, after all, is watching whom:

> But what I particularly observed, before I had been half-an-hour in the house, was the close and attentive watch Miss Dartle kept upon me. . . : So surely as I looked towards her, did I see that eager visage, with its gaunt black eyes and searching brow, intent on mine. . . . In this lynx-like scrutiny she was so far from faltering when she saw I observed it, that . . . I shrunk before her strange eyes, quite unable to endure their hungry lustre.                          (365–66)

And yet he suffers the sight of Rosa constantly; later in the same chapter we witness through David's eyes and ears Rosa's music-playing:

> I don't know what it was, in her touch or voice, that made that song the most unearthly I have ever heard in my life, or can imagine. There was something fearful in the reality of it. It was as if it had never been written, or set to music, but sprung out of the passion within her; which found imperfect utterance in the low sounds of her voice . . . I was dumb when she leaned beside the harp again.                          (369)

For David, Rosa's allure renders a crisis in meaning, evident in the phrases ''I don't know'' and ''I was dumb,'' in the vague term ''something,'' and in the use of the subjunctive in the third sentence.

It is curious that David's dreams at Highgate are dreams of language in which Rosa's voice seizes control of his tongue—''I found that I was uneasily asking all sorts of people in my dreams whether it really was or not—without knowing what I meant'' (255). Both Rosa's dream-conjuring and harp-playing are only two of the numerous scenes of articulation in which these women use their rage to generate alternative voices of protest, voices that arrest the male eye and silence the dominant discourse. Bodily expressions of rage—Rosa's scar, Miss Wade's striking of her breast and seizure of Tattycoram—are the overt, anatomical manifestation of a pysche in pain; however, rage for these women also manifests itself as voice. Miss Wade's tale within the tale, her "History of a Self-Tormentor," is certainly a striking instance of rage grown articulate. Interrupting the novel with her own tale, Miss Wade shows how these characters, in body and in voice, repeatedly disrupt the narrative, taking it in new directions—not only in what they say (which I will turn to later) but also in how they say it, in the subversive ways they use language. For example, both Miss Wade and Rosa are deft at using irony to learn as well as to reproach. And Rosa's greatest rhetorical strategy is her use of indirection: "It appeared to me that she never said anything she wanted to say, outright; but hinted it, and made a great deal more of it by this practice" (251). Even to the disadvantage of his beloved Steerforth, David attributes to Rosa a sharpness, a cleverness: "Miss Dartle insinuated in the same way: sometimes, I could not conceal from myself, with great power, though in contradiction even of Steerforth" (252). Such an utterance as Rosa's "That sort of people.—Are they really animals and clods, and beings of another order?" underscores the dark ramifications of Steerforth's charms (252). Through sarcasm and irony, through being "all edge" and a "grindstone," Rosa offers an alternative voice critical of Steerforth, one that exposes his indifference and cruelty long before any other voice in the novel can—if, indeed, it ever can.[8]

As the wound that cuts through her mouth, Rosa's scar physicalizes the linguistic "edge" she wins through her tortured discourse of insinuation. So, too, in turn does Dickens' use of linguistic imagery to describe her scar reinforce the conflation of Rosa's passion, pain, and body with her language. The instrument of her speech is the locus of her pain is the space of her arousal:

> I observed that [the scar] was the most susceptible part of her face, and that, when she turned pale, that mark altered first, and became a dull, lead-colored streak, lengthening out to its full extent, like a mark in invisible ink brought to the fire. . . . I saw it start forth like the old writing on the wall.          (253)

In fact, Rosa's entire body becomes a semiotic tissue:

> The mere vehemence of her words can convey, I am sensible, but a weak impression of the passion by which she was possessed, and which made itself *articulate* in her whole figure.          (400, my emphasis)

Time and again, voice and body come together for Rosa, whether it be in the moment of playing harp music that appears to usher forth from her body rather than her instrument or when she seems to caress the very words of Littimer's report on Steerforth (564). Such an articulate body supports contemporary feminist theory's claim for the intimate connections between pain and women's discourse. Elaine Scarry in *The Body in Pain* argues more broadly that "the story of expressing physical pain eventually opens into the wider frame of invention" (22). And specifically about Brontë's *Villette,* Rachel Brownstein writes, "The language of Lucy Snowe [is] the language of the sensual self that has been denied expression and has acquired, in consequence, strange new energies that can transform conventional signs" (62).

Madame Defarge's knitted register, the creation of her ability to "transform conventional signs" into "her own stitches and her own symbols," is another image of voice, here expressing the counterforce of Revolution: "It would be easier for the weakest poltroon that lives, to erase himself from existence, than to erase one letter of his name or crimes from the knitted register of Madame Defarge" (202). Out of her clothes Madame Defarge constructs symbols, such as the "rose in her headdress" and the pattern she picks out on her sleeve. As other women join Defarge in her work, knitting becomes the novel's central image, symbolic of the Revolution in its inception: "So much was closing in about the women who sat knitting, knitting, that they their very selves were closing in around a structure yet unbuilt, where they were to sit knitting, knitting, counting dropping heads" (216). And this work comes from pain—"The fingers of the knitting women were vicious, with the experience that they could tear" (250–51); their knitting, we learn, is a displacement for their hunger (215). Always at work, Madame Defarge is an author of "shrouds," a maker of "portraits," and her masterpiece is a script concerned with the payment of old, aristocratic debts (imaged in the counting of money and tabulation of accounts).[9]

But it is her body and her gender themselves that make Madame Defarge the most eloquent figure in *A Tale of Two Cities,* contrary to Slater's following dismissal of her:

> Her vitality derives from one totally dominating passion. . . . We know all about her, once we have understood this, and never feel in the way she is presented that there is any transcending of the immediate requirements of the story. The figure of this implacable knitting woman does not come to seem symbolic of some aspect of human experience or the human condition.                    (291)

The embodiment of life under the Terror, Defarge is an image of political desire and class fear that horrifies because she provokes in Dickens and his narrator a more primal sexual desire and fear. Madame Defarge holds for the narrator the "terrible attraction" that Paris holds for Darnay. Identifying Madame Defarge's beauty as "that kind of beauty which not only seems to impart to its possessor firmness and animosity, but to strike into others an instinctive recognition of those qualities" (390–91), Dickens implies, first, that Defarge's beauty endows her with rage and, second, that the observer will instinctively see the intimacy of rage with beauty. From the bloody bosom of St. Antoine to the Guillotine—"that sharp female newly-born" (282), "the great sharp female" (307)—to the Gorgon's head that turns Monsieur the Marquis's chateau to stone to the Revolutionary "men devilishly set off with spoils of women's lace and silk and ribbon" (291), Dickens feminizes the Revolution (and masculinizes the aristocracy represented by Monseigneur). Like Carlyle in his *French Revolution* (Dickens' historical source for *A Tale of Two Cities*), Dickens is fascinated with the revolutionary women, those Carlyle calls "Menads" in his seventh book, "The Insurrection of Women." "The men," writes Dickens, "were terrible . . . but, the women were a sight to chill the boldest" (252). He makes us hear "the women passionately screeching" and witness their "frenzy" as they "whirled about, striking and tearing at their own friends until they dropped into a passionate swoon" (254, 252).

In "Orgasm, Generation, and the Politics of Reproductive Biology," Thomas Laqueur calls the Revolution "the argument made in blood that mankind in all its social and cultural relations could be remade" and argues it "engendered both a new feminism and a new fear of women" (18). Dickens fears Madame Defarge and her counterpart, La Guillotine, in their power to decapitate and its symbolic and psychological equivalency, to castrate, perhaps most directly acknowledged in the chapter title "The Gorgon's Head." Defarge's ability to mutilate transfixes the narrator and appropriately serves as subject matter for the novel's most violent moment:

> [T]here was but one quite steady figure, and that was a woman's . . . [she] remained immovable close to him when the long-gathering rain of stabs and blows fell heavy; was so close to him when he dropped dead under it, that, suddenly animated, she put her foot upon his neck, and with her cruel knife—long ready—hewed off his head.    (249)

Lucie's failed appeals to Madame Defarge as "wife," "mother," and "sisterwoman" reveal how far removed she is from the Dickensian ideal of feminine service to others; her furiously knitting hand rests impassive to Lucie's womanly kiss. When Dickens describes the Carmagnole, his vocabulary reveals his horror: he calls the dance "a fallen sport—a something, once innocent, delivered over to all devilry"; formerly "healthy" now "angering" and "bewildering," now "warped" and "perverted"; the pastime of a time of "hazard," of a "disjointed time" (307–08). Seemingly, Dickens' faith in the renovating power of the female body leads easily into his fear of the uncontrollable fecundity produced by the female body as an image for the Revolution. Madame Defarge is necessarily childless, enabling her to engage in the new, demonic type of proliferation (replete poverty and plentiful death) for which the Guillotine is responsible.

Although *David Copperfield, Little Dorrit,* and *A Tale of Two Cities* seem widely divergent novels, all three are definitive nineteenth-century novels in their concern with the formation as well as the potential mis-formation of identity. While *David Copperfield* is the only traditional *Bildungsroman* of the three, *Little Dorrit* tells the tale of an arrested adult protagonist finally prepared to form(ulate) his identity, and *A Tale of Two Cities* depicts the growing pains and growing concerns of a developing British empire—allegorically coded in Carton's and Darnay's struggles. According to all three texts, one of the obstacles to healthy growth is misalliance, particularly the threat of aristocratic leanings and sympathies lurking in Steerforth's "tasteful easy negligence," Clennam's family secret that cancels out forgiveness, and the French aristocracy. Against such moneyed masculinity, then, rises enraged femininity as the retributive voice, as the punisher of such dangerous tendencies. An etiology of their pain reveals that all three enraged, beautiful women share origins in dependency and rejection and/or violence at the hands of privileged males. Madame Defarge's motive for violence, we discover, is avenging her servant-class family and violated sister—"imbued from her childhood with a brooding sense of wrong, and an inveterate hatred of a class, opportunity had developed her into a tigress" (391). Discarded by Steerforth and Gowan, Rosa and Miss Wade share similarly orphaned lives of social and monetary dependency. Their social uselessness—Rosa considers herself a "mere disfigured piece of furniture"—and impoverishment are stressed time and again. As if Rosa's scar were not a sufficiently eloquent expression of her neglect, Steerforth himself imparts to David Rosa's brief life-story:

> She was the motherless child of a sort of cousin of my father's. He died one day. My mother, who was then a widow, brought her here to be company to her. She has a couple of thousand pounds of her own, and saves the interest of it every year, to add to the principal. There's the history of Miss Rosa Dartle for you.                                                                 (253)

Pancks's narrative of Miss Wade's life is all too similar:

> She is somebody's child—anybody's—nobody's. Put her in a room in London here with any six people old enough to be her parents, and her parents may be there for anything she knows.... She knows nothing about 'em. She knows nothing about any relative whatever.... [Mr. Casby] has long had money (not overmuch as I make out) in trust to dole out to her when she can't do without it.                                                                 (524–25)

The slimness of their lives as narrated by others, however, does not capture the potency of Rosa's irony, Miss Wade's self-penned history, and Madame Defarge's knitted register as subversive discourses: Rosa is able to implicate David in the Steerforth/Emily tragedy, Miss Wade sharpens the pangs of guilt Arthur feels in his breast, Madame Defarge can alter political structures. They mesmerize and rage and articulate in order to punish. Their identity is a rebuff, particularly to gender and class expectations. While Lucie comforts her six-year-old child, the very next page depicts Madame Defarge sporting a pistol, resisting submission to her husband for whom she plays the catechist in aggression, stern when his appetite for violence flags. Miss Wade challenges the currency of the word "gentleman" (516), and both she and Rosa interrogate what is "natural" for women (*Little Dorrit* 22, *David Copperfield* 367–68). The visual vocabulary that describes Miss Wade's home life—the bare garden, the London and Calais flats posted with "to let" signs—is shorthand certainly for her rejection of the conventional community afforded by bourgeois family life (she lives in a house that is home to no one) and possibly for what some readers interpret as her iconoclastic choice to lead a coded lesbian existence with Tattycoram. Neither nurturers nor comforters, these stern and unforgiving females are thus freed to assault privilege in its numerous manifestations. As Miss Wade asserts in *Little Dorrit*'s opening pages, a prisoner does not forgive his prison; and, indeed, she keeps returning, a sort of choric presence in the novel, like destiny to punish the wrongs of the past. She does not let the amnesiac Clennam forget; her incriminations that force Clennam into accountability facilitate one of Dickens' key purposes for the novel, clearly stated in the novel's former title, "Nobody's Fault." So too does Madame Defarge play the part of Fate, the Furies, or—much like her lieutenant—Vengeance. Although one of her taglines is "and she saw nothing," we quickly learn that she sees everything, including prophetically that which is "inaudible and invisible" (195). Miss Wade's tagline "I understood," much like Rosa's clever appeals "to know," underscores their similar abilities to acquire and possess information that will turn out to be central to the novel's resolution. Both are figures of curiosity, blackmailers of sorts who hunt down knowledge, for Rosa pays Littimer for his words just as Miss Wade rewards Blandois for information concerning Gowan. For all three, Miss Wade makes the claim, "I have the curse to have not been born a fool," and their erotic potency is matched only by this kind of authority. They pose the riddle and hold the answer. As Helena Michie claims, "If women's bodies are written transcriptions of cultural problems, they are also, consciously or not, repositories of secret knowledge that must be processed to be understood" (120).

Although Rosa, Miss Wade, and Madame Defarge protest in order to punish the protagonists for their dangerous connections, the battle between narrated and narrator takes a final turn when these retributive voices are themselves ultimately punished. Self-avowal eventually leads to disavowal, the somatic expression of which is, again, succinctly contained in Rosa's scar. As a mark of erasure, Rosa's scar invalidates her—WOMAN or WOMAN's MOUTH—she is present in the text only to be vanquished and disappear. So too Miss Wade's "The History of a Self-Tormentor"—in one way powerful in its refusal to be assimilated—also cancels itself out to remain at best an act of self-betrayal, harmless to others and defeating to the self. Dickens' working notes for *Little Dorrit* remind him to revise in order to isolate Miss Wade's narrative, to "change this to two chapters, getting the Self-Tormentor narrative by itself" (822). The writing, thus, resides in its chapter, socially and fictionally alienated, much like its author. Miss Wade's history, "From her own point of view," does not ultimately liberate her character nor does it rescue a feminine, buried discourse; rather it is an anatomy—"Dissect it," Dickens instructs—of a perspectival disease. What begins as a feminist revision of the word "hate"—"You don't know what I mean by hating"—concludes as Miss Wade's embarrassing, purposeless self-exposure to Arthur Clennam. "Unconsciously laying bare all her character" is Dickens' plan for "Miss Wade's story"; and the resulting confession drawn from her bosom, inscribed on the papers from her bureau's inner drawer, reveals a self guilty of her own torment, a clinically drawn case study of neurosis and repression.

One by one, these voices of protest expire. What should mark Rosa's long-awaited triumph, her confrontation with Emily in Martha's London room, is in fact the beginning of her demise. This scene is one of the novel's most intensely visual scenes with abundant, if unintentional, charged references to what characters can and cannot see. Although Rosa's incrimination of Emily takes on specular shape—"I have come to see James Steerforth's fancy"—it is actually David who visually steals the scene, strategically positioned, as he is, at an aperture afforded him by a special back door.[10] In what stands as the novel's voyeuristic climax, we watch David watch Rosa gaze upon Emily:[11]

> [Her tone's] mastered rage, presented her before me, as if I had seen her standing in the light. I saw the flashing black eyes, and the passion-wasted figure; and I saw the scar, with its white track cutting through her lips, quivering and throbbing as she spoke.        (604)

When Rosa attempts to strike Emily, the gesture seems purposeless—"[t]he blow, which had no aim, fell upon the air" (606). Here and elsewhere, Dickens emphasizes the purposelessness of such rage. Rosa repeatedly strikes only her own wound, and Miss Wade continually places "that repressing hand upon her own bosom." In order to limit the scope of these women's influence even further, Dickens uses doubling or coupling, most evident in Miss Wade's and Tattycoram's alliance—here, appropriately, an object of Clennam's eye:

As each of the two handsome faces looked at the other, Clennam felt how each of the two natures must be constantly tearing the other to pieces. . . . Arthur Clennam looked at them, standing a little distance asunder in the dull confined room, each proudly cherishing her own anger; each, with a fixed determination, torturing her own breast, and torturing the other's.                    (642, 643)

In each novel, the enraged women fall at the hands of a female tribunal (purging female rage with female rage). Rosa's punishment is to endure an eternal incarceration with Mrs. Steerforth—"Thus I leave them; thus I always find them; thus they wear their time away, from year to year" (735). Miss Wade is betrayed by Tattycoram who rededicates her love for the Meagleses and bears witness against Miss Wade: "I have had Miss Wade before me all this time, as if it was my own self grown ripe—turning everything the wrong way, and twisting all good into evil" (787). And Madame Defarge dies in battle with Miss Pross, branding her killer's face with "the marks of griping fingers" (398).

So too are Dickens' texts "branded" with marks remaining to tell the story the enraged, female body tries to tell. Such textual and somatic traces locate the rupture in the text wherein lies an unstable discursive space where body, pain, and expression intersect. Signifying parts of the body—Madame Defarge's knitting hand, Miss Wade's breast, and most vividly Rosa's scarred mouth—seem to confirm both what Helena Michie argues specifically about Esther Summerson, "The body and sexuality assert themselves . . . through pain and scarring. In learning to read the scars we read desire" (29), and what Peter Gay writes in his opening line of *The Cultivation of Hatred:* "The scars that aggression has left on the face of past are indelible"(3). As I have argued, Rosa, Miss Wade, and Madame Defarge attract, repel, and even stand in for Dickens' own imaginative and psychic states even though the eventual eradication of these violent females, upon whom the gaze ultimately turns hostile, will ensure the triumph of good Dickensian heroines. After completing the novel's unpleasant task of denouncing Emily as the unpalatable female and thus diffusing the threat of a rekindled childhood love for David, Rosa ushers in Agnes. Tattycoram receives a new role model into her malleable life, Amy Dorrit. She is thus able to learn the womanly lesson, for as Mr. Meagles professes, "Yet I have heard tell, Tattycoram, that [Amy's] young life has been one of active resignation, goodness, and noble service" because she always focused upon "duty" (788). And, in *A Tale of Two Cities,* the "poor little seamstress," as a reworking of the image of Madame Defarge, is the unexpected heroine. In her "work-worn, hunger-worn young fingers" (384), we see Dickens' rescue of the images of sewing, work, gender, and body.[12] As a vocational, dutiful essence, she is "girlish," "patient," self-sacrificing ("I am not unwilling to die"), "uncomplaining," enduring, "constant." On the other side of Dickens' enraged, beautiful women stands this "poor little seamstress" ready to die so that her cousin might "profit" and have a better life by it.

# NOTES

1. Or little that is positive. Long ago, Forster set the trend when he identified the "curiously unpleasant" Rosa Dartle as the single flaw in an otherwise perfect novel; and in similar impatience he called the "surface-painting" of both Miss Wade and Tattycoram "anything but attractive" (II: 132, 226).

2. These categories come from Merryn Williams's *Women in the English Novel, 1800–1900;* another set can be found in Patricia Ingham's *Dickens, Women, and Language.*

3. In his chapter "Women Passing By" in *From Copyright to Copperfield: The Identity of Dickens,* Alexander Welsh analyzes the ways in which *David Copperfield* "stresses 'woman' " (124), citing how "much energy in *Copperfield* is expended in positioning the hero with respect to the women in his life" (129). Welsh continues, "All this positioning in respect to women . . . represents most of the work in plotting the novel; the men in this personal history, even Steerforth, fall more readily in and out of place." Of course, almost as provocative is the chapter's title itself, with its implied visual exchange; I disagree only with Welsh's sense that, as in the case of Emily and David, when women pass by in *David Copperfield* males "try . . . **not** to look" (131).

4. A generation ago, John Carey catalogued Dickens' attraction to violence in "Dickens and Violence" from *The Violent Effigy.* When he moves from such violent forces as fire and cannibalism to the potential for human violence, however, Carey speaks exclusively of Dickens' violent men.

5. In her article "Victorian Women and Insanity," Elaine Showalter recounts Dickens' visit to St. Luke's Hospital where he found himself fascinated with the female inmates, particularly "one old-young woman, with her dishevelled long light hair, spare figure, and weird gentility" (157). Both visually and linguistically charged, this moment from Dickens' life appears to inform the fictionalized scene here.

6. This famous phrase indicates my debt to Luce Irigary's *Speculum of the Other Woman,* even though I will go on to argue that these characters give challenge, if indeed temporarily so, to her claim that "[w]oman has no gaze, no discourse for her specific specularization" (224).

7. Of course, Freud's "The Medusa's Head" and the interpretation it has generated make such an irony far from unexpected. For example, Laura Mulvey writes, "Thus, the woman as icon, displayed for the gaze and enjoyment of men, the active controllers of the look, always threatens to evoke the anxiety it originally signified" (21).

8. Many generations of readers have noted David's love for Steerforth, which fuels his desire to identify with his affluent friend and even to become him. Yet Rosa's

presence admonishes David for such a desire, feminizing him, making him see what it is not to be the seducer but rather the seducer's victim.

9. It is not pushing the point too far to argue that these women are figures of the author. Given their way with words, given their familiarity with accounts of all kinds and, as I will later claim, accountability, Rosa, Miss Wade, and Madame Defarge are invested with the powers of authorship. Perhaps this is clearest in the case of Miss Wade, whose greatest act is the penning of an autobiographical novel in miniature, inserted in one of Dickens' own numerous autobiographically charged novels.

10. Precisely because David cannot actually see Rosa's attack but rather is able to conjure up the tableau based only on what he hears, this scene, as evident in the passage I quote, showcases his visual command of the moment. This scene is the first time in the novel that David watches Rosa without her knowledge of it or without her returning the gaze.

11. Although Welsh claims that David in this scene "stands idly by" (139), and Slater writes, "Worse still, [Dickens] determines, despite the great implausibility involved, to have David overhear the tremendous tongue-lashing that Rosa administers to Em'ly" (268), David's spectatorship here is far from idle or implausible and is, in fact, the scene's key element. As Slater later allows, this scene is for Dickens "irresistible," and such moments of irresistibility are precisely the focus of this article. In his essay "From Outrage to Rage: Dickens's Bruised Femininity," U.C. Knoepflmacher is drawn to this very scene as illustrative of Dickens' "orchestration of male and female anger," here veiling masculine anger "by displacing it onto the female" (85). Although my gloss of the precise nature of David's and Dickens' fascination for Rosa will differ from Knoepflmacher's biographical/psychoanalytical focus on Dickens' hostility towards his mother, I relish Knoepflmacher's close examination of the subtleties of this scene.

12. A "cleansing" of the imagery is also apparent in Dickens' description of Lucie Manette as "the golden thread" in her father's life (110).

# WORKS CITED

Auerbach, Nina. *Woman and the Demon.* Cambridge: Harvard UP, 1982.

Brooks, Peter. *Body Work.* Cambridge: Harvard UP, 1993.

Brownstein, Rachel. *Becoming a Heroine.* New York: Penguin, 1982.

Carey, John. *The Violent Effigy.* London: Faber and Faber, 1973.

Dickens, Charles. *Bleak House.* Introduction, Sir Osbert Sitwell. New York: Oxford UP, 1962.

———. *David Copperfield.* Ed. Jerome Buckley. New York: Norton, 1989.

————. *Dombey and Son.* Introduction H. W. Garrod. New York: Oxford UP, 1960.

————. *Little Dorrit.* Ed. Harvey Peter Sucksmith. New York: Oxford at Clarendon P, 1979.

————. *Our Mutual Friend.* Ed. Stephen Gill. New York: Penguin, 1971.

————. *A Tale of Two Cities.* Ed. George Woodcock. New York: Penguin, 1970.

Forster, John. *The Life of Charles Dickens.* New York: Charles Scribner's Sons, 1899.

Gay, Peter. *The Cultivation of Hatred.* New York: Norton and Co., 1993.

Guerard, Albert. *The Triumph of the Novel: Dickens, Dostoevsky, Faulkner.* New York: Oxford UP, 1976.

Ingham, Patricia. *Dickens, Women, and Language.* Toronto: U of Toronto P, 1992.

Irigary, Luce. *The Speculum of the Other Woman.* Ithaca: Cornell UP, 1985.

Knoepflmacher, U. C. "From Outrage to Rage: Dickens's Bruised Femininity." *Dickens and Other Victorians.* Ed. Joanne Shattock. New York: St. Martin's, 1988. 75–96.

Laqueur, Thomas. "Orgasm, Generation, and the Politics of Reproductive Biology." *Representations* 14 (1986): 1–41.

Michie, Helena. *The Flesh Made Word.* New York: Oxford UP, 1987.

Mulvey, Laura. *Visual and Other Pleasures.* Bloomington: Indiana UP, 1989.

Scarry, Elaine. *The Body in Pain.* New York: Penguin, 1982.

Showalter, Elaine. "Victorian Women and Insanity." *Victorian Studies* 23. 2 (Winter 1980): 157–181.

Slater, Michael. *Dickens and Women.* Stanford: Stanford UP, 1983.

Welsh, Alexander. *From Copyright to Copperfield: The Identity of Dickens.* Cambridge: Harvard UP, 1987.

Williams, Merryn. *Women in the English Novel, 1800–1900.* New York: St. Martin's, 1984.

Wilson, Edmund. *The Wound and the Bow.* New York: Oxford UP, 1970.

# Becoming Poor to Make Many Rich: The Resolution of Class Conflict in Dickens

*Steven Hake*

Class conflict worried Dickens. He announced that the purpose of *Household Words* was no less than " 'to bring the greater and lesser in degree, together . . . and mutually dispose them to a better acquaintance and a kinder understanding.' In a word, he was promising to root out social disharmony" (Marlow 145). Myron Magnet, in *Dickens and the Social Order,* argues that Dickens believed that the upper classes have a responsibility to educate and humanize the lower classes: "No ruling class has a right to withhold the means—material, social, spiritual—of raising life above the merely brutal and savage" (200).

However, if we look carefully at his novels, we can see that it is often the "brutish" lower classes who humanize those above them. Marxists also see "salvation" as coming from below—the lower classes overthrow the upper—but Dickens' views are not necessarily those of Karl Marx. Perhaps this explains why the socialist playwright and critic George Bernard Shaw sees a gap in Dickens at this point. Dan H. Laurence and Martin Quinn observe that, "although both Shaw and Dickens were extremely sensitive to social disorder. Shaw, the Socialist, had a cause while Dickens—and, by extension, Shakespeare—did not" (xxii).

Because Dickens' "cause" was not that of socialism, it went unrecognized by critics such as Shaw. English and American critics in general have been very slow to recognize the depth of Dickens' Christian faith, particularly as reflected in his major novels.[1] His resolution of class conflict is a striking instance of this.

In Dickens, class tensions are resolved by a Christian concept of salvation through a forgiving and self-sacrificing love. Christianity always works from the bottom up. God was not incarnated as an aristocrat, but rather as a son in a poor, working-class family. Christ, though He was rich, became poor that He might make many rich (cf. II Cor.8:9). We see this pattern reflected in the way working-class people in Dickens suffer for and save the rich and sophisticated, or those who aspire to be rich and sophisticated. Dickens thus reflects the Bible's emphasis that it is often the poor and socially despised who are the first to enter the kingdom of God (Matt. 21:31 and Luke 7:29) and the rich and sophisticated who are scarcely able to enter at all (Matt. 19:24, Mark 10:25 and Luke 18:25). In Dickens it is most often the poor who are portrayed as having solid Christian values (cf. the Peggottys, Ham, Joe Gargery, and Lizzie Hexam). The rich, however, are seen as vain, tormented and in need of salvation (cf. Steerforth, his mother, Estella, Miss Havisham and Eugene Wrayburn). Those who aspire to "raise" themselves to a higher class (cf. Emily and Pip) are often seen as losing in the attempt much more than they gain. I will examine this aspect of *David Copperfield,* yet also make comparisons to *Great Expectations* and *Our Mutual Friend.*

Not only can we see class conflict resolved by the suffering and death of the poor for the rich, but we can also see a definite development of this idea as it took deeper root in Dickens' mind and art. Emily aspires to be a lady even before she meets Steerforth. She is thus ripe for Steerforth's deceptive promises and plunges herself into misery. She is saved by her own repentance and by the suffering love of Mr. Peggotty and Ham. Neither Emily nor the Peggotties, however, are able to save Steerforth, though Ham dies in the attempt, perhaps because there is a tinge of Steerforth even in them. They also encouraged Emily, though inadvertantly, in her desires to be a lady, and they were also deceived by Steerforth. In this they are in significant contrast to both Joe and Biddy in *Great Expectations,* who were consistently aware of what was happening to Pip. Pip aspires to be a gentleman only after meeting Estella and only in order to win Estella. He too is saved by the long-suffering, forgiving love of Joe Gargery, no less real than, though not so dramatic as, the wanderings of Mr. Peggotty and the death of Ham. As Pip's warped values come back into focus, he is able in turn, by the vivid example of his own suffering and forgiving love, to rescue first Miss Havisham and finally even Estella[2] from their own unbending aristocratic pride and bitterness. So the upwardly aspiring person in *David Copperfield,* Emily, is able only barely to save herself and not able to save her aristocratic lover. In *Great Expectations,* Pip is not so early set on upward aspirations and so is able to save both himself, Estella, and Estella's mother.[3] In Dickens' last completed novel, *Our Mutual Friend,* Lizzie Hexam does not aspire to be a lady at all and so in a sense needs no salvation herself, and she succeeds in redeeming her Steerforth-like lover, Eugene Wrayburn. That social station to which Lizzie did not aspire, she is yet granted as the novel concludes, in that Eugene makes her a lady. Yet what she gives to Wrayburn is infinitely greater than what he gives to her. Wrayburn lifts her up socially, but she lifts him up spiritually.

He makes a "lady" of her, but she makes a man of him. So we can see a clear progression in the art of Dickens in which the poor grow in confidence in their spiritual riches in Christ, and thus in their ability to withstand the temptations of the deceptive worldly riches of the upper classes.

## EMILY'S "FALL" INTO THE UPPER CLASS

In *David Copperfield* Mr. Peggotty and Ham suffer for and save the would-be lady, Emily. Emily aspires to be a lady long before she meets Steerforth. When she and David first meet as little children, she already has very definite ideas about the clothing she would give to her uncle if she were a lady. Although she expresses this desire in generous terms, David even as a child can see the inappropriateness of this method of expressing her gratitude to her uncle. Perhaps the fact that she was "spoiled by them all [e.g., all the Peggottys]" (141) accounts in part for this aspiration. They set her apart, and in this way perhaps contribute, however inadvertently, to her later fall. Mr. Omer observes that she has "elegant taste in the dress-making business" (305), so much so that no duchess can touch her, and that all the village women are jealous of her beauty and resentful of her aspirations to be a lady.

David, Mr. Peggotty, and Ham also contribute, albeit unwittingly, to Emily's fall in that they are first captivated by Steerforth: Emily learns of him through these men already so close to her. As they praised him, she sat "listening with the deepest attention" (143). When she meets him, she, too, is captivated: "She soon became more assured when she found how gently and respectfully Steerforth spoke to her; how skilfully he avoided anything that would embarrass her" (316). David says that Steerforth brought them all, "by degrees, into a charmed circle" and Mrs. Gummidge says she felt "bewitched" (316).

Emily is thus removing herself gradually from the solid world view of the working-class Peggoties, and transforming her allegiance to the outwardly impressive but ultimately empty values of the upper-class Steerforth. Even she has already begun to do this before meeting him in her desire to become a "lady"; his appearance accelerates, gives specific focus to, and completes the process. Dickens continues to prepare us for Emily's outward flight and to chronicle her gradual inward fall in many subtle ways. After meeting Steerforth, Emily keeps away from Ham in his presence. Martha also appears as a "disturbing shadow" (325) of a fallen woman. Emily is associated with the devouring sea and shipwrecks. Mr. Peggotty cannot bear to see Emily and Martha side by side "for all the treasures that's wrecked in the sea" (337). Steerforth's boat was originally named the "Stormy Petrel," a harbinger of trouble, as the petrel was believed to be most active before a storm (suggesting

Steerforth's feverish activity before the abduction). The name petrel itself is believed to be a diminutive form of Peter, alluding perhaps to his attempt to walk on the stormy waters and his sinking when he took his eyes off Christ and looked rather at the more impressive wind and waves (as Emily takes her eyes off Ham and is fascinated by the more impressive Steerforth).[4] These associations are reinforced when Steerforth renames the boat "The Little Em'ly" (325). There is one final reminder of this imagery when Mr. Peggotty finds Emily in Martha's room, and David notices that there are ships on the walls.

Emily experiences one final struggle as she talks with Martha, taking a last look at the people and values she is rejecting. She thinks she is not as good or as thankful as she ought to be for the opportunity to marry a good man and lead a peaceful life. In a slight but symbolic action, Peggotty "recall[s] her [Emily's] stray ringlets," even as Emily "innocently kiss[es] her chosen husband on the cheek, and creep[s] close to his bluff form as if it were her best support" (340). Both the Peggottys and David put the best construction on things, as David thinks that Martha's effect on Emily only intensifies her purity and grace (341), and Mr. Peggotty thinks that Emily's trembling and clinging to him "even to the avoidance of her chosen husband" is a result of the fact that Barkis is dying (443). Even the repetition of the word "chosen" before husband heightens for the reader the struggle in Emily's mind.

When Emily abandons the Peggottys and Ham for Steerforth, the contrast between the two families, and the two world views they represent, becomes increasingly clear. She hopes initially that Steerforth will make her a lady, but this hope is gradually abandoned. Her low spirits and his restlessness reflect the rapid breakdown in their foundationless relationship—she is unable to respect him and he is unable to commit himself to her in love. David says to Mrs. Steerforth:

> . . . if you suppose the girl, so deeply wronged, has not been cruelly deluded, and would not rather die a hundred deaths than take a cup of water from your son's hand now, you cherish a terrible mistake.                    (673)

The cup of water image, taken from the gospels of (cf. Matt.10:42 and Mark 9:41) suggests that the salvation Steerforth holds out to Emily, in his invitation to her to become his "lady" and join the upper class, is a bogus one of which she no longer wants any part.[4]

This is confirmed when Rosa confronts Emily. For all her shrewdness, Rosa completely misreads Emily's personality and motives when she calls her "bold, flaunting [and] practiced" (718) and thinks that Emily can use her money to console the Peggottys. Emily is re-entering, or perhaps entering for the first time, the Christian world of the Peggottys, a world about which Rosa knows nothing. Emily alludes to the Lord's prayer as she desperately pleads with Rosa, "... for Heaven's sake spare me, if you would be spared yourself" (719), but it is precisely this forgiving love that Rosa never receives and can never give. Emily says that Rosa knows, perhaps, Steerforth's power with a weak, vain girl. (The reader is vividly shown Steerforth's ability to soften even Rosa in his final time with her before running off with Emily—Rosa too is taken in and then recoils in disgust). Emily then goes on to say that Steerforth "used all his power to deceive me, and that I believed him, trusted him, and loved him!" (720).

Emily abandons the world of the Peggottys before she realizes the full value and inner beauty of that world, even as Pip abandons the world of Joe Gargery in *Great Expectations* without beginning to understand what it is he is walking away from until it is almost too late. Both Emily and Pip eventually see through the superficially impressive world of Steerforth and Estella and are brought back to their senses by the long-suffering and sacrificial love of the Peggottys and Joe Gargery. As the Old Testament tabernacle was ordinary-looking on the outside, but resplendent on the inside, so one of the deepest movements in both these novels is toward the eventual recognition of one's true self and true home in that which at first is despised as outwardly common and unimpressive.

## EMILY'S REDEEMERS: MR. PEGGOTTY AND HAM

Mr. Peggotty resolves, as soon as he learns of Emily's flight, not simply to wait for his prodigal daughter as the father does in that gospel story (Mrs. Gummidge does that, with the candle burning), but to seek her over land and sea.[5] His one message for her (that he sends out in every way he can) is one not of condemnation, but of love and forgiveness, a message that Steerforth intercepts and prevents Emily from receiving.[6] Mr. Peggotty's willingness to sacrifice himself to save Emily is shown in many ways. He confronts Mrs. Steerforth with her son's responsibility and demands that if Emily is low Steerforth should "raise her up!" (468). He is even willing never to see Emily in this life, if that would embarrass her new family, "till all of us shall be alike in quality afore our God!" (468). He asserts that he suffers as much as Mrs. Steerforth does and he despises her attempt to offer him "compensation." In all these things he reminds us strongly of the contrast between inner and outer nobility seen when Joe Gargery stands before Miss Havisham.

As Emily lies near death in the home of the Italian peasant woman, her one desperate need is for some word of forgiveness, and she fears she will not receive it. Mr. Peggotty remarks that this woman who helped Emily at such a time of need will have "treasure in heaven" (728), a reference to

Matthew 6 and a further reminder of the eternal perspective that characterizes his own outlook as well as that of Ham. When Mr. Peggotty finally does find Emily, she faints and he covers her face with a handkerchief and carries her home. This covering serves as an emblem of atonement and forgiveness.[7] He also returns every shilling of money that he ever received from the Steerforths so that his motives are perfectly clear to all. Finally, he takes Martha with him as well as Emily to a new life in a new world. David says, " . . . if ever I have loved and honored any man, I loved and honored that man in my soul" (811). Steerforth's influence on David is profound, but that of Mr. Peggotty and Ham is even more so, and it is this good influence that enables him finally to see Steerforth in the right light (as I hope to show below). As the ship leaves, taking the emigrants away, David reflects: "Aye, Emily, beautiful and drooping, cling to him with the utmost trust of thy bruised heart; for he has clung to thee with all the might of his great love" (812).

Emily's eventual redemption is accomplished not only by the forgiving and self-sacrificing love of Mr. Peggotty, but also by that of Ham. Just as Mr. Peggotty contrasts strongly with Mrs. Steerforth as the inwardly noble parent figure, so Ham contrasts strongly with Steerforth as the inwardly noble lover. Ham is described as "iron-true" to Emily, enabling Mr. Peggotty to die in peace with Emily in Ham's care (314), as opposed to Steerforth, who causes Mr. Peggotty to suffer so much for his falseness to Emily. We are told that "nature had given [Ham] the soul of a gentleman" (443), though not the wealth and articulate speech of one.

Ham's redemption or reclamation of Emily is developed along the lines of the lost childhood motif. In her initial note, Emily tells Ham to think of her as someone who died as a child and "was buried somewhere" (452). In a later letter, she speaks of Ham as "so brave and so forgiving" (587). This courage and forgiveness enable her to rise from the dead, as it were, and recover the lost innocence of her childhood, as can be seen in her near death by fever after her flight from Steerforth, her crying out for forgiveness, and her final experiencing of the "weakness of the littlest child" (727). We are reminded of Jesus' words, " . . . unless you change and become like little children, you will never enter the kingdom of heaven" (Matthew 18:3).[8]

Shortly before his death, Ham is described as the "serenest of the party" (736). As he is being prepared for sacrifice, he is described as broken-hearted, yet full of courage, sweetness, and a willingness to work harder and better than others. He talks of Emily as a child, but not as a woman, as her entrance into womanhood coincides with her yielding to the false values of Steerforth. In his last letter to her, he attempts very delicately both to ask Emily's forgiveness for pressing his affections and putting her in a difficult position, and also to assure her that he is not too greatly hurt by her betrayal. He hopes finally to see Emily "without blame, where the wicked cease from troubling and the weary are at rest'' (738). This reference to Job 3:17 is both apt for obvious reasons and interesting, as Job also refers to a pre-Steerforth-like innocence and joy of childhood when he asks, '' . . . why was I not hidden in the ground like a stillborn child, like an infant who never saw the light of day?'' (vs. 16).

Though the sea is portrayed in the novel most frequently as an angry devourer and devours Ham himself, a detail suggests a heaven beyond it for Ham, as he concludes his final message to Emily and ''turns his face towards a strip of silvery light upon the sea'' (738). David later says of Ham's last message to Emily that it consisted of a ''deep fidelity and goodness not to be adorned'' (785). This is thoroughly consistent with the novel's presentation of Ham's character and perhaps explains the decidedly unadorned way in which Ham's death is recorded. The event contains within itself its own eloquence which does not need rhetorical heightening. If this is true, then the understated description of Ham's death, which might be taken as implicitly favoring the upper classes, confirms rather the novel's view that it is the rugged, self-sacrificing nobility of the poor, inward, and unadorned, that redeems the upper classes. Emily says of this last message that its very goodness is like ''sharp thorns'' (785) that hurt, but also heal, like the crown of thorns worn by Christ at his trial. She says finally, ''When I find what you are, and what uncle is, I think what God must be, and can cry to him. . . . In another world, if I am forgiven, I may wake a child and come to you'' (785). Emily learns of God's love and mercy through Ham and Mr. Peggotty, and makes one final reference to her hope of eventually recovering fully through this love and mercy the innocence of her lost childhood.

Ham's death can be seen as a sacrificial, even substitutionary, death for Emily. The angry sea demands Emily, but Ham offers himself instead, so that the sea can take Emily rather to a new life far away. David says of Ham as Ham is getting ready to save the drowning sailor, that ''the determination in his face, and his look out to sea—exactly the same look as I remembered in connexion with the morning after Emily's flight—awoke me to a knowledge of his danger'' (793). While this look refers most specifically to Ham's attitude toward Steerforth (I discuss this in detail below), it can also be thought of as bringing to mind Ham's willingness to die for Emily when he learns of her flight:

> ''My love, Mas'r Davy—the pride and hope of my heart—her that I'd have died for, and would die for now—she's gone!''. . . .
>     The face he turned up to the troubled sky, the quivering of his clasped hands, the agony of his figure, remain associated with that lonely waste, in my remembrance, to this hour.                                                    (451)

Ham finally has his opportunity to lay down his life for Emily. Mr. Peggotty's last news of Emily at the novel's end shows her to be as she was in childhood, only better (i.e., without foolish aspirations to become "a lady"). His carrying to her, at her request, some grass and earth from Ham's grave, shows that Mr. Peggotty has not lived for her, and Ham has not died for her, in vain.

## STEERFORTH REDEEMED AS WRAYBURN

Having looked at how Emily is first lost then found, let us look at how Steerforth is lost in *David Copperfield,* but redeemed as Wrayburn in *Our Mutual Friend.* Perhaps the two things that most characterize Steerforth are his many abilities and his waste of those abilities. The very first time his name is mentioned in the novel, David sees it cut deep and often in the table top (79), suggesting Steerforth's inflated view of himself. Steerforth replaces Mr. Mell briefly as a teacher and teaches "in an easy amateur way, and without any book (he seemed to know everything by heart)" (101). Both his abilities and his underuse of them are suggested by this detail. At Yarmouth David praises Steerforth's abilities as athlete, speaker, singer—it seems there is nothing he cannot do. David thinks Steerforth could distinguish himself at Oxford as a scholar, but he has no interest in this, almost a contempt for it, and his manner is again characterized by "carelessness and lightness" (291). Steerforth proposes a toast: " . . . and the lilies of the valley that toil not, neither do they spin, in compliment to me—the more shame for me!'' (295). His mother says of their choice of Mr. Creakle's school that they looked for one where Steerforth would be deferred to, that he soon became king there and could have totally broken out, but rather he "haughtily determined to be worthy of his station" (296). This school gives Steerforth an opportunity to make a somewhat more constructive use of his abilities, at least for awhile. Mrs. Steerforth further says of him that he "can always [when he wants to] outstrip every competitor" (296). At Yarmouth Steerforth also shows himself to be a good sailor who loves rough toil just as a change of pace.

Eugene Wrayburn is also characterized as someone with many abilities that are not being used. He drifts through life until he meets Lizzie Hexam. She gives him at last something to strive for and someone to live for. Her goodness acts as a moral rebuke to him, gradually undermining his cynicism. In his efforts to clear her father's name and help with Lizzie's education he begins to experience the satisfaction of doing things for others. Even his elaborate tormenting of Bradley Headstone, while perverse in motivation, gives him an opportunity to exert himself over a sustained period of time with a sense of vigor so new to him that it surprises his friend Mortimer Lightwood. His final death and rebirth are dramatized in his being struck from behind by Headstone (hence his name, I suppose, both as blow to the head and as gravestone), his near drowning in the river, and his protracted battle with death before his eventual recovery. The old, indolent Eugene dies forever and a new, resolute one emerges, willing to sacrifice everything for his wife:

> I will fight it out to the last gasp, with her and for her, here, in the open field. When I hide her, or strike for her, faint-heartedly, in a hole or a corner, do you [Mortimer Lightwood] whom I love next best upon earth, tell me what I shall most righteously deserve to be told—that she would have done well to turn me over with her foot that night when I lay bleeding to death, and spat in my dastard face. (*OMF* 885, 886)

Lizzie is the one who rescues Eugene from drowning and who inspires him to pull through the deep waters of his fever and illness. She is able to do this for him because she, unlike Emily, does not cave in to his twisted values, but rather raises him up to her healthy ones. She, like Mr. Peggotty, Ham, and Joe Gargery, believes in her loved one no matter what, and willingly risks her own life to save him.

Wrayburn gets Lizzie only after a very long, difficult and life-changing struggle, and only on Lizzie's own terms. Steerforth gets Emily all too easily, and on his own terms. His pursuit of her is a game, a momentary excitement, "a mere wasteful careless course of winning what was worthless to him, and next minute thrown away" (311). Lizzie's goodness rebukes and inspires Wrayburn. Steerforth sees goodness in David, but this is not enough to stop him: "I believe you are in earnest, and are good. I wish we all were!" (318).

In a final revealing scene before their separation, David comes upon Steerforth looking at pictures in the fire, anticipating a similar scene involving Lizzie Hexam in the later novel. But Lizzie sees salvation for Eugene in the fire, while Steerforth sees only ruin for himself and Emily. Lizzie reveals what she sees to her friend Jenny Wren, but Steerforth hides what he sees from David; he spoils the fire and strikes out of it a "train of red-hot sparks that went careering up the little chimney, and roaring out into the air" (321), suggesting the train of disastrous events about to take place.

Steerforth wishes that he had been better guided and could guide himself better. He sees himself as the boy in the nursery tale who "didn't care" and became food for the lions (322). Wrayburn's father is no more "steadfast and judicious" (*DC* 322) than Steerforth's and is also a primary cause of his drifting lifestyle. David marvels that Steerforth can master anything so easily, yet make such a fitful use of his powers. In a final irony, Steerforth exhorts David to "Ride on over all obstacles, and win the race!" (426), and David "wished, for the first time, that he [Steerforth] had some worthy race to run" (426). The contrast between Steerforth's pursuit of Emily and Wrayburn's of Lizzie could scarcely have been focussed more sharply. In Steerforth's final meeting with David, he wishes that David could give to him freshness and innocence—it is just these qualities that Lizzie gives to Wrayburn.

## STEERFORTH'S WOULD-BE RESCUER: HAM

Having looked at Emily, her rescuers, and Steerforth, it remains only to look briefly at his would-be rescuer, Ham. The roles of worthy and unworthy lover reverse themselves. Ham, as the worthy lover who humbles himself, is of the lower class, while Steerforth the unworthy lover is of the upper class. Eugene as the worthy lover who humbles himself is of the upper class, while Headstone as the unworthy lover is of the lower class, aspiring in foolish pride to exalt himself. There is an interesting contrast too in Ham as the diligent and skillful boat builder (recall the Emily-as-boat imagery) and Steerforth as the boat buyer and stealer.

Ham's initial response to Steerforth's abduction of Emily is to condemn him as "a damned villain" (453). Mr. Peggotty's initial response is no less violent and vengeful: he is ready to sink Steerforth's boat and wishes he could sink him instead. David himself is ready to curse Steerforth. At this critical point Mrs. Gummidge intervenes and first asks Mr. Peggotty to forgive her for all the grief she's ever caused him. She then reminds him of how he had pity on her, on Ham, and on Emily, and how he has sheltered them all these years. Finally, she reminds him of the promise, "As you have done it unto one of the least of these, you have done it unto me" (454, cf. Matthew 25:31–40). This passage in Matthew is one of the most moving in all the Bible on the subject of mercy, and this finally moves Mr. Peggotty (and David) to tears and to mercy as they yield to "better feeling" (454). David remembers Steerforth at his best not necessarily because he is unwilling to denounce him because he is of the upper class (he is ready to curse him, and even now says that the fascination, the evil spell, is gone; 454), and not simply because Steerforth himself asked him to do so, but most of all because he is moved to mercy. He feels "as weak as a spirit-wounded child" (454), recalling again the childhood motif of humility where mercy triumphs over judgment.

Dickens introduces a deliberately misleading ambiguity in his description of Ham's response to Emily's disappearance that functions in a way analogous to his treatment of Mrs. Strong's innocence. Dickens casts doubt on Mrs. Strong, not to tease the reader, but to make the eventual disclosure of her faithfulness the more powerful. So David wonders whether revenge or mercy are uppermost in the mind of Ham, to make the nobility of his final sacrifice the more pronounced. Ham, after Emily's flight, is described as living a good life, though cut very deeply, as always strong to face danger to help and save others, yet very gentle. Yet the morning after the flight David sees a look, not of anger, but of determination in Ham's face and thinks the determination is to kill Steerforth (456). Later David asks Mr. Peggotty about Ham's state of mind and what he might do if he met Steerforth. Mr. Peggotty replies that he can't plumb the deep waters of Ham's mind on that point and would rather not ask him, but that he thinks its best if they never meet (677). Mr. Omer, on the other hand, says "all [Ham's] life's a kindness" (735).

In the climactic tempest chapter David suggests that many disparate threads of his story are to be brought together by an event to which he is "bound by an infinite variety of ties" (784). Ham's conduct continues tender, manful, quiet, even serene, though he is most tried. As the storm builds, the wreck is spotted, and the sailors on it begin to perish, the expectation of the narrative is that Ham will risk his life again to save others as he has so often in the past. As Ham is preparing to do so, indications that the last survivor is Steerforth begin to appear. The look of determination on Ham's face reminds David of the look that he originally took to be a murderous one. He says that this woke him up to a knowledge of Ham's danger, and he implores the other men on the beach "not to do murder" (793) by allowing Ham to go after the man about to drown. The men on the beach no doubt understood his words to mean murder in the sense of allowing Ham to throw his life away in a hopeless situation, but the suggestion is still there that Ham might be motivated as much by justice as by mercy in his determination to go out after Steerforth. Yet if Ham merely wants to ensure Steerforth's death, all he need do is wait a few moments, as Steerforth's death is immanent. He could easily have simply stood on the beach with the others, thinking that Steerforth is at last being justly destroyed by the sea over which he carried Emily away. Yet his last words are words, not of revenge, but of blessing: "Mas'r Davy,' he said, cheerily grasping me by both hands, 'if my time is come, 'tis come. If 'tan't, I'll bide it. Lord bless you, and bless all! Mates, make me ready! I'm a-going off!' " (793). Ham's valiant attempt fails, and David says of him that "his generous heart was stilled for ever" (794).

Steerforth speaks of his greatest nightmare as his own self (322). Like Kurtz in *Heart of Darkness,* he looks inside himself and is horrified. He is to an almost satanic extent taken up with himself and his own desperate fancies, no matter how destructive. He bewails his upbringing and his inability to break free from this bondage to self. His mother, too, is like him in her unbending pride. As she learns of his death there is some indication that her stony heart might be beginning to break. As Rosa justly rebukes her pride, Mrs. Steerforth's mouth is rigid and her teeth are closed, "as if the jaw were locked and the face frozen up in pain" (799). She finally feels the hammer blow to the face that Rosa felt so many years before. Rosa says, "Now is your pride appeased, you madwoman? Now has he made atonement to you—with his life! Do you hear?—His life!" (799). Class conflict is resolved in Dickens in a distinctively Christian way. The poor suffer and die for the rich, often succeeding in rescuing them from their mad pride and bondage to self:

God chose the foolish things of the world to shame the wise; God chose the weak things of the world to shame the strong. He chose the lowly things of this world and the despised things—and the things that are not—to nullify the things that are, so that no one may boast before him.        I Cor. 1:27–29

# NOTES

This essay was published in a shorter version in the *Sun-Yat Sen Journal of the Humanities* (April 1993).

1. As early as his preface to *Pickwick,* Dickens made it clear that while he was a severe critic of the *abuses* of religion, he maintained a deep respect for religion itself. While his own faith had many weaknesses, it was still very real, particularly as reflected in his novels. Such astute foreign readers as Leo Tolstoy and Fyodor Dostoevsky recognized this.
2. Even Estella, though suffering is stressed as her teacher, is helped in the end by Pip's example. While I merely assert Pip's influence over Miss Havisham and Estella here, I demonstrate it in my as yet unpublished doctoral dissertation "The Power of a Life: *Great Expectations* as a Christian Novel.
3. Grahame Smith, in *Dickens, Money, and Society,* stresses both the greed for money and the intense class consciousness in G.E. (171).
4. Some readers might find this suggestion somewhat fanciful. I make is because I think it has critical merit. However, my overall argument does not depend upon it.
5. The New Testament metaphor "fishers of men" (cf. Matt. 4:19 and Mark 1:17) is perhaps in the background here.
6. Cf. John 8:1-11 and the woman taken in adultery.
7. The ideas of covering and atonement are closely linked in the Bible. We are covered with the blood of Christ even as the mercy seat covered the ark of the covenant.
8. Taken from the *Holy Bible: New International Version* copyright 1978 by the New York International Bible Society, used by permission.

# Works Cited

Dickens, Charles. *David Copperfield.* London: Oxford UP, 1960.

———. *Our Mutual Friend.* Harmondsworth, Middlesex: Penguin Books, 1985.

Magnet, Myron. *Dickens and the Social Order.* Philadelphia: U of Pennsylvania P, 1985.

Marlow, James E. "Social Harmony and Dickens' Revolutionary Cookery." *Dickens Studies Annual* Vol. 17. New York: AMS, 1988.

Shaw, Bernard. *Shaw on Dickens.* Ed. Dan H. Laurence and Martin Quinn. New York: Frederick Ungar, 1985.

Smith, Grahame. *Dickens, Money, and Society.* Berkeley: U of California P, 1968.

# The Civilizing Mission at Home: Empire, Gender, and National Reform in *Bleak House*

## Timothy L. Carens

In *Bleak House* (1852–53), Dickens creates a world in which the "condition of England" belies the presumed distinction between the "civilized" imperial metropole and the "savage" periphery. Consider the description of Captain Hawdon's burial in the "pestiferous and obscene" graveyard to which the narrative obsessively returns. "Into a beastly scrap of ground which a Turk would reject as a savage abomination, and a Caffre would shudder at," the narrator explains, "they bring our dear brother here departed, to receive Christian burial" (202). Although Hawdon is enfolded within the rhetorical embrace of Christian kinship as "our dear brother," his corpse receives treatment that even representative heathen, a "Turk" and a "Caffre," would recognize as "a savage abomination."[1] The narrator concludes that the graveyard will provide "a shameful testimony to future ages, how civilization and barbarism walked this boastful island together" (202).[2] The novel documents this lamentably intermingled "civilization and barbarism" in its effort to chasten the pride of the "boastful island" which, Dickens suggests, inaccurately perceives itself to be entirely civilized. The "heart of a civilized world," as Allan Woodcourt refers to London, conceals pockets of primitive darkness (691).

Passages such as this one certainly register what Patrick Brantlinger (1988) refers to as the "reformist point that savagery or barbarism in the heart of civilization is as bad as anything" encountered on the periphery (117). This "reformist point," in fact, emerges very explicitly in a letter (9 July 1852) in which Dickens responds to the Rev. Henry Christopherson, a reader of *Bleak House* who objected to its satiric attack on overseas philanthropy:

> If you think the balance between the home mission and the foreign mission justly held in the present time—I do not . . . I am decidedly of opinion that the

two works, the home and the foreign, are *not* conducted with an equal hand; and that the home claim is by far the stronger and the more pressing of the two. Indeed, I have very grave doubts whether a great commercial country holding communication with all parts of the world, can better christianise the benighted portions of it than by the bestowal of its wealth and energy on the making of good Christians at home and on the utter removal of neglected and untaught children from its streets, before it wanders elsewhere.     (*Letters* VI: 707)

The sense of dire need at the very center of empire underlies the novel's effort to unveil the "boastful island['s]" own forms of barbarism, which Dickens calls in the same letter the "darkest ignorance and degradation" at "our very doors" (*Letters* VI:707). He constructs an imperial economy of reform which redirects the "civilizing mission" first and foremost to England's own benighted "natives."[3]

In the letter to Christopherson, Dickens focuses on the problem of "neglected and untaught children" who roam the streets "at home." *Bleak House* develops the correspondence implied here, between an imperial metropole tainted by barbarism and an unruly domestic sphere, in satiric portraits of women philanthropists, most notably Mrs. Jellyby, who devote themselves to the "foreign mission." The critique of the nation which "wanders elsewhere" before attending to the "home mission" converges with the critique of women who seek public duties before attending to their homes. Esther Summerson articulates the novel's antidote to such varieties of "telescopic philanthropy" when she explains that she strives "to be as useful as [she] could . . . to those immediately about [her]; and to try to let that circle of duty gradually and naturally expand itself" (154). Bruce Robbins (1990) argues that the figure of the gradually expanding circle privileges a proximate, amateur model of influence, in which "all action remains continuous with and answerable to its originary center," over Mrs. Jellyby's attempt to reform distant problems through professional institutions and projects (215). He demonstrates how the novel's endorsement of "concentric gradualism" reveals an (inevitably imperfect) effort to replace systematic reforms with "personal" responsibility (215).[4] My concern in this essay is to show how Esther's theory of reform represents, like the satire on Mrs. Jellyby which it complements, a rhetorical intersection of anxieties related to the location of philanthropic duties in the context of empire and the division of those duties into gendered spheres of influence. The figure insists that the civilizing mission begins "at home" for both the imperial nation and the middle-class woman. Particular conceptions of the proper way for a middle-class woman to extend her influence thus sustain the imperial economy of reform.

The gradually expanding circle, however, fails to account for all of the novel's approved reform procedures. Dickens is ultimately unwilling to enforce Esther's rejection of "telescopic" concerns to the extent that he precludes the possibility of readjusting the imperial relationship so that the periphery benefits the metropole rather than vampirically sapping its reform energies. He explores this beneficial possibility primarily in representations of male characters such as Woodcourt and George Rouncewell, both of whom conspicuously revise Esther's formula by establishing their authority on distant colonial ground before demonstrating their altruism at home. The novel thus maps two very different procedures for national reform. The first works by restricting benevolent influence, for the imperial nation as for the middle-class woman, to the "domestic" sphere. The second charts a path for reform-minded men that links (albeit, for the most part, abstractly) imperial adventure and military service to the recivilization of the savage metropole. Charity only necessarily *begins* at home, as we shall see, for the middle-class woman.

This essay seeks to analyze how Dickens works to resolve his ambivalence about empire, specifically about the effect of empire on social reform "at home," by plotting alternative, gendered procedures for reforming the inadequately civilized metropole. Sections of the novel which relocate the nation's civilizing mission to the imperial center provide fascinating examples of how, as Deirdre David (1995) formulates it, "writing about empire both appropriates and elaborates Victorian gender politics" (5).[5] The extent to which discourses of empire and gender are intertwined, indeed, makes it virtually impossible to give appropriative authority to either one; they are, as David perceives and as the relocation of the imperial nation's civilizing mission in *Bleak House* confirms, mutually constitutive.

A character of central importance to my argument, Mrs. Jellyby introduces the forms of disorder which the novel struggles to repair in its representation of the civilizing mission as properly conducted, "at home." The satire on Mrs. Jellyby reveals how Dickens adapts contemporary material to construct an ideological nexus of gender and empire, creating a sub-plot that both rebukes the woman who fails to manage her domestic sphere before acquiring other projects and disparages a philanthropy that attends to peripheral barbarism.[6] Dickens bases the portrait of Mrs. Jellyby on Mrs. Caroline Chisholm, founder of the Family Colonization Loan Society, an organization that sponsored emigration to Australia.[7] While Dickens endorses her association in *Household Words* (30 March 1850), privately he blames her for neglecting her children. "I dream of Mrs. Chisholm, and her housekeeping," he confesses in a letter; "[t]he dirty faces of her children are my continual companions" (*Letters* VI:53). Haunted by what he perceives as signs of the professional woman's domestic failings, Dickens transforms Mrs. Chisholm and her neglected children into the Jellyby family.

Dickens also switches the site of the emigration scheme from Australia to Africa, where Mrs. Jellyby ambitiously proposes to civilize a section of the untamed continent and, simultaneously, to provide an outlet for British families in search of work.[8] Her plan, as sketched by Mr. Kenge, entails "the

general cultivation of the coffee berry—*and* the natives—and the happy settlement, on the banks of the African rivers, of our superabundant home population'' (82). The actual colony, of course, travesties both the civilizing mission
and emigration scheme. Despite Mrs. Jellyby's optimistic assurance that Borrioboola-Gha offers ''[t]he finest climate in the world!'' Esther eventually
reports that the colony has failed ''in consequence of the king of Borrioboola
wanting to sell everybody—who survived the climate—for Rum'' (86, 933).
The savagery of Africa defeats the mission to tame it. Those who withstand
the climate, rather than ''cultivating'' the ''natives'' by teaching them the
virtues of wage labor, are themselves nearly enslaved.

Several years before the publication of *Bleak House,* Dickens anticipates
his depiction of Borrioboola-Gha in a review published in *The Examiner* (19
Aug. 1848) of the *Narrative of the Expedition sent by Her Majesty's Government to the River Niger, in 1841* (1848). A crucial supplement to the novel,
this text illuminates another aspect of the satire on Mrs. Jellyby and her
colony. Dickens takes the opportunity of reviewing the *Narrative* to excoriate
what he depicts as the wildly ambitious abolitionist and missionary goals of
the ill-fated expedition, a project sponsored by the government and supported
by the African Civilization Society and many missionary groups.[9] He dismisses the effort to civilize Africa, significantly, with language that anticipates
Esther's description of the appropriate way for a woman to spread domestic
order.[10] In *The Examiner,* he insists that ''the work at home must be completed
thoroughly, or there is no hope abroad'' (533). In *Bleak House,* Esther timidly
submits that ''it is right to begin with the obligations of home . . . and that,
perhaps, while those are overlooked and neglected, no other duties can possibly be substituted for them'' (113). Her image of a gradually and naturally
expanding circle of female influence also recycles the metaphor Dickens uses
in the earlier essay to advocate for a ''natural expansion'' of civilization.
Admonishing those committed to the ''foreign mission,'' he argues that
''[g]ently and imperceptibly the widening circle of enlightenment must stretch
and stretch, from man to man, from people unto people; but no convulsive
effort, or far-off aim, can make the last great outer circle first, and then come
home at leisure to trace out the inner one'' (533). The gradually expanding
circle constructs a model of gradual, proximate reform which Dickens uses
to regulate the imperial nation's extension of enlightening civilization as well
as the woman's extension of domesticating influence. Distance from the primary locus of concern, whether nation or home, invalidates the reform
project.

Both texts in which the gradually expanding circle appears, however, make
gender-based exceptions to its repudiation of ''telescopic'' concerns; both
texts focus scorn on middle-class women philanthropists, while finding it
possible to praise men who perform adventurous forays on the periphery. In

*The Examiner,* Dickens blames unnamed women involved in the planning of the expedition, the "weird old women who go about, and exceedingly round-about, on the Exeter Hall platform" (531).[11] These witch-like figures have blithely overstepped the "inner circle" of home, both domestic sphere and nation, and are further contemptible for having staged an unequal battle between British men and Africa, personified as an "enemy against which no gallantry can contend" (531). On the other hand, Dickens eulogizes with "a glow of admiration and sympathy" the "brave men" who "sacrificed themselves to achieve [the expedition's] unattainable project" (533). These men, represented as admirable, self-sacrificing heroes, escape censure for their role in a project that ignores the exigency of the gradually expanding circle. When he considers these figures, the discourse of social criticism, which exposes the "weird old women" who expend money and energy on futile reform projects abroad, gives place to sentimental tribute. A similar double standard emerges in *Bleak House,* in which Dickens rebukes Mrs. Jellyby for planning the civilizing mission to Africa, but praises Woodcourt for his gallant performance on the imperial periphery.

Dickens satirizes Mrs. Jellyby with a pattern of metaphors carefully designed to highlight her transgression of boundaries. Although the fate of the Borrioboola-Gha colonists reveals an alarming result of her hubris, he shows much less concern with the unfortunate colonists than with the "home population" that stays at home. Neglecting her household duties by spending all of her time on the project designed to "cultivate" Africans, Mrs. Jellyby ironically transforms her home into a wilderness, her family into savages, reproducing in her British domestic sphere the very conditions she claims to redress in Africa. Esther describes Mr. Jellyby as a "mild bald gentleman" who "seemed passively to submit himself to Borrioboola-Gha, but not to be actively interested in that settlement. As he never spoke a word, he might have been a native, but for his complexion" (89). By figuring the dominated husband as a passive "native," Esther records an instance of the irony that repeatedly subverts Mrs. Jellyby's philanthropic project, which merely reproduces versions of Africa within her home. Note, particularly, that Dickens attributes the appearance of the "native" at home to Mrs. Jellyby's inversion of normative sexual power relations and refusal to respect gendered spheres of activity. Overwhelmed by his domineering wife, Mr. Jellyby, throughout the novel an object of sympathy, can only "passively . . . submit himself" to her distant project. The points at which Mrs. Jellyby diverges most egregiously from the meek and dutiful housewife become chinks in the barrier between forms of distant savagery and the British domestic sphere.

If Mrs. Jellyby transforms her husband into a passive "native," her rejection of the duties Dickens prescribes for her as mother threatens to produce children who are never acculturated at all. Peepy, the youngest child, contentedly plays "at Wild Beasts" beneath a piano he thinks of as his "den" (237).

Mr. Jellyby describes his children as "Wild Indians" and concludes that "the best thing that could happen to them was, their being all Tomahawked together" (472). When pressed by Esther to interpret this nihilistic despair, Caddy Jellyby translates her father's comment to mean simply that her siblings "are very unfortunate in being Ma's children" (472). Attributing the children's savagery to Mrs. Jellyby's inadequate mothering, Dickens again calls attention to the ironic effect of the professional woman's overseas mission.

While Mrs. Jellyby neglects her young children in order to devote herself fully to Borrioboola-Gha, Mrs. Pardiggle takes the reverse approach, forcing her offspring to participate in all of her philanthropic schemes. Notably, she achieves the same result as her colleague. As Mrs. Pardiggle recites the "contributions" she has exacted from her children, Esther notices that the children grow "absolutely ferocious with discontent. At the mention of the Tockahoopo Indians, I could really have supposed Egbert to be one of the most baleful members of that tribe, he gave me such a savage frown. The face of each child, as the amount of his contribution was mentioned, darkened in a peculiarly vindictive manner" (151). Both of these professional women produce "darkened" savages in their own families by sympathizing with peripheral savages before their own children.

An illustration on the cover of the monthly numbers of *Bleak House* shows a white woman protectively enfolding two African children in her arms. While this illustration does not refer to any episode in the plot, it functions as another jibe against women who supposedly care more for distant savages than for their own offspring.[12] In the satire on Mrs. Jellyby and her ilk, Dickens more specifically suggests that women who undertake philanthropic missions before attending to their families erase differences between children in Africa and their own children beneath the piano. The mothers who refuse to conform to the gendered procedure for exerting their influence produce "savage" children whose faces are "darkened" by dirt and anger, thus contributing to the problem of intermingled "civilization and barbarism" at home.

Caddy Jellyby, forced to labor as a secretary, suffers from her mother's despotism rather than her indifference. She, too, acquires a "complexion" suggestive of racial difference. Esther finds her, after a day of generating Borrioboola-Gha correspondence, using vinegar to remove the "ink stains on her face" (92).[13] Caddy herself provides a context in which to understand her symbolically discolored skin. "Talk of Africa!" she exclaims, "I couldn't be worse off if I was a what's-his-name—man and a brother" (236). Referring to the image popularized by abolitionists, of a shackled African who asks "Am I not a man and a brother?" Caddy suggests that her mother creates slaves at home as well as furnishing them for the sinister king of Borrioboola-Gha.[14] Unlike her father, the passive "native," she determines to revolt. Remembering the appropriate name for her oppressed condition, she declares,

"I won't be a slave all my life" (238). Caddy rebels against treatment that, Dickens suggests, negates the difference between her and the objects of her mother's philanthropic concern in distant Africa. The woman who claims the authority to establish civilization in distant Africa ironically converts her entire family—through emasculation, neglect, and enslavement—into varieties of the native Other.

Catherine Gallagher (1985) demonstrates that when Caddy refers to herself as a "slave" she appropriates a trope often used by critics of industrialism to focus attention on the "white" slaves, the disenfranchised workers of England's factories (4). Dickens claims in a letter (20 Dec. 1852) that "Mrs. Jellyby gives offense merely because the word 'Africa', is unfortunately associated with her wild Hobby. No kind of reference to slavery is made or intended, in that connexion" (*Letters* VI:825). Caddy's metaphors, however, show that Dickens is being somewhat disingenuous here. In fact, he adopts the same rhetorical practice used by critics of industrial exploitation, although in *Bleak House* he documents abuses that transform the middle-class girl, rather than the industrial laborer, into a slave.

Dickens uses Esther, of course, to illustrate the efficacy of his approved model of female reform, a "civilizing mission" in which domestic order expands incrementally from a well-managed domestic sphere. Emphasizing her role as an effective manger of the household economy at Bleak House, he shows her radiating order from that site gradually and naturally, like the "summer sun" to which her surname refers. Esther functions in the novel as a domesticator, one who brings certain of the "savages" she encounters within the fold of civilization, but Dickens describes her method as natural. The paradox reflects the effort to represent Esther's mode of influence as the "natural" one for women, in relation to which Mrs. Jellyby's procedures represent an unnatural alternative. Deeply involved in the cultural machinery of societies, committee meetings, and ever-circulating documents, Mrs. Jellyby rejects the "natural" way for a woman to extend her influence, ironically ensuring that the household over which she presides returns steadily to nature.

Esther first proves her ability to reverse the professional woman's disastrous effect in the Jellyby household, in which the distinction between British home and untamed wilderness remains precarious. "[T]he rooms," she notes, "had such a marshy smell" (87). Misplaced, misused, and broken objects signify a general disregard for the implements that mark the advances and enable the comforts of the "civilized" domestic sphere. The drunken "cook" even fails to ensure that the family's food enters the realm of culture. "We had a fine cod-fish, a piece of roast beef, a dish of cutlets, and a pudding," reports Esther, enumerating dishes which would have made "an excellent dinner, if it had had any cooking to speak of, but it was almost raw" (88). Although at first somewhat discomposed by these primitive conditions, she soon begins

to fight back the darkness by imposing domestic order. Esther reveals a remarkable skill for establishing the fundamental comforts of civilization,
"coaxing a very cross fire that had been lighted, to burn; which at last it did,
quite brightly" (90). Recognizing her friend's aptitude, Ada claims that Esther
"would make a home out of even this house" (90). Esther's stay in the
Jellyby wilderness is brief, but while there she begins to reclaim the territory
for domesticity.[15]

Her influence on the Jellyby children is more significant than her limited
assault on the "waste and ruin" of the household (476). While Mrs. Jellyby
plans the "happy settlement" in Africa, Esther fulfills the role of mother that
her host has rejected, reading stories to the children and, significantly, washing
Peepy. When Esther awakes after her first night in the Jellyby household, she
opens her eyes "to encounter those of a dirty-faced little spectre" (94). Peepy
seeks out the woman who, temporarily fulfilling the duties of motherhood
ignored by Mrs. Jellyby, washes away the filth that obscures the difference
between the "complexion" of the British boy and the child of Borrioboola-
Gha. Esther achieves a more lasting accomplishment by transforming Caddy
from a sullen and disempowered "slave" into a competent middle-class wife
(476). In The Examiner, Dickens mocks the Niger Expedition's impossible
objectives, among the most naive of which he finds the intention to substitute
"free for Slave labour" (532). By focusing her attention on a British woman,
Esther actually achieves the goal represented by Dickens as insanely ambitious
when applied to distant Africa. Caddy suffers, he suggests, not only because
the labor she endures as her mother's secretary is unpleasant in itself, but
also because that labor supplants an education in those skills with which the
middle-class woman manages the domestic sphere. As Caddy complains to
Esther, "I can't do anything hardly, except write" (93). At first, Caddy can
only vent her frustration by exclaiming bitterly "I wish Africa was dead!"
(92). Esther helps her to overcome this rebellious anger, the response of an
embittered "slave." She "soften[s] poor Caroline" over the course of their
first meeting and continues, through the course of the novel, to perform the
modified civilizing mission of facilitating Caddy's transition from rebellious
"slave" to a position at least approximating that of the middle-class housewife (114).[16] While Mrs. Jellyby's treatment of her daughter gives slavery a
foothold in the nation, Esther works to "liberate" Caddy into the role of
affectionate and dutiful wife and mother.

The forms of savagery which Esther encounters in the Jellyby wilderness
provide her with a reform project located within what Dickens constitutes as
the circle of her concerns. The middle-class woman's proper civilizing mission, he suggests, consists of performing and imparting the duties which
sustain the middle-class British domestic sphere and thus preserve distinctions
between "home" and Borrioboola-Gha. Although the figure of the gradually

expanding circle suggests the potential for incrementally extending "civiliza-tion" beyond that sphere, Dickens remains suspicious of projects in which middle-class women attempt to carry the torch too far beyond the ideological locus of their concerns.

The episode in the brickmaker's house tests the extent of the middle-class woman's civilizing influence. Compelled to accompany Mrs. Pardiggle on her philanthropic excursion beyond the "iron barrier" of class, Esther and Ada encounter a world far more foreign and violent than the mismanaged Jellyby household (159). The drunken brickmaker, himself "all stained with clay and mud," proudly owns responsibility for his wife's "black eye" (156). Filth and bruises discolor the skin of the working-class characters, revealing further types of "darkened" British savages in need of reform. Mrs. Pardiggle of course entirely fails to enlighten them, sacrificing what effect she might have by adopting the combative authority of the "inexorable moral police-man" (158). Although Esther continues to feel that she has overstepped the outer limit of her "circle of duty," she and Ada have somewhat better success. When Mrs. Pardiggle retreats, they stay behind to ask Jenny, the bruised mother, if her baby is ill. The baby, in fact, dies just at that moment, but Ada's naive compassion produces a response that Mrs. Pardiggle fails to achieve. "Such compassion, such gentleness," reflects Esther, "might have softened any mother's heart" (160). The same verb that conveys Esther's effect on Caddy recurs as Dickens suggests that the middle-class woman's moral influence relies on conventionally female emotions as well as duties. Here, Ada's spontaneous expression of sympathy partly bridges the divide between classes and creates a channel for civilizing enlightenment. While Mrs. Pardiggle's evangelical lesson produces only hostility, Esther and Ada gently whisper to Jenny "what Our Savior said of children" (160). By repudi-ating Mrs. Pardiggle's "businesslike and systematic" philanthropy and seiz-ing the opportunity to exploit the supposedly natural bond between women of different classes, they advance civilization a tiny step into the dark places of working-class life (156).

The civilizing influence of the middle-class woman is, however, severely curtailed on this foreign ground. The glimmer of light which Esther and Ada bring to the benighted home only momentarily comforts Jenny and has no lasting effect on the family. Although the brickmaker's family represents a much more legitimate concern than, for example, the natives of Borrioboola-Gha, Dickens remains highly skeptical about the viability of missionary forays conducted by middle-class women beyond the "outer circle" of the middle-class domestic sphere. Indeed, Esther articulates the intention to devote herself to "those immediately about [her]," the procedure for reform offered as the sharpest alternative to Mrs. Jellyby's "telescopic philanthropy," as an argument against accompanying Mrs. Pardiggle to the brickmaker's.

If *Bleak House* represents foreign missions—exemplified most clearly by projects designed to "cultivate" such foreign savages as the "natives" of Borrioboola-Gha (and more ambiguously by those to reform such domestic savages as the brickmaker and his family)—as potentially disastrous distractions for the middle-class woman, the novel does not by any means categorically reject all "telescopic" projects. In fact, exceptions to the procedure endorsed by Esther, that "it is right to begin with the obligations of home," quietly emerge throughout the novel, delimiting the logic of the gradually expanding circle. If Mrs. Jellyby and Mrs. Pardiggle, at their worst, confuse the distinction between British civilization and peripheral savagery, certain other characters help to repair that distinction, apparently by reapplying the skills they have acquired in imperial outposts to social problems encountered upon their return.

Consider, as an initial example, Mrs. Bagnet, a character who provides an important exception to the rule that pits "far-off-aims" specifically against the woman's "work at home." Her mode of regulating her household, with a no-nonsense authority that reflects her experience as a soldier's wife, demonstrates an effective alliance between certain "telescopic" concerns and domestic life in London. Just as her kitchen utensils, which "have done duty in several parts of the world," prove equally useful in London, the duties Mrs. Bagnet learns abroad serve her well when attending to the spiritual and physical well-being of her household (442). She says grace "like a military chaplain" and develops "an exact system" for apportioning food with "the kit of the mess" (442). An act of charity she performs also reflects the utility of experience gained as an imperial soldier's wife. Famous for the ease with which she accomplishes arduous journeys, Mrs. Bagnet sets off at a moment's notice to find George's mother. She returns to London with Mrs. Rouncewell, herself appearing "quite fresh and collected—as she would be, if her next point, with no new equipage and outfit, were the Cape of Good Hope, the Island of Ascension, Hong Kong, or any other military station" (805). Resourceful Mrs. Bagnet, whose experience shuttling from one imperial "military station" to another facilitates her benevolence, marks another important contrast to Mrs. Jellyby. Esther responds to the ironic discrepancy between Mrs. Jellyby's professional concerns and the state of her domestic sphere by bringing the civilizing mission home, so to speak. By successfully integrating the "telescopic" military duties of empire with the "obligations of home," Mrs. Bagnet begins to reveal Dickens' strategy for distinguishing between the "foreign mission" and other, apparently less objectionable demonstrations of imperial power. While overseas philanthropy distracts the woman from her gendered responsibilities, the military control of distant territories helps her perform them.

If the representation of the Bagnet household reveals an alliance between female duty and empire, a productive coalition between imperial military operations and gendered responsibilities "at home" particularly emerges in the depiction of certain male characters who are actively involved in what Dickens represents as the civilizing mission in the public streets of the savage metropole. Woodcourt and George Rouncewell, who undertake responsibilities which complement Esther's reform work in the middle-class domestic sphere, indirectly reconcile "far-off" military objectives with the effort to enlighten and alleviate the suffering of the "darkened" characters they encounter in "the great wilderness of London" (718). The careers of these men are particularly significant, in fact, because they help to overcome a conflict that develops between national reform and empire. By fashioning a masculine version of compassionate philanthropy that incorporates imperial experience, Dickens reserves a place for empire in the civilizing mission at home.

The novel's satire on the foreign mission crystallizes in the portrait of Jo, tragically neglected on the very "door-step of the Society for the Propagation of the Gospel in Foreign Parts" (274). In the letter to Christopherson, Dickens defends such scenes by insisting that missions to "christianise" distant heathen ignore the "darkest ignorance and degradation" at "our very doors." Although he does not in that letter explicitly object to other varieties of imperial influence—military conquest, political control, or economic domination—wielded by the "great commercial country holding communication with all parts of the world," the irony attending that grandiose phrase hints at a buried fault line. At one striking point in *Bleak House,* this fault line becomes visible in an expressed ambivalence about the extent of England's empire in relation to its domestic collapse. Surveying the ugliness of Tom-all-Alone's, the narrator suggests that "in truth it might be better for the national glory even that the sun should sometimes set upon the British dominions, than that it should ever rise upon so vile a wonder as Tom" (683). A crucial moment in the novel's effort to imagine solutions to an inadequately civilized "heart of a civilized world" occurs here as the narrator deflates the hackneyed expression of imperial pride. Refusing to derive comfort from the fact that the "sun never sets upon the British Empire," he insists that urban slums at the imperial metropole must be factored into the equation from which "national glory" is derived. Implicitly, the passage represents the burden of maintaining a vast empire of "dominions," a term denoting territory under formal governance, as competing with the reform of the conditions which have produced Jo. The logic of the gradually expanding circle achieves a rhetorical momentum which carries it into a different ideological arena. Having served to reject the overseas philanthropic missions initiated by middle-class women, it here begins to cast suspicion on the state-sponsored acquisition and rule of distant territories.

It is important to note, however, the relatively restrained tone of the passage, so unlike the scathing invective with which the narrator denounces overseas philanthropy. The satire here is moderate, almost hesitant. The imperial center has decayed to such an extent that it "even" may justify a reconsideration of imperial expansion. The narrator submits that "it might be better" and that the sun should only "sometimes set" upon the British empire. These careful expressions of doubt reveal a lingering commitment to the concept of empire that weathers the rejection of "pretence[s] afar off for leaving evil things at hand alone" (696).[17]

While the novel in this passage tentatively groups unspecified "dominions" with Borrioboola-Gha as distractions from the effort to solve social problems "at home," it also works to contain the harmful effects of devoting attention to matters "afar off" in the representation of overseas philanthropy and its agents. It does so by demonstrating an effective alliance between military imperialism and national reform. Dickens indirectly justifies the possession of "dominions" abroad in the careers of men who return from adventure and military service on the imperial periphery equipped to reform savagery "at home." Woodcourt and Rouncewell both help to enforce the geographic boundary on compassion by attending to the destitute natives of England rather than those of Borrioboola-Gha. As Dickens depicts them performing their compassionate missions, however, he repeatedly demonstrates that imperial experience both permeates their charity and reinforces their masculinity.

The description of Woodcourt's heroic performance in "those East-Indian seas" signifies a remarkable departure from the novel's effort to focus attention on problems close at hand. While the men of the Niger Expedition succumb to the savagery of Africa, Dickens ensures that Woodcourt emerges victorious from his harrowing experience as surgeon on a navy ship which founders off the coast of India. "Through it all," as Miss Flite describes the adventure to Esther, "my dear physician was a hero. Calm and brave through everything. Saved many lives, never complained in hunger and thirst, wrapped naked people in his spare clothes, took the lead, showed them what to do, governed them, tended the sick, buried the dead, and brought the poor survivors off at last" (556). Unlike the Africa of The Examiner article, the "enemy against which no gallantry can contend," India provides a site where the British man can prove his mettle without meeting "certain destruction" (531).[18]

If Dickens sheds a "glow of admiration and sympathy" on this instance of male imperial adventure, he is particularly concerned to illustrate the indirect benefit the metropole accrues from it. As in many Victorian imperial adventure novels for boys, Woodcourt discovers his authority, his "intrepidity and humanity," when tested by extreme circumstances in tropical locales (675). In this novel, however, the adventure abroad prepares the hero for the civilizing mission which awaits him at home.[19] When Woodcourt "seems half inclined for another voyage," Jarndyce observes that to let him leave England again would be "like casting such a man away" (743). Once his authority is established, further adventures on the imperial periphery would waste a resource needed at the center.[20]

The novel demonstrates the need for a compassionate hero prepared to alleviate the suffering of those exposed to savage nature in descriptions of public streets which, like the Jellyby household, confuse distinctions between urban civilization and savage "wilderness." *Bleak House* opens with the memorable picture of a London so inundated by mud that the supposedly modern capital resembles a primeval swamp. What has not, I think, been noted about the novel's description of urban decay is that it collapses geography as well as time, and recalls in particular the description of Africa in *The Examiner*. In that journal, Dickens represents the continent as a site of malignancy, decay, and, particularly, disease, noting with distaste the "slimy and decaying earth" and the "rotting vegetation" of the "pestilential land" (533). The fever that eventually kills Jo and threatens Charley and Esther, carried by the "pestillential [sic] gas" of Tom-all-Alone's, evokes the fever described in *The Examiner*, suspended in the "pestilential air" of Africa (683). Savage nature, intimidating enough when located in distant Africa, deteriorates and overwhelms the monuments of civilized life in England. The "decaying earth" of Africa becomes the "decaying houses" of England; the pavements of London disappear beneath "crust upon crust of mud" (49). Snagsby walks along "a villainous street, undrained, unventilated, deep in black mud and corrupt water . . . and reeking with such smells and sights that he, who has lived in London all his life, can scarce believe his senses" (364). His reaction marks the condition of Tom-all-Alone's as a geographical anomaly, a puzzling intrusion of savage nature in the supposedly civilized metropolis.

Just as the description of the Jellyby household constructs a domestic wilderness for Esther to civilize, the "Africanization" of public London supplies Woodcourt with a terrain in which to exercise his "intrepidity and humanity" at home. Braving the "black mud" and "pestillential gas" of the London slum, Woodcourt searches for destitute individuals in need of aid.[21] In fact, immediately after the narrative represents the responsibility for "British dominions" as a potential hindrance to the project of reforming Tom-all-Alone's, it begins to defuse the conflict between empire and national reform in the description of Woodcourt walking through the heart of urban darkness:

> A brown sunburnt gentleman, who appears in some inaptitude for sleep to be wandering abroad rather than counting the hours on a restless pillow, strolls hitherward at this quiet time. Attracted by curiosity, he often pauses and looks about him, up and down the miserable by-ways. Nor is he merely curious, for in his bright dark eye there is compassionate interest; and as he looks here and there, he seems to understand such wretchedness, and to have studied it before.
> (683–84)

Dickens at first identifies Woodcourt only as "a brown sunburnt gentleman." The physical trace of the doctor's recent imperial tour significantly emerges as he makes this philanthropic excursion through the London slum. The reference, at this juncture, to the sign of experience gained "afar off" provides an initial indication of the utility of male involvement in empire to the reform of social problems in the public sphere "at home."

After his return, Woodcourt devotes himself to conducting a "civilizing mission" on a small scale and in a local setting. Mrs. Jellyby wastes time, money, and British lives on a doomed plan to "cultivate . . . the natives of Borrioboola-Gha, on the left bank of the Niger" (86). Woodcourt, on the other hand, ministers to the woman he finds "on the banks of the stagnant channel of mud which is the main street of Tom-all-Alone's" (684). Applying experience gained abroad, where he has encountered wretchedness and "studied it before," he attempts to sooth the miseries he discovers while "wandering abroad" at home. Woodcourt assures Jenny, the brickmaker's wife, as he bandages her head, "I wouldn't hurt you for the world" (684). His cliché expresses a sentiment approved by Dickens, a compassion for the destitute British subject that seems to outweigh an acquisitive interest in "the world." The sentiment, however, masks the link established between an adventure deeply implicated in a system of territorial acquisition and surveillance and the treatment of suffering in London. The fact that Woodcourt's imperial adventure becomes in effect an apprenticeship to the "work at home" helps to accommodate the possession of "British dominions" with the impulse, at least, to reform "so vile a wonder as Tom."

Even more explicitly than the Jellyby and Pardiggle children, Jo exhibits the collapse of distinctions between the savage periphery and the "heart of a civilized world." His garments, recalling Dickens' reference in *The Examiner* to the "rotting vegetation" of Africa, look like a "bundle of rank leaves of swampy growth, that rotted long ago" (274, 686). The narrator indignantly compares the "genuine foreign-grown savage" to Jo, the "ordinary home-made article," whom he describes as

> Dirty, ugly, disagreeable to all the senses, in body a common creature of the common streets, only in soul a heathen. Homely filth begrimes him, homely parasites devour him, homely rags are on him: native ignorance, the growth of English soil and climate, sinks his immortal nature lower than the beasts that perish.                                                        (696)

While Dickens claims in *The Examiner* review that "between the civilized European and the barbarous African, there is a great gulf set," *Bleak House* once again indicates just the reverse. The categories have become lamentably confused: Jo's ignorance collapses the privileged distinction between the "native" Briton and the African "native."[22]

The alliance that Woodcourt and George Rouncewell form to care for Jo reveals the impress of their imperial careers. Indeed, the two men form a kind of impromptu military unit as they take responsibility for Jo's welfare. When Woodcourt brings Jo to the shooting gallery, the "trooper" detects the "air" of a sailor in the doctor; he mistakes him for a "regular blue-jacket" and, translating Woodcourt's class position into military authority, defers to him with a respectful "military salute" (693). George suggests, "in a martial sort of confidence, as if he were giving his opinion in a council of war," a plan for washing and clothing Jo (697). Traces of George's military experience, like Woodcourt's adventure, emerge as the narrative depicts a compassionate corrective to the indifference that has produced "savages" like Jo.

Dickens emphasizes that George and Woodcourt address those aspects of the outcast's miserable life that erode distinctions between the "home-made" and the "genuine" savage. They relieve Jo of his "homely filth . . . homely parasites" and "homely rags," the physical signs, for Dickens, of savage life in England. Woodcourt also redresses the spiritual neglect that has left Jo "in soul a heathen" by teaching him the Lord's Prayer. Although Jo expires midway through the prayer, Dickens intimates that the last-minute missionary work smooths the spiritual progress of the "home-made savage." After Jo dies, the narrator announces that "light is come upon the dark benighted way" (705). Woodcourt thus follows the policy Dickens articulates in the letter to the Rev. Christopherson, bestowing his "energy on the making of good Christians at home."

The concern for Jo, of course, comes too late to bring him within the pale of civilized life. George's protection of "dirty-faced" Phil Squod represents a more successful and longer-lasting example of the civilizing work Dickens reserves for men in "the great wilderness of London." Another variety of "home-made savage," Phil is discolored by a series of industrial accidents that leave him a crippled beggar. George discovers him, "blackened all over," hobbling down the street of a slum, and immediately adopts him as his general subaltern (404). The returned imperial soldier provides Phil with a healing sanctuary from the unfeeling world of industrial labor, which, having eroded distinctions between the native Briton and his African counterpart, abandons him to the streets. Phil expresses his loyalty by referring to George as "Governor" or, significantly, "Commander," a title which corresponds to Miss Flite's nickname for him, "General George" (693). The humble "trooper" never rises to a position of military authority. However, those touched by his kindness in London, recognizing the extent to which military training sustains the authority he does command in charitable matters, award him the commission he could not earn as a soldier of empire.

Imperial military service does not, of course, represent an absolute prerequisite for male altruism. John Jarndyce, to take the most notable exception, does not rely on imperial experience as he extends benevolent aid to those in need.[23] The link that does emerge between imperial military service and the compassionate duties performed by certain men in the public wilderness of London is significant not because it sets an unbroken pattern, but because it clarifies the ideological limits of the gradually expanding circle as it constructs an alternative rhetorical intersection of empire and gender, one with its own set of contingencies and priorities. As Woodcourt and Rouncewell perform their civilizing duties in the public sphere, having gained experience on the "outer circle first" before returning home to maintain "the inner one," they enact a procedure for reform that simultaneously justifies the possession of distant "dominions" and defines a masculine type of compassionate philanthropy.

Woodcourt and Rouncewell perform their civilizing work in the public streets of the imperial metropole rather than the middle-class domestic sphere. They extend their influence across the "iron barrier" of class without expressing anxiety about forsaking "those immediately about [them]." Despite these crucial distinctions between the male and female versions of the civilizing mission at home, the charitable services the men provide closely approximate those provided by Esther. The washing and clothing of Jo recalls, for example, her nurturing care of Peepy. The military vocabulary with which Dickens describes the male version of the civilizing mission reminds readers, however, that the same men who gently attend to the "home-made savage" have also proven their courage on distant colonial ground. Vestiges of imperial heroism prevent compassion, that is, from eroding manliness.

Just as Dickens repudiates the "foreign mission" partly by applauding the unassuming femininity supposedly exemplified by Esther's intention to devote herself to "those immediately about [her]," he justifies the military control of distant "dominions" by paying homage to the masculinity of the male reformers. Imperial service and manliness mutually reinforce each other. George's robust physique, like his philanthropic duty, advertises his previous career as a soldier of empire. Indeed, the description of his manly body in relation to the wizened Smallweeds reveals Dickens indulging in a morally uncomplicated, if displaced, approval of empire. The narrator discovers "the strongest and the strangest opposition" in a comparison of "[h]is developed figure, and their stunted forms; his large manner, filling any amount of room, and their little narrow pinched ways; his sounding voice, and their sharp spare tones" (349). The "developed figure" of the British soldier provides an occasion for admiring the imperial expansiveness or "large manner" which, when considered as national policy in relation to urban neglect, forces a reappraisal of "national glory." As the scene develops, the withered miser significantly acquires the connotation of a savage opponent. Mr. Smallweed, who holds the mortgage on George's shooting gallery, looks up at the towering

soldier "like a pigmy" (356). If the trope of "home-made" savagery generally identifies subjects in need of civilizing compassion, it here suggests the
impulse to destroy. Dickens shapes the moral opposition between these characters as an imperial confrontation between a powerful, forthright representative of British empire and a dwarfish, malevolent savage.

While Woodcourt remains physically rather indistinct, imperial adventure
endows him with a courageous fortitude that translates into sexual desirability.
It is only when Esther hears of his valor in "those East-Indian seas" that she
confesses her romantic interest in him, "part[ing] with the little secret" at
which she has thus far only hinted (557). Feeling "such glowing exultation
in his renown," she "so admired and loved what he had done; that [she]
envied the storm-worn people who had fallen at his feet" (556). Esther
significantly directs her erotic impulse to Woodcourt's heroic performance,
"what he had done" on the periphery of empire, projecting her own passion
onto the idolatrous gesture of the grateful survivors. Imperial adventure functions economically in the characterization of the male hero, constructing
Woodcourt as a man equipped both to counteract metropolitan savagery and
to fulfill the romantic desires of Esther.

The trajectory of Richard Carstone's dissolute career provides a crucial
corollary to segments of the novel which associate social utility and manliness
with imperial experience. Dickens measures Richard's failure, in fact, by the
yardsticks established by Woodcourt and George. Before Richard becomes
enmeshed in Chancery, he impresses Ada with a reckless disregard for the suit:

> "I can go anywhere—go for a soldier if that's all, and never be missed. I would
> sell my best chance, if I could, on the shortest notice and the lowest terms."
> "And go abroad?" said Ada.
> "Yes!"
> "To India perhaps?"
> "Why, yes, I think so," returned Richard.                    (108)

Ada obligingly supplies Richard with an appropriate locale for imperial service, fashioning for him a fantasy of male adventure in an exotic colonial
site. He begins to balk, however, as soon as she gives concrete shape to his
bravado. The fact that he "return[s]" his hesitant acquiescence suggests the
extent to which it is *her* fantasy, not his, and anticipates his inability to make
good on his boast. Esther later visits Richard in the port town where he is
stationed as an army officer, hoping to persuade him to escape Chancery by
serving in Ireland. Richard, who has just resigned his commission, can only
ask plaintively, "how could I have gone abroad?" (676). While Woodcourt
acquires compassionate authority on the imperial periphery and then reapplies
it to good effect "at home," Richard, unable to extricate himself from the
court case, cannot help himself, much less participate in any aspect of the
"home mission."

Although exploited financially by the "pigmy" Smallweed, George possesses a moral rectitude, affiliated with his soldiering career, that fortifies his opposition to the usurer. Richard, without such resources, is much more vulnerable to the attack of another villain figured as an African savage. References to the somber black attire worn by Vholes, Richard's tenacious exploiter, gradually transmute into suggestions of threatening racial Otherness. The lawyer removes his "close black gloves as if he were skinning his hands" and gazes at Richard "as if he were making a lingering meal of him"; the narrator compares Vholes and his family to "minor cannibal chiefs" (607, 605). The nightmarish inversion of the civilizing mission, the consumption of the missionary by black-skinned cannibals, is significantly displaced onto the cash of the male character who cannot bring himself to "go abroad."[24]

Dickens presents a clear-cut distinction between the invigorating effects of imperial adventure or service and the emasculating influence of Chancery. Woodcourt, who becomes a "hero" on the Indian island, and George, whose powerful body displays signs of his soldiering career, mark high points of moral and physical masculine development intimately associated with empire. Richard, on the other hand, remains oddly "boyish" to the end of his life, his sexual development arrested by the influence which, as Esther soon perceives, blights "all his manly qualities" (675, 378). Increasingly enmeshed in the suit, Richard becomes helpless and etiolated, "thin and languid," his body and manner announcing the extent to which Chancery has compromised his development as a gendered subject (878). Dying soon after Esther notices him in this condition, he proves himself unable to support the family he has started, only ensuring that Ada's inheritance as well as his own feeds the cannibalistic Vholes. This pathetic end sharpens the contrast between Richard and Woodcourt, whose imperial adventure draws forth the compassionate heroism that proves as useful to others in England as in "those East-Indian seas."

In the conclusion to *Bleak House,* Dickens reveals a final effort to imagine an ideal alternative to the disastrous civilizing mission organized by Mrs. Jellyby. Esther and Woodcourt begin their married life in the strangely duplicated second Bleak House, an offshoot settlement of the home established by John Jarndyce. This "colony," unlike Borrioboola-Gha, extends the circle of a middle-class, domestic civilization *within* the nation and reinforces rather than subverts traditionally gendered spheres of influence.[25] By respecting the distinctions offended by Mrs. Jellyby, it secures the blessing of nature. Dickens replaces signs evocative of his descriptions of a malignant African swamp with references to the "rich and smiling country" that surrounds the second Bleak House, which is propped up by colonnades "garlanded with woodbine, jasmine, and honey-suckle" (912). The second Bleak House exists in harmony with indigenous English plants, emblematic of a nature vastly different from the mud and decay which have invaded London and the Jellyby household.

The missions which Esther and Richard perform in their "colony" of Bleak House continue to reflect the gendered procedures for reform endorsed by Dickens. Having already proven her ability to impart the skills with which the middle-class woman sustains civilization within the domestic sphere, Esther will surely repeat the educational process with her own "two little daughters" (933). While her influence has limited effect in the habitat of the working class, she does preside over the marriage of Charley to a "well to do" country miller and thus completes the rescue of a girl nearly engulfed by the savagery of London (933). This event suggests that the middle-class woman best exerts her benevolent influence over the working class by guiding select individuals through stints of domestic service in the middle-class home. The fact that Charley's sister becomes Esther's new maid indicates that a new cycle has begun. Esther extends the circle of civilization by ensuring that the young women who come under her benign supervision find a secure position within a domestic sphere of a suitable class.

As "medical attendant for the poor," Woodcourt undertakes a duty in the public sphere that provides an outlet for his "compassionate interest" for the destitute among the natives of Yorkshire (872). Although the scene of his service is far removed from the island in "those East-Indian seas," the affiliation persists between male adventure abroad and compassionate service at home. Jarndyce correctly predicts that Woodcourt will secure the position, confiding to Esther that, in the district where the job awaits, her lover's "reputation stands very high; there were people from that part of the country in the shipwreck" (873). The compassionate treatment of British poor is once again enabled by the hero's imperial adventure.

If Dickens uses the "happy ending" of *Bleak House* to privilege the civilizing methods practiced by Esther and Woodcourt, he notably locates their colony at a farther remove than the first Bleak House from the problems which, he suggests, produce varieties of "home-made" savagery in the "heart of a civilized world." Esther's sketch of the picturesque Yorkshire village excludes feminist philanthropists who neglect their children as well as the grinding poverty of Tom-all-Alone's. These conditions, on the other hand, presumably persist in the sites that have been left behind. Although Jo has died, the other tenants of the slum continue to suffer its brutalizing effects. Mrs. Jellyby has forsaken overseas philanthropy only to take up "the rights of women to sit in Parliament" (933). Dickens indicates that the new mission, no less than the old, will compromise her ability to care for her children and household. In *The Examiner* review, Dickens advocates abandoning Africa to its own excessive savagery, a barbarism too powerfully resistant to the inroads of civilization. Through the rarefied atmosphere of the Yorkshire village, it is possible to glimpse a similar despair. The "colony" of Bleak House finally suggests less an outpost of progress than a tactical retreat to an ideal place in which the social forces which necessitate the civilizing mission "at home" can be easily controlled. Ironically, the novel which excoriates Mrs. Jellyby for envisioning an idealistic colony rather than solving problems at hand reaches for closure by practicing its own variety of utopian evasion.

## NOTES

I am indebted to John Maynard and the anonymous reader of *Dickens Studies Annual*, both of whom gave me insightful comments on this paper.

1. Critics often note that *Bleak House* insists upon the interconnectedness of the society represented, without remarking that Dickens defines community with borders that conspicuously exclude those identified as foreign "savages." This strategy of course relies on a fundamentally imperial and ethnocentric perspective which presumes a geography composed of "civilized center" and "savage periphery." Since most readers perceive, at this point, the ideological contingencies of such supposedly natural oppositions, I will most often omit the cautionary quotation marks in the rest of the essay.

2. An early issue of *Household Words* (6 April 1850) includes an essay entitled "Heathen and Christian Burial" which perhaps influences Dickens in his treatment of Hawdon's burial. "If from the heights of our boasted civilisation," the article begins, "we take a retrospect of past history, or a survey of other nations—savage nations included,—we shall, with humiliation, be forced to acknowledge that in no age and in no country have the dead been disposed of so prejudicially to the living as in Great Britain" (1:43). This writer also finds in the condition of metropolitan burial grounds an indication that England cannot fulfill the "boast" of imperial civilization by demonstrating its superiority to "savage nations."

3. Norris Pope (1978) shows how, throughout his novels and other public and private comments, Dickens represents the foreign missionary effort as occupied "with useless and vexatious projects, while ignoring urgent social problems at home" (127). R. Bland Lawson (1991) traces the influence of Carlyle in Dickens' general contempt for overseas missions, arguing that both *Bleak House* and *Past and Present* (1843) ridicule the practice of "devoting time and money to causes that are continents away rather than taking care of the distressed and impoverished at home" (25).

4. Robbins suggests that Dickens undercuts the "politics of presence" by representing egregious problems that cannot be solved by individual measures, implicitly endorsing supposedly disparaged forms of institutional responsibility. The spiritual and educational neglect of Jo, for example, indicates a social problem that cannot be solved by any single person.

5. In her reading of Dickens, Suvendrini Perera (1991) also focuses on the "interplay between the continually evolving discourses that constituted and managed both gender and empire" (65). Both David and Perera, particularly the latter, make interesting comments about *Bleak House*, but both focus primarily on *Dombey and Son* in their analyses of Dickens.

6. In *Dickens at Work* (1958), Butt and Tillotson note that Dickens uses the satire on Mrs. Jellyby to disparage both "female emancipation" and the type of "misguided philanthropy" that ignores domestic duties in favor of distant projects (194). Also see A. Abott Ikeler (1981) and Brahma Chaudhuri (1988).

7. See Harry Stone's introduction to Dickens' article "A Bundle of Emigrants' Letters" (1850) for a description of the collaboration between Dickens and Mrs. Chisholm.

8. In "A Bundle of Emigrants' Letters," Dickens observes that "there are strong reasons in favor" of emigration to Australia, particularly for those who are "ready and willing to labour," but cannot find work at home (Stone I: 88). The fictional counterpart of this statement is found in *David Copperfield* (1850), in which Australia provides an ideal destination for the disgraced Peggotty family and the restless Micawbers. For Dickens, Australia holds the potential for fulfilling the colonial dream which Africa thwarts.

9. See Pope for a fuller description of the Niger Expedition and contemporary responses to it (99–108).

10. Robbins also notes the correspondence of this language, although he does not call attention to its significance as a gendered procedure for reform.

11. Pope describes Exeter Hall, the meeting place of many philanthropic societies, as "the accepted monument to the missionary and charitable zeal of English Protestantism" (1). He provides the most thorough account of Dickens' animosity for the organizations that used the building as their forum. Perera uses Dickens' review of the *Narrative* primarily to support her analysis of the link between gender and imperial trade in *Dombey and Son,* but also briefly considers it in relation to *Bleak House* and confirms my general point about the twin priorities of the gradually expanding circle. Both texts, she argues, suggest that the "usurpation of the masculine platforms of economy and colonial policy by 'weird old women' (both politicized women and men feminized by humanitarianism) simultaneously perverts the ideology of gendered spheres of influence at home and guarantees disaster abroad" (61).

12. In Elizabeth Barrett Browning's poem "Aurora Leigh" (1857), Aurora partly justifies her rejection of Romney to herself by imagining that he could force her to make a similar transaction. His commitment to social justice, she fears, would lead him to rupture the "natural" bond of maternal affection by "chang[ing] my sons . . . for black babes / Or piteous foundlings" (99).

13. Jeffrey Spear aided my argument with this observation. Dickens later suggests that Caddy's baby inherits the "stain" of her enforced labor. He describes the child as having "curious little dark veins in its face, and curious little dark marks under its eyes, like faint remembrances of poor Caddy's inky days" (736). Captain Hawdon's experience renews the association of secretarial work with Africa. Although he does not himself undergo a metaphoric racial transformation, his

desk, "a wilderness marked with a rain of ink," suggests another intrusion of the tropical desolation Dickens associates with Africa (188).

14. Joel J. Gold (1983) argues that Dickens covertly associates Mrs. Jellyby herself with African slave dealers. He assumes that Dickens read a passage from a travel narrative entitled *Egypt and Nubia,* published six years before *Bleak House,* in which the author describes seeing "a caravan of Jelabi, or slave pedlars, who are in the habit of trafficking between Darfour and Cairo" (37).

15. In the representation of Esther's civilizing mission, Dickens subtly undermines absolute distinctions between public and private roles for the middle-class woman—much in the same way that Ruskin does when, in an often quoted passage from "Of Queen's Gardens" (1864), he observes that "[a] woman has a personal work or duty, relating to her own home, and a public work or duty, which is also the extension of that . . . what the woman is to be within her gates, as the center of order, the balm of distress, and the mirror of beauty; that she is also to be without her gates, where order is more difficult, distress more imminent, lovliness more rare" (136–37). While it is important to perceive that Esther undertakes "public work" in the Jellyby household, it is equally important to notice that it occurs within the private sphere. Dickens does imagine the middle-class woman performing charitable work outside her own house, but represents *the* home as her proper sphere of influence.

16. Caddy takes a step down on the class ladder in her marriage to Prince Turveydrop, in whose dancing school she takes a leading role. Dickens significantly approves of the mother who works outside the domestic sphere in response to economic necessity, as long as she expends her compassion on her family. Esther describes, in her final comments on Caddy, how the circle of domestic civilization expands through maternal affection. Having herself "softened" the bitter girl, she notes approvingly that "there never was a better mother then Caddy, who learns, in her scanty intervals of leisure, innumerable deaf and dumb arts, to soften the affliction of her child" (933).

17. Lillian Nayder (1992) claims, perhaps responding to this passage, that "in *Bleak House,* Dickens holds the imperial mission partly accountable for the failure of social reform in England" (691). As we shall see, however, Dickens works to distinguish between the civilizing mission, which certainly conflicts with social reform at home, and imperial adventure and military service, which indirectly facilitate it.

18. Dickens' attitude toward India becomes much darker after the "Mutiny" in 1857. In a letter to Angela Burdett-Coutts (4 Oct. 1857), he imagines becoming a "Demoniacal" tyrant in India. "I wish I were Commander in Chief in India. The first thing I would do to strike that Oriental race with amazement (not in the least regarding them as if they lived in the Strand, London, or at Camden Town), should be to proclaim to them in their language, that I considered my holding that appointment by the leave of God, to mean that I should do my utmost to exterminate the Race upon whom the stain of the late cruelties rested" (Osborne, 188). For a discussion of how Dickens imagines unifying classes in England through opposition to mutinous India, see Nayder.

19. Patrick A. Duane (1980), in his analysis of late-Victorian imperialist boy's literature, notes the popularity of the theme in which young heroes "became authorities
in their own right and vented their energies by expanding the Queen's realms or
by defending her possessions overseas" (108). Woodcourt's adventure marks an
early instance of the Victorian hero who finds his authority on the periphery of
empire, but Dickens significantly shows Woodcourt using that authority and vent-
ing his energies by reforming the queen's inadequately civilized territories in
London.

20. Dickens also remains wary of too much experience on the imperial periphery.
Woodcourt becomes a hero on a specifically imperial tour, but one that apparently
involves no direct contact with the continent itself or its indigenous people. While
"those East-Indian seas" provide a theater on which to stage the development
of compassionate heroism in *Bleak House,* Dickens reveals in other contexts
reservations about the effect of imperial power on British men. His reservations
surface, for example, in *Dombey and Son* (1848), in which he represents Colonel
Bagstock as a sadist who perpetually abuses a "dark servant" (451). In *The
Mystery of Edwin Drood* (1870), the hot-tempered Neville attributes his haughti-
ness to contact with "abject and servile dependents, of inferior race" (90). Both
of these characters, Dickens suggests, have been contaminated by the imperial
hierarchy of power.

21. Judith Walkowitz (1992) argues that "urban explorers" like Dickens and Henry
Mayhew "adapted the language of imperialism to evoke features of their own
cities. Imperialist rhetoric transformed the unexplored territory of the London
poor into an alien place, both exciting and dangerous" (18). Her description of
Dickens himself as one of the "engaged urban investigators of the mid- and late-
Victorian era" who patrolled the backstreets of the metropolis with the "earnest
(if still voyeuristic) intent to explain and resolve social problems" might also be
applied to Woodcourt (18).

22. In a letter to John Forster (7 Oct. 1849), Dickens considers possible subjects for
articles in *Household Words.* Among other projects, he imagines writing "a history of Savages, showing the singular respects in which all savages are like each
other; and those in which civilised men, under circumstances of difficulty, soonest
become like savages" (*Letters* V: 622). He perhaps fulfills the second part of this
project in the portrait of Jo, "under circumstances of difficulty" in a society more
concerned with the "foreign-grown savage" than with its own variety.

23. Dickens offers Jarndyce as a responsible father figure in relation to Skimpole in
the same way that he opposes Esther to Mrs. Jellyby. Significantly, Skimpole
demonstrates his irresponsibility partly by revealing aesthetic interests in matters
far afield. Considering the "Slaves on American plantations," he light-heartedly
declares, "they people the landscape for me, they give it a poetry for me" (307).
On the one hand, this revery reveals the questionable morality of Skimpole's
aesthetic detachment. Esther's reaction to it, however, enforces the novel's effort
to generate sympathy for the neglected and exploited "at home" before considering injustices abroad. Rather than criticizing Skimpole for drawing pleasure from
the plight of exploited Africans, she substitutes the more immediate objects of
concern, wondering whether he "ever thought of Mrs. Skimpole and the children,

and in what point of view they presented themselves to his cosmopolitan mind''
(307–8). The irresponsible dilettante, like the impractical philanthropist, meets
with censure from the character who remains always mindful of the "obligations
of home.''

24. In *The Night Side of Dickens* (1994), Harry Stone establishes the centrality of the
cannibal metaphor in the work of Dickens. Stone documents how Dickens associates cannibalism both with foreign or peripheral savagery, as in the case of
Vholes—whose black gloves, indistinguishable from his skin, signify racial Otherness—and with an indigenous variety, in the tradition of Hogarth and fairy
tales. Arguing that cannibalism in one of its manifestations taints most of the evil
characters in *Bleak House,* he proposes that the novel's lesson is that "all obey
society's golden rule: eat or be eaten—or, more exactly, eat *and* be eaten. We
consume our neighbors, we even batten on our progeny and our progenitors,
Dickens is saying, instead of loving them. Mr. Vholes' cannibalism is only the
most unadorned representation of this grim truth and of society's law'' (150).

25. The second Bleak House recalls Dickens' idealized description of Australian colo-
nies in the *Household Words* article in which he endorses Mrs. Chisholm's Family
Loan Colonization Society. Dickens imagines that "from little communities thus
established other and larger communities will rise in time, bound together in a
love of the old country still fondly spoken of as Home'' (Stone I: 88). Esther
manifests the emigrant's nostalgia when she reports that, after Jarndyce has given
the second Bleak House to herself and Woodcourt, "all three went home'' to the
first Bleak House.

# WORKS CITED

Brantlinger, Patrick. *Rule of Darkness: British Literature and Imperialism, 1830–1914.*
Ithaca: Cornell UP, 1988.

Butt, John and Kathleen Tillotson. *Dickens at Work.* Fair Lawn, NJ: Essential
Books, 1958.

Carlyle, Thomas. *The Works of Thomas Carlyle.* 30 Vols. London: Chapman and Hall,
1898. Rpt. New York: AMS Press, 1980.

Chaudhuri, Brahma. "Dickens and the Women of England at Strafford House.'' *English Language Notes* 25 (June 1988): 54–60.

David, Deirdre. *Rule Britannia: Women, Empire, and Victorian Writing.* Ithaca: Cornell UP, 1995.

Dickens, Charles. *Bleak House.* New York: Penguin Books, 1971.

———. "A Bundle of Emigrants' Letters.'' *Household Words.* 30 March 1850:19–24.
Rpt. in *Charles Dickens's Uncollected Writings from Household Words 1850–1859.*
Ed. Harry Stone. 2 vols. Bloomington: Indiana UP, 1968:85–96.

——. *David Copperfield.* New York: Penguin Books, 1966.

——. *Dombey and Son.* New York: Penguin Books, 1970.

——. *The Mystery of Edwin Drood.* New York: Penguin Books, 1974.

——. *The Pilgrim Edition of the Letters of Charles Dickens.* Ed. Madeline House and Graham Storey. 6 vols. Oxford: Clarendon Press, 1965–1981.

——. "Review of the *Narrative of the Expedition sent by Her Majesty's Government to the River Niger in 1841.*" *The Examiner.* 19 August 1848:531–33.

——. *To the Baroness Burdett-Coutts.* Ed. Charles C. Osborne. New York: E. P. Dutton, 1932.

Duane, Patrick A. "Boy's Literature and the Idea of Empire, 1870–1914." *Victorian Studies* 24 (1980:1): 105–22.

Gallagher, Catherine. *The Industrial Reformation of English Fiction: Social Discourse and Narrative Form.* Chicago: U of Chicago P, 1985.

Gold, Joel J. "Mrs. Jellyby: Dickens's Inside Joke." *Dickensian* 79 (Spring, 1983): 35–38.

"Heathen and Christian Burial." *Household Words* 1.2 (1850): 43–48.

Ikeler, A. Abbot. "The Philanthropic Sham: Dickens' Corrective Method in *Bleak House.*" *College Language Association Journal* 24 (June 1981): 497–512.

Lawson, R. Bland. "The 'Condition of England Question': *Past and Present and Bleak House.*" *The Victorian Newsletter* 79 (Spring 1991): 24–27.

Nayder, Lillian. "Class Consciousness and the Indian Mutiny in Dickens's 'The Perils of Certain English Prisoners.' " *Studies in English Literature 1500–1900* 32 (1992): 689–705.

Perera, Suvendrini. *Reaches of Empire: The English Novel from Edgeworth to Dickens.* New York: Columbia UP, 1991.

Pope, Norris. *Dickens and Charity.* New York: Columbia UP, 1978.

Robbins, Bruce. "Telescopic Philanthropy: Professionalism and Responsibility in *Bleak House.*" *Nation and Narration.* Ed. Homi K. Bhabha. New York: Routledge, 1990. 213–30.

Ruskin, John. "Of Queen's Gardens." *Sesame and Lillies.* Vol. 18 of *The Works of John Ruskin.* Ed. E. T. Cook and Alexander Wedderburn. 39 vols. New York: Longmans, Green, 1905.

Stone, Harry. *The Night Side of Dickens: Cannibalism, Passion, Necessity.* Columbus: Ohio State UP, 1994.

Walkowitz, Judith. *City of Dreadful Delight: Narratives of Sexual Danger in Late-Victorian London.* Chicago: U of Chicago P, 1992.

# Signification and Rhetoric
# in *Bleak House*

*Paul A. Kran*

The large body of critical work on Dickens' *Bleak House* is extremely diverse
and hence difficult to characterize with any degree of accuracy. If one element
can be singled out as common to most analyses, it would be a distinct tendency
to view the text in terms of twos. A more "traditional" school of criticism
sees *Bleak House* as a series of parallels and analogies in both plot and
character; it argues that the novel's two narratives represent complementary
parts of a unified aesthetic and social vision, while a school of critics influenced by deconstruction sees those same parallels and analogies as binaries
that fall apart upon close reading. Such critics see the two narratives as irrecon-
cilable and argue that the text's vision is ultimately fragmented and incoherent.

Its dual narrative structure makes the schematization of *Bleak House* into
a series of binaries almost inevitable, and, despite the fluctuations in critical
interests and methodologies, the way in which the two narratives either work
together or negate one another will probably always remain the central formal
issue in criticism of the text. Even if the issue remains unresolved—and
unresolvable—the commentary on the text generated by both schools of criticism has provided significant insights into not only the text, but into the
pitfalls of both the traditional humanist critique and the radical anti-humanist/
formalist critique as well. If the New Critics were never entirely successful
in their attempts to reconcile the two narratives, deconstructionists have been
a little too quick to use the dual narrative structure of *Bleak House* as evidence
of Dickens' retrograde binary thinking; both schools share the traditional,
rather snobbish view of Dickens as an "entertainer" in their insistence on
his utter lack of insight into what he was doing. I do not point this out in order
to suggest that we take Dickens' intentions more seriously in our criticism, but
rather to express a certain impatience with readings that exult in having

"caught" Dickens at something of which he himself would not be the least surprised to be told. One of the tenets of deconstructive criticism is the assumption that before its advent, everyone, with a few notable exceptions, was straitjacketed by binary thinking. But what their best work on *Bleak House* proves is less the inadequacies of Dickens' binarism than the inadequacy of binarism as a means of comprehending the complexities of Dickens. A more flexible methodology consisting of more than two categories needs to be brought to bear on the novel.

One approach that seems to have potential for fulfilling this requirement is that of Jacques Lacan, particularly his theories on the linguistic determination of the subject and intersubjectivity elaborated in the "Seminar on 'The Purloined Letter'." Lacan develops his theory of intersubjectivity through the analysis of another plot-driven narrative, Poe's "The Purloined Letter," by tracking the movement of the signifier (the letter of the title) and noting how its position in the text dictates the behavior of the actors in the story. From this analysis he concludes that

> the displacement of the signifier determined the subjects in their acts, in their destiny, in their refusals, in their blindness, in their end and in their fate, their innate gifts and social acquisitions notwithstanding, without regard for character or sex, and that, willingly or not, everything that might be considered the stuff of psychology . . . will follow the path of the signifier.
>
> (Muller and Richardson 43–44)

This conception of psychology is more useful in a text where considerations of individual character are subordinated to the characters' role in the plot than the more humanistic psychological notions of identity, trauma, neurosis and defense mechanisms that have dominated certain discussions of *Bleak House,* especially those concerning the "nature" of Esther Summerson.

Even the most cursory reading of *Bleak House* reveals any number of highly charged signifiers that function in an analogous manner to that of the letter in Poe's text, including, but not limited to, Esther's handkerchief, smallpox, Lady Dedlock's letters to Hawdon, and the documents in the Jarndyce suit. It is through the circulation of these signifiers, rather than through the active agency of any of the characters, that the complex plot(s) of the novel unfold, and their passing between and among characters creates the system of personal and social interconnections the text makes explicit it wishes to establish:

> What connexion can there be, between the place in Lincolnshire, the house in town, the Mercury in powder, and the whereabout of Jo the outlaw with the broom . . . ? What connexion can there have been between the many people in the innumerable histories of this world, who . . . have . . . been very curiously brought together!          (*BH* 272)[1]

It could be and has been said of both Lacan's and Dickens' conceptions of the relationship of character to plot (or of subject to Signifier) that they hold extremely pessimistic views of the possibilities of agency, activity, and self-determination in human life.[2] Such a view can only be maintained if one holds a mimetic theory of narrative; the work of Peter Brooks, for example, demonstrates that plot, when considered as a cognitive rather than a mimetic activity, affirms the subject's ability to create meanings and comprehend the world. Although Lacan's "Seminar" argues that subjects are completely and irrevocably formed by the path of the signifier, his text admits of a position in the signifying chain that one can hold at least temporarily which permits the subject to perceive and comprehend its path. The "Seminar," in addition, speaks quite often—and in terms quite similar to Brooks's—of Poe's active, shaping role in the production of his text, without any crude recourse to his intentions or his individual psychology. The combination of a non-mimetic theory of narrative and the possibility of a self-reflexive subjectivity makes Lacanian theory, at least in this instance, a useful middle ground between humanist and formalist theories of textuality.

Lacan's work, particularly the "Seminar on 'The Purloined Letter'," has of course been very influential in literary studies, but generally speaking, the most important Lacanian-inspired literary scholarship has not simply transposed the terms of Lacanian psychology as if they were directly and unproblematically applicable to texts, but has combined Lacan with the work of other thinkers more directly concerned with issues of language and literature.[3] As my own attempt to address these issues, I propose yet another encounter, in this instance between Lacan and historiographer Hayden White. White's thought also builds upon the work of structuralists such as Saussure, Jakobson, and Lévi-Strauss, but in contrast to Lacan, White's work is fundamentally concerned with the effect of the narrative act upon the narrated, and he uses specifically literary concepts and methodology to analyze those effects in historical writing.

The four major tropes of classical rhetoric—metaphor, metonomy, synechdoche and irony—dominate White's work, where they function less as figures of speech than as fundamental psychological and epistemological categories. In the introduction to *Metahistory,* White links each of these tropes to the four major literary genres (or modes of emplotment), to the four modes of historical argument, and to the four major ideologies (taken from Frye, Mannheim, and Popper, respectively). White has certain reservations about these formulations; he stresses that the typology of historical consciousness he derives from them is not nearly as neat in practice as in his introduction, and warns the reader not to use them too rigidly. Nonetheless, as a means of approaching *Bleak House,* White's introduction provides us with a fairly precise set of terms and lets us think in fours rather than twos.[4] White's main argument, that the figures of rhetoric and the major narrative genres constitute the conceptual modes by which we comprehend and impose order upon reality, acknowledges the limitations language places upon understanding; yet, as Lacan to subjectivity and Brooks to plot, White attributes a certain amount of productive force to those limitations. The concepts and terminology that inform White's arguments make his model fairly easy to extend to a discussion of a literary text such as *Bleak House*.[5] In combination with Lacan's notion of a signifying path, White's model allows us to track the major signifiers of the text in terms of systematic differences in the meanings their movements create, the nature of the relationships between characters that they establish, and to identify and discuss the ideological implications of those meanings and relationships, implications that critics of the novel, always thinking in twos, have long found to be confused.

## I. Signifier Displacement in the Metaphoric Mode: Esther's Handkerchief

Esther's handkerchief first appears in *Bleak House,* chapter 8, "Covering a Multitude of Sins," in which Esther and Ada are escorted by Mrs. Pardiggle to the squalid home of the brickmakers on a mission of "charity." They arrive to find the husband drunk and extremely resentful of Mrs. Pardiggle's repeated intrusions; Jenny, his wife, shows signs of a recent beating and is struggling to administer to the needs of a sick baby on her lap with the help of her neighbor, Liz. While Mrs. Pardiggle proselytizes the family in a voice "much too businesslike and systematic" (*BH* 156) about the virtues of hard work, "as if she were an inexorable moral policeman" (*BH* 158), Jenny's baby quietly dies. This death occasions a spontaneous outburst of grief and sympathy from Ada and from Esther, who, in order to "make the baby's rest the prettier and gentler" (*BH* 160) lays the dead child on a shelf and discreetly covers it with her handkerchief. Mrs. Pardiggle is characteristically unmoved by this spectacle of actual human suffering in all its particularity. The other four women in the room share a recognition of Jenny's very specific grief, which they grasp nonetheless as a primary component of human experience that transcends the class differences that the text has carefully foregrounded throughout the chapter.

The scene at the brickmakers' is a key moment in the text's ideological structure. Mrs. Pardiggle's brand of rigid, institutionalized charity is shown to be utterly inadequate and inhuman, and is opposed by Esther's spontaneous, dignified gesture of covering the dead baby, one of the "individual acts of responsibility and love" that Joseph Fradin, in an oft-quoted article, argues the text advances as the only possibility for human happiness (63). Insofar as such spontaneous and localized acts are advanced as an ideal of human behavior, Fradin finds that *Bleak House* stresses the impossibility of reform on an institutional level and holds a resolutely anarchist ideology, an argument D. A. Miller will cast into different terms in *The Novel and the Police*. In Hayden White's model, anarchism is one of four primary ideological positions, which he links to the trope of metaphor as its basic conceptual mode and to a romantic mode of emplotment. After this first appearance of the handkerchief in a symbolic gesture that validates an anarchist ideological position, it functions as a powerful metaphor and creates what could be deemed the "family romance" of *Bleak House* as it moves throughout the text.

One might argue that the symbolic force of the handkerchief in the text is based on either metonomy or synechdoche, as a signifier associated with Esther's charitable act, or as representing one in the series of such acts and gestures that define Esther's total character. However, since the covering of the dead baby with the handkerchief actually constitutes the charitable act, there exists a relationship of identity between the act and the signifier, hence a metaphoric relationship. The handkerchief becomes a cherished keepsake for Jenny "partly because it was yours [Esther's] . . . and partly because it had covered the baby" (*BH* 497). The value the handkerchief holds for Jenny reaffirms one of the text's primary metaphors, Esther as "the dead child," both in the eyes of the law that has no official way of recognizing her and in the eyes of her mother, Lady Dedlock, for whom Esther has very literally been dead.

As the handkerchief passes from Jenny's hands into those of Lady Dedlock, its metaphoric force changes. At this point in the plot, Lady Dedlock has had her suspicions about Esther's true identity confirmed by Guppy's insinuations; the handkerchief adds nothing to her knowledge. Her possession of it has another, symbolic value for her, as the only means by which she can acknowledge and celebrate her relationship to her daughter, which the strictures of society otherwise force her to keep secret. The handkerchief transforms Esther from a "dead child" in Lady Dedlock's mind into a living, breathing entity; moreover, Jenny's story of how the handkerchief came to her and the almost transcendent esteem in which she holds Esther form the sum-total of what Lady Dedlock knows of her daughter. For Jenny and Lady Dedlock alike, the handkerchief stands as an irrefutable symbol of Esther's goodness. That goodness stands in defiance to the greater structures of society which render ineffectual the genuine human impulses behind charity by turning it into "system," and the handkerchief attests to Esther's value in a society that refuses to recognize her.

The ultimate condemnation of social organization comes in the recognition scene between mother and child in chapter 36. Since their first encounter in chapter 18, Esther herself has had certain vague suspicions about her relationship to Lady Dedlock. She has also heard, through Charley, that a woman had made inquiries about her at the brickmakers' cottage and had taken the handkerchief away with her. When Lady Dedlock approaches her in the woods around Chesney Wold in an agitated state unprecedented in her, handkerchief in hand, Esther has an instinctual awareness of the significance of the moment that renders language, the most pervasive mode of social organization, if not entirely superfluous, certainly extremely inadequate: "I cannot tell in any words what the state of my mind was, when I saw in her hand my handkerchief, with which I had covered the dead baby" (*BH* 565).

It is easy to see how Esther's reticence at this crucial moment in her life's history could be construed as evidence of her repression in a humanist psychological critique, but this reticence cannot be divorced from the more generalized doubt Esther has of the ability of language to express genuine human emotion and to convey the truth, nor from the seriousness with which she uses language herself (Young 68–69). If Esther shies away from relating her own feelings at all the crucial moments in her story, it must also be remembered that she also shies away from the direct dramatization of any highly charged emotional scene, including her interview with Richard at Deal, where her own feelings are not of primary concern. On the whole, Esther seems less repressed than suspicious; language, as a systematic and social means of expression, is inadequate in its ability to convey the truth of the most basic and important human experiences. The handkerchief thus becomes an iconic, and hence less arbitrary, means of communication. This suspicion of language reinforces the text's more global suspicion of "system" and contributes to its incipient anarchism, as does the entire scene between Esther and Lady Dedlock. It is the only moment in *Bleak House* in which the women are allowed to acknowledge their relationship, a perfectly "natural" relationship that social organization has invalidated, something made explicit very early on in the text by Conversation Kenge: "Aunt in fact, though not in law" (*BH* 67).

The naturalness of the blood tie and its oppositions to society are underscored by the setting of their meeting, in the woods, far from the censuring eyes of society. Indeed, Esther's narrative is filled with the idyllic and awed descriptions of nature, and these come almost invariably within close proximity to an encounter with Lady Dedlock (e. g., the descriptions of the terrain and the weather in chapter 18, in which Esther, Ada and Jarndyce find themselves in the same shed with Lady Dedlock, and, later, during Esther's and Bucket's pursuit of Lady Dedlock through a snowstorm). The predominance of nature imagery during Esther's meetings with her mother are consistent with a romantic mode of emplotment, and of course, the search for and return to one's parents is the plot of romance par excellence. As is true of many romances, the subplot that revolves around Esther's true parentage culminates in the woods. This "recognition scene" conforms closely to how Hayden White characterizes the anarchist point of view: "Anarchists are inclined to idealize a *remote past* of natural-human innocence from which men have fallen into the 'corrupt' social state in which they currently find themselves'' (*Metahistory* 25, White's emphasis). In terms of creating a romantic subplot, the signifying path of Esther's handkerchief is completed in this scene, having created a metaphoric bond between three women who have been utterly alienated by their society and having affirmed bonds and ties that stand in complete opposition to that society.

If Esther's handkerchief has completed its circuit in the romantic subplot, it has not made its last appearance in the text. After they part in the woods, Lady Dedlock retains the handkerchief and keeps it among her private possessions as her sole souvenir of her daughter. There it stays until it is found by Inspector Bucket when he searches her rooms after her flight. Bucket is entrusted in the text to uphold and, quite literally, to police the society that invalidates the ties between Esther and Lady Dedlock, and as such, the handkerchief acquires a different status and meaning in his hands than it had previously. No longer does the handkerchief represent a spontaneous "act of responsibility and love," nor does it affirm a maternal love that society refuses to recognize. By this point, Bucket has already heard the entire story of Lady Dedlock's relationship to Esther, albeit in convoluted form, from Mrs. Snagsby, Smallweed, and the Chadbands, so the handkerchief reveals nothing to him in that regard. It says nothing to him about qualities, but serves simply as an indication that Lady Dedlock has some affection for her daughter and that Esther might be of some assistance in finding her. This change in the handkerchief's status from symbol to that of a "clue" or "lead" takes it out of the realm of metaphor and places it in the realm of metonymy.

## II. Signifier Displacement in the Metonymic Mode: Smallpox

Esther's handkerchief has very little chance to operate as a metonomy in *Bleak House*. True, it leads Bucket to Esther and leads them both to the discovery of Lady Dedlock's body, but Bucket already had sufficient reason to seek out Esther before its discovery. Nonetheless, even this brief deployment of the handkerchief as a metonymic signifier seems to confirm Hayden White's linkage of the trope of metonymy to a tragic mode of emplotment and a radical ideology. A far more extensive deployment of metonymy occurs in the text in the form of the smallpox subplot.

White, building on Jacobson, sees metonomy as the trope of cause and effect, and hence of both narrative and scientific explanation (*Metahistory* 35). Although in the largest context of *Bleak House,* smallpox becomes a symbol of all the ills of Victorian society, its particular properties and the movement/spread of the infection throughout the text is much more indicative of metonomy than metaphor. Smallpox exists in a relationship of contiguity with those who carry it and is passed from one character to another. Moreover, it is associated in the text with the squalor of poverty, caused by the unsanitary conditions of Tom-all-Alone's and Nemo's graveyard. The circulation of smallpox through the text occurs through a readily discernible series of causes and effects: Jo goes to visit Nemo's graveyard and contracts the disease; Inspector Bucket causes Jo to "move on" to St. Albans, where he passes the disease on to Charley, et cetera.

F. S. Schwarzbach praises the accuracy with which Dickens portrays the symptoms and the spread of smallpox in *Bleak House* (93–96). This attention to such details is consonant with what White calls "The Mechanistic theory of explanation" which "turns upon the search for the causal laws that determine the outcomes of processes discovered in the historical field" (*Metahistory* 17). As a theory of explanation concerned with causal laws, White sees it as a metonymic mode, and the one most likely to be used by those who hold a "scientific" view of history, such as Hegel, Taine, and Marx. Science attempts to understand the causes of processes so as to predict their eventual effects in order to be in a position to intervene where necessary, which makes Mechanism an hospitable theory to a radical ideology. As a theory that emphasizes determinism in historical phenomena, it will tend to use a tragic mode of emplotment, depicting a man's, a nation's, a class's inevitable submission to the inexorable laws of history. The depiction of smallpox in *Bleak House* isolates causes, as opposed to the circulation of the handkerchief, which is a much more generalized indictment of social structures based on a priori suspicion of them; it is also opposed to the treatment of Chancery as an institution, which D. A. Miller amply demonstrates cannot be localized, and whose origins in time cannot be specified (59–62).

Miller argues that *Bleak House* becomes a detective story in order to localize and put a face on evil so that it can be combatted, but he ignores the way in which the deployment of smallpox performs the same function. It is by no means insignificant that smallpox infects ("connects") three orphans, who, as the traditional "innocent victims" of society can easily be invoked for pathos in a rhetoric of reform. Dickens' depiction of the causes of smallpox leaves little doubt as to what needs to be done to check its spread: large-scale improvements of sanitary measures in poor districts and graveyards, which would entail public funds and government intervention; in short, radical means. In addition, Esther's voluntary isolation proves the efficacy of quarantining victims. Radical ideology, according to White, via Mannheim, sees the possibilities of social improvement as imminent and concerns itself with devising revolutionary means to bring change about now (*Metahistory* 25). It is easy to recognize the rhetorical efficacy of invoking a lethal epidemic to convince the public of the need for immediate and radical intervention, and would have been especially compelling in Dickens' day, when an effective vaccine against the disease had been available for more than fifty years, but universal immunization had been blocked by arguments that smallpox was an effective and indispensable means of controlling the poor population (Schwarzbach 97). Thus the means of effective intervention were already available, but not being used due to government inaction and the cynicism of the ruling classes. Almost all of the imagery and rhetoric surrounding the smallpox epidemic in *Bleak House* impresses the reader with a sense of urgency, perhaps nowhere more clearly than in Jo's death scene with its famous concluding words: "And dying thus around us every day" (*BH* 705).

There is, however, a certain amount of ambiguity in the deployment of smallpox as an ideological signifier, especially when considered in its relation to the rest of the text. The spontaneous sympathy and desire to help that Jo's illness inspires in Esther and Charley ultimately backfires and they themselves become stricken with the disease. In spite of their help, Jo is "moved on" and eventually dies; Esther is severely disfigured. In the long run, the text appears to support Skimpole's assessment of the situation. As callous and cruel as it seems, Skimpole's providential logic is usually flawless (Garrett 68), and his voice is the conservative one of self-interest (much of what he says sounds like a grotesque parody of Adam Smith). This textual support of Skimpole's ideology makes it a bit more difficult to dismiss than Esther's narrative would have it. Moreover Garrett, along with more recent work by Marcia Goodman and Barbara Gottfried, all make extremely interesting arguments about parallels between Esther and Skimpole. Although the degree of sincerity with which they make their claims is suspect, both claim to base their actions upon providence, a belief that asserts the existence of a divine plan, benevolent in design, which renders human effort to control its own destiny superfluous and doomed to failure; hence, as an ideological position, it is essentially conservative.

Since, thus far, most of what has been taken to be the anarchic and radical impulses of *Bleak House* have been largely contained to Esther's narrative, this conservativism in her point of view needs to be acknowledged, but in the long run, it does not need to be taken that seriously. For the most part, analyses of Esther's narrative have long recognized that its content undercuts the validity of her highly conventional opinions. However, smallpox, to the extent that it functions in the text more or less as Skimpole warns it will, changes those social ties and connections that a large part of the text tries to foreground and celebrate into a source of pain and even death. Esther's famous dream during the critical moment of her illness makes the malevolent quality of these ties very explicit:

Dare I hint at that worse time when, strung together somewhere in great black space, there was a flaming necklace, or ring, or starry circle of some kind, of which *I* was one of the beads! And when my only prayer was to be taken off from the rest, and when it was such inexplicable agony and misery to be a part of the dreadful thing?                                                    (*BH* 544)

In retrospect, she can call the desire "to be taken off from the rest" her "worse time," a moment when her normal values of charity and duty desert her. Esther is the one character in the text who is constantly aware of her relationship to others—indeed, she defines herself almost completely through those relationships—and the one character who takes seriously the obligations they confer upon her. Yet her fondest desire, in this key moment of the text, is to be free of those obligations, to exist independently of them, a desire that seems to assert that the greatest happiness, contrary to what much of the text and Esther herself try to demonstrate, lies not in fulfilling the obligations that living a social existence entails, but rather in being entirely free from them. True, it would be difficult to cite a single instance where the text advocates setting those obligations aside in the pursuit of one's own interests in the manner of a Skimpole or a Vholes, but this image of the horror of social existence becomes part of the text's dominant "bleakness," like the mud and fog that surround Chancery Court in chapter One. *Bleak House* consistently portrays human existence on earth as a fallen one that must be endured rather than a world gone astray through human error that can, in the long run, be perfected through human effort. Such existential pessimism underlies the text's shrillest and most poignant calls for action and reform.

### III. Signifier Displacement in the Synechdochal Mode: Lady Dedlock's Letters

Any discussion of the ideological meaning of *Bleak House* eventually runs into a conflict between radical and conservative impulses of the sort outlined above (e.g., Fradin, D. A. Miller and a great many feminist readings). Peter Garrett locates the crux of this conflict in Jarndyce's advice to his wards in chapter 13: "Trust in nothing but Providence and your own efforts. Never separate the two" (Garrett 68). It appears self-evident to Garrett that providential design and human effort cannot be reconciled except in an act of faith, but in Dickens' day, efforts to reconcile the two logically had by no means been given up—if indeed they ever have. I would prefer to see this yoking of two apparently mutually exclusive philosophical positions as an active attempt to negotiate between them, and not as an unconscious and inevitable lapse into a logical aporia. In other words, ideological conflict in *Bleak House* is allowed to develop and play itself out and does not occur primarily as the product of logical inconsistencies inherent in any a priori ideological message the text seeks to transmit. Some logical and/or conceptual inconsistency does, of course, play a role in *Bleak House,* as in any other text, and it could be argued in accordance with the categories I have thus far established that the ideological conflict detected in the deployment of smallpox stems from the close proximity of the trope of metonomy to synechdoche, which White sees as the trope most conducive to conservativism. On the whole, however, it seems to me less productive to look at the way Dickens' rhetoric of radicalism slips inevitably into a certain conservativism when there is at least one signifier, Lady Dedlock's letters to Hawdon, which, as it is displaced throughout a signifying chain and among figures in the text, creates, quite actively, an entire subplot and set of meanings that support a conservative ideology.

There may at first appear to be a certain incongruity in the claim that Lady Dedlock's letters circulate through the text in a synechdochal mode, especially according to White's topology, which links synechdoche to both a conservative ideology and to a comic emplotment, on the basis that all three assert a harmonious integration of part to whole, of individual to society (*Metahistory* 36). The letters, after all, give rise to events that lead to Lady Dedlock's death, a state rather far removed from the harmonious integration into society that White claims always occurs at the end of a comedy. It is here, perhaps, that White does the most violence to Frye's theory of modes; the discussion of comedy in *The Anatomy of Criticism* is far more modulated than White would have it—there is more than one type of comedy, and Frye himself is not unaware of their possible ideological underpinnings. His discussion of ironic comedy is particularly relevant to *Bleak House.* Ironic comedy, according to Frye, has as its central theme the driving out of a *pharmakos,* or scoundrel, from society as a means of restoring order (the examples he gives are *Volpone* and *Tartuffe*); an element declared alien or deviant is cast out rather than reconciled to society (Frye 45). A great deal of the secondary literature on the novel supports this view of Lady Dedlock as *pharmakos,* especially Michael Ragussis's arguments that all evil stems from Lady Dedlock's original transgression with Hawdon and many feminist readings that use the text's scapegoating of Lady Dedlock as evidence of Dickens' or the period's sexism.

Frye warns that "[i]nsisting on the theme of social revenge on an individual, however great a rascal he may be, tends to make him look less involved in guilt and the society more so" (Frye 45). Thus the *pharmakos* in comedy can easily turn into a tragic figure (e.g., Shylock), and the particular difficulties of the form of ironic comedy may help to explain the ambiguous responses Lady Dedlock's death provokes both within the text and within readers. In spite of the difficulties inherent in ironic comedy, Frye insists that it is alive and well today in the guise of the detective story. At this point, Frye's arguments anticipate—in quite a surprising way—those advanced by D. A. Miller in *The Novel and the Police.*[6] Miller's reading of the detective story aspect of *Bleak House* as an attempt to localize and identify sources of evil that the text earlier characterizes as ubiquitous and faceless clearly attempts to identify a function very similar to that performed by the *pharmakos* in Frye's typology,[7] and ideologically, this function is clearly conservative.

Now that the detective story has been established as a comic genre, we are in a better position to examine the signifying chain created by Lady Dedlock's letters. They become important in the text as a piece of evidence, and evidence, as we have already seen in reference to the significance that Esther's handkerchief holds for Bucket, is always a piece or *part* that must be related to the *whole* of the story—in other words, they function synecdochally. In *Bleak House,* the letters themselves reveal only half the truth; they are proof of Lady Dedlock's affair, but not of the existence or the identity of her illegitimate child, which come to light through other sources. Yet one need not be completely convinced of Frye's classification of the detective story as a comic genre to realize the comic elements created by the circulation of the letters; their path serves to connect the most grotesquely comic characters of the novel and places them in specifically comic situations. Moreover, of the three signifiers discussed so far, the letters most closely resembles the purloined letter of Poe's story, and their displacement comforms most closely to Lacan's reading.[8] Sir Leicester remains in the first position, that of the king, oblivious to what most closely concerns him and takes place beneath his very eyes, while the other characters alternate between the second and the third positions, either holding the letters or scrambling for their possession. Characters are determined in their course of action based on what they perceive to be their position in relation to the letters' location; for example, Guppy believes Krook to have them, so he installs Jobling/Weevle in Nemo's now vacant room in order to gain his confidence. As is true in Poe's story, possession of the letters never appears to confer the power they are expected to; they are coveted and hoarded by Krook, who cannot read them (and hence make use of them), and he dies just as their significance is about to be revealed. Tulkinghorn is similarly prevented by his murder from making use of their contents, and even Grandfather Smallweed, who has made money by giving them to Tulkinghorn, comes too late for him to gain anything but negligible funds through his extortion attempt. The plotting, if not the actual portrayal, of the events brought about by the displacement of the letters, to the extent that it relies upon cheated expectations, plans gone awry, bad timing, is profoundly comic.[9]

The displacement of Lady Dedlock's letter's throughout the text serves to illustrate the unavoidable role of contingency in human affairs and the impossibility of human efforts either to minimize or profit from that contingency, a view compatible with at least certain varieties of conservative ideology, for example, laissez-faire capitalism; at any rate, it is certainly incompatible with any ideology that stresses intervention and reform. In final analysis, the letters do not even do what it had been assumed throughout the text that they would do, bring about Lady Dedlock's downfall. The letters do lead to her exposure, though via a highly circuitous route, but the revelation of their contents to Sir Leicester does not lead to her condemnation. Sir Leicester, caricatured throughout the text for his conservative values, suddenly becomes a highly sympathetic, even "noble" character, forgives his wife and, contrary to all expectations, begs Bucket to return her safely to him. One possible reading would see this as an enlightened moment in the text, a recognition that sexual transgression is not the horrible crime against god and society that the Victorians held it to be. However, in terms of plot, Sir Leicester's forgiveness means that Lady Dedlock's flight and death occur not because they seem preferable to enduring the retribution society would exact once her transgressions became a matter of public record—a tragic ending—but because she errs in her estimation of Sir Leicester's response to the truth. Though we might feel that her death at Nemo's graveyard is unduly harsh, the events that lead to it are emplotted in such a way as to make it nobody's fault but her own,[10] the result of a fatal misapprehension of the truth rather than of fear of society's unjust censure. Guilt and responsibility are privatized, one of the most important strategies in any conservative ideology. Moreover, Sir Leicester's "surprising" choice of Lady Dedlock as a wife and his later forgiveness, both of which run completely counter to what one would expect given the point of view he espouses, insist on possibilities for human action and feeling that exist independently of social institutions and the roles that individuals are given to play within that society.[11]

### IV. Signifier Displacement in the Ironic Mode: Jarndyce and Jarndyce

It might be noted at this point that the displacement of Lady Dedlock's letters is given much more space and involves more characters than that of either Esther's handkerchief or the smallpox infection, and the signifying chain it creates traverses almost the entire text, as opposed to the other two, which are largely confined to the first half. This leads me to suggest that conservative ideology enters the text more self-consciously and less as the result of the slippage of meaning or the play of *écriture* than is usually found to be the case in postmodern readings. Lest we jump to the conclusion that the text ultimately advocates a conservative ideology, we ought first to examine the movement of its most pervasive signifier, the Jarndyce suit in Chancery.

There is a certain irony in speaking of the "movement" of the Jarndyce suit, since it never seems to "go" anywhere and is described almost entirely in images of stagnation and entanglement. Unlike the handkerchief or Lady Dedlock's letters, or even the letter in Poe's story, the suit cannot be located at a specific point in place and time, and as virtually all the characters in the text discover, its path through the text is well near impossible to follow. This irony is only to be expected, since the Jarndyce suit functions in an ironic mode throughout the text, and to the extent that the suit dominates *Bleak House,* although the point seems almost too self-evident to mention, irony is the text's dominant trope, above and beyond the more localized functionings of metaphor, metonomy, and synecdoche that have been outlined above. The many arguments that the two narratives of *Bleak House* work together by encouraging the reader to make connections between them that the text itself does not make explicit (of which Donovan and Harvey are the most prestigious) all acknowledge the dominance of irony, a trope that means without saying what it means, whether or not it is the term they use for it.

In spite of the fact that the suit or any of the documents associated with it do not really move from one place to another in the text, they nonetheless function in an analogous manner to the letter in Lacan's reading of Poe. It need not be pointed out that the existence of the suit has priority over and supersedes individual desires and inclinations; clearly all the characters involved in the suit act and plan according to what they perceive to be its importance and how they conceive their relation to it. Richard is an obvious example of how the suit creates character,[12] the various lawyers in Chancery are others. Even John Jarndyce's resolute decision to have nothing to do with the suit can be said to be the ruling passion of his life, so he, too, can be said to be determined by his involvement in it, and that involvement lies at the root of his decision to take Richard and Ada as wards, the first significant action of the Chancery plot. Moreover, as is true of the letter in "The Purloined Letter," the reader of *Bleak House* knows very little of the actual content or origins of the suit; it is known primarily through its effects, actual or anticipated, on individuals and institutions. The text shows little concern for the "truth" of the case.

The position of power in Lacan's triad is a position of highly self-reflexive subjectivity, an ironic consciousness that follows the path of the letter and recognizes its significance in relation to the other two positions. This power, in Lacan's formulation, is purely epistemological; it is lost the moment the figure in possession of it tries to derive any practical benefit from his or her knowledge. Lacan emphasizes that this third "ironic" position can be occupied only momentarily and that the power it confers is both precarious and dubious. In White's typology, irony "represents a stage in consciousness in which the problematical nature of language itself has become recognized" (*Metahistory* 37). The mediating role of language between consciousness and historical reality is foregrounded and thus ironic historiography is suspicious of the "naive" theory of language implicit in the other three tropological modes, and of its own results as well.[13] It is the mode of skepticism, and thus the only appropriate mode for Jarndyce and Jarndyce, which almost systematically eludes any and all efforts to comprehend it, although certain lawyers know how to profit from it.[14]

The generic mode irony favors is satire, which works by negating the positive assertions of one of the other genres. Hence satire incorporates the other genres into itself in order to exist. This raises the issue of whether or not the romantic, tragic and comic plots discernable in *Bleak House* are present only in order to be undermined. Certainly there is much irony on a local level in the comic plot engendered by the movement of Lady Dedlock's letters, yet as that plot nears its end, the ironical distance between narrator and character disappears and the overall tone of the text becomes sympathetic rather than detached. The more isolated moments of the text in which the handkerchief and smallpox are at issue are remarkable as one reads them for the absence of the irony that is all-pervasive elsewhere (though many readers have probably felt that Oscar Wilde's remark about Little Nell's death is equally applicable to Jo's); I thus conclude all three exist in the text as positive elements not meant to be negated. However, the Chancery case engenders a number of different subplots itself, and it seems possible to read Richard's story as a satirical tragedy and Esther's marriage as a satirical comedy, which would at least be able to account for the disturbing effect the marriage has had on certain critics.[15]

That *Bleak House* contains a great deal of satire has long been recognized (see Butt and Tillotson in works cited), and in reference to our efforts to understand the meaning and function of the suit in the text, White's discussion of the relationship of satire to irony is less useful that his discussion of contextualism, the ironic mode of historical argument. White sees Contextualism as a medium ground between Formism, which sees any given historical period or phenomenon as irreducibly unique, and Mechanism or Organicism, which see history as the product of certain trans-historical laws or as tending toward a specific "telos." A contextualist argument will isolate some element of the historical field and then trace the "threads" that link the event to be explained to different areas of the context. The relationship between event and context is seen as *actual* rather than rule-governed, existing at a specific time and place, and there is an a priori assumption in all Contextualist thought that the first, final and material causes of historical events are unknowable (*Metahistory* 18). As a mode of argument that isolates events from the flow of time and tries to comprehend them in terms of other objects in the historical field, contextualism is synchronic/structuralist in nature. The clear parallel between irony as a trope that stresses the limitations of historical knowledge makes this particular part of White's model more readily acceptable than others. White also points out that although there are no epistemological grounds for preferring one model over another, the ironic/contextualist position, with its self-reflexivity and awareness of its own limitations, appears to him to be the one most hospitable to the ''mature'' modern sensibility, though it recurs at different historical moments (*Metahistory* 26).

The above has fairly clear and direct application to both the Jarndyce suit and to the novel as a whole. The present tense of the third person narrative obscures the location in time of the events it describes, and the chronology between chapters can for the most part only be established through references to Esther's story. The famous opening of the novel, which places Chancery within the context of its London environs, further divorces the narrative from the flow of time through the use of verbs in their participle form, where verbs occur at all. ''[I]t would not be wonderful to meet Megalosaurus, forty feet long or so, waddling like an elephantine lizard up Holborn Hill,'' (*BH* 49) precisely because time plays no discernible role in the world as it is depicted in these first pages—everything is as it has always been, and presumably always will be. The introduction to Jarndyce and Jarndyce, and the subsequent ''development'' of the case as a signifier in the rest of the text conforms closely to White's characterization of the ironic/contextualist mode:

> Jarndyce and Jarndyce drones on. This scarecrow of a suit has . . . become so complicated that no man alive knows what it means. The parties to it understand it least; but it has been observed that no two Chancery lawyers can talk about it for five minutes without coming to a total disagreement as to all the premises. Innumerable children have been born into the cause; innumerable young people have married into it; innumerable old people have died out of it. Scores of persons have deliriously found themselves made parties in Jarndyce and Jarndyce, without knowing how or why . . . but Jarndyce and Jarndyce still drags its dreary length before the Court, perennially hopeless.          (*BH* 52)

The most that can be said of Jarndyce and Jarndyce is that it comes up regularly in Chancery proceedings, it has existed for an unspecified but clearly considerable duration, has caused immeasurable suffering, and is utterly incomprehensible. There are no positive terms by which it can be grasped; no one knows where it came from, where it will lead, or why it is the way it is.

Jarndyce and Jarndyce exists in such a state until it consumes itself in its own costs, having defeated any and all attempts to bring it to a close through human agency. The suit, like Lady Dedlock's letters, is deployed in the text so as to ''dissolve all belief in the possibility of positive political action,'' which is how White describes the ultimate effects of irony as the basis of a world view (*Metahistory* 38). But the comic plot in which Lady Dedlock's letters figure unravels in such a way so as to reassure the reader that ''positive political action'' is unnecessary in a providential universe. The ironic denouement of Jarndyce and Jarndyce offers no such reassurance; the Chancery plot locates and acknowledges the gross inequalities of Victorian society but does not offer positive strategies for its improvement. Change is felt to be necessary but there are no possibilities for envisaging viable alternatives; we are simply and hopelessly stuck in the mud and fog of the human condition. Miss Flite, perhaps the most pathetic and abused victim of Chancery in the text, articulates this dilemma. In a scene at her room at Krook's she describes to Esther, Ada, and Jarndyce Allan Woodcourt's kindness to her following Nemo's death and expresses a desire to repay him after her cause will have finally been decided: "I expect a Judgement, on the day of Judgement. And then I shall confer estates" (*BH* 251). The rich biblical resonances of this speech have received much critical attention, but within the context of *Bleak House,* its more literal meaning must not be overlooked. Presumably, what Miss Flite means is that she will remember Allan in her will, a will that will inevitably need to be probated *in Chancery,* quite possibly resuming the cycle from which she will have only just been freed. In her desperation, she cannot imagine things to be other than they actually are. Miss Flite, like Richard, Gridley and almost all the other characters to a greater or lesser degree, cannot conceive of good and evil independently of the terms Chancery has used to define them, which places them all in the almost intolerable position of having to trust in the *eventual* ability of the institution to set things right, in spite of all evidence to the contrary. Though White argues that the negational strategies of irony can be appropriated to the ends of any ideological position, he sees it as most appropriate to a liberal position, which recognizes the need for change but cannot conceive of that change occurring outside the already-established perimeters of society. The data for change is thus projected to an unspecified point in the distant future ("Judgement Day") with the rationale that society will adjust itself given the time to do so (*Metahistory* 25). Richard, Gridley, Miss Flite, and even Esther's anxious optimism that justice exists and will eventually be served reflects exactly such an ideological orientation.

If, as certain theorists would have it, postmodern criticism at its best re-enacts, rather than merely explicates, the text, to the extent that the above arguments resemble the "loose baggy monsters" of Victorian fiction that Henry James so despised, my reading of *Bleak House* has been a success. It would be wonderful indeed if I felt myself able to synthesize my various observations and draw some final conclusions about the ideological meaning of the text, but, as another ironic Contextualist, my aims are more modest. I do not feel that the ideological positions discernible in the text can be seen in dialectical tension with one another—there are simply too many of them, and it would be forcing matters to find a resolution to ideological conflict in the text. The novel's ending in an ellipsis almost seems to defy the reader in such efforts. One can make assertions about the relative amount of space each ideological position is given to elaborate and develop itself and conclude that the liberal ironic/contextualist position surpasses all the others in the attention it receives and its centrality to the plot, themes and imagery of the novel, but I have a painfully ironic awareness as I say so that—given my own ideological predispositions and professional training—this is exactly what I *would* say. I have cast my arguments about the ideological import of *Bleak House* in terms of rhetoric out of the sense that choice between them is less a matter of evaluating their proximity to the truth than in deciding which one is the most persuasive.

If the above analysis of the plots of *Bleak House* ends, in a typically deconstructive fashion, by insisting that their ideological meaning is ultimately conflicted and undecidable, that analysis also convinces me that these ideological conflicts and complexities are not just the accidental by-products of the play of *écriture,* but active and productive elements of the text. Another—perhaps more historicizing—account of the text is needed in order to get at the meanings generated by its conflicting ideological paradigms. This task, I believe, can only be carried out after certain critical orthodoxies concerning the text have been problematized, specifically the insistence that the dual narrative structure of *Bleak House* is evidence of its submission to a binary logic that ultimately undermines itself and the intentions of its author. I do not necessarily want to suggest that we need to take Dickens' intentions more seriously in our criticism, but as a simple matter of justice, the text amply demonstrates that we can attribute to Dickens an ironic self-consciousness at least as acute as that of our most subtle critics. If Dickens has been credited for his ability to provide a panoramic vision, on the mimetic level, of Victorian society, it seems like a short step to credit him with the ability to provide a an equally broad vision of the conflicted ideological paradigms of his day as well.

# Notes

1. All references to *Bleak House* are to the Penquin edition of 1971.
2. Critics are divided on the issue of action in Dickens. Robert Caserio builds an entire chapter out of his belief in Dickens' ultimate faith in the efficacy of human action, while the deconstructive school argues precisely the opposite.
3. Julia Kristeva's fruitful combination of Lacan with Bakhtin and Shoshona Felman's work with Lacan and Searle are perhaps the two most important examples. The persistent need of critics to modify and adapt Lacanian thought before making use of it in textual analysis probably stems from Derrida's attack on the "Seminar," "The Purveyor of Truth," which fault's Lacan's reading of Poe as insufficiently "literary," ignoring the story's status as text and the effect of the narration upon the narrated.

4. The work of Kristeva and Barthes provides me with a precedent for arguing that there exists more than one signifying chain; the "Seminar" itself, typical of Lacan's monological thought, discusses only one.

5. The introduction to *Metahistory* expresses some reservations about the utility of its model to the analysis of literary texts, but White will go on to use the model in a reading of Flaubert's *Éducation sentimentale.*

6. Note the following statement on p. 47 of *The Anatomy:* "We should have to say, then, that all forms of melodrama, the detective story in particular, were advanced propoganda for the police state . . . if it were possible to take them seriously." Except for Frye's rather snobbish declaration of immunity from the seductive appeal of popular forms, this sentence could have come straight out of *The Novel and the Police,* which, given the vast differences in Frye's and Miller's critical orientations, strikes me as almost uncanny. Miller nowhere mentions Frye or his work in his book.

7. Miller himself does not appear to recognize how the Lady Dedlock subplot functions in the text in more or less the same way he argues Bucket and the murder subplot function—possibly because a thorough discussion of this issue would weaken his main arguments. If the text ultimately assigns guilt to more than one source, it becomes harder to maintain that it seeks to localize that guilt. Moreover, Miller implicitly argues that the conservative ideological content of the detective story comes at the end of the text as a kind of (inevitable) reactionary response to the complex social problems *Bleak House* reveals. However, Lady Dedlock and her letters introduce elements of a detective story as early as chapter 2. If we accept Miller's (and Frye's) linkage of the detective story as a genre and conservative ideology, the fact that the mystery surrounding Lady Dedlock spans the entire novel suggests that its conservative elements are far more pervasive—and far more actively embedded—than Miller would have it.

8. This should hardly be surprising. Poe's story is, after all, one of the first detective stories.

9. Even though, to many reader's, Lacan's intersubjective model seems an excessively "bleak" view of human psychology, there is certainly ample evidence that Lacan himself saw something intrinically comic about it (cf his use of the ostrich image as a description of the triad in the "Seminar" [Muller and Richardson 32]).

10. And of course, "Nobody's Fault" was the working title of *Bleak House.*

11. Mrs. Woodcourt's final acceptance of Esther as a daughter-in-law in spite of her questionable origins can be read as another plot element tending in the same direction.

12. I would argue that both Dickens and Lacan ultimately embrace the notion character=action that derives from Aristotle's *Poetic* and *Ethics.* This would take some spelling out; I only mention it in order to sidestep endless speculation about whether Richard's downfall can be entirely attributed to the suit, or if the suit merely brings out qualities that were latent within him all along.

13. The suspicion of language's efficacy that emerges through the displacement of Esther's handkerchief suggests at least the possibility of a positive means of communication based upon iconic/metaphoric signifiers that have more than an arbitrary relationship to their signifieds; any suggestion that viable alternatives

exist is impossible in an ironic/contextualist mode, as I point out below. Certainly none emerge from the novel's treatment of the Chancery suit.

14. Presumably it is the self-conscious (or at least self-interested) activity of the lawyers which eat up the estate, but once the case ceases, so do their profits, and perhaps their professional reputations, so the "end" of Jarndyce and Jarndyce ultimately defeats everyone.

15. Among them, Frank, Kearns and Zwerdling.

# Works Cited

Axton, William. "The Trouble with Esther." *Modern Language Quarterly* 36 (1965): 545–57.

Blain, Virginia. "Double Vision and Double Standard in *Bleak House*: A Feminist Perspective." In Bloom 139–56.

Bloom, Harold, ed. *Modern Critical Interpretations: "Bleak House."* New York: Chelsea House, 1987.

Brooks, Peter. *Reading for the Plot: Design and Intention in Narrative.* New York: Random House, 1984.

Butt, John and Kathleen Tillotson. *Dickens at Work.* London: Methuen, 1957.

Caserio, Robert L. *Plot, Story and the Novel: From Dickens and Poe to the Modern Period.* Princeton: Princeton UP, 1979.

Daleski, H. M. "*Bleak House.*" In Gilbert 13–40.

Dickens, Charles. *Bleak House.* Introduction by J. Hillis Miller. Harmondsworth: Penguin, 1971.

Donovan, Robert A. "Structure and Idea in *Bleak House.*" In Jacob Korg, ed. *20th Century Intepretations of "Bleak House."* Englewood Cliffs: Prentice Hall, 1968.

Fradin, Joseph I. "Will and Society in *Bleak House.*" In Gilbert 40–64.

Frank, Lawrence. " 'Through a Glass Darkly': Esther Summerson and *Bleak House.*" In Gilbert 64–83.

Frye, Northrop. *The Anatomy of Criticism.* Princeton: Princeton UP, 1959.

Garrett, Peter K. *The Victorian Multiplot Novel: Studies in Dialogic Form.* New Haven: Yale UP, 1980.

Gilbert, Elliot L., ed. *Critical Essays on Charles Dickens's "Bleak House."* Boston: G. K. Hall, 1989.

Goodman, Marcia Renee. " 'I'll Follow the Other': Tracking the (M)other in *Bleak House.*" *Dickens Studies Annual* 19. (1990): 147–67.

Harvey, W. J. "*Bleak House.*" In A. E. Dyson, ed. *Dickens: Modern Judgements.* London: Macmillan, 1968.

Miller, D. A. *The Novel and the Police.* Berkeley: U of California P, 1988.

Muller, John P. and William J. Richardson. *The Purloined Poe: Lacan, Derrida and Psychoanalytic Reading.* Baltimore: Johns Hopkins UP, 1988.

Ragussis, Michael. "The Ghostly Signs of *Bleak House.*" In Gilbert 143–63.

Schwarzbach, F. S. "*Bleak House*: The Social Pathology of Urban Life." *Literature and Medicine* 9 (1990): 93–104.

White, Hayden. *Metahistory: This Historical Imagination in Nineteenth-Century Europe.* Baltimore: Johns Hopkins UP, 1973.

———. "The Problem of Style in Realistic Representation: Marx and Flaubert." In Berel Lang, ed. *The Concept of Style.* Ithaca: Cornell UP, 1979.

Young, Saundra K. "Uneasy Relations: Possibilities for Eloquence in *Bleak House.*" *Dickens Studies Annual* 9 (1981): 67–85.

Zwerdling, Alex. "Esther Summerson Rehabilitated." In Bloom 37–56.

# On Goods, Virtues, and *Hard Times*

*Valerie L. Wainwright*

Dickens, Orwell decided, was a nineteenth-century liberal; a "generously angry" writer, but one whose criticism was above all moral: "in reality his target was not so much society as human nature".[1] Since Orwell wrote, in 1939, not only has Dickens' political stance continued to be the subject of debate, but doubts have been raised as to whether his treatment of moral/political issues in the novel can be taken as the expression of a coherent and consistent viewpoint. I propose to examine *Hard Times* while bearing in mind recent reflections on the enduring features of liberalism, on its core tenets, principle concerns, goods, and virtues. Current controversy centers on the limitations and potential of this complex and multifaceted body of thought. Once we place *Hard Times* firmly within the context of the ongoing *critique and defence* of the moral and political implications of liberalism, more favorable claims can be made for both novel and novelist. Dickens' satire becomes more focussed.

We can contest, for a start, both of Roger Fowler's oft remarked and damaging conclusions. In the first place, according to Fowler, Dickens "attacks an unmanageably large and miscellaneous range of evils (utilitarianism in education and economics, industrial capitalism, abuse of unions, statistics, bad marriage, selfishness, etc.); . . . he mostly oversimplifies them . . . ; [and] is unclear on what evil causes what other evil" (91–108). One of the problems with this criticism is that it fails to conceptualize adequately the problems Dickens is addressing, and hence cannot trace the relations between the "evils." So that, for example, two of the issues mentioned are misrepresented as "industrial capitalism" and "bad marriage." In the first case, Dickens is concerned with the illiberal practices of capitalists who self-advertise themselves as liberals; and in the second, with the lack of opportunities for divorce in a society in which independence and freedom are key issues. Divorce is still a class privilege, a liberty denied to the dispossessed majority. The last item in the list, "selfishness," could be replaced by "a concern for self-interest," the unlovely character trait that liberalism condones. For Dickens,

169

the liberal discourse of character can breed strong (as regards determination) but strange offspring. The other "evils," with the exception of "trade unionism," are part and parcel of the manifold problems associated with the widespread influence of liberal utilitarianism. What the trade union "abuse" highlights is the threat to the key values of liberalism that is posed by an increasingly important source of power. All these issues have some bearing, then, on the complex problem of the dangers to and the limits of liberalism.

Secondly, Fowler asserts that Dickens' "proposed palliatives are feeble, misconceived in terms of purely individual initiatives and responsibilities and sentimentally formulated" (106). Fowler is not alone in denigrating Dickens' "remedies," and other critics have found the other "solutions" that their readings provide equally untenable. For Gallagher, *Hard Times* seems to suggest that the ideal family is a model for a deeply fractured society. But the novel itself then reveals doubts about this project and ultimately "the job of reforming society falls on Sissy's slight shoulders."[2] According to Raymond Williams, *Hard Times* withdraws into personal feeling, exalting a childish innocence that "shames the adult world, but also essentially rejects it" (109). A better understanding of Dickens' enterprise may be gained, however, if, eschewing the widespread preoccupation with "solutions" and "reforms", we conceive of his novel as revealing the need for a variety of essential "goods" that pertain to both private and public spheres. If in *Hard Times* Dickens identifies certain distinctive strands of modern liberal theory and practice, it is to gauge their impact on personal well-being broadly conceived. If two of the novel's many concerns are: what contributes to human flourishing? and, has all that could be done to promote it been done? then Dickens' answer is not simply that what is largely missing from people's lives and hence required is amusement and/or affection, the "palliatives" to which Fowler refers. In this reading the range of Dickens' "positives" is seen as far wider in scope, encompassing both life goods and a fundamental good, a constitutive good, an innate quality or disposition that makes for virtue or excellence.

In Dickens' view, virtue is a fundamental element in, though only partially constitutive of, well-being. But yet again among modern critics the forms his conception of moral excellence takes have also found little favor. Barbara Hardy's assessment that Dickens' picture of "domestic proficiency and concentrated virtue has happily dated" may be taken as representing what many readers feel (10). As an ideal, the Angel of the House is, unsurprisingly, unpopular, and perhaps this accounts for a failure to examine in any detail Dickens' articulation of moral personality, of the moral economy of the psyche. But are either angels or self-sacrificing saints really to the point? Arguably the question that interests Dickens is not What makes for saintliness? but What are the ingredients that together ensure effective moral agency? Typically, Dickens' moral exemplar or model is described simply as a noble

innocent whose happiness consists in spreading joy around her and in satisfying the needs of others.[3] Of the various aspects of moral character that
might engage the attention of the moral analyst (motives, perception, judgment, attitudes, emotions, commitments, ideals, inclination, self-conception),
it appears that for Dickens the salient features are impulse, instinct, and
inclination. I shall try to show that Dickens' picture of the psychological
make-up of moral excellence is more complex; that by adopting the technique
of repetition with variation, involving different combinations of key psychic
elements, Dickens constructs a neat typology of moral character, and points
up the right relationship between the different human capacities that are essential both to moral agency and to a "thick" or robust identity. Pre-eminent
among moral components are the capacities for accurate perception and emo-
tive attachment or commitment, and these are foregrounded in his strategies
of representation. Each of these categories is crucially, and more or less
explicitly, related to the will. A good will is foundational, the bedrock of an
effective moral personality. Clearly, then, the strict relation prominent liberals
postulated between the impetus to further self-interest and the will was problematic. For Dickens, it was essential to re-affirm the function of the will as
a moral source, an empowering force for the good; a force which is manifest
in the quality and fitness of the moral response to others.

This reading will reject views of Dickens as proposing or endorsing spiritual
exaltation, over-ambitious altruism, benign paternalism, or the self-defeating
resort to privatism or self-sacrifice. Dickens' novel is the expression of a
troubled liberal: a liberal whose misgivings embrace on the one hand disregard
for basic liberal standards, principles and goods in social life, and on the
other, the pretensions, complacency, narrowness, obtuseness, the limited
moral vocabulary and vision of hegemonic liberal capitalists and theorists.
Dickens' polemic attests to his belief that "liberals and liberalism are forever
in need of ideas and images that protect and invigorate, disturb, disrupt and re-
fashion their thinking and its arrangements and practices" (Flathman, *Willing
Liberalism* 15).

"Mankind is clueless about how to live, what to do."[4] The idea that liberal
theory provides no solutions to the key questions: what is the purpose of life
or what are the ends of life? what are the goods that we should be seeking
and that constitute a good life, a life of well-being? finds expression in the
novel in the predicament of Louisa Gradgrind. Asked by her father whether
she will accept the marriage proposal of the blustering bully Bounderby,
Louisa voices for the first, but not the last, time one of the novel's major
preoccupations: "what does it matter?"[5] Her statement/question articulates
the modern sense of inner emptiness, of weariness, the idea that nothing is
worth doing. Gradgrind's response is typical of the man: though not totally
uncaring, he looks to his theory to provide an answer. His theory favors

radical detachment, viewing life and life's decisions from a purely universal or abstract point of view; and he is either unable or unwilling to suggest a course of action involving the "aspirations and affections" (136) that might offer some prospect of personal fulfilment. In Gradgrind's version of utilitarianism, Reason—here conceptualized as mental clarity and austere disengagement or detachment—has attained the status of an end in itself. It has become a hypergood. But commitment to a hypergood is, as Dickens realised, highly problematic in that it usually determines the whole direction of one's moral orientation; encouraging an exclusivity of moral vision, it limits the focus of action.

Life goods should be abundant and diverse.[6] What the citizens of Coketown lack are various life goods that can satisfy basic human needs and confer dignity and self-respect. Certain of these goods belong to the social or political sphere, where principles regulate the relations that connect people from different walks of life, people possessing unequal shares of power like Bounderby and Blackpool. Dickens underscores dramatically the need for values which with hindsight we have come to view as central to the theories of liberalism as it was evolving in this period. Toleration or forebearance, open-mindedness, freedom of speech, and mutual respect, the goods which protect the dignity of the individual, promote understanding among people and preserve social harmony and order, are in short supply in the world of *Hard Times*. The governing classes, represented by Gradgrind and Bounderby, have erred in so far as they have failed to live up to traditional liberal ideals.

Dickens shares doubts about prevailing social codes and practices with Elizabeth Gaskell. But the issues and ideals Dickens delineates in *Hard Times* differ in significant respects from those of *North and South*, which was written at the same time. In Gaskell's portrayal of the developing relationship between her male and female protagonists, John Thornton and Margaret Hale, the ideals of classical liberalism are pitted against a revised form of paternalism, though Gaskell's own overarching discourse points the way past both ideologies towards a revised liberalism that has much in common with the new liberalism that J. S. Mill was formulating in this period (Wainwright 149–65). *Hard Times*, on the other hand, dramatizes the power, the influence, the need for, and the limits of, a wide range of liberal notions, while it is also envisions the practice of "community" values and virtues and explores some of the implications of certain "communitarian" forms of life.

It is the firm conviction of modern communitarian thinkers, like Alasdair MacIntyre, that the community model provides its members not only with essential life goods (security, solidarity, fraternity) but also, and significantly, with a robust sense of personal identity, with a "thick" self firmly rooted in his or her environment and capable of affection and empathy. By cooperating in community projects and sharing community ideals and practices, alienation, loneliness, and anxiety—the psychological distemper to which the liberal is prone—is kept at bay. The self flourishes when nourished on a diet of intimacy and care, when it finds purpose and direction in commitments to the well-being and aims of community members. But for liberal theorists like Stephen Holmes this cosy picture of community life is unreal, implausible. It fails to fill in the shadows, the dark side of solidarity. So where communitarians stress the therapeutic gains of communal life, liberals translate "embeddedness" into restriction and restraint and find that the liberal goals of personal freedom and individuality are ditched in the cause of belonging.[7] As the critics Gallagher and Bodenheimer both point out, the model of the cohesive family, whether extended or compact, constitutes for Dickens a locus of much that is worthwhile and admirable in social life (Gallagher, 160–61; Bodenheimer 199–202). Yet it is equally the case that the novel insists on the difficulties involved in "belonging." As a social idea the circus stands for communal practices set in contrast with the aggressively libertarian drives of all those characters for whom the family counts for little or nothing (Bitzer, Bounderby, and Tom Gradgrind). Potent images of the collective action of the circus folk (as a tower of strength, demonstrating mutual interdependence, as a welcoming refuge for the abandoned Sissy, as a repository of stories of developing family life) imply that this kind of family-community provides an intimate moral dimension where nuturing and sustaining is an habitual practice, where certain virtues, such as loyalty, trust, and love, endure and abound. These are the virtues, the moral imperatives, that Sissy has learnt in the circus and finds impossible to unlearn later in Gradgrind's world. But it is Sissy herself who relates to Louisa a story—of her early life with her father—that is, at one and the same time, an account of loyalty and attachment and love, and of what happens when one ceases to "fit into" the group.

Moreover, just as Sissy's father's sense of failure and shame, compels him to leave his community, so does Stephen Blackpool's open dissent mean that he is expelled from the working-class community of Coketown. Stephen's experiences highlight the costs of solidarity when unity is obtained through conformist bigotry. "Private feelings must yield to the common cause" (175), maintains the obnoxious Slackbridge. And among the workers of Coketown, the shared goals and values of the community and the association to which they belong require "severe conditioning and control"[8]; eccentricity of behavior or thought, differences of outlook, are not tolerated. It is this insight that distinguishes Dickens, the journalist, who actually went to the north of England to investigate the mechanisms of working-class solidarity, and who reported on the peace and concord he found there, from Dickens, the theorist, who wrote *Hard Times* (553–59). The trade union scenario in the novel is the representation of Dickens' liberal fear of the use of the concentrated power of associations to incubate fanaticism and promote "insiduous and individuality-diminishing influence'' (Flathman, *Willing Liberalism* 8). At the trade union meeting Stephen experiences at one and the same time the force of community pressure and the loss of a fundamental liberal good. Indeed, twice Stephen is effectively deprived of the right to freedom of speech by those with the power to curb his prospects of earning a livelihood, the trade union leader and the factory owner. In analogous scenes, Slackbridge and Bounderby both invite Stephen to speak out, though Slackbridge only grudgingly after demands from the workers. But when Stephen refuses to endorse their views, their vindictive reactions—they are able to punish him, the trade union leader significantly ''silencing'' him—make a mockery of the idea of freedom of expression or discussion. Furthermore, just as Bounderby has the power to say whatever he likes, however outrageous, with impunity, so can he, to all effects and purposes, dissolve his marriage bonds when he pleases. Stephen, on the contrary, is denied any prospect of gaining the freedom to remarry and hence to create a family of affect.

The long suffering Stephen challenges Louisa's special status as the character whose condition of deprivation is most disabling. Desolate and despondent, both appear for the first time voicing similar desires, desires ''to see'' that are effectively needs: ''Wanted to *see* what it [the circus] was like,'' (57) Louisa tells her father. ''Yet, I don't *see* Rachel, still'' (103), says Stephen (emphasis added). Let us turn then to questions relating to the nature and function of perception and of a closely connected moral category, the will.

## II

In *Hard Times* modes of perception generate theme and design. Out of the act of seeing, or desiring, or failing, or refusing, to see, a network of connotations develops, structuring the novel at the levels of plot and theme, connecting, often by means of the trope of *peripeteia,* or ironic reversal, scenes represented sequentially.[9] We may consider briefly some of the implications of a few notable examples. At the very beginning of the novel, Gradgrind forcibly prevents Tom and Louisa from watching the circus, judging the whole set-up a dangerous distraction, only in ''Whelp-hunting'' to be compelled to see Tom dressed up in circus garb; now a tragi-comic figure, his son acts a farcical role in a farcical ending to a ridiculous system. Tom's disguise is meant to help him avoid capture for the crime he has committed. In the planning of this crime, Tom Gradgrind sets Stephen to watch the bank and so attract suspicion. But, while in the same building, Tom is being closely watched himself by Bitzer. In both cases the same self-interested motives prompt the ''watchful'' activities. Then there is Mrs. Sparsit who sees in her imagination a ''mighty staircase'' down which Louisa Gradgrind moves inexorably towards disgrace and shame. Mrs. Sparsit "kept unwinking watch and ward over" Louisa. She follows Louisa when she takes flight from her husband's house only to lose sight of her at the crucial moment Louisa turns in the direction of her father's house. Despite not having seen which way Louisa went, such is Sparsit's faith in her knowledge of Louisa (paralleling Bounderby's presumed knowledge of his workers) that she recounts the wrong story to Bounderby. The moment marks the beginning of her own fall "from her pinnacle of exultation into the Slough of Despond" (281). Rather than making an attempt to understand the "real" Louisa, Sparsit lets her uncontrolled and unsympathetic imagination provide her with one insight too many. Thematically, perception functions therefore in ways that are crucial to Dickens' conception of moral personhood. In such a compressed or schematic work the activity of the eyes is rarely merely descriptive, but expresses instead a precise attitude, a state of responsiveness that is more often than not ethical in its implications. The eyes, always important in a Dickensian physiognomy—one thinks for example of the oft' remarked "pityful and plaintive look" of Amy Dorrit (bk. 1, ch. 7) or the "glaring" and "staring" that characterizes the revolutionaries in *A Tale of Two Cities*—are especially telling here. In *Hard Times* the body language that talks loudest is that of the eyes, and the messages they send are indicative of moral stature or sensibility. Characters are differentiated and defined by their varying capacities for the discernment or understanding that in moral situations may be achieved through "a just and loving gaze," an "act of attention" that is undistorted by prejudice or malice.[10] They watch, gaze, strain their eyes, have trusting eyes, or hawk's eyes or dark eyes of the mind; or the mind itself is capable of looking over and beyond [the tempter's distracting smile]; they look carelessly out, keep a sharp look out, use cunning scrutiny, steal looks remarkable for their intense and searching character, glance anxiously, look to, desire to look on, possess marvellous acuteness of countenance, stare, glimpse, peep or envision; and all the manifold modes of perception involved are certain short cuts to a reading of the inner self, a key element in the expression of desire, attitude, moral responsiveness.

Exemplary in this respect are the ways in which Sissy Jupe is perceived by the Gradgrinds. Early on in the novel at Louisa's request Sissy begins to relate the story of her life with her father. Tom, who enters the room stares at them both but then does not care enough about Sissy even to look at her again. He is totally unmoved by her story, viewing others instrumentally as means for achieving his own ends, and Sissy, it seems, is useless to him. But both Louisa and Bounderby have their uses, and his repeated demand that Louisa "look sharp for Bounderby" (101), is at one and the same time a command that Louisa disregard Sissy and hurry to find Bounderby.

Gradgrind is certainly not manipulative in this way, but, as in his dealings with his daughter, he fails to pay sufficient attention to the person before him.

Worshipping the hypergood Reason, Gradgrind has installed in the place of "gods as great as itself" "a grim idol, cruel and cold, with its victims bound hand to foot, and its big dumb shape set up with *a sightless stare,* never to be moved by anything but so many calculated tons of leverage" (233, italics added). Averting his gaze at crucial moments, Gradgrind misses the signs related by the eyes.

Louisa, however, closely regards Sissy as she tells her story, evidently trying to understand what her life was like; she comes to feel compassion for Sissy; and then significantly, moves towards her: "Louisa saw that she was sobbing; and going to her, kissed her; took her hand, and sat down beside her" (100). Her attentiveness followed by her caring response—given emphasis in the text by the mention of several separate and yet linked actions—parallels Sissy's own watchful attention and opening towards Louisa at the moment of her greatest need. "Accurate moral perception is a good in its own right, but like other goods it is so only ceteris paribus," writes Lawrence Blum.[11] And his observation takes us precisely to that aspect of Dickens' narrative that merits greater attention: the modes he adopts to articulate his ideas about the relation of perception to other psychic capacities that pertain to moral personhood. Louisa "would have been self-willed . . . but for her bringing up" (57), her father thinks with satisfaction. She has lost her willfulness, but the vital power of her will ("the animating source," "essential to spirited, challenging and hence engaging" human life) has not been impaired (Flathman, *Willing Liberalism* 11). Appropriate moral responsiveness is, the novel implies, a function of necessary connections being made between good perceptions, the capacity to care, and a good will.

But before focussing closely on the ways in which Dickens' narrative strategies engender ideas and elaborate his argument on this subject, I should like to consider a few influential and contrasting points of view relating to the controversy surrounding the significance of the will at the time Dickens was writing his novel.

## III

Edward Tagart, the officiating minister at the Unitarian chapel in Little Portland St., which Dickens attended regularly, had become by the 1850s a close friend (Dickens, *Letters* 3:449). During the period when Dickens was preparing *Hard Times,* Tagart, a scholar of repute, was at work on a defence of John Locke against those who accused him of propagating atheistic views. Earlier, in 1843—the year Dickens sent note of his "earnest and grateful feelings for your eloquent and charming discourse of last Sunday"—Tagart had published an introduction to a reprint of the renowned sermon the neo-platonist Ralph Cudworth had preached in 1647 before the House of Commons. In both works passages are devoted to the disposition of the will.

"There is nothing in the whole world able to do us good or hurt but God and our own will, neither riches nor poverty, nor disgrace nor honour, nor life nor death, nor angels nor devils; but willing or not willing, as we ought to do."[12] "As we ought to do"; the terminus to Cudworth's statement on the significance of the will and its unique role in promoting the good, is crucial. How ought we to will? or what ought the will to be like? Cudworth feared and condemned "the blind, dark, impetuous Self will" (102). He, like the other neo-platonists, held that only those Christians who had power over their own wills, who, moving the mover, could direct this energy to virtuous ends (and above all to complying with God's will or commandments), could live happily and be said to be free.[13] In *Hard Times,* as we shall see, a similar antithesis or contrast between an "anarchic" will obedient above all to impulse or inclination, and a will that is vital but in crucial respects subject to control and restraint, informs and shapes characterization at a fundamental level.

In proposing the work of Ralph Cudworth to his Victorian readers and listeners, Tagart reaffirmed the salience of the power of the good will in moral life, thus disputing the influential Augustinian belief in the fundamentally corrupt nature of the human will. But by so doing Tagart not only offered an argument against Saint Augustine, he also engaged in discussion with John Stuart Mill. In the same year in which Cudworth's sermon was re-published by the Unitarian association (which attracted many prominent liberals to its meetings), John Stuart Mill argued in his *System of Logic* that "Volitions are not known to produce anything directly except nervous energy" (362). Mill's attempt "to reduce the will to the level of physical sciences" clearly angered Tagart greatly; and in his book on Locke he engaged in indirect combat, reasserting his belief in the primacy of the will in personal and social life: "Be it what it may, be it the direct product of volition, still the indirect or ultimate products are far more important; nay, the only products of any importance; nervous action being a very insignificant and subordinate part of the phenomena dependent for existence upon the human will. . . . The pleasures and pains, the happiness or misery of inappreciable multitudes for long periods of time have been and may continue to be affected by the states of an individual will, commingled with other assisting conditions. All the interests of our intellectual, moral and social being are wrapped up, so to speak, in its character and agency" (139).

But arguably, far more damaging to the moral status of the will as well as pernicious to attempts at self-understanding, were the widely diffused convictions of the great liberal's father, James Mill. In Cudworth's sermon the "Self will" inspires loathing. In James Mill's matter-of-fact analysis this is clearly not the case. When disciplined and directed, the "Self will" has a valuable role to play. Prompting enterprise, it is the necessary spur to self-improvement of a social and economic nature, and hence the moving force behind national prosperity. "It is indisputable," claimed James Mill, "that the acts of men follow their will, that their will follows their desires; that their desires are generated by their apprehension of good and evil; in other words by their interests."[14]

Liberalism has taught us that both political economy and justice require that every man has a right to pursue his own self-interest within certain well-defined bounds. The modern liberal apologist Richard E. Flathman argues that: "developing, pursuing, and satisfying interests and desires are positive goods, are characteristics that deserve to be valued, protected, and promoted. They are made central to conceptions of individuality, of equality, and of freedom and hence are fundamental to a society suitable to human beings as liberals had come to conceive of them. We are not to apologize for our "desirousness" and "interestedness"; we are to insist upon them."[15] And insist upon them is precisely what Bitzer does. In "Philosophical" Bitzer lays bare his motives for wishing to arrest Tom." I wish to have his situation, sir, for it will be a rise to me, and *will do me good*" (303, emphasis added). Like any good liberal where questions of justice are concerned, Bitzer acts, not in the spirit of rancor, but from a position of detachment: "You seem to think that I have some animosity against young Mr Tom; whereas I have none at all. I am only going, on the reasonable grounds I have mentioned, to take him back to Coketown". Bitzer may well be right on all counts. Nevertheless, there seems little to like in him, or little that might qualify as good. Yet Dickens has endowed him with many virtues: liberal virtues, fully versed in the laws of political economy, independent, self-disciplined, prudent, courageous, conscientious, and industrious; Bitzer is determined to get on. As a description of our ambivalence towards the archetype that Bitzer represents, Iris Murdoch's, in *The Sovereignty of Good,* can hardly be bettered: "how familiar to us [he is] . . . the offspring of the age of science, confidently rational . . . He is the ideal citizen of the liberal state, a warning held up to tyrants. He has the virtue which the age requires and demands, courage. . . . The sovereign moral concept is freedom, or possibly courage in a sense which identifies it with freedom, will, power. Act, choices, decision, responsibility, independence are emphasized in this philosophy of puritanical origin and apparent austerity. It must be said in its favour that this image of human nature has been the inspiration of political liberalism. However, as Hume once wisely observed, good political philosophy is not necessarily good moral philosophy" (80). *Hard Times* is the expression of Dickens' agreement with Hume.

Bitzer does not just live by liberal tenets; he is the abstract individual at the very center of the classic theory of individualism. Demanding his rights and respect for contracts (the "bargain" made for his schooling) detached in outlook and pursuing his solitary quest for independence, advancement, and profit, Bitzer stands for all that liberalism's critics hold to be most deleterious. In the view of MacIntyre, Sandel, et al., the self for whom these are the values that count can only be thin, insubstantial, volatile.[16] *Hard Times* anticipates their accusation: Bitzer is "colourless" and "transparent," Bounderby, "blustery," a lot of hot air, while Harthouse "drifts." With the drifting Harthouse we return firmly to the subject of the will; for within the novel's comprehensive moral discourse Harthouse's is the personality that is vitiated by a wanton will.

## IV

In his admirable introduction to *Little Dorrit*, the novel composed immediately after *Hard Times*, Lionel Trilling observed that in that novel: "The whole energy of the imagination . . . is directed to finding the non-personal will in which shall be our peace" (xv). More recently, Harold Bloom has commented on the centrality of the will throughout Dickens' fiction, but has expressed doubts about Dickens' belief that there can be different kinds of will. "The aesthetic secret of Dickens appears to be that his villains, heroes, heroines, victims, eccentrics, ornamental beings, do differ from one another in the kinds of will that they possess. Since that is hardly possible for us, as humans, it does bring about an absence of reality in and for Dickens." It is Bloom's opinion that Dickens refuses "to offer us any accurately mimetic representations of the human will" (4). On Dickens' view, what is undeniably real is the immanent sustaining power of a good will. But "purposive" self-wills and wanton wills are also characterized and encapsulated in the dynamics of his narrative, albeit in a somewhat rudimentary manner. And it looks promising for Dickens' theory that a close fit can be traced between his narrative account of the operations of the will and the acute and rigorous analyses of the will developed recently by philosopher Harry H. Frankfurt. For both Dickens and Frankfurt "the character of a person's will constitutes what he most centrally is . . . the boundaries of his will define his shape as a person ("On the Necessity" 24).

To begin at the beginning, Frankfurt observes, in *The Importance of What We Care About*, that "Reason has usually been regarded as the most distinctive feature of human nature and the most sharply definitive." And of course the (problematic) Gradgrindian educational project is based on this Enlightenment intuition. "I believe, however," continues Frankfurt, "that volition pertains more closely than reason to our experiences of ourselves and to the problems in our lives that concern us with the greatest urgency'' (viii). In Frankfurt's lucid exposition of his own belief, we have the underlying premise upon which Dickens' typology of character is constructed. As an illustration of Frankfurt's conception of a "rational wanton," Harthouse, the languid aristocrat from beyond Coketown, is exemplary. "What distinguishes the rational wanton from other rational agents," observes Frankfurt, "is that he is not concerned with the desirability of his desires themselves. He ignores the question of what his will is to be" (17). Pursuing whatever course of action he is most strongly inclined to pursue, Harthouse clearly "does not care which of his inclinations is strongest." Harthouse the libertine is free. He is free from all ties, free to come and go as he pleases, free to choose his occupation, free to change his mind. But such freedom is not an unambiguous good; "since nothing is necessary to him, there is nothing that he can be said essentially to be" (25).

Where Harthouse's wanton will is simply "anarchic," moved by mere impulse and inclination, the good will, as personified in Sissy and Rachel, is at once free and constrained. Among the most important characteristics of the two women are their capacities for loving and caring; and it is a characteristic of this love that it willingly accepts the ties that are thereby created. The Neoplatonic preacher Cudworth, in the sermon to which we have already referred, described the paraxodical nature of this love with great clarity: "Love is at once a Freedome from all Law, a state of purest Liberty, and yet a Law too, of the most constraining and indispensable Necessity" (Patrides 125). In the novel, the "natural restraint" that the good will, susceptible to love, imposes on the loving contrasts with the "system of *unnatural* restraint" (165, emphasis added) that Gradgrind has forced upon his children.

Once taken into the Gradgrind household, Sissy becomes subject to the same oppressive system, the same bombardment of facts: "It hailed facts all day long so very hard, and life in general was opened to her as such a closely-ruled cyphering book, that assuredly she would have run away, *but only for one restraint*" (emphasis added, 95) The "restraint" that prevents Sissy from running away is precisely the kind of "necessity" to which Frankfurt refers in his study on the will: "About certain things that are important to him, a person may care so much, or in such a way, that he is subject to a kind of necessity. . . . To the extent that a person is constrained by volitional necessity there are certain things he cannot help willing or that he cannot bring himself to do" ("On the Necessity" 20). Sissy's desire for freedom—"her strong impulses . . . to run away"—is effectively overruled by a stronger desire which is related to what she most cares about, and that is her father. The source of the power that compels Sissy to remain with the Gradgrinds, is none other than her own will. It is "lamentable," records the narrator ironically, that "this restraint was the result of no arithmetical process, was *self-imposed* in defiance of all calculation . . . " (emphasis added, 95). Underlying Dickens' description of Sissy's predicament is the notion that her action is free in so far as it involves this decisive moment of assent or repudiation, when the power governing the will assents to or refuses to consent to the proposed impulse. This decisive moment constitutes a commitment of the true self which is rooted in her deepest desire.

Sissy stays in Coketown, as both her own good nature and the plot require, to play a saving role in the lives of the Gradgrind children. The sustaining relationship she offers Louisa at the moment of her breakdown is replicated in the story of Rachel and Stephen. But in developing his dramatic interpretation of the powers of the will in the scene where Rachel saves both Stephen and his wife, Dickens' account becomes at once more complex and enigmatic, and undoubtedly for some readers more problematic. Although as regards plot, the scene in Stephens's house is virtually irrelevant, thematically, it is centrally important, bringing together in a unity of interconnection Dickens' ideas on the moral efficacy of good perceptions, firm commitments and a vital will. Unlike Sissy's "just and loving gaze", however, Rachel's "act of attention"[17] belongs to a different ontological order, for Rachel is asleep at the critical moment in which Stephen's wife reaches out for the poison.

Rachel, we learn, has hurried to Stephen's house in response to a message that someone needed "looking to"; both looking at and looking after. To Stephen and the reader she articulates the nature of her motivation in coming in terms of commitment: her ready response to the call was made in the cause of a friendship formed long before. Urging Stephen to sleep, she tells him she will "watch" over his wife. Rachel's capacity to care and moral competence is contrasted at every turn with Stephen's moral helplessness, expressed repeatedly in his need to see her: "Let me see thee. . . . Let me see thee. . . . Let me see thee. . . . I can never see thee better than so . . . " (122). Stephen's fears are transformed into his monitory nightmare, in which, "subject to a nameless, horrible dread", he can neither see "one pitying or friendly eye," nor "look again" "on Rachel's face or hear her voice." Waking up he realizes that Rachel has fallen asleep and watches as his wife reaches out for the poison. But "Dream or reality, he had no voice, *nor had he power to stir*" (emphasis added). Stephen is powerless, his will to act immobilized by his conflicting feelings for his wife: "He was motionless and powerless, except to watch her" (124). But Rachel awakes and acts. Her action can only be interpreted in terms of clairvoyance; Rachel possesses insight, the profound, even mysterious, capacity for perception or knowledge which powers the will.

Dickens' delineation of moral personality highlights its vital, assertive nature, a nature which gains resolution through adherence to the Christian virtues of love, faith, and hope. Through his representation of effective moral agency, Dickens registers his distance from all those who, like J. S. Mill, found the Christian ideal "essentially a doctrine of passive obedience" (*On Liberty* 112–13). Sharing the Neoplatonic dislike of Quietism, Dickens endows his liberators with a life-enhancing energy. In his moral agents, opposing characteristics are paradoxically reconciled; innocent and mature—in the responsible giving of care and attention—spontaneous and self-disciplined, they are both free and yet obedient.

# NOTES

1. "Charles Dickens," in *The Collected Essays, Journalism and Letters of George Orwell*, vol. 1 (London: Secker & Warburg, 1968) 413–60.

    As Stephen Pulsford observes "there has never been critical consensus about Dickens' politics." Pulsford provides a good summary of the different perspectives on this issue in "The Aesthetic and the Closed Shop: The Ideology of the Aesthetic in Dickens's *Hard Times*," *Victorian Review*, 21:2 (winter, 1995): 145–60. Pulsford concludes that "the politics of *Hard Times* are ultimately not contradictory but unconstructive . . . the novel can sense the institutions that infringe its own values, but not see its way towards practical solutions" (157). The tension within Dickens' thought is the subject of Nicholas Coles's "The Politics of *Hard Times*: Dickens the Novelist versus Dickens the Reformer," *Dickens Studies Annual*. 15 (1986): 145–79.

2. According to Catherine Gallagher, *Hard Times* embodies the contradictions of the paternalist metaphor it is keen to promote. It is, in Gallagher's opinion, "frought with ambiguities." "Up to its very last page, *Hard Times* is a book that simultaneously flaunts and discredits its metaphoricality, calling into question both the possibility of paternalist reform and the validity of its own narrative practice"; *The Industrial Reformation of English Fiction: Social Discourse and Narrative Form, 1832–1867* (Chicago: Chicago UP, 1985) 155, 166.

3. Thus F. R. Leavis: "Sissy stands for vitality as well as goodness—they are seen, in fact, as one; she is generous, impulsive life, finding self-fulfilment in self-forgetfulness—all that is the antithesis of calculating self-interest . . . the life that is lived freely and richly from the deep instinctive and emotional springs [is contrasted with] the thin-blooded, quasi-mechanical product of Gradgrindery"; *The Great Tradition*, (London, 1948) reprinted in *Hard Times*, ed. George Ford and Sylvère Monod (New York: W. W. Norton, 1966, 1990) 344.

4. Stephen Holmes sums up the anti-liberal position of philosopher Alasdair MacIntyre in a way that strongly recalls the concerns of Dickens in *Hard Times*: "Vital social relations have been desiccated by arid individualism. A warm solidary and emotionally satisfying communal order, has yielded to a chilly, egoistical and morally hollow one. The social faculties of prelapsarian souls have been grieviously damaged by western rationalism. Generosity, friendship and joy have nearly

vanished. Niggardliness and misery are all-pervasive. Idyllic normative consensus has been supplanted by sickenly endless disagreement. Thick pre-industrial forms of social identity have been replaced by thinner and more universal ones. As a result *mankind is clueless how to live, what to do.* Modernity has few if any redeeming features, according to the tenets of deprivation history in this its purest form." *The Anatomy of Anti-Liberalism* (Cambridge: Harvard UP, 1993) 89–90; emphasis added.

5. All page references in the text are taken from *Hard Times for These Times*, ed. David Craig (Harmondsworth: Penguin, 1969).

6. Particularly relevant here is Charles Taylor's essay "The Diversity of Goods," in *Utilitarianism and Beyond*, ed. Amartya Sen and Bernard Williams (Cambridge: Cambridge UP, 1982) 129–44.

7. The literature on this topic is vast, among the many and important works are those by Michael Walzer "The Communitarian Critique of Liberalism," *Political Theory* 18:1 (February, 1990): 6–23; Will Kymlicka, *Liberalism, Community and Culture* (Oxford: Clarendon P, 1989); and Stephen Holmes, "The Permanent Structure of Antiliberal Thought," in *Liberalism and the Moral Life*, ed. Nancy L. Rosenblum (Cambridge: Harvard UP, 1989) 159–82.

8. Nancy L. Rosenblum points out ("Pluralism" 219) that "the idea of a self constituted by communal forces can point to severe social conditioning and control that is all the more efficient if it operates through self-discipline."

9. David Lodge observes that the use of peripeteia contributes to the "didactic, illustrative import of the story," but he does not discuss the ways in which this device allows Dickens to develop the thematic concerns of the novel; "How successful is *Hard Times?*" in *Working with Structuralism* (Boston: Routledge and Kegan Paul, 1981) reprinted in the Norton edition of *Hard Times*, ed. George Ford and Sylvère Monod, 384–85.

10. Iris Murdoch's penetrating discussion of the nature of moral agency may serve as a gloss for Dickens' concerns in this novel: "As moral agents we have to try to see justly, to overcome prejudice, to avoid temptation, to control and curb imagination [one thinks of Sparsit] to direct reflection. Man is not a combination of an impersonal rational thinker and a personal will. He is a unified being who sees, and who desires in accordance with what he sees, and who has some continual slight control over the direction and focus of his vision . . . the chief enemy of excellence in morality . . . is personal fantasy: the tissue of self-aggrandizing and consoling wishes and dreams [like those of Bounderby and Gradgrind] which prevents one from seeing what there is outside one." From *The Sovereignty of Good,* (London: Routledge, 1970) 40, 59. For Murdock "true vision occasions right conduct," though she also believes that "suppression of the self is required before accurate vision can be obtained," (66).

11. Lawrence A. Blum in *Moral Perception and Particularity* (Cambridge: Cambridge UP, 1994), 34. Blum acknowledges his "intellectual debt" to Iris Murdoch, whose views are discussed in his book.

12. Ralph Cudworth, *A Discourse Preached Before the House of Commons,* printed and sold by the Unitarian Association, 1843; all references cited are from the

version edited by C. A. Patrides in *The Cambridge Platonists*, (London: Edward Arnold, 1969) 90–127.

13. Cudworth's fellow Neoplatonist John Smith maintained in "The Excellency and Nobleness of True Religion" (in Patrides 162) that "The Second *Property or Effect of Religion,* whereby it discovers its own *Nobleness . . . is this, That it restores a Good man to a just power and dominion over himself and his own Will, enables him to overcome himself, his own Self-will and Passions, and to command himself & all his Powers for God. . . .* There is nothing in the World so boisterous as a man's own *Self-will,* which is never guided by any fixt or steddy Rules, but is perpetually hurried to and fro by a blind and furious impetus of *Pride and Passions* issuing from within it self."

14. *Essay on Government,* (1828) cited by Steven Lukes in *Individualism* (Oxford: Basil Blackwell, 1973) 82–83.

15. "Liberalism and the Human Good of Freedom" in *Liberals on Liberalism* ed. A. Damico (Totowa, N.J: Rowman and Littlefield, 1986) 82–83. The point made by Amy Gutmann in "Communitarian Critics of Liberalism," *Philosophy and Public Affairs,* 14 (1985): 317, that "the real and recognized dilemma of modern liberalism . . . is not that people are naturally egoistical, but rather that they disagree about the nature of the good life," is central to Elizabeth Gaskell's conception and portrayal of attitudes and relationships in *North and South.*

16. Alasdair MacIntyre, *After Virtue,* (London: Duckworth, 1981), 216–21. Michael Sandel (in *Liberalism and the Limits of Justice,* [Cambridge: Cambridge UP, 1982] 16), berates the separateness of liberal individuals, their "openness" or "lack of a received or fixed identity".

17. Key terms in Murdoch's conception of the moral personality, *On the Sovereignty of Good* 34.

# Works Cited

Bloom, Harold. Introduction, *Modern Critical Views: Charles Dickens.* New York: Chelsea House, 1987.

Blum, Lawrence A. *Moral Perception and Particularity.* Cambridge: Cambridge UP, 1994.

Bodenheimer, Rosemary. *The Politics of Story in Victorian Social Fiction.* Ithaca: Cornell UP, 1988.

Coles, Nicholas. "The Politics of *Hard Times*: Dickens the Novelist versus Dickens the Reformer." *Dickens Studies Annual,* 15 (1986): 145–79.

Craig, David, ed., *Hard Times for These Times.* Harmondsworth: Penguin, 1969.

Cudworth, Ralph. *A Discourse Preached before the House of Commons.* Printed and sold by the Unitarian Association, 1843.

Dickens, Charles. *The Letters. The Pilgrim Edition.* Vol. 3, Ed. Madeline House, Graham Storey, & Kathleen Tillotson. Oxford: Clarendon P, 1974.

————. "On Strike." *Household Words,* 11 Feb. 1854:553–59.

Flathman, Richard E. "Liberalism and the Human Good of Freedom" in *Liberals on Liberalism* ed. A. Damico. Totowa, N.J: Rowman and Littlefield, 1986.

————. *Willing Liberalism: Voluntarism and Individuality in Political Theory and Practice.* Ithaca: Cornell UP, 1992.

Fowler, Roger. "Polyphony and Problematic in *Hard Times,*" in *The Changing World of Charles Dickens* ed. Robert Gittings. Totowa: Barnes and Noble, London: Vision Press, 1983. 91–108.

Frankfurt, Harry H. *The Importance of What We Care About.* New York: Cambridge UP, 1988.

————. "On the Necessity of Ideals," in *The Moral Self,* ed. G. Noam and T. E. Wren (Cambridge: M.I.T. Press, 1993), 16–27.

Gallagher, Catherine. *The Industrial Reformation of English Fiction: Social Discourse and Narrative Form, 1832–1867.* Chicago: Chicago UP, 1985.

Hardy, Barbara. *Charles Dickens: The Later Novels.* London: Longman, 1968.

Holmes, Stephen. *The Anatomy of Anti-Liberalism.* Cambridge: Harvard UP, 1993.

————. "The Permanent Structure of Antiliberal Thought, in *Liberalism and the Moral Life,* ed. Nancy L. Rosenblum. Cambridge: Harvard UP, 1989 159–82.

Kymlicka, Will. *Liberalism, Community and Culture.* Oxford: Clarendon Press, 1989.

Leavis, F. R. *The Great Tradition.* (London, 1948) reprinted in *Hard Times.* ed. George Ford and Sylvère Monod. New York: W. W. Norton, 1966, 1990.

Lodge David. "How Successful Is *Hard Times?*" in *Working with Structuralism* Boston: Routledge and Kegan Paul, 1981, rpt. in the Norton ed. of *Hard Times* ed. George Ford and Sylvère Monod. New York: W. W. Norton, 1966, 1990. 384–85.

MacIntyre, Alasdair. *After Virtue.* London: Duckworth, 1981.

Mill, James. *Essay on Government.* (1828).

Mill, John Stuart. *On Liberty.* Harmondsworth: Penguin Books, 1974.

————. *A System of Logic,* in *Collected Works of John Stuart Mill,* vol. 7, ed. J. M. Robson. Toronto: Toronto UP, 1973.

Murdock, Iris. *The Sovereignty of Good.* London: Routledge, 1970.

Patrides, C. A. *The Cambridge Platonists.* London: Edward Arnold, 1969.

Pulsford, Stephen. "The Aesthetic and the Closed Shop: The Ideology of the Aesthetic in Dickens's *Hard Times*," *Victorian Review* 21:2 (winter, 1995): 145–60.

Rosenblum, Nancy L. "Pluralism and Self-Defence" in *Liberalism and the Moral Life,* Cambridge: Harvard UP, 1989.

Sandel, Michael. *Liberalism and the Limits of Justice.* Cambridge: Cambridge UP, 1982.

Tagart, Edward. *Locke's Writings and Philosophy Historically Considered.* London: Longman, Brown, Green and Longmans, 1855.

Taylor, Charles. "The Diversity of Goods" in *Utilitarianism and Beyond,* ed. Amartya Sen and Bernard Williams. Cambridge: Cambridge UP, 1982. 129–44.

Trilling, Lionel. Introduction. *Little Dorrit.* Oxford: Oxford UP, 1953.

Wainwright, Valerie. "Discovering Autonomy and Authenticity in *North and South*: Elizabeth Gaskell, John Stuart Mill, and the Liberal Ethic." *Clio* 23:2 (winter, 1994): 149–65.

Walzer, Michael. "The Communitarian Critique of Liberalism." *Political Theory* 18:1 (February, 1990): 6–23.

Williams, Raymond. *Culture and Society: 1780–1950.* New York: Harper & Row, 1966.

# On History, Case History, and Deviance: Miss Wade's Symptoms and Their Interpretation

*Anna Wilson*

> you were a mystery to all of us, and had nothing in common
> with any of us when [Tattycoram] unfortunately fell in your
> way. I don't know what you are, but you don't hide, can't
> hide, what a dark spirit you have within you. If it should
> happen that you are a woman, who, from whatever cause,
> has a perverted delight in making a sister-woman as
> wretched as she is (I am old enough to have heard of such),
> I warn her against you, and I warn you against yourself.
>
> (*Little Dorrit* 379)

There is a thread in Dickens criticism which addresses the interpretation of Miss Wade, the deviant woman accused in the above passage from *Little Dorrit* of seducing Tattycoram for dark purposes; it will be part of my task to recontextualize that tradition. But given that a recent boom in lesbian and gay studies has led to the discovery of lesbians in places and at times where we used to think there could be no hope (or fear) of finding them, it is surprising that no attempt has been made by this new constituency to read Miss Wade as another heretofore unacknowledged precursor. The absence of any such identification can in part by explained by the early focus of lesbian historical studies on the exhumation of examples of self-conscious lesbian identity, essentially a search for a transhistorical, and hence validating, model of sexuality. The recent shift in criteria from identity to "same-sex erotic attraction" allows for a much more fluid and more historically-nuanced typology of desire. It is only with a further move toward an interest in how the concept of intra-female desire might operate culturally, however, that Miss Wade becomes visible as a significant player in the mid-Victorian cultural imaginary.[1]

Miss Wade has always been an anomaly, and her awkward position subject to explanation. The presence in *Little Dorrit* of her "History of a Self-Tormentor," in which she reveals her alienation and hatred, is itself narratively problematic. It provides no answers to the questions Arthur Clennam has asked, substituting her own personal revelations for the documentary secrets Clennam needs to unravel his past. The placement of this under-motivated confession gave Dickens some trouble in his construction of the novel: his outline for the original serialization is studded with the repeated note "Miss Wade? No!!" before the "History" finally emerges.[2] John Forster inaugurates a critical tradition of discomfort in suggesting excision of what he called "the least interesting part" of the novel. Dickens acknowledged it as "interpolated," but nonetheless defended Miss Wade's "History" as crucial to the whole: "the introduced story so fit[s] into surroundings impossible of separation from the main story, as to make the blood of the book circulate through both" (qtd. in Forster 626). This paradoxical narrative positioning—somehow at the heart of things, and yet both excisable and having no natural place—parallels, I shall argue here, Miss Wade's position in history. By replacing Miss Wade's "History" within an historical context from which it has hitherto been separated, I hope to show how the blood of Miss Wade might be said to circulate through the narrative of mid-Victorian culture.

The history I have in mind, that against which Miss Wade has not been read, are those contemporary discourses on governesses and on madness with which, as I shall show, Miss Wade's self-revelation complexly intersects. The historical status of any reading of Miss Wade as lesbian is much more equivocal, and yet it is all these various possibilities that I shall seek to intertwine here. The truth value of "Miss Wade as lesbian" will be questionable to some readers, not only because of the presumed absence of Victorian lesbians but also because of the invested nature of any "lesbian reading." In fact, previous readings of Miss Wade could be said to demonstrate counter-investment; they are, if anything, anti-lesbian readings: twentieth-century criticism is definite in differentiating Miss Wade from whatever "lesbian" may be taken to mean. Both Miss Wade's account of her passionate, consuming, and destructive love for her school friend Charlotte and her subsequent attempt to corrupt Tattycoram have been read as manifestations of paranoia rather than of sexual deviance. While these accounts are written in the presence of "lesbian" as a conceptual category, it is held to be important that we not fall into misinterpretation of the nature of Miss Wade's strangeness. We are variously assured that Miss Wade is no lesbian because it is people she hates, not just men, that Miss Wade is on "a masculine rampage," or that Tattycoram is a surrogate daughter and hence in no eroticized relation to her companion. What is singularly consistent is the unanimity of feeling that there is nothing right and perhaps something faintly disreputable about looking at Miss Wade through a lesbian glass.[3]

Criticism seems to be replicating, in fact, the ways in which psychology, having once produced the lesbian as a category, has proceeded to deconstruct it as a motivating mechanism of desire: thus the lesbian move in psychoanalytic discourse is always in the end something else, an imaginary retriangulation of objects and identities that turns out to be the inhabitation of masculine desire. The effect of critical accounts of Miss Wade's sickness as anything but lesbianism is two-fold, keeping both history and critics ("nothing in common with any of us" as Mr. Meagles is quick to assert) safe from lesbian taint. One might justify such denials as attempts to reproduce an historical reading, reanimating the purity available to the original nineteenth-century reader whose mind is unpolluted by sexologists' discourse on homosexuality as deviance. However, Mr. Meagles' comments on the possible sources of Miss Wade's action ("perverted delight"), and his claim to a secret knowledge that is perhaps an open secret ("I am old enough to have heard of such"), at least raise the question of female homosexuality as cultural concept for Victorian readers. Critics are, furthermore, markedly untroubled by the ahistorical nature of their own interpretations of Miss Wade, based on Freudian theory.

It is not my intention to discount psychological readings of Miss Wade, but rather to render visible the consequences of such an interpretation—the consequences, for example, of insisting upon the priority of psychotic rage over lesbian rage. The "History" seems to ask for interpretation as a psychological text, an interpretation that has laid bare Miss Wade and her paranoia, has found, as Edmund Wilson put it, "a sort of case history of a woman imprisoned in a neurosis which has condemned her to the delusion that she can never be loved" (57). One might imagine Freud submitting Miss Wade's confession to an analytic process similar to that he performed on Schreber's *Memoirs*.[4] Her symptoms have also illuminatingly been read as the shadows of others in the text, her unconscious as a key to the novel's secrets.[5] But what is elided by this familiar and persuasive angle of view is the possibility of Miss Wade as disruptive figure in another system, the unconscious of the text. Rather than simply rereading Miss Wade's symptoms in a lesbian light, I propose a symptomatic reading—of Miss Wade *as* symptom—within a larger cultural context. A symptomatic reading converts text into analysand in order to arrive at a hypothetical diagnosis of the causes of neurosis: it reads the text's necessarily deformed response to historical circumstances that surround and engender it.[6] The focus shifts from the revealing excesses of the confession to that confession as itself a disruption which has had to be explained or repressed. It is thus, of course, a psychological method, but one applied in search of a social rather than an individual narrative of development. This seems to me a potentially illuminating critical strategy for explication of Miss Wade, not least because there can be no removal of psychology from this case; paranoia will not simply disappear nor history simply appear in its place.

There are two cultural categories against which Miss Wade as fictional construct comes into play for the Victorian reader, the governess and the madwoman. That Miss Wade is a governess has not itself been much dwelt upon, but it is a defining factor of her experience in as much as it is this role which comes at mid-century to be the locus of discussion of the stability and nature of the middle class. It is through the governess that the necessary social inequity that accompanies and upholds the middle class is insistently figured. And it is the governess who, on leaving the middle class, goes mad. While for twentieth-century readers Miss Wade's paranoia is the primary explicatory mechanism through which her identity is read, for contemporaries the two conditions of being, "governess" and "insane," are causally linked.

The governess, and the difficulties of her social position, appear everywhere, in periodicals and conduct manuals as well as fiction, in the mid-nineteenth century. Although the immediate problem presented by the governess is the likelihood of her destitution, it is the flexibility of her own status and what that flexibility suggests about how the middle class is constituted and upheld that is ultimately at issue. The governess is at once the symbol of social advance (for the upwardly mobile family that employs her) and the troubling trace of the threat of social decline (in her own devalued person). Her presence is thus a material reminder of the constructed nature of the class she serves.[7]

In the context of a perceived general increase in the lunatic population (and an overall increase in the percentage of female inmates), the "fearful fact" of the destitute and deranged governess generated disproportionately intense interest and explanation, even given that the 1861 census, reinforcing earlier census findings, showed that a higher proportion of governesses than of any other female occupational group were institutionalized.[8] Pondered and reiterated in every contemporary discussion are "the dreadful stories that we all hear, every year of our lives, of old governesses, starved, worn out, blind, paralytic, insane" (*Once a Week* qtd. in Neff 159). Various causes were adduced for this cultural phenomenon. Medical opinion held that the governess's inability to satisfy natural maternal instincts predisposed her to a slide into madness. The Governesses Benevolent Institute, focusing its reforming efforts on providing annuities to the aged and destitute governess, emphasized the debilitating effect on the governess's sanity of a long-drawn out attempt to stave off an inevitable penury. The feminist journalists who took up the governesses' cause spoke of the effect on the governess's nerves of her great isolation within her employer's family, always ostracized and resented, endowed with middle-class sensibilities but never allowed to gratify them. All agreed, however, on the readiness with which, faced with whatever difficulty, the governess's grip on sanity would loosen.

Fiction, conduct books, and journalism alike represent the governess as downtrodden victim. This ubiquitous figure can be understood in part as a reaction formation to that other familiar creature, the usurping social climber. But whether or not the pathetic governess is a cloak for middle-class fears of invasion, it is overwhelmingly as victim that the governess appears in contemporary discussion.[9] While accounts of the penniless, abused governess, genteel target of neglect and exploitation, in *Household Words* or feminist newspaper campaigns seem designed to promote social reform, the fictional governess, whose narrative trajectory is always away from this incongruent description towards a return to middle-class status, seems to aim at imagining a resolution of the governess problem by means of its disappearance. Where fiction privileges the fantasy of social movement, the conduct book is a manual of stasis. The individual reworks herself into reconciliation with her social position by applying to her situation the hermeneutic of Christian duty. For example, in her *Principles of Education,* Elizabeth Sewell acknowledges the "real discomfort" of the governess's "unpleasant position"; but the governess's not inconsiderable problem, "the impossibility of being happy," is then redefined in terms of the burden of worldly suffering imposed not on governesses in particular but fallen mankind in general. Anna Jameson, a sympathetic observer, active in promoting better conditions for governesses and a spokeswoman for feminist causes, still produces only resignation as the individual's solution: "the best preparation is to look upon the occupation to which you are devoted (I was going to say *doomed*) as what it really is,—a state of endurance, dependence, daily thankless toil" (40). Jameson's account, explicitly addressed to would-be governesses, is uniformly grim: in the light of the asylum that threatens, the governess who would survive must be desensitized by a painful adjustment in her expectations of life.[10]

Both these and other writers routinely invoke madness as the end which their warnings and advice are designed to avert. And while unhappiness may be simply an unavoidable occupational condition, it is resentment—the unresolved desire to return to your former position—which will send you mad. The threat of madness thus operates as a form of social control in conduct book discourse, persuading young women of the necessity of abandoning a status into which they were born. The conduct book presents the status quo as a monolith against which the individual cannot sanely struggle, while popular fiction produces an equally monolithic structure of social and individual possibility into which the displaced governess can reenact her return.

Dickens' portrayal of Miss Wade evidently departs from the downtrodden victim convention.[11] Equally clearly, Miss Wade has failed to heed the advice of those who counsel acceptance of one's lot lest insanity ensue. Although Miss Wade is not (quite) destitute she may indeed be mad: is she, then, in contemporary terms, a warning of what might befall those who do not take up their allotted burden? Or does Miss Wade speak, as if she were Jane Eyre and Bertha Mason both, of social injustice? Reading symptomatically, all these seem plausible as conversations created with other representations, interventions operating simultaneously at different levels of textual consciousness. But how does Miss Wade as mad governess play in the novel itself?

In *Little Dorrit* the explanatory category "unhappy temper" can readily be seen as a mechanism whereby social inequity and protest at that inequity are alike rewritten as individual psychological failure. Yet social discomfort is not simply redefined as individual difficulty. The parallel accusations of unhappy temper made of Tattycoram and Miss Wade by their employers, and of Arthur Clennam by his mother, establish a social network, material circumstances which produce a general oppression and which motivate the victims' resentment and suspicion. At the same time, some unhappinesses of temper are more justified within the narrative than others. Clennam's paranoid conviction of the existence of family secrets is confirmed within the text itself: he is thus perspicacious rather than mad. The novel's treatment of Tattycoram suggests that the individual is appropriately unhappy in the face of institutional pressure, when crushed in the uncomfortable spaces where classes intersect.

Miss Wade and her "History" in fact operate as the structure in distinction from which Tattycoram must define herself if she is to solidify her new status. Leaving Miss Wade, Tattycoram must produce a counter-History, her own confession, in order to gain admittance to the family:

> "Oh! I have been so wretched," cried Tattycoram, weeping much more, "always so unhappy, and so repentant!.... I have had Miss Wade before me all this time,... finding no pleasure in anything but keeping me as miserable, suspicious, and tormenting as herself... " (880.)

Tattycoram's version of the history of self-torment departs radically from Miss Wade's; her reentry into the social is signalled by this crucial identification of resentment as sickness rather than protest. She need make no other statement of wholesome integration. She need only signal her awareness of the personal consequences of rebellion: to fail to internalize one's allotted place in the social structure is to condemn oneself to torment, and it is this recognition that enables Tattycoram's return.

Her recantation also encourages us to read Miss Wade's unhappy temper as a sign of internal corrosion rather than social injustice. Tattycoram represents herself as having been goaded into class consciousness:

> It was a madness in me, and she could raise it whenever she liked. I used to think, when I got into that state, that people were all against me because of my first beginning; (880)

In Tattycoram's final self-analysis it is madness that produces awareness of class inequity; and then again it is this knowledge that leads to madness. Miss

Wade, in an interesting shift of agency, becomes not the victim of insanity but its propagator; she stands between the individual and her goal of social adjustment.

Another way of understanding Tattycoram and Miss Wade is as lunatics under treatment. Tattycoram's reeducation at the Meagles'—the self-imposed counting, the lectures, the analysis of her troubles as stemming from her mother's passion—closely resembles the moral treatment regimens of the Victorian asylum. Like the rehabilitated inmate, Tattycoram learns to inhibit herself and hence is released into social acceptability.[12]

The structure of the novel seems, then, to do two things—to delegitimize Miss Wade's "History" as authentic narrative of social injustice, rendering it legible rather as madness self-inscribed, and to set Tattycoram up in contrast to Miss Wade as the model of successful negotiation of social difficulty. The narrative pathologizes Miss Wade, a process that subsequent critical readings only repeat and intensity. In as much as Miss Wade becomes an ideological construct for Tattycoram's instruction, her capacity to illuminate and reflect the historical situation of the governess is extinguished: Miss Wade moves outside history.

Would a lesbian reading of Miss Wade do the same thing, again keeping Miss Wade away from history? How might Miss Wade's "History" read, were the possibility of a lesbian position given conceptual room? The patterns of her story (love for another of the same sex; rejection by the beloved; ostracism from the community) follow the stages of the early lesbian coming-out narrative: one can read Miss Wade's confession as a precursor of a lesbian genre. The will to self-damnation which the urge to confess projects might be an anticipation of Radclyffe Hall's influential fictionalization of Krafft-Ebing's doomed invert in *The Well of Loneliness*. Miss Wade's self-hatred, the corrosive abuse of power turned upon the innocent love-object, are familiar aspects of 1950s pulp fiction. Read through the coming-out story as it developed in the 1970s, a form producing a narrative trajectory through self-realization in oppression to liberation, Miss Wade's confession begins to look like a self-consciously resistant text. It looks, in any event, at least like Foucault's reverse discourse, that move whereby newly-identified deviants reclaim the terms of their description as the basis for a discovered sense of community. My point is not that Miss Wade's "History" "is" any of these things, but rather that there are interpretative possibilities that have been foreclosed not by the absence of awareness of lesbian ways of reading but by a reluctance to read that way. One can imagine that the history of lesbian identity, and of lesbian narrative, would look different, were it to include Miss Wade. But can this reimagined literary tradition have any impact on Miss Wade and her historical context?

The Victorian reader, for whom the category "lesbian" and the concept of same sex love as pathology were alike unknown, would not of course have either produced or avoided a lesbian reading as such. Although it is possible to line up the ''History'' with confessions produced in response to the new discourses of homosexual deviance, *Little Dorrit* predates the science of sexology; if there is a buried narrative of desire, it is not one written within the conceptualizations provided by Havelock Ellis or Krafft-Ebing.[13] But it seems clear that, despite the lack of a specifically lesbian context, both Miss Wade's attachment to her young friend Charlotte and her influence over Tattycoram are relations of suspicion in *Little Dorrit* and perhaps also, one could therefore assume, for the contemporary reader outside the text. It is possible that some discomfort, although we cannot yet specify its nature, reigns in Victorian as in modern readers, faced with Miss Wade's pursuit of young women.

Relations between women are certainly matter for comment and investigation. Fictional representations of female friendship often depict it positively, as a necessary socializing precursor to marriage. Friendship is the relation in which women learn to feel, and where they acquire the feminine traits that will equip them for heterosocial relations. It is in the company of women that girls learn to be feminine. Yet this necessary cultivation of a proper feminine emotionalism is not without its complications; other sources suggest that friendship could also dangerously become an end in itself.[14] Sewell's conduct book begins from the position of addressing a universally-recognized problem: ''Who has not known . . . the evils of an exaggerated or unwise friendship?'' (131). Her account of friendships apparently places them firmly in the sphere of the natural and inevitable: mothers must accept their daughters' shift of loyalty to an older female mentor as a part of the maturation process. Nonetheless, the emotional connection between women who are not mothers and daughters but who reoccupy those positions is both natural and not natural:

> When romantic friendship puts itself forward as having a claim above those ties which God has formed by nature, it becomes the source of untold misery to all who are connected with it.
> And this is, of course, its tendency. Overpowering feeling of any kind naturally claims to be its own law, in opposition to the definite laws of God . . . and persons will neglect the plainest, most paramount duties of their homes, for the sake of some self-chosen friend, because the feeling on both sides is so strong.
> (140)

While granting the naturalness of attachment between women, Sewell thus reasserts a distinction between nature as sanctified by God and an oppositional form: emotion used not to hold together the domestic, but rather to disrupt it. Martha Vicinus suggests in *Independent Women* that while friendships were sanctioned and encouraged between schoolgirls as a means to their internalizing self-control, in adult women special friendship was seen as more threatening: women able to chose the alternative of romantic friendship would be empowered to escape the duty (and the sanction) of marriage. Such relationships threaten to create alternative affective structures and alternative economic units.

It is noticeable that in *Little Dorrit* Miss Wade's attempt to attach Tattycoram, having been unable to submit herself to marriage, is not tolerantly looked upon. There seems to be no hint of acceptance in the narrative for the need, which Miss Wade expresses, for a companion "who knew what she knew" (734). Sewell's warning that "romantic and overweening friendships between governesses and pupils are often found to be objectionable . . . [and] to be guarded against carefully," is suggestive, perhaps, although neither Charlotte nor Tattycoram is actually Miss Wade's pupil. Their relation, rather, is disturbing because it cannot quite be explained in terms of either such anticipated excesses or the middle-class daughter's maturational choice of a mother-substitute. Mr. Meagles responds to the possibility of same-sex bonding with horror. In his confrontation with Miss Wade over Tattycoram, Miss Wade's influence is represented as that of a basilisk whose baleful drawing eye consumes what it fixes, "as if she took possession of her for evermore" (379). Is it the devouring power of female sexuality, strongly evoked by this grotesque image, which motivates Mr. Meagles's acute anxiety, faced with the proposed partnership of Miss Wade and Tattycoram? He says:

> My child, whatever you may think, that lady's influence over you—astonishing to us, and I should hardly go too far in saying terrible to us to see—is founded in passion fiercer than yours, and temper more violent than yours. What can you two be together? What can come of it? (378)

What can come of it? It is tempting, for the feminist reader, to ascribe Mr. Meagles's fear to the prospect of female bonding, and to an apocalyptic vision of networks of connection between women which will subvert the family, microcosm and building block of industrial capitalism. This is the aspect of cultural anxiety for which both Sewell and Vicinus prepare us. Taken thus far, a modern lesbian reading of Miss Wade, and contemporary constructions of romantic friendship, in fact suggest a similar interpretation of Miss Wade's relations, first with Charlotte and subsequently with Tattycoram, both producing a resistance that takes the form of the diversion of women's affection and loyalty from husband to friend. While Sewell writes of unsanctified emotions, and contemporary lesbian discourse of women who desire women, Miss Wade figures in both as that aberrant desire which needs to be repressed and, as the novel's anathema, as the means to that repression.

But there is an additional element at back of Mr. Meagles's anxiety which also needs to be addressed. Miss Wade's "History" tells us that her attempt to engage Charlotte's loyalties away from a familial "crowd of cousins and acquaintances'' (726) is thwarted by a vigilant aunt. The case of Tattycoram is different, for Tattycoram has no family to which she is loyal. Miss Wade explains her power as coming from that mutual lack: "the foundation of my influence here [is] . . . founded in a common cause. What your broken plaything is as to birth, I am. She has no name. I have no name. Her wrong is my wrong" (379). Miss Wade's language here is the rhetoric of group identification. A common condition of origin unites Tattycoram and Miss Wade, and it unites them in a "common cause," a phrase that covers the idea of a shared (political) aim as well as a shared source. What threatens and appalls Mr. Meagles, the organ of control through benevolence, is not, then, merely the prospect that what Miss Wade and Tattycoram might "be together" is some species of alternative marriage. Their bond, as Miss Wade defines it, is not that of two individuals escaping from the limits of the family, but rather that between two members of a class.

In the vacuum created by the absence of family, class loyalties emerge to fill the void. Mr. Meagles's position as architect of social control thus becomes clear. Vigilantly keeping the peace, he is flexible enough to permit a selective program of absorption into the middle class on the part of the appropriately socialized individual. It is better, his aversive reaction to the conjunction of Miss Wade and Tattycoram implies, to allow individual upward mobility than to countenance a joining of forces. Mr. Meagles intervenes to break up the pairing of Tattycoram and Miss Wade because a nascent structure of liberation must be contained, one that can thus be understood as involving connections between both embodied (sexualized) individuals and disembodied (theoretical) social units.

Dickens' account of free-floating female radicals has little confidence in the power of regulation provided by middle-class hegemony and the self-discipline it promotes. The novel is flexibly aware of social possibility, and precisely because of this awareness, actively interventionist. Potentially disruptive subversives can most successfully be contained by the psychologized reading which the novel promotes.

Opening up the lesbian reading possibilities of Miss Wade enables an enhanced conception of how and what Miss Wade resists, linking her "History" to other threats to class and gender stability. Miss Wade's passion is not in any simple way a precursive lesbian sensibility, or her confession a coming-out story. Yet reading her thus produces both a forward impact—that imaginary lesbian tradition which will look different—and a backward one. Despite the pleasures of a lesbian appropriation of history, however—creating perverts where none had been before—this is not quite the gesture I had in mind. For the process of "outing" Miss Wade, while politically engaged, ultimately repeats the methodology of the psychologizing reading—it declares the inner self (the lesbian) the ultimate reality. I suggest that a lesbian identity be seen not as the ultimate truth of Miss Wade's "History" but rather as its major metaphor. It thus impartially renders both psychological and social forms of disruption. It unites the threat of a subversive female sexuality *and* of the capacity to connect with others in a newly-formed, newly-aware, class.

In pointing out the absence of both history (in the form of the governess) and psychology (in the form of the lesbian) from accounts of Miss Wade, I have sought to disrupt a continuity of strategy between text and critic, and between Victorian and twentieth-century mediations of resistance. A symptomatic reading of Miss Wade, unlike readings of Miss Wade's symptoms, does not amount to a definitive diagnosis. Instead, what is produced is a diagnostic weapon which operates upon analyst (there being no appropriate escape from this metaphor) as well as subject. "The History of a Self-Tormentor" can thus finally become a text that turns its critique outward to its readers, who must torment themselves with questions about texts, history, and how to read.

# NOTES

I want to thank Sharon Marcus for valuable comments on a earlier version of this paper, and Nancy Klancher for bringing her clarity to bear on tormented ideas and prose.

1. Martha Vicinus's " 'They Wonder to Which Sex I Belong': The Historical Roots of Modern Lesbian Identity" provides a useful critique of the earlier process as well as making a detailed case for the transhistorical nature of same-sex attraction. While hers is a very useful model for historical research, it has the obvious problem of being based on the assumption of the existence of a single, transhistorical, entity "same sex," a category which other work tends to deconstruct (see, for example, David M. Halperin, "Is there a History of Sexuality?"). For an example of what I take to be a current trend, the move away from the search for either actual lesbians or actual women engaged in erotic behavior towards a search for cultural representations of these phenomena, see Lisa Moore's " 'Something More Tender Still Than Friendship': Romantic Friendship in Early-Nineteenth-Century England."

2. See *Dickens' Working Notes for His Novels,* ed. Henry Store. Chicago: U of Chicago P, 1987. Dickens considers, and defers, Miss Wade for numbers 3, 4, 6, & 7 of the novel's serial publication. The "History" appeared in number 8.

3. For an example of denial of the validity of a lesbian reading, see John Lucas: "I think it is a mistake that Miss Wade should be spoken of as a lesbian. Dickens' daring does not lie in any suggestion of her sexual nature. Indeed, Miss Wade hates society as a whole, not just men (269). For "masculine rampage," see Edward Heatley: "if Miss Wade herself seduces the young females with whom she comes in contact, it is less the seduction of one female by another than the exertion of the mesmeric will . . . (158)"; for the maternal Miss Wade, see Randolph Splitter: "Miss Wade inflames Tattycoram's resentment and also, in effect,

"seduces" her, becoming the mother she would like to have had to the child she once was (125)." Much seduction, definitely no lesbians, and not much in the way of same-sex erotic attraction.

4. I would suggest, however, that Freud's case history of Miss Wade would focus on her account as evidence of an example of the etiology of paranoid delusion, to which female object choice would be incidental (although in the Schreber account paranoia is causally linked to homosexuality, Miss Wade does not fit this pattern, in which persecution is employed "as a means of warding off a homosexual wishful phantasy" ("The Case of Schreber," 59)). There are aspects of Freud's argument in his most extended analysis of lesbianism, "The Psychogenesis of a Case of Homosexuality in a Woman," that Miss Wade's confession can be said to anticipate: like the subject of his analysis, she moves through a series of love objects, substituting one for another as her hopes are disappointed, arriving at Tattycoram only after the failure of heterosexual attachement. But the lesbian as Freud depicts her (both in the individual case and as a general rule established by his treatments of others) is a notably cheerful, well-adjusted individual; he is constrained to point out that cures are unlikely, since most subjects are happy with their affective practices. The tradition which discounts lesbianism as an explanation while pathologizing Miss Wade might be said, therefore, to have a percursor in Freud's own omission of the vengeful female deviant from his gallery of perverts.

5. See, for example, Diane Sadoff, "Storytelling and the Figure of the Father," where Miss Wade's narrative "acts out Clennam's self-hatred" (129–30).

6. I am following Rosemary Hennessy here in seeing symptomatic reading as a means of return to history: "symptoms appear as 'excesses' in the narrative, disruptions in its logic or linearization which are either suppressed or 'explained' (articulated onto preconstructed categories) so as to quell their disruptive force. These 'shadowy' excesses which haunt the coherence of the text point to the play of history beyond the secured edges of ideological closure" (94).

7. Mary Poovey's account of mid-century representations of the governess in *Uneven Developments* clarifies the importance of this figure as a point of articulation of contested assumptions about female nature and separate spheres. In Poovey's analysis, the governess, constructed as a bulwark between middle and working class, tends to collapse the very gender and class distinctions she is pressed to uphold. For Poovey, the significance of the ubiquitous mad governess lies in her synecdochal relation to the fallen woman: the danger of the governess is the danger of (the existence of) female sexuality; the threat she poses is thus ultimately to the concept of the bourgeois female subject. My interpretation of the figure of the governess diverges from Poovey's on account of a different angle of approach: rather than consider the governess as the other against which a hegemonic middle class defines itself, I am more concerned here with how that ideological construct defines and constrains those women who became governesses.

8. For an account of the shift to a female population, see Showalter. Mad governesses were a separate category for the first time in the 1851 census; for details of census statistics on governesses in lunatic asylums, see Hammerton (26).

9. The most notable exception to this trend is Lady Eastlake's vitriolic review of *Jane Eyre*, in which Jane is convicted of both lower-class traits and the desire for social mobility. It should be noted, however, that Eastlake's review, which covers *Vanity Fair* and the Annual Report of the Governesses Benevolent Institute for 1847 as well as Brontë's novel, is a negotiation of competing resolutions of the governess problem. Eastlake makes clear that Jane's sin is her identification of her struggle with organized class conflict, and finally reiterates the victim model as that into which the approved governess must fit herself, and as that which makes her a suitable object for charity. By declining a class identification, by acknowledging themselves neither middle nor working class, governesses render themselves worthy beneficiaries of the GBI's aims. The GBI serves to ameliorate governesses' living conditions and simultaneously to reinforce a categorization of them as individuals whose needs will be addressed as individuals, and by others, not governesses themselves.

10. Freud's account of treating a governess is markedly consonant with the problem and resolutions offered by conduct manuals: Miss Lucy R., who is troubled by olfactory hallucinations, is cured when, realizing that her hopes of marrying her employer are futile, she accepts her lowered social status and lot in life. See "Case 3: Miss Lucy R., Age 30" in *Studies on Hysteria* 106–24.

11. That Dickens was also comfortable operating within this convention can be seen from his address to the GBI in 1844, in which he lauded their mission "to render governesses more respected" (Fielding 66). Articles arguing for a revision in governesses' conditions—where governesses appear as the gentle victims of unfeeling, exploitative female employers who neglect their own womanly duties—were published in *Household Words* in the 1850s. (For example, see "Only a Governess," *HW* 19:546–49, 7 May 1859, and "Two-pence an Hour," *HW* 14:138–40, August 23, 1856.) From these evidences one might infer Dickens' alignment with the notion that governesses' status incongruence could be regarded as a social problem amenable to the operations of middle-class benevolence. Yet the treatment of Miss Wade obviously complicates any such positioning. The inconsistency of Dickens' approaches to the governess as between fiction and non-fiction raises the problem of how different narrative modes should be understood as interacting. While Eastlake's use of the GBI Annual Report to counter *Jane Eyre*'s a version of her situation suggests reliance on the superior scientific quality of documentary evidence, it can hardly be assumed that the truth value of *Household Words* will be implicitly greater for Dickens or his readers than the imaginary Miss Wade—especially when she so thoroughly inhabits certain (medical and scientific) aspects of contemporary representations of governessal madness.

12. For details of these coerced activities of self-reform, and of wayward mothers as an explanatory tool in the Victorian moral treatment movement, see Bynum, ed. *The Anatomy of Madness.*

13. While Krafft-Ebing was a crucial influence in the emergence of inversion as a telling narrative of individual identity, his attention to abnormal governesses per se seems to have been focused on social causes of insanity rather than psychopathology: "Homesickness, unpleasant family and social relations that often drive

these poor creatures away from home; insulting, harsh treatment; in general, depressing social position; disappointed love, over-exertion in work usually appear as causes" (*Textbook of Insanity, Based on Clinical Observations* 154).

14. For an extended account of female friendship's treatment in Victorian fiction, see Tess Cosslett, *Woman to Woman.*

# Works Cited

Bynum, W. F. et al., eds. *The Anatomy of Madness: Essays in the History of Psychiatry,* Vol 3: *The Asylum and its Psychiatry.* London: Routledge, 1988.

Cosslett, Tess. *Woman to Woman: Female Friendship in Victorian Fiction.* Atlantic Highlands, NJ: Humanities Press International, 1988.

Dickens, Charles. *Little Dorrit.* 1857. Ed. John Holloway. Harmondsworth: Penguin, 1967.

Eastlake, Elizabeth, Lady. *"Vanity Fair*—and *Jane Eyre." Quarterly Review* 84 (1848): 153–85.

Fielding, *The Speeches of Charles Dickens.* Ed. K. J. Fielding. Atlantic Highlands, NJ: Humanities P, 1988.

Forster, John. *The Life of Charles Dickens.* 1874. Ed. J. W. T. Ley. NY: Doubleday, 1928.

Freud, Sigmund and Joseph Breuer. *Studies On Hysteria.* [1893] trans. James Stratchey. London: Hogarth Press, 1955.

———. "The Case of Schreber" [1911]. trans. James Stratchey. London: Hogarth Press, 1955.

———. "The Psychogenesis of a Case of Homosexuality in a Woman." [1920] In *Collected Papers,* Vol 2., New York: Basic, 1959.

Halperin, David M. "Is There a History of Sexuality?" *History and Theory* 28 (1989): 257–74.

Hammerton, A. James. *Emigrant Gentlewomen: Genteel Poverty and Female Emigration 1830–1914.* London: Croom Helm, 1979.

Heatley, Edward. "The Redeemed Feminine of *Little Dorrit." Dickens Studies Annual* 4 (1975): 153–64.

Hennessy, Rosemary. *Materialist Feminism and the Politics of Discourse.* NY: Routledge, 1993.

Jameson, Anna. *The Relative Position of Mothers and Governesses.* 2nd ed., London, 1848.

Johnson, Wendell Stacey. *Charles Dickens: New Perspectives.* Englewood Cliffs, NJ: Prentice Hall, 1982.

Krafft-Ebing, R. von. *Textbook of Insanity, Based on Clinical Observations.* Philadelphia, 1904.

Lucas, John. *The Melancholy Man: A Study of Dickens's Novels.* Brighton: Harvester, 1980.

Moore, Lisa. " 'Something More Tender Still than Friendship': Romantic Friendship in Early-Nineteenth-Century England." *Feminist Studies* 18, Fall 1992:499–520.

Neff, Wanda F. *Victorian Working Women: An Historical and Literary Study of Women in British Industries and Professions, 1831–1850.* 1929. New York: AMS P, 1966.

Peterson, M. Jeanne. "The Victorian Governess: Status Incongruence in Family and Society." Vicinus, Martha, *Suffer and Be Still: Women in the Victorian Age.* Indiana UP, 1972.

Poovey, Mary. *Uneven Developments: The Ideological Work of Gender in Mid-Victorian England.* Chicago: U of Chicago P, 1988.

Sadoff, Dianne F. "Storytelling and the Figure of the Father in *Little Dorrit.*" In Johnson: 121–41.

Sewell, Elizabeth. *Principles of Education Drawn From Nature and Revelation and Applied to Female Education in the Upper Classes.* London: Longman, 1865.

Shelston, Alan. *Charles Dickens: Dombey & Son and Little Dorrit: A Casebook.* Basingstoke: Macmillan, 1985.

Showalter, Elaine. "Victorian Women and Insanity." *Madhouses, Mad-Doctors, and Madmen.* Ed. Andrew Scull. Philadelphia: U of Pennsylvania P, 1981, 313–38.

Splitter, Randolph. "Guilt and the Trappings of Melodrama in *Little Dorrit.*" *Dickens Studies Annual* 6 (1977): 119–33.

Store, Henry. *Dickens' Working Notes for His Novels,* Chicago: U of Chicago P, 1987.

Vicinus, Martha. *Independent Women: Work and Community for Single Women, 1850–1920.* Chicago: U of Chicago P, 1985.

———, ed. *Suffer and be Still: Women in the Victorian Age.* London: Methuen, 1980.

———. " 'They Wonder to which Sex I Belong': the Historical Roots of the Modern Lesbian Identity." *Feminist Studies* 18, Fall 1992:467–97.

Wilson, Edmund. *The Wound and The Bow.* Boston: Houghton Mifflin, 1941.

# The Narrator's Shame: Masculine Identity in *Great Expectations*

*Kathleen Sell*

Robert Newsom, in his article "The Hero's Shame," observes that "indeed there would be no question about discussing shame in the novel were it not for all the critics who have emphasized guilt at the expense of shame" (18). If we may define guilt as uneasiness over one's actions and shame as uneasiness over one's self, shame, indeed, does seem to be at the heart of what motivates many of the conflicts in *Great Expectations,* and the emphasis on guilt, while productive of insightful readings,[1] has served to obscure the role of shame that is central to the narration and thematics of identity in the novel.[2] Fundamentally, shame has to do with who and what one is, the sense of self, and not simply or only with what one does. Therefore, because identity is a central concern of *Great Expectations,* and shame is closely allied to the development of a sense of self, it is, perhaps, the more productive of the two concepts for this novel. In fact, I would argue that what motivates Pip's narrative is the desire to reverse the structure of shame, to turn the shaming gaze away from himself and onto others, and simultaneously to indulge in the most extreme version of the shame fantasy—total self-exposure, interpellating the reader as witness.

What the narrative sets in motion is a dynamic of shame that has class, sexual, and gendered aspects, and Pip, in his desire to become a gentleman, will feel two types of shame. The first is class shame, or what Newsom calls "social shame" (19), provoked by his desire for Estella and her contemptuous dismissal of him as a coarse and common laboring boy. This is a shame linked to his body, to the necessity of work and to his companionship and camaraderie with Joe, whom Pip comes to see, too, as coarse and common. The second type of shame Pip feels is moral shame, that aspect of shame most closely allied to guilt, and provoked, often by Biddy, in response to his treatment of Joe. The purpose of the narrative is to expose his younger self's

203

folly in experiencing the first type of shame, to displace the blame for his past actions, and to demonstrate the growth of the narrator in the emphasis on the second type.

It is Pip's act of narrative confession that allows him both to indulge in maximum self-exposure and to manipulate the presentation of his self so that shame is diverted from the self in the act of narrating. Estella, and the narration of Pip's awakening desire for Estella, are central to this project, for Estella becomes the focal point of the narration's representation of shame, heterosexual desire, and class ambition. The question is why and how does she become so central? Ultimately, I would argue that Pip's shame stems from his desire to abandon the world of masculine bonding and labor at the forge for a narrative of upward class mobility and heterosexual union. Thus, Pip's desires for class mobility and for Estella involve a shift from homosocial to heterosexual bonds. It is the failure to complete this shift successfully and establish a secure masculine identity through financial independence and marriage to Estella that provokes the lingering shame that motivates the narrative. The narrative's insistence on Estella as central to Pip's development, and on the failures of women in the novel, are an attempt to mitigate this shame and to represent himself as reformed, though the efficacy of this reformation remains an open question. Several issues in the novel to be examined, then, in order to understand what I am calling the shame linked to Pip's failure of identity: first, the role of shame in Pip's representation of himself in the narrative; a clearer picture of the gentlemanly ideal that Pip aspires to and the problematic status of labor in this ideal; the emergence of shame and desire simultaneously and the dependence of masculine identity on fulfilling a heterosexual narrative of desire; the failure of women to play their roles and consequently their failure to underwrite masculine identity; and finally, the text's ambivalence over the version of masculinity based on the model of a competitive male sphere balanced and compensated for by a "safe" feminine, domestic sphere.

I

Pip's representation of himself in the narrative is a process of distancing his present from his past self and accounting for the past self's errors by displacing blame for them. This process of distancing centers around the narrative's changing definition of the term gentleman, whose use corresponds clearly with Victorian practice and in particular, the middle-class use of the term to denominate a gray rather than precisely defined area that covers not only economic status but also demeanor and moral character. One understanding of the term is based on the qualities of a person's character, the other on the amount of property one owns and the freedom from the need to labor.

Initially, Pip sees in Joe's character qualities which elicit his admiration. But with Pip's exposure to Satis House, he comes to define "gentleman" as someone who would be worthy of Estella's attentions, in other words someone with a genteel veneer both in manners and body, and as someone with expectations. This leads him to repudiate his "former" life. He says at the end of chapter 13, "Finally, I remember that when I got into my little bedroom, I was truly wretched, and had a strong conviction on me that I should never like Joe's trade. I had liked it once, but once was not now" (119).³ That being a gentleman involves distancing himself from Joe and the forge is confirmed by Jaggers's pronouncement that "it is the desire of the present possessor of that property that he be immediately removed from his present sphere of life and from this place, and be brought up as a gentleman—in a word, as a young fellow of *Great Expectations*" (154). For Pip, being a gentleman involves not honest labor, but the expectation that one will be freed from the necessity of labor forever. Once in London, Pip discovers that he is "not designed for any profession" (214), and the meaning expressed by the term "gentleman" here is clearly grounded in class and economics.

Yet Biddy, always a voice that expresses the narrator's present consciousness of his past self's shame, remarks on the paucity of this class-based definition, saying "Yet a gentleman should not be unjust neither" (166). She emphasizes the moral qualities of character a gentleman should have rather than his material wealth. Similarly, Herbert reminds Pip of his father's maxim "that no man who was not a true gentleman at heart, ever was, since the world began, a true gentleman in manner" (197). The shame that motivates the narrator is his younger self's simultaneous awareness of and vacillation between these two poles, which can be seen in the conflicting pull of class shame and moral shame that he feels throughout the narrative. The material wealth he comes into gives him a genteel veneer, but fails to make him a true "gentleman at heart," or to make him just to Joe, Biddy, Magwitch, and even Herbert. The character's true understanding of the term gentleman comes, of course, when the narrator shows himself finally recognizing Joe's worth: ". . . I lay there, penitently whispering, 'O God bless him! O God bless this gentle Christian man!' " (497). However, Pip's understanding here is fragile, and he cannot rid himself of the haunting class shame that has defined his identity. The older narrator is at pains to show up Pip's failure to see "gentleman" as, more importantly, implying an ethical code of behavior, one that recognizes the worth of a person and is free of the distancing effects of class prejudice. The narrative is given as evidence that Pip has indeed learned the true meaning of "gentleman," and he accomplishes this by both denigrating and justifying the past self from whom he distances himself.

While it is commonplace to argue that there is distance and difference between the narrated and narrating self in a first-person narrative, this distance is exacerbated in *Great Expectations* by the narrator's shame. One attribute of shame is the desire both to hide, to efface the self, and to exhibit, to expose the self to humiliation. Silvan Tomkins explains that "In shame I wish to continue to look and to be looked at, but I also do not wish to do so" (137).[4] The narrator of *Great Expectations* is simultaneously working through both ends of the shame dynamic, and he does so by creating two selves: the character on display in the narrative and the narrator, effaced from the narrative by his reticence, obliquity, and refusal to bring the narrative contemporaneous with the scene of narration. The desire to escape the gaze and divert it onto others, and the desire to expose the self both characterize the activity of the first-person narrator of *Great Expectations*.

What is at stake, here, is the very identity of the narrator. Robert Newsom explains that the source of shame is one's awareness "that one has not met the requirements of the ego-ideal, which is an idealized image of the self one would like to be and in some senses believes oneself to be," and thus, "shame . . . touches upon the very sense of self, being, and identity" (6).[5] For shame to be activated, then, one must have a sense of a self differentiated from others, and one for which an ideal has been constituted: shame becomes activated when one becomes conscious of a self that deviates from an ideal self. This awareness of self is negative, based not on success but on a perceived failure of the self. Throughout the text, Pip reacts to his actions and desires not just with guilt, but with shame—with a painful self-awareness that he is not measuring up to some imagined ideal. Thus, his experiences of shame constitute the borders of his identity as criminal, thief, liar, common laboring boy, apprentice, gentleman, and narrator. He constructs shameful labels of identity rather than just confessing to guilty acts. Because Pip's reactions to his actions, and to events out of his control, take shape as questions about who he is, not simply guilt over what he has done, it is himself that he objects to.

However, it is clear that the "painful and exaggerated awareness" of self that occurs in response to shame in inherently communal. Implicit in the structures and dynamics of shame is the watchful other, whose gaze, whose witness of the self in the act of not meeting an imagined ideal, is what produces the intense affect. In fact, Eve Kosofsky Sedgwick argues that:

> Shame floods into being as a moment, a disruptive moment, in a circuit of identity-constituting identificatory communication. Indeed, like a stigma, shame is itself a form of communication. Blazons of shame, the "fallen face" with eyes down and head averted—and to a lesser extent, the blush—are semaphors of trouble and at the same time of a desire to reconstitute the interpersonal bridge.                                    (*"Performativity"* 5)

Paradoxically, the exaggerated awareness of self in shame leads to a desire to reduce or terminate communication with others, but at the same time may heighten communication by enhancing the visibility of the self. Shame, then, like narrative, is a communicative act, and it works both to individuate the individual and to put the individual in relation to others. It serves to mark the *boundaries* of identity, functions indeed as proof *of* an identity.[6] For Pip, the shaming gaze operates on two levels: within the text in response to other characters' especially Estella's, assessment of him, but also in the structure of the narrative itself, in which he first turns the shaming gaze on his past self.

From the first, the narrative makes clear that his younger self's identity is founded on misinterpretation: he names himself Pip and then writes that he formed his "first fancies regarding what [his parents] were like . . . unreasonably . . . from their tombstones" (1). But his misinterpretation continues more seriously once he has been exposed to Satis House, and it is here that the narrative of identity is linked to the narrative of class and heterosexual desire through shame. On being informed of his expectations, Pip exclaims "My dream was out; my wild fancy was surpassed by sober reality; Miss Havisham was going to make my fortune on a grand scale" (154), and the other characters simply confirm in him this tendency to assume that Miss Havisham has made his fortune. Moreover, the coincidences of the narrative, especially the connection Pip discovers between Magwitch and Estella, underscore the falsity of identities founded only on appearance. The misinterpretations founded on these appearances profoundly affect the identity of the narrator, especially in the shame that results from his discovery of the discrepancy between his "wild fancy" and reality and his realization that his expectations led him to mistreat first Joe and then Magwitch when he learns the true source of his expectations. Clearly, the narrator's intention is to show, through the act of confession, his recovery from such wild fancies, and to exculpate himself by exposing and admitting his past errors. The narrator's authority in *Great Expectations,* then, is constituted in ambivalent and complex ways. The addresses to the reader that the narrator makes seem designed to draw attention to and to expose his past shame, but this attempt to bolster his narrative authority at the expense of his younger self leads one to ask why the narrator is at such pains to divert scrutiny from himself.

At times the narrator takes an almost third-person approach to his younger self, which allows him to achieve an authorial superiority and distance which authorizes his voice. He clearly expresses confidence in his moral reform, explicitly asserting his moral superiority, as narrator, to his self as character. He says at the conclusion of the first stage of his expectations, "Heaven knows we need never be ashamed of our tears, for they are rain upon the blinding dust of earth, overlying our hard hearts. I was better after I had cried than before—more sorry, more aware of my ingratitude, more gentle. If I had cried before, I should have had Joe with me then" (177). The narrative is itself an act of contrition designed to elicit from the reader the sympathetic, softening tears that may "overlay" any hearts disposed to hardness toward the narrator. His desire to appear contrite also appears at the end of chapter 29 when he writes, "Ah me! I thought those were high and great emotions. But I never thought there was anything low and small in my keeping away from Joe, because I knew she would be contemptuous of him. It was but a day gone, and Joe had brought tears into my eyes; they had soon dried—God forgive me!—soon dried" (264). Passages such as these expose the character both to the narrator's irony and to the anticipated "shame-on-you" of the reader. The narrator creates, then, a distance between himself as subject and object, and through that very distance abrogates moral authority to himself.

This assumption of moral authority is especially clear in the tone of moral superiority that characterizes his manipulation of his younger self's language. Barry Westburg writes, "the narrator seems to reconstruct the boy's language so that it unconsciously reveals a state of mind that everyday speech does not often so clearly reveal"; moreover, "this state of mind, disclosed here in Pip's patronizing repetitions, is something Dickens evidently wishes us to think of as revealed for us by a narrator whose intimate knowledge of the boy allows him to 'adjust' the boy's speeches . . . in the interest of a truth that could not emerge in a literal, autobiographical record" (120). This is clear, at one level, in the speech tags the narrator attaches to his younger self's speech: " 'How do you spell Gargery, Joe' I asked him, with modest patronage" (55); "Said I, in a virtuous and superior tone" (166), et cetera. The adjustment and detachment of these sorts of tags underscore the fact that the narrative includes two Pips, two selves: one whose history is told in the narrative and a hidden second self that the narrative in effect seeks to conceal. The reader is implicitly called on to question Pip's interpretation of events, of his younger self and of other characters.

Certainly, the very ease with which the older narrator shows up his younger self's failings should lead the reader to question the tacit assumption that the narrator has, at the time of the narration, reached some sort of moral superiority. At times the narrator comments explicitly on Pip's failings, inviting the reader's condemnation and highlighting his more mature self's awareness of and condemnation of these failings. Of the lies Pip tells on returning from his first visit to Satis House, the narrator parenthetically comments, "(I beg to observe that I think of myself with amazement when I recall the lies I told on this occasion)" (79). But concomitant with the narrator's condemnation of his part self, is his justification of his past self. He asks, "What could I become with these surroundings? How could my character fail to be influenced by them? Is it to be wondered at if my thoughts were dazed, as my eyes were, when I came out into the natural sunlight from the misty yellow rooms" (109)? The questions implicitly reach out to the reader, Pip goes on to excuse his behavior himself:

*Perhaps* I might have told Joe about the pale young gentleman, *if* I had not previously been betrayed into those enormous inventions to which I had confessed. *Under the circumstances,* I felt that Joe could hardly fail to discern in the pale young gentleman or appropriate passenger to be, put into the black velvet coach; therefore, I said nothing of him.
*Besides,* that shrinking. from having Miss Havisham and Estella discussed which had come upon me in the beginning grew much more potent as time went on. I reposed complete confidence in no one but Biddy; but U told poor Biddy everything. Why it came natural for me to do so, and why Biddy had a deep concern in everything I told her, I did not know then, *though I think* I know now.                                                          (109, italics mine)

This is the language of justification. The conditionals, the explanation of circumstances, the subtly suggested uncertainty of "I think" are all designed both to expose and to excuse, eliciting sympathy from the reader for his younger self and approval for the narrating self.

In a similar vein, at the beginning of chapter 14 he writes "How much of my ungracious condition of mind may have been my own fault, how much Miss Havisham's, how much my sister's, is now of no moment to me or to any one. The change was made in me; the thing was done. Well or ill done, excusably or inexcusably it was done" (120). Here, the question of blame is deferred, but the fact that he raises the possibility of blame in his sister or in Miss Havisham dilutes the blame the reader may assign to him, while at the same time he maneuvers to win the sympathy and approbation of the reader by appearing not to assign blame at all. His dismissals of his younger self occur along with self justification, and the narrator vacillates between contempt and shame, his own relation to his younger self unresolved.

The very fact of the narration itself, however, indicates a desire to divert shame and a continuing sense of shame that leads one to suspect the narrator's motives. Pip's authority as a narrator is constructed ambivalently, and it is clear that the text asks us to question Pip's authority as narrator of his own life. What Pip is trying to achieve through narrating his story is the power to control his own story and the power to construct his own identity through the manipulations of the narrative. This is clear from the first page of the story where Pip names himself and "writes" his own identity. The ambivalence of the narrator, his inability finally to "write" a definitive identity for himself, is evident in the text's duplication and reduplication of selves, and this ambivalence is linked specifically to his inability to construct a secure masculine identity for himself. The reasons for this failure become evident in the novel's treatment of the narratives of class ambition and heterosexual desire.

## II

The question of class is evident throughout the narrative, in the equivocation about what it means to be a gentleman, in Pip's desire to distance himself from Joe in order to be worthy of Estella. But it is evident as well in the narration itself, and it is here that the irresolution of the questions raised about class in the novel become clear. The narrator's primary activity, writing his story, is potentially shameful because writing, or literacy more generally, is used throughout the novel to mark class distinctions. As Pip becomes more literate, language comes to mark a distance based on class, and language learning is associated with his shame of Joe and desire for Estella. He uses language to try to change Joe, failing to recognize in him any worthiness inherent in his character, instead seeking to varnish him and give him a more genteel veneer: "Whatever I acquired, I tried to impart to Joe. This statement sounds so well that I cannot in my conscience let it pass unexplained. I wanted to make Joe less ignorant and common, that he might be worthier of my society and less open to Estella's reproach" (123–24). Literacy for Pip, then, is an issue of class and identity. Murray Baumgarten writes that "For Pip as for us reading and writing are not just skills but semiotic codes constitutive of personality and social order;" they shape not only the "self" but the social context in which that self comes to exist, and "the ability to use them is the mark of gentility" (64). Yet the narrator, who felt such shame over his coarse, common laboring hands, now has ink-stained hands—the mark of his need to labor first as a clerk and now as a writer. While writing is an intellectual labor, and thus could be seen as gentlemanly, the novel, by focusing on links between labor, literacy, and class, makes even this sort of intellectual labor somewhat ambivalent. At issue here is the problematic status of labor—the need to work for money as opposed to working for one's own satisfaction or enjoyment—and its relation to class. Moreover, throughout the novel, Pip's understanding of what it means to be a "gentleman" is based on leisure, the freedom from the need to work at all.

Links between labor and literacy and literature and class in this novel are complex, for the context in which Pip wishes to "become" a gentleman is a complex one in the nineteenth-century, and it is the use to which literacy is put that makes the difference. In *Great Expectations* the *work* of writing is insistently effaced; this is labor that is invisible and takes place in a narrative in which the achievement of literacy is supposed to free one from labor, make one a gentleman, and yet the act of writing is itself, as Mary Poovey has shown, labor.[7] I agree with William Cohen, who argues that "writing is . . . as much a mark of the protagonist's class descent (the economic necessity of writing) as of his rise (the intellectual ability to do so.)" (226). Pip, then, is finally unable to free himself from labor by finding a true benefactor, nor is he able to find a safe domestic space and a wife of his own to ameliorate the fact that he must work and compete in the marketplace. Thus writing, the labor Pip takes up and simultaneously makes invisible, is a form of labor where the pressures and inconsistencies involved in representations of labor

and the representation of the "individual," and of masculine identity in particular, become clear. That Pip ends up writing his narrative but hiding the scene
of literary labor, then, is a clear sign that the tensions raised by class in this
novel are left unresolved. But Pip's failure to be a gentleman and the continuing uneasiness over class are related to the more central irresolution in the
novel—his relationship with Estella. It is through Estella that his failure of
identity is connected to the failure of the feminine in the novel that threatens
to undermine the possibility of masculine identity.

Pip learns distance and contempt from Estella, and these are directly related
to the class shame he develops in response to her scorn of him. Moreover,
he responds to Estella's scorn with an internalized self-contempt: "Her contempt for me was so strong that it became infectious, and I caught it" (70).
The image of disease makes clear the distance, distaste, and fear of taint
involved in the class shame that comes to replace his close companionship
with Joe. It is only when he is able to bridge the distance between himself
and Joe, and himself and Magwitch that he can replace scorn and contempt
with empathy.[8]

Pip is clearly in a state of equality with Joe as a child at the forge; they
share mutual understanding and identify with each other as fellow sufferers.
Pip says that he "always treated him as a larger species of child, and as no
more than my equal" (15), and that they share a "freemasonry as fellow-
sufferers" (17). It is in Pip's relationship with Joe that the drive of the
narrative to replace male companionship with heterosexual desire first becomes clear. Joe's first visit to Pip in London makes the distance between
them painfully obvious. That Pip is aware that his behavior fails to be "gentlemanly" is clear, though he admits that he "had neither the good sense nor
the good feeling to know that this was all my fault, and that if I had been
easier Joe, Joe would have been easier with me" (240). Joe is clearly aware
of Pip's disease, concluding that " 'Diwisions among such must come' "
(244). But Pip emphasizes that Estella is at the root of this "diwision" and
that his behavior would have changed with knowledge of Joe's purpose in
coming: "I felt my face fire up as I looked at Joe. I hope one remote cause
of its firing, may have been my consciousness that if I had known his errand,
I should have given more encouragement" (243). In an earlier visit to Satis
House Estella made the connection between change in station and change in
companions irreversibly connected for Pip: " 'Since your change of fortune
and prospects, you have changed your companions,' said Estella. 'Naturally,'
said I. 'And necessarily,' she added, in a haughty tone; 'what was fit company
for you once would be quite unfit company for you now' " (257). Pip must
learn a definition of gentleman based on sympathetic identification and not
on class superiority before he is able to empathize with Joe and with Magwitch
and to feel the shame that motivates his narrative.

This empathy, however, becomes possible not just because of the narrator's presumed moral regeneration but because, in spite of her contempt, and perhaps because of it, Pip's desire for Estella has remained central in the narrative. The very empathy Pip feels for Joe and Magwitch puts him in another potentially shameful position, which is only mitigated by the narrative's insistence on Estella's centrality. Pip's relationships, at various points, with Joe, Herbert, Orlick, Drummle, and Magwitch are dangerously intense, "a form of contact too close for comfort" (Cohen 238), and the "increasingly savage violence" of the confrontations between men in the novel, the increasing discomfort of such close male contact—what Cohen terms the "novel's homophobia" (238)—is both a source of shame in the narrative and, I would argue, a reason for the narrative's elevation of Pip's undying, Byronic desire for Estella. She is necessary in the narrative to displace the charge of other less clearly named desires.[9] Ultimately, Pip is not able to fulfill his desire for Estella unequivocally, nor is he able to go back to an idyllic world of male friendship and bonding.

Thus, Pip feels shame not only because he fails to become a gentleman in both senses of the word, but also because in Victorian ideology the key for grounding this identity is based on the creation of a heterosexual dyad, which Pip fails to do.[10] Pip's development is arrested because his desire is left unfulfilled, outside the safe harbor of marriage, and it is only vicariously domesticated through his attachment to Herbert and Clara. It is the shame over Pip's failure to consolidate securely a masculine identity, economically or sexually, that the narrative must account for. The narrator accomplishes this by turning the shaming gaze onto the women of the novel.

## III

While the successful containment of potentially transgressive male desires and aggressive competitiveness should be assured by marriage, in this novel it is not, for women refuse to play the role of domestic angels, and they certainly provide no safe haven. Domestic space in *Great Expectations* more often disrupts and provokes violent competitiveness rather than ameliorating it. Thus, Pip's shame, and his failure to fulfill the narrative of desire required of the typical Victorian hero whose identity must be underwritten by a woman to succeed, are linked. One reason for the failure of identity in the novel, the reason the narrator most emphatically insists on, is that women in *Great Expectations* refuse to play the role assigned to them by an ideology that demanded, at least in theory, a strict separation of private and public in order to compensate for the dangers of class antagonism and unbridled economic competition in the public world. That it is now commonplace to assert that this separation was never really in effect, not even in fiction, doesn't undermine the imaginative power it had and the impact it had on representations of gender and appropriate gender behavior. Women in this novel fail to provide a safe haven from the competitiveness that underlies the social and economic field in which the male defines his identity and thus they fail to underwrite masculinity. The women in this novel are represented as a nightmare version of the domestic ideal of womanliness.

Recent work on this novel abundantly documents this point. Susan Walsh describes Miss Havisham as "a voluptuary of pain, spokeswoman for the masochistic dark side of domestic ideology" (89). Curt Hartog writes that "throughout the novel, feminine identity collapses because the major female characters deny love instead of giving it" (249) and "the failure of feminine identity leads inevitably to the failure of masculine identity" (253).[11] Similarly, Gail Turley Houston argues that in *Great Expectations* "the key women in the protagonist's life are anything but maternal . . . the long suppressed Dickensian female defies her maternal role" (14), and Alison Milbank writes that "women use their domestic space either as a reformatory for punishment of male misdeeds or as a weapon in some sexual power game" (122), so what exists in *Great Expectations* is a "demonic matriarchy" that fails to play its allotted role in the Victorian ideology of hearth and home. Victorian women are supposed to be selfless, and in that selflessness, be able to provide a space safe from the competitiveness and self-interest of the public world. In this novel, by contrast, femininity fails utterly. Mrs. Joe, Miss Havisham, Estella, Molly, Mrs. Pocket become the target of the narrator's shaming gaze and are ruthlessly exposed to the gaze of the reader. Their failures are not, finally, balanced for Pip by the few good women in the novel—Biddy, Clara, Miss Skiffins. Yet the narrator clearly uses and narrates this failure for his own ends, displacing any blame of himself onto the catalog of women who failed to be womanly and who are thus accountable for the character's and the narrator's failings.

Mrs. Joe is the first and most obvious failure of femininity in the novel, and her failures is linked to two central aspects of femininity: first, a failure of maternal instincts, that aspect of femininity Poovey argues the Victorians saw as central to defining women as selfless; and second, a failure to ameliorate class conflict and the violent competition potentially provoked by this conflict. The domestic space that should provide a haven for Pip is instead a scene of violence, discomfort, and humiliation for him. While the adult narrator's recounting of the young Pip's encounters with "Tickler" are distanced by the tone of ironic detachment, Pip's suffering and Joe's ineffectual attempts to curb it are indicative of a home pervaded by violence: by temper, "rampages," pins accidentally stuck into bread, dosings with tar water and "Tickler" (15–18). Moreover, Pip's lessons about social status are learned early, even before he goes to Satis House, for as he labors as a child as "odd-boy about the forge" and does other jobs for the neighbors, his labor is accounted for in such a way as to avoid the appearance that they need the wages he earns, so that their "superior position might not be compromised" (52). Thus for Pip, the necessity of laboring for wages is associated with a sensitivity to appearances and class position that Estella will bring painfully into consciousness. And finally, rather than alleviating and compensating for the violent competitiveness between men, Mrs. Joe provokes it in the fight between Joe and Orlick. Mrs. Joe inflames the conflict and casts it in sexual terms; the issue becomes one of whether Joe will fight to defend his wife's honor, not Orlick's dissatisfaction over Pip's preferential treatment. She eroticizes the violence in much the same way Estella does.

Miss Havisham, as Susan Walsh has clearly argued, also fails to play the appropriate economic and maternal roles allotted her in Victorian ideology in withdrawing her capital from circulation and in refusing to play benefactress to her young male relatives (90–91), and, in the case of Pip, damagingly pretending to play that role when in fact she does not. While initially the misinterpretation is Pip's, she capitalizes on his mistake in order to provoke the jealousy of her rapacious relatives when she says, for instance, " 'Good-bye, Pip! You will always keep the name of Pip, you know' " (175), deliberately alluding to a condition of Pip's expectations and confirming his belief that she is his patron. Miss Havisham also represents a failure of the feminine in her perversion of the maternal instinct. Miss Havisham's adoption of Estella is motivated not by selflessness, but by her appetite for revenge, for she raises Estella to "wreak revenge on all the male sex' " (193), as Herbert tells Pip. Thus, Miss Havisham represents a failure of the feminine in her failure to underwrite the aspirations of men financially (the notable exception coming when she finances Herbert and leaves a legacy for his father), and in her perversion of the maternal role, which perpetuates her failure of femininity by damaging Estella, which by extension also damages Pip.

That Miss Havisham asks Pip to play so that she can train Estella in how to shame, humiliate, and humble men is clear. In the game "beggar your neighbor," in Estella's refusal to call Pip by his name, referring to him only as "boy," and in the way he is fed like an animal and provoked into expressing his mortification in tears, the entire scene is one designed to elicit and provoke shame. Estella's insults change his perception of himself. As he now looks at his "coarse hands and . . . common boots," he finds that his new "opinion of those accessories was not favorable" (71). He resolves "to ask Joe why he had ever taught me to call those picture-cards jacks which ought to be called knaves," wishing "Joe had been rather more genteely brought up, and then I should have been so, too" (72). Estella's goading creates a painful and new self-consciousness of his body, his clothing, and his social status as a laborer, a future apprentice. This painful self-awareness and shame is "the smart without a name" (72) that he feels as he walks home, humiliated and painfully self-aware.

It is this first self-consciousness that sets in motion Pip's shame of his home and it creates an ego-ideal for him that is tied to the narrative of desire and the class ambition that accompanies this desire. Pip himself acknowledges in his "lunatic confession" to Biddy, his desire to be a gentleman and his desire for Estella are inextricable linked: " ' . . . I want to be a gentleman on her account' " (144). Thus, Pip becomes aware of himself as a desiring subject, but one who is "subject" to contempt from the object of his desire. His ideal self now is one that would be above Estella's scorn and would be worthy of her. This necessarily entails for Pip a shame that is not only sexual but social, one that relates not only to his person but to his identification with a certain class of people. The narrator, with a clearly ironic sense of the distinction between his younger self and his narrating self's shame, recalls that

> I did not forget Joe's recommendation, and yet my young mind was in that disturbed and unthankful state that I thought long after I laid me down, how common Estella would consider Joe, a mere blacksmith: how thick his boots, and how coarse his hands. I thought how Joe and my sister were then sitting in the kitchen, and how I had come up to bed from the kitchen, and how Miss Havisham and Estella never sat in a kitchen, but were far above the level of such common doings. I fell asleep recalling what I "used to do" when I was at Miss Havisham's; as though I had been there weeks or months, instead of hours—and as though it were quite an old subject of remembrance, instead of one that had risen only that day. (82)

Thus, Pip's shame is generalized not just to himself, but to the forge and to Joe as well. He learns a system of distinctions based on class, which he internalizes, from Miss Havisham and Estella. The "used to do" subtly acknowledges the way this experience has caused him to revise his understanding of his past, of his life and identity up to this point. They are now retrospectively seen through Estella's contemptuous eyes, and Joe's influence cannot withstand the power of Pip's desire for Estella. Pip's belief that the forge represents "the glowing road to manhood and independence" (129) changes under the pressure of Estella's influence, provoking in Pip the character class shame, and in the narrator, moral shame over his betrayal of Joe.

What makes the narrator's confession of his shame of home and its source in Estella even more painful in his assertion that even then he knew his desire for Estella would produce only misery, and yet he could not give it up. It is clear throughout the narrative that the one thing Pip *cannot* give up is his desire for Estella. He writes in Chapter 29: " . . . when I loved Estella with the love of a man, I loved her simply because I found her irresistible. Once for all; I knew to my sorrow, often and often, if not always that I loved her against reason, against promise, against peace, against hope, against happiness, against all discouragement that could be. Once for all; I loved her none the less because I knew it, and it had no more influence in restraining me than if I had devoutly believed her to be human perfection'' (253). Even after her marriage, he avoids the final knowledge that would put an end to any hope: '' . . . I avoided the newspapers, and begged Herbert (to whom I had confided the circumstances of our last interview) never to speak of her to me. Why I hoarded up this last wretched little rag of hope that was rent and given to the winds, how do I know? Why did you who read this commit that not dissimilar inconsistency of your own, last year, last month, last week?'' (409–10). Through his repeated references to his fascination with Estella, the narrator manages to divert the shaming gaze from himself, and his passion becomes the all encompassing excuse for his behavior, the blame is subtly shifted from him to his love for Estella to Estella herself.

In the end, Pip cannot, even in response to Biddy's question in chapter 57, answer honestly that he has lost all interest in Estella. He tells Biddy ''But that poor dream, as I once used to call it, has all gone by, Biddy, all gone by!' '' (518). However he continues, in Dickens' revised ending[12] to say: ''Nevertheless, I knew while I said those words that I secretly intended to revisit the site of the old house that evening alone, for her sake. Yes, even so. For Estella's sake'' (518). Dickens' revision in fact makes even more clear that Pip cannot give Estella up. While in the first ending, she is married to another man and thus again completely out of reach, the second ending makes that separation less unequivocal. I will not rehearse here the long debate over the merits or demerits of the two endings or whether or not Dickens' oblique second ending implies that they will be married, for even if they do marry they cannot reproduce at this stage the sort of fireside closing scene that ends *David Copperfield*, for example. What is more important, I think, is that the ending's very obliquity and the revisions which make it more ambiguous, clearly indicate that perhaps Pip hasn't come as far as he would like us to think.[13] He hasn't given up his ''wretched hankerings,'' and cannot, still cannot give up Estella.

At least twice in the narrative he attempts to transfer his interest from Estella to Biddy, realizing that Estella makes him miserable, but he is unable to do so. His most obvious attempt to substitute Biddy for Estella comes in chapter 57 when he leaves for home to propose to Biddy, but his hope in regards to Biddy is baffled because she is always associated for him with home, Joe, the forge, everything he has left behind in his attempt to become a gentleman and become worthy of Estella. E. Pearlman argues that in this novel ''there is a disparity between ideology and implicit moral,'' between the narrator's supposed reform and the resolution of the plot in that while

"Dickens masquerades as the enemy of class bias and social snobbery. . . . The novel itself speaks counter to that profession," for "by transforming the gentle Agnes into the proletarian Biddy, and by forestalling the marriage, Dickens has called his own bluff" (201). Ultimately, Pip cannot completely recover from the distance imposed by his desire to rise, to be a gentleman, which has made Biddy "unworthy" in the same way that he is unworthy of Estella. Class remains, to the end of the narrative, an important determinant of Pip's desire, but this desire itself isn't so easily accounted for.

The very insistence on his inability to give up his desire for Estella leads one to ask, especially once it becomes clear that this desire is doomed, why it is made so prominent. One answer is that the work of the narrative of heterosexual desire in *Great Expectations* is to separate Pip from a masculine world bonded against a dangerous and distasteful femininity. Clearly, the masculine identity founded on the domestic ideal, so often upheld in the nineteenth-century novel, cannot exist if the hero will not leave home (and in this case his masculine mother, Joe), and cannot find a woman to establish a new home for him. Pip fails to find this in Estella, and the drastic consequences of this failure can be seen in the increasing violence in the novel against women and between men. The savage and violent confrontations between men in the novel, and the association of these with criminality as well as the strong residue of resentment of women, indicate the increasing strain in the narrative as it insists on the narrative of heterosexual desire in the face of a nightmare version of the feminine ideal. While the bonds that Pip has with men are more intimate than any he has with women, they are proscribed, and the novel's irresolution clearly indicates this tension between ambivalent desires. Thus, Pip's desire for Estella becomes even more paramount the less likely it is to be fulfilled, for it is the desire itself which comes to bear the burden of doing the work of the domestic ideal: shorting up masculine identity, legitimating and normalizing heterosexuality, delegitimating other desires, and ameliorating the consequences of economic competition. Estella is a way to divert the shaming gaze from himself by placing the blame, even for his very identity, on her.

For Pip, it is clear that more is at stake than losing Estella. What is at stake is his very identity. He says of her:

> Truly it was impossible to dissociate her presence from all those wretched hankerings after money and gentility that had disturbed my boyhood—from all those ill-regulated aspirations that had first made me ashamed of home and Joe—from all those visions that had raised her face in the glowing fire, struck it out of the iron on the anvil, extracted it from the darkness of night to look in at the wooden window of the forge and flit away. In a word, it was impossible for me to separate her, in the past or in the present from the innermost life of my life. (256)

In an uncomfortable way, Estella lives in Pip, blurring the gender boundaries that the domestic ideal insists must be kept rigidly divided and complicating his ability to achieve a securely masculine identity of his own. Again in chapter 34 he writes "Yet Estella was so inseparable from all my restlessness and disquiet of mind that I really fell into confusion as to the limits of my own part in its production. That is to say, supposing I had had no expectations, and yet had had Estella to think of, I could not make out to my satisfaction that I should have done much better" (294). Her being a part of him means he need not take full responsibility for his faults, for she " 'cannot choose but remain part of [his] character, part of the little good . . . part of the evil' " (391).

Yet it would be a mistake to see Estella as all powerful in Pip's life, holding all the cards that can make him good or bad, happy or miserable. What the narrator accomplishes in so magnifying the role Estella plays in his development is precisely a shift in blame; he diverts responsibility and shame from himself by making himself a victim of Estella's influence and behavior. As Gail Turley Houston observes, "the reasoning of *Great Expectations* is that, not the devil but Estella made me do it" (17). The narrator makes clear that Estella, is certainly, as Susan Walsh points out, no "moral 'guarantor' " [14] who provides a safe domestic haven from the public world of masculine competition. In fact, she does quite the opposite, not merely provoking rivalries as would a coquette, but provoking violent competition that she, at least in one instance, rewards with a kiss. But Estella herself is certainly a victim as well, of Miss Havisham's manipulations, of Bentley Drummles's abuse, and of the narrator's spiteful insistence that she is to blame for his moral failings.

Estella's role is a complex one, especially since she is made to seem unworthy of Pip's insistent devotion. As Gail Turley Houston has noted, Estella is raised by Miss Havisham to be a perfect, too perfect, nightmare version of the selfless, undesiring Victorian heroine: "trained in the accomplishments of the ideal Victorian woman, Estella as Dickensian heroine has finally necessarily become what Victorian and Dickensian expectations must naturally—or, rather, unnaturally—result in: she is the nightmare version of the Victorian female bred to have no desires, no appetites, trained to be desired and to be the object of appetite" (17), but as such, she is incapable of returning love or affection. Miss Havisham "stole her heart away and put ice in its place' " (429), taking from her all that makes the selfless Victorian heroine human. The narrator narrates Estella's perversion at the hands of Miss Havisham, but then emphasizes her power to pervert his identity in turn. The narrator aggrandizes and exaggerates Estella's influence on him and his desire for her, turning her into the novel's ultimate scapegoat.

## IV

Estella's central relation to Pip's story illustrates most clearly the interconnections between sexual and class conflict—the narrative of class ambition, of heterosexual desire and the relation of both to the narrator's shame. It is through her that Dickens is able to expose the fiction of domestic ideology's attempt to resolve such conflicts through a woman. This is most obvious in the fight scene between Herbert and Pip in the ruined garden of Satis House. That Pip sees the potential consequences of his fight with Herbert in class terms is clear when he says "I felt that the pale young gentleman's blood was my head, and that the law would avenge it. Without having any definite idea of the penalties I had incurred, it was clear to me that village boys could not go stalking about the country, ravaging the houses of gentlefolks and pitching into the studious youth of England, without laying themselves open to severe punishment" (106). But Estella eroticizes this violence and finds it exciting rather than seeking to ameliorate it, rewarding Pip with a kiss (104), and the fight itself is a prelude to the sort of competition Pip must engage in in order to rise. And while in truth he hasn't displaced Herbert's own expectations, both young men believe this to be the case, though Herbert magnanimously refuses to be bitter about it. Thus Estella confirms Pip in his desire to be a gentleman for her sake and in the conviction that competition and male-male competitiveness rather than camaraderie, such as he has with Joe, is the only way to rise. Estella's influence is a way for Pip to explain and excuse this desire to rise, and also a way to ensure that he learns the proper way to relate to other men—through competition rather than through camaraderie.

However, this scene is certainly complex in other ways as well, and one reason for Pip's overpowering desire for Estella and his need to blame her for his moral failings can also be seen here. This scene is a clear example of the way in which Pip's uncomfortably close encounters with men, friendly as well as competitive or even violent, are retrospectively displaced onto a narrative of heterosexual desire. This scene serves as an occasion for "more provoking touches" than Estella's kiss, as Pip and Herbert begin their combat with a "curiously cruising scrutiny" as Herbert undresses under Pip's watchful eye in preparation for their fight (Cohen 234–34). Thus, while "in the logic of the novel's plot, fights interpose at junctures of fierce romantic rivalry, the *narration* of the battles consistently provides the occasion for the playing out of erotic contact, both homo- and hetero-sexual, between combatants" (Cohen 233). These battles, as well as the failure of the domestic ideal in the novel, constitute the reason the narrator's desire for Estella is so important. The failure to establish a safe domesticity and the continued close, and for

Pip uncomfortable, contact with other men, are symptoms of the narrative's uneasiness over Pip's inability to clearly delimit his relationships with men or to make them safe. Through marriage, he would rule out the potentially shameful quality of his close relationships with men and ameliorate his need to compete and labor.

The novel, however, is unable to resolve Pip's complex desires and the increasing intensity of the violence, between Orlick and Pip and Magwitch and Compeyson, correspond to an increasingly intense insistence on an undying desire for Estella, though that has been made impossible by her marriage. As in so many other Dickens novels, the strain between the different directions in the narrative makes ending nearly impossible and certainly ambivalent. Unfulfilled desire for Estella is only one source of Pip's "wretched hankering," and it is the very fact that he is unable to resolve his desire for her that is shameful. Throughout the novel, too close relations between men, especially between Pip and other men, are mediated through a woman. Biddy is both the occasion and the excuse for Orlick's violent assault on Pip, and Estella mediates Pip's ambivalent desires. Thus, Estella serves not only to divert blame from the narrator, but also to mediate other potentially shameful relationships, and his insistence on his desire for her is an attempt to resolve these.

The fragility of the narrator's resolutions can be seen most clearly in his relationship to Magwitch. His apparent conversion from contempt to empathy for Magwitch is in a complex relation to his desire for Estella, and again one is led to question the insistent gesture which makes Estella so central to the narrative's project. Paradoxically, it is the fact that she *is* installed so centrally in his narrative, even though she is unattainable, that allows him to recover his closeness with Magwitch and then Joe. Pip notes that his growing affection for Magwitch might stem from the interest he holds for Pip in light of Pip's discovery of Estella's parentage. He emphasizes that it is Estella, throughout his ordeal with Magwitch, who motivates his responses, both his abhorrence, his pity, and his devotion. He asks in chapter 43, "Why should I pause to ask how much of my shrinking from Provis might be traced to Estella?" (379), and the answer is that by doing so, he can excuse himself and blame Estella while appearing to be taking the moral high ground in exposing his past injustices. His adamant refusal to renounce his interest in Estella, however, can be seen as another instance of the displacement of other unsettling relationships onto his desire for her. The peculiarly physical intensity and virulence of Pip's revulsion for Magwitch leave a residue that cannot be completely accounted for, even in the face of the destruction of his expectations. Magwitch's signs of affection, his pleasure at seeing Pip "has a perilously overt sexual charge," and "Pip's gag reflex serves to bolster, not to diminish the eroticism of the episode, for it demonstrates his revulsion to be as highly cathected as the convict's attraction" (Cohen 243). Pip is only able to sympathize with and show affection to Magwitch when he is able to transpose his discomfort onto his desire for Estella by finding the link between her and the convict.

Pip's gradual change of heart towards Magwitch is accounted for by his attempt to bridge the "abyss" between him and Estella created by her marriage. The narrator assures this interpretation when he says of his search for the truth of Estella's parentage: "I really do not know whether I felt that I did this for Estella's sake, or whether I was glad to transfer to the man in whose preservation I was so much concerned some rays of the romantic interest that had so long surrounded me. Perhaps the latter possibility may be nearer to the truth" (439). Pip sees a reduction of distance between him and Magwitch as a way to avoid completely renouncing his interest in Estella in spite of her marriage and despite the devastation of his own expectations that are the consequence of Magwitch's return and revelations. Clearly, then, Pip's change of heart towards Magwitch is carefully qualified and legitimated by his emphasis on his continued desire for Estella.

Pip's relationship with Estella would signify his successful acquisition of gentility and a securely heterosexual masculine identity. Absolutely essential to his project is the economic freedom he assumes comes from Miss Havisham. The relationships which he most values with other men—Joe and Magwitch—represent a "dire sliding away from gentility, wealth and power" (Sedgwick *Between Men* 168). Pip must believe that the plot of ambition and the plot of heterosexual desire are necessarily linked, the one legitimated and sanctioned by the other. His discovery that this is not true is devastating. The source of his wealth pulls him back down as his desire for Estella becomes out of reach, and finally, the discovery of Estella's parentage exposes the utter artificiality of gentility and the falsity of an ideology that necessarily links a domestic ideal with class status. Pip discovers not just that his, but also Estella's, gentility is "forged," inescapably linked to the taint of criminality. The foundation of his desire for her, of his very identity, is false, yet it is too late for him to go back. He cannot completely recover his comfortable domesticity with Joe, nor marry Biddy, and the irresolution of the ending leaves the plot of heterosexual desire permanently unfinished for Pip.

Thus, while Pip is able ultimately to learn the simple Victorian lesson that being a gentleman means more than not having to work, he cannot entirely undo the identity that has been forged out of his shame. He cannot return to live and work at the forge, to marry Biddy and have a little Pip of his own; he instead is condemned to a sort of half life, exiled from England, and without a family of his own, a permanent bachelor guest in Herbert and Clara's home. Even Joe and Herbert, who both fulfill the narrative of heterosexual desire, do so in a space clearly outside the competitive marketplace of Victorian England while Pip is left altogether outside both narratives—that of heterosexual desire and that of a successful Victorian hero. The novel's insidious misogyny is both the product and the symptom of Pip's shame over all of his "wretched hankering," so violently repudiated in the narrative. Pip is left in what is, as the nineteenth-century wears on, the increasingly ambiguous and multivalent role of the "bachelor."[15] In this novel, the emergence of this "type" has its source in the increasing untenability of an impossible domestic ideal that insists on rigidly demarcated gender roles and desires.

Clearly, then, Estella functions more as a scapegoat than as an object of erotic desire. Pip's self-imposed exile at the novel's end indicates the extent to which he is alienated from both the socially sanctioned world of marriage and from the close bonds with other men that the novel shows to be so problematic. *Great Expectations* marks a moment in Dickens' work, and in Victorian culture, in which the strain placed on ideals based on a specific gender, sexual, and class politics erupts into insurmountable and irresolvable inconsistencies. It is the very fact of irresolution itself, narrated in the conclusion, that constitutes Pip's failure of identity and his shame. The complexity of his conflicting desires and the shame that these provoke, leave him unable to fulfill the plot of heterosexual desire, and in order to explain away this shame, he turns the shaming gaze of the narration on the women of the novel, unable or unwilling to acknowledge his own continuing ambivalence.

# NOTES

1. The most important article on guilt in *Great Expectations* is, of course, Julian Moynahan's seminal essay "The Hero's Guilt: The Case of *Great Expectations*," in *Essays in Criticism* 10 (1960): 60–79. Other critics who take guilt explicitly or implicitly to be a crucial to the novel's thematics are Michal Peled Ginsberg, "Dickens and the Uncanny: Repression and Displacement in *Great Expectations*," *Dickens Studies Annual* 13 (1984): 115–24; Barry Westburg, *The Confessional Fictions of Charles Dickens,*, esp. pp. 155–78; and J. Hillis Miller who in *Charles Dickens: The World of His Novels,* writes that " . . . the Dickensian hero becomes aware of himself as guilty" (251).

2. Though, of course, shame and guilt are closely allied. Silvan Tomkins argues that "shyness, shame and guilt are not distinguished from each other at the level of affect . . . ," yet "the conscious awareness of each of these experiences is quite distinct," and thus "it is the difference in the other components which accompany shame in the central assembly or, in other words, which are experienced together with shame, which make the three experiences different" (118). Moreover, shame is also "related to and easily confused with contempt, particularly self-contempt; indeed, it is sometimes not possible to separate them" (119). He says later again in regards to the usage of the terms guilt and shame that "we commonly speak

of being ashamed of moral infractions, but we do not ordinarily speak of feeling guilty for our inferiority'' (152). Robert Newsom argues that '' 'Shame' almost always refers to a feeling as opposed to a state or fact'' (5), while guilt is clearly a ''state,'' something that results from one's actions. See Eve Sedgwick below for the link between shame and identity formation in relation to reading literature. I owe this insight to her seminar at the School of Criticism and Theory in 1992 and to her recently published article on Henry James which I was fortunate to read at an earlier stage.

3. I am quoting from the 1980 Signet Classis edition of *Great Expectations,* page 119.
4. Similarly, Newsom argues ''that to feel shame involves being looked at and that one's reaction to shame is to want to escape the gaze and hide'' (7). Newsom goes on to explain the history of the word shame to make this connection even clearer: ''The connection between shame and being visible is intrinsic'' since shame ''deriving from a root meaning 'to cover' '' (8). Sedgwick in ''Queer Performativity: Henry James's *The Art of the Novel,*'' argues that ''shame effaces itself; shame points and projects; shame turns itself skin side outside; shame and pride, shame and self-display, shame and exhibitionism are different interlinings of the same glove: shame, it might finally be said . . . *is performance.* I mean theatrical performance' (5). The issue of performativity is central to understanding shame's relation to narration as narration is performative: it constitutes the identity it purports to describe, and helps to constitute a self for the reader as well by engaging them in reconstructing that performance, repeating it.
5. Newsom further clarifies this, quoting Gerhart Piers: ' ''Whereas guilt is generated whenever a boundary (set by the superego) is touched or transgressed, shame occurs when a goal (presented by the ego ideal) is not being reached. It thus indicates a real 'shortcoming'. Guilt anxiety accompanies transgression; shame, failure' '' (6).
6. Sedgwick argues that ''Shame, as opposed to guilt, is a bad feeling that does not attach to what one does, but to what one is''; thus, ''one therefore *is something,* in experiencing shame'' (''Performativity'' 12).
7. Poovey's analysis in *Uneven Developments* illustrates how the labor of literature, writing itself as a special form of labor, came to be a way to trope and to work through these contradictions: ''Precisely because literary labor exposed the problematic nature of crucial capitalist categories, writing, and specifically the representation of writing, became a contested site during this period, a site at which the instabilities implicit in market relations surface, only to be variously worked over and sometimes symbolically resolved'' (104–05). The contradictions that need to be worked through are those inherent to the idea of the individual: ''But because of a paradox central to the concept of the individual in class society, the individualization of authorship actually 'solved' the contradiction between two images of writer—the 'genius' and the cog of the capitalist machine—at the same time that is assured the writer a constructive and relatively lucrative social role,'' and she goes on to link this solution to the establishment of an identity, of a name: ''On the one hand, by its very nature, the successful promotion of a marketable 'name' depended on distinguishing between this writer and all other competitors. But on the other hand, arguments advanced to discriminate a writer's

personality so as to enhance the value of his work often referred to his ability to appeal to or represent the taste of all his readers—to be, in other words, like everybody else'' (106, 108).

8. The relationship between shame and class in the novel can best be understood through the distinction between contempt and self-contempt. Tomkins writes: "Shame-humiliation is the negative affect linked with love and identification, and contempt-disgust the negative affect linked with individuation and hate. . . . Whenever an individual, a class or a nation wishes to maintain hierarchical relationships, or to maintain aloofness it will have resort to contempt of the other. Contempt is the mark of the oppressor. . . . In a democratic society, contempt will often be replaced by empathic shame'' (140–41).

9. Eve Sedgwick argues that "By the time of *Great Expectations, Our Mutual Friend,* and *Edwin Drood, . . .* Dickens' writing had incorporated the concerns and thematics of the paranoid Gothic as a central preoccupation. Specifically, each of these novels sites an important plot in triangular, heterosexual romance—in the Romance tradition—and then changes its focus as if by compulsion from the heterosexual bonds of the triangle to the male homosocial one, here called " 'erotic rivalry' " (*Between Men* 162). I agree with her analysis, but I want to look at this dynamic from a different angle, trying to account for the novel's shrill insistence on Pip's desire for Estella and her centrality to his motivations and behavior. As the male homosocial bonds become increasingly uncomfortable, the insistence on Estella increases proportionately.

10. Mary Poovey argues that in *David Copperfield* "The kind of subject described and reproduced by David Copperfield is individualized, psychologized, and ahistorical; it is also gendered. In fact (masculine) gender is the constitutive feature of this subject; identity here takes the form of a physical and emotional development in which the male subject tempers his sexual and emotional desires by the possibilities of the social world. This . . . also entails a specific model of desire . . . [which] is insatiable and potentially transgressive; it begins in the home as the condition of the individual's individuation and growth; it motivates his quest for self-realizations; and, ideally, it is stabilized and its transgressive potential neutralized in the safe harbor of marriage'' (90).

11. While I would argue that Hartog himself repeats the gesture of scapegoating the feminine in the novel, I do agree with his conclusion that masculine identity is represented as succeeding or failing in the novel based on the success or failure of feminine identity.

13. I agree with John O. Jordan who writes that it is "emptiness or absence that motivates his narrative'' (80), an emptiness whose source Jordan sees in the narrator's still unfulfilled desire for Estella.

14. Walsh argues, "Set loose in the world like an enemy agent, Estella is no moral 'guarantor,'. . . . Rather she is a cold-blooded anti-monitoress who seems to atomize rather than harmonize the competing interest of covetous men'' (89–90).

15. Eve Sedgwick writes that "with Thackeray and other early and mid-Victorians, a character classification of 'the bachelor' came into currency, a type that for some men both narrowed the venue, and at the same time startlingly desexualized the question of male sexual choice'' (*Epistemology* 188).

# Works Cited

Baumgarten, Murray, "Calligraphy and Code: Writing in *Great Expectations.*" *Dickens Studies Annual* 11 (1983): 61/72.

Cohen, William A. "Manual Conduct in *Great Expectations.*" *ELH* 60 (1993): 217–59.

Crawford, Iain. "Pip and the Monster: The Joys of Bondage." *SEL* 28 (1988): 625–47.

Ginsburg, Michal Peled. "Dickens and the Uncanny: Repression and Displacement in *Great Expectations.*" *Dickens Studies Annual* 13 (1984): 115–24.

Hara, Eiichi. "Stories Present and Absent in *Great Expectations.*" *ELH* 53 (1986): 593–614.

Hartog, Curt. "The Rape of Miss Havisham." *Studies in the Novel* 14 (1982): 248–65.

Houston, Gail Turley. " 'Pip' and 'Property': The (Re)Production of the Self in *Great Expectations.*" *Studies in the Novel* 24 (1992): 13–25.

Jordan, John O. "The Medium of *Great Expectations.*" *Dickens Studies Annual* 11 (1983): 73–88.

Milbank, Alison. *Daughters of the House: Modes of the Gothic in Victorian Fiction.* New York: St. Martin's P, 1992.

Miller, J. Hillis. *Charles Dickens: The World of His Novels.* Cambridge: Harvard UP, 1958.

Moynahan, Julian. "The Hero's Guilt: The Case of *Great Expectations.*" *Essays in Criticism* 10 (1960): 60–79.

Newsom, Robert. "The Hero's Shame." *Dickens Studies Annual* 11 (1983): 1–24.

Pearlman, E. "Inversion in *Great Expectations.*" *Dickens Studies Annual* 7 (1978): 278–93.

Poovey, Mary. *Uneven Development: The Ideological Work of Gender in Mid-Victorian England.* Chicago: U of Chicago P, 1988.

Romig, Evelyn M. "Twisted Tale, Silent Teller: Miss Havisham in *Great Expectations.*" *Dickens Quarterly* 5 (1988): 18–22.

Sedgwick, Eve. *Between Men: English Literature and Male Homosocial Desire.* New York: Columbia UP, 1985.

———. *Epistemology of the Closet.* Berkeley: U of California P, 1990.

———. "Queer Performativity: Henry James's *The Art of the Novel.*" *Gay and Lesbian Quarterly* 1 (1993): 1–16.

Stein, Robert A. "Pip's Poisoning Magwitch, Supposedly: The Historical Context and Its Implications for Pip's Guilt and Shame." *Philological Quarterly* 67 (1988): 103–16.

Tambling, Jeremy. "Prison-bound: Dickens and Foucault." *Essays in Criticism* 36 (1986): 11–31.

Tomkins, Silvan. *Affect Imagery Consciousness vol. 2 The Negative Affects.* New York: Springer, 1963.

Walsh, Susan. "Bodies of Capital: *Great Expectations* and the Climacteric Economy." *Victorian Studies* 37 (1993): 73–97.

Westburg, Barry. *The Confessional Fictions of Charles Dickens.* Dekalb, IL: Northern Illinois UP, 1977.

# "Dashing in Now": *Great Expectations* and Charles Lever's *A Day's Ride*

## Jerome Meckier

Thanks to Charles Lever's unpopular serial, circulation of *All the Year Round* declined for the only time during Dickens' life. His new periodical in jeopardy, the novelist had to rescue the editor by writing *Great Expectations* which reversed the slump in sales. Consequently, *A Day's Ride: A Life's Romance* is chiefly remembered as the reason Dickens' thirteenth novel appeared in weekly installments instead of monthly parts as originally planned. But Lever's disaster sheds light on the nature of Dickens' countermeasure, not just its genesis; it helps to explain what Dickens wrote as well as when and why.

The consensus is that Dickens behaved handsomely. His "proposed remedy," inserting *Great Expectations* to accompany *A Day's Ride,* was "not drastic," Lionel Stevenson decided (*CL* 243). Edgar Johnson went further: dreading the "blow" to Lever's self-esteem from news of negative public response, Dickens strove "generously to assuage the wound" (*J* 2:965). Instead of terminating *A Day's Ride,* J. A. Sutherland commented, Dickens permitted Lever's serial to complete its run out of "a spirit of collegiality."[1]

Actually, editorial policy at *All the Year Round* prejudiced Lever's chances. When sales began falling, Dickens' decisions precluded recovery from a bad start. In addition, the novelist capitalized imaginatively on a rival's fiasco: *A Day's Ride* reminded Dickens of pitfalls to avoid and furnished a convenient target for parodic revaluation. Instead of one serial buttressing the other, a disgruntled Dickens wrote his story to cancel Lever's, in effect to repeal the latter's unrealistic world view. *Great Expectations* is primarily a satire on Victorian expectancy, an anti-Cinderella fairy tale in which Pip's rise and fall warns an entire nation against snobbish overconfidence; but it also achieves a thoroughgoing revision of the candy-coated comedy in *A Day's Ride.* Admitting an editorial mistake, Dickens set out to prove that he was still the period's most trenchant social critic and finest serialist. Lever was forced to compensate aesthetically for the financial losses he had caused. Having been costly to Dickens, he found himself in no position to retaliate. *Great Expectations* eclipsed *A Day's Ride* so completely that the final, most interesting chapter of the Dickens-Lever rivalry has remained hidden.[2]

The permanent decline in Lever's reputation has obscured parallels between his younger self and the early Dickens, who were frequently regarded as contenders for preeminence. In 1830, Lever began contributing sketches of city life to *The Dublin Literary Gazette* not unlike those Boz set in London a few years later. *Harry Lorrequer,* Lever's first novel, was serialized in the *Dublin University Magazine (1837)* shortly after Mr. Pickwick commenced his travels, then reissued in monthly parts to take advantage of Dickens' success.

Critics occasionally ranked Lever above Dickens. The popularity of *Charles O'Malley* (1841), Edgar Allan Poe wrote, "surpassed even the inimitable compositions of Mr. Dickens" (WJF 1:274).[3] One reviewer professed that he "would rather be the author of *Harry Lorrequer* than of all the 'Pickwicks' and 'Nicklebys' in the world" (*CL* 91). When Lever's publishers advertised this comment, Dickens protested and Lever wrote an apologetic letter "to his rival" (*CL* 95). According to W. J. Fitzpatrick, Lever in pink wrappers, Thackeray in yellow, and Dickens in green were "the three most popular novelists of the day" (WJF 2:185). Lever considered himself a match for Dickens. Thus *Tom Burke of "Ours"* attempts a Dickensian rendition of the Paris slums; *St. Patrick's Eve* (1845) resembles a Dickens Christmas book. Dickens and Lever were frequently mentioned for the same jobs. In 1841, Richard Bentley asked Lever to edit his *Miscellany,* a post Dickens held first. After Dickens suspended *Household Words* and commenced *All the Year Round,* Bradbury and Evans, publishers of the earlier venture, tried to persuade Lever to spearhead "a rival journal" (*CL* 238).

Given this prolonged public competition, the invitation to contribute a serial to *All the Year Round* is puzzling. The editor surely did not plan from the outset to embarrass an old foe of the novelist. Dickens was beginning a new phase in which he reoriented his melodramatic realism toward the tragicomic and the psychological. Not so Lever, whose views on comedy and composition (i.e., structure) never changed.[4] This prolific, Dublin-born novelist's early novels vividly portrayed Irish military and fox-hunting society, but he was slipping past his prime—if not already *passé.* Nevertheless, Dickens courted him, as this lavish solicitation shows: "believe, my dear Lever—not only that I 'want' you now, but that I have 'wanted' such a generous spirit in a man, many a long day" (*CL* 241). Presumably, Dickens had never heard Lever's prediction, years earlier to Alexander Spencer, that "fast writing and careless composition'' in *Dombey and Son* had "set the gravestone" on Dickens' fame (*ED* 1:204). Nor did Dickens realize how jealous Lever was of his rival's ever-increasing reputation. A gambler and spendthrift, Lever envied Dickens' securer financial position, which, ironically, he was fated to endanger.

Most likely, Dickens regarded Lever as a stopgap. His novel was to follow either Collins's *The Woman in White* or, preferably, its successor, which Dickens hoped would be a story by Elizabeth Gaskell or George Eliot. But Gaskell, who had already contributed three serials to *Household Words,* reneged; Eliot decided against what she considered the serial format's "terseness and closeness of construction" (J 2:956). Had Lever followed Eliot or Gaskell, for whom suspenseful construction was not the sine qua non, he might have seemed more at home in Dickens' rotation. Instead, he succeeded one of the cleverest serialists the century produced. *A Day's Ride* went against the tone of the journal's previous offerings without measuring up to their excitements.

On-again, off-again negotiations may have been responsible for Lever's late start and lackadaisical approach. Discussions began in October 1859, but Dickens did not offer terms until January 1860; the starting date still depended on Eliot. Uncertain when he would be needed, Lever had no motive to work in earnest until February 1860, when Dickens requested four installments by June. Although Lever had a tentative title, his general idea, and three full months, his resolve seems to have eroded: as late as April, he was ransacking *Tales of the Trains* (1845), one of his weakest productions, "to see" if he "could steal any of the incidents" for the "new tale" he had promised Dickens (*CL* 241).

Perhaps Lever mistook Dickens' off-hand manner during the preliminaries for a nonchalance equal to his own. Perhaps Dickens underestimated the amount of strong handling the undisciplined Lever required. Dickens was not extending carte blanche in conceding that Lever could write "anything grave or gay about anything in the wide world"—as long as the material filtered through his "bright and keen eyes" (*CL* 241). From the editor's manner of expressing confidence in his contributor's judgment, however, Lever assumed that he could rely on last-minute improvisation. He had published nineteen serials since 1837 (more than Dickens' entire output), yet he proceeded to ignore the lessons about scrupulous planning that Dickens' successes up to 1860 should have taught him. Lever may have trusted the popularity of Dickens' periodical to carry him no matter how indifferently he composed: "The *Ride* I write as carelessly as a common letter," he boasted to Spencer on 17 September 1860, "but I'd not be the least astonished to find the success in the inverse ratio to the trouble" (ED 1:362).

As a result of so cavalier an approach, *A Day's Ride* is an episodic novel in which events succeed each other according to whatever Lever thought of next. Algernon Sydney Potts, the son of a Dublin apothecary is an upstart like Pip, discontented with his lot and anxious to appear genteel. In chapter 38, we learn that he is 23 years old—Pip's age by the "Third Stage." The novel chronicles Potts's ludicrous daydreams, his snobbish pretensions; it savors the embarrassments these repeatedly cause him as he travels from Ireland to London, then through parts of Belgium, Germany, Switzerland, and Austria, going as far east as Russia before returning to Great Britain (i.e., Wales) by way of Paris. These meanderings begin during the long vacation from Trinity College, Dublin, after an undistinguished first year. Armed with a small legacy from his uncle, Potts sets out as if for a ride of a day or so but is on the road approximately three years.[5]

Loosely connected mishaps, the stuff of picaresque, were foreign to the serial novel's increasing emphasis on a tight plot full of suspense and surprise. Based on Potts's itinerary, Lever's story literally rambled. Incidents were often amusing and the n'er-do-well hero is always likeable, but Lever's casually unfolding tale could not incite readers to clamor for the next issue. One can skim chapters without losing the storyline: 6, 8, 12, 14, 17, 22, and 26, all from the novel's looser first half, fall into this category. Dickens eventually said as much: in a letter for 6 October 1860, he suggested that the tale was "too detached and discursive"; it was not "strung . . . on the needful strong thread of interest" (L 3:183–84)—accurate criticisms that he would keep in mind for Great Expectations but ought to have leveled sooner, not after Lever's novel had been running for almost two months.

Dickens had asked Lever "to give him something lively" for his year-old journal; the editor wanted to "infuse some new blood" lest he and Collins remain its only serialists. Previously a successful contributor of shorter pieces to Household Words, Lever responded with a novel intended to "record the life of a fool."[6] In 1860, however, Potts (or Pottinger as he restyles himself in chapter 9) was an anachronism.[7] The Irish equivalent of a Cockney picaro, Potts is an undergraduate version of the sporting grocer, whose disasters on horseback were ridiculed by Robert Smith Surtees in sketches collected as Jorrocks's Jaunts and Jollities (1838). Instead of a transfusion, Lever took the Victorian novel two decades into its past.

Surprisingly, Dickens exhibited no editorial misgivings prior to publication. He assured lever that the nondescript title was "a very good one" and warned him not to write down to a periodical audience as if it were not to be trusted "with anything good" (J 2:956–57)—strange advice to a veteran serialist even if All the Year Round was several notches above the Dublin University Magazine. Although Dickens recommended "condensation" as a general principle, he simply wanted assurances that Lever's hero would commence his wanderings before the end of the first installment (chs. 1–2). As of June 1860, Dickens was delighted with the "vivacity, originality, and humour" of the opening chapters, especially "the rising invention in the drunken young man" (i.e., the hero's attempts in chapter 3 to pass as someone noteworthy—the finest swordsman in Europe, a friend of the emperor of Russia. Actually, Potts drinks too much and loses his rental horse in a backgammon game). This episode, Dickens wrote Lever, "made me laugh to an extent and with a heartiness that I should like you to have seen and heard" (J 2:957).

For a decade, Dickens was urged to abandon social criticism for the Pickwickian manner that had made him famous. But when he reverted to something in a lighter vein, even if he did not write it himself, his audience objected. Dickens may have been drawn to *A Day's Ride*'s atavistic qualities: having pacified the Pickwickians in his readership with Lever, he would be at liberty to continue the epic critique of Victorian society that spans the 1850s from *Bleak House* through *Hard Times* and *Little Dorrit* to *A Tale of Two Cities*. For economic reasons, two novels in this Juvenalian onslaught had to be weekly serials—*Hard Times* to prop up *Household Words, A Tale of Two Cities* to inaugurate *All the Year Round.* With the weekly serial department entrusted to Lever, Dickens could reestablish the novel in twenty monthly parts as his primary vehicle for social analysis.

When *A Day's Ride* commenced (18 August 1860), it was forced to compete with installment 39 of *The Woman in White,* which still had another climactic installment to go. That Lever did not capture readership from the beginning is not entirely his fault; no match for the accumulated interest in Wilkie Collins's novel, his humbler fare was bound to debut inauspiciously. While Potts was renting Blondel and setting out, Walter Hartright finally cornered Count Fosco. Besides Fosco's confession to the conspiracy against Laura Fairlie, next week's final installment included Hartright's account of her vindication and his subsequent discovery of the murdered Fosco's corpse in the Paris morgue. No wonder Potts's misadventures at the "Lamb," the inn where his first and only day on horseback ends with the loss of his mount, went unnoticed.

During a previous overlap (26 November 1859), *The Woman in White* debuted on the third page of *All the Year Round* (95–104), immediately after the last installment of *A Tale of Two Cities.* It ran a mere two pages (93–95), posing little threat to Collins's suspenseful beginning (chs. 1–4). His longer installments kept Lever's tale far from the front page for *two* weeks: after opening on the ninth page on 18 August (441–47, following Collins on 433–41), *A Day's Ride* was pushed back to the twelfth page on 25 August (469–74, following Collins on 457–68).

Distracted by Collins, few readers probably turned directly to Lever on either 18 or 25 August. Some may not have read Lever's first two installments, so the fixing power of his third installment, Potts's meeting with the Croftons (ch. 5), assumed greater importance than could have been anticipated. Reading Lever after finishing either of Collins's last two installments only served to magnify the former's deficiencies as a serialist—no economy, little suspense. Thus every conceivable course of action on the reader's part prevented *A Day's Ride* from grabbing hold. Lever's story would have begun to greater advantage had Dickens waited until September before starting its run. But it seems to have been editorial policy to launch a new serial before the old one had concluded.[8] This fostered a sense of continuity implicit in the journal's title. Instead of providing momentum for transition, however, *The Woman in White* refused to relinquish the spotlight.

On 27 October 1860, Dickens announced the December starting date for *Great Expectations.* He encouraged readers to look past Lever instead of struggling to come to terms with him. *A Day's Ride* still had five months to go. On 9 February 1861, well in advance of Lever's last installment (23 March) and with *Great Expectations* less than a third in print, Dickens announced that the end of *A Day's Ride* was in sight.[9] It was customary to reveal when one serial would end and another begin, but pointing to a conclusion *seven* weeks beforehand seems premature. Dickens timed his announcement to coincide with the "great expectations" chapter (ch. 18). The same week that Jaggers informed Pip of his improved prospects, Dickens told readers of theirs.

Dickens first mentioned *A Day's Ride* as a coming attraction on 21 July 1860, a month before its commencement. There were three reminders of its approaching inaugural: 28 July, 4 and 11 August. Thus the advent of Lever's novel and that of *Great Expectations* received similar emphasis, but the latter was promoted as an anodyne to be administered months before the former terminated. Collins's *The Woman in White* had only five more installments to go after 21 July. Readers no doubt surmised that it was nearing conclusion, but this was not made official until 18 August 1860, one week before the end. As Lever's first two chapters appeared along with Collins's penultimate installment, Dickens included this notice: "In pursuance of the plan announced at the commencement of THE WOMAN IN WHITE, we have the pleasure of presenting to the reader a New Story by Mr. CHARLES LEVER. After the completion of The Woman in White next week, A DAY'S RIDE will occupy its place on the first page of each weekly number, and will be continued from week to week until finished." Less than four months later, *Great Expectations* appropriated the top spot that Collins had enjoyed uninterruptedly for 39 weeks. Dickens' serial automatically took precedence, banishing Lever into the recesses of *All the Year Round* for a second time: to the twelfth page again on 1 December 1860. The displacement of *A Day's Ride* has been dismissed along with Dickens' early announcement of its termination date as "minor irritations" for Lever (*CL* 244). But his installments were soon relegated to the last pages. On 2 February 1861, for example, the issue began with chapters 16 and 17 of *Great Expectations*; then came features such as "Volunteers at Hythe," "Hard Frosts," and "In Praise of Bears." Chapter 36 of *A Day's Ride* ran last.

The "plan" divulged on 26 November 1859 did not specify Lever's novel as Collins's successor. On 18 August, Dickens was alluding to his editorial pledge only to publish "sustained works of the imagination." The "plan" was clearly intended to mean that Dickens' periodical would never contain another of his novels after *A Tale of Two Cities*. On the other hand, it offered assurance that the inaugural serial had established the standard. By October 1860, Dickens must have accused himself of having broken the covenant made with his readers less than a year before. That the introduction of *Great Expectations* was a slap in the face to Lever seems not to have worried Dickens nearly as much as repairing the sacred bond he had forged with the public.

Dickens' talent as a serialist guaranteed that his troubled journal would rebound. Bolstering *All the Year Round* was impossible, however, without sinking a fellow novelist—a case of the editor deciding, in effect, to deliver the coup de grâce to a floundering contributor. Opportunities to outshine a rival proved irresistible. Lever had sealed his fate in the more than three months before *Great Expectations* was introduced. Nevertheless, it is difficult to imagine readers persisting with *A Day's Ride* during the four months the stories ran concurrently. When the opening chapters of *Great Expectations* outclassed *A Day's Ride* as unmercifully as the final episodes of *The Woman in White* had, Lever's sense of déjè vu must have grown acute: first one melodramatic realist prevented his novel from catching on; then a second made certain it never did.

In a letter for 15 October 1860, Dickens lectured Lever about a serial's obligation to "fix the people in the beginning" (*L* 3:186–87). Two and a half months later, making his point a second time, he demonstrated how this fixing should be done. Contrary to Lever's casual commencement, Dickens began with a confrontation as momentous as Walter Hartright's encounter with the ghostly Anne Catherick in Collins's opening installment. Lever's hero gets underway slowly and seems equally foolish at start and finish, but Pip's life is changed forever by an arresting apparition when Magwitch starts "up from among the graves" within seconds of the novel's beginning (*GE* 4).

Dickens took readers' divided expectations to heart. "The opening," he insisted to Forster in a letter for "October 1860," is "exceedingly droll" in that the "relations" between "a child and a good-natured man" (Pip and Joe) "seem to be very funny" (*L* 3:186). At the same time, he had set up "the pivot on which the story will turn," Pip's long-term affiliation with

Magwitch. In the first installment, Dickens supplied Pip and Joe (ch. 2) for diehard Pickwickians, Pip and Magwitch (ch. 1) for sensational realists.[10] A counterpoint of comedy and terror resulted from the compression into adjoining chapters of two parallel father-son relationships sharply different in tone and significance. Outshining Lever's loosely constructed story, Dickens' bildungsroman's first two chapters indicated that Pip's growth and development would meet the definition of tragicomedy by alternating serious and humorous episodes. Dickens' brand of melodramatic realism had tragicomic possibilities—it belonged to a higher genre than Lever's picaresque novel.

"Four weekly numbers have been ground off the wheel" and a fifth is imminent, Dickens wrote Collins on October 24 (L 3:188). He was doing the first visit to Satis House (ch. 8) and would soon move on to Pip's exaggerated account of this event: under Pumblechook's "bullying" cross-examination, Pip describes Miss Havisham's "black velvet coach," "cakes and wine" eaten from "gold plate," dogs fighting "for veal-cutlets out of a silver basket," and the waving of flags and swords (GE 68–69). After opening dramatically, Dickens rescinded the praise he had lavished on Potts's "rising invention" in chapter 3 of A Day's Ride. The superiority of the eight-year-old's imagination to the intoxicated undergraduate's tall tales symbolizes the relationship that Dickens quickly established between the creative faculties of their respective authors.

Closeted with distinguished company at the "Lamb," Potts feels removed "from all accidents of his situation"—that is, free to masquerade as anyone he pleases (ADR 22). Soon this scion of apothecaries is bragging about estates in his family since the Magna Charta. Had Pip been quizzed further, however, there would have been no limit to his fabrications: "a balloon in the yard," "a bear in the brewery" (GE 70). Both episodes use lying to expose the hero's inferiority complex, but social pressures to rise above the ordinary are harsher on Pip. Potts lies to Hammond, Oxley, Lord Keldrum, and Father Dyke to gratify an inflated sense of personal worth. Younger, poorer, and defenseless, Pip is forced to satisfy the unreasonable expectations of Pumblechook and Mrs. Joe. His subsequent desire for ascendancy, as sharp as Magwitch's, is both an internal drive and the result of exhaustive social conditioning since childhood. Potts fails to deceive his companions; Pip easily bamboozles Pumblechook and Mrs. Joe, who want their illusions confirmed. When Pip confesses his lies, even Joe seems culpable, wishing for a flag at Satis House if no coach; if no "immense" dogs to pull it, then at least a "puppy" (GE 71).

In chapter 9 Dickens served notice that he intended to broaden, deepen, and, above all, darken Lever's themes. His method of revaluing rivals was to substitute bleaker renditions that reduced to frivolity their alleged mishandling of similar materials. This process of parodic reconsideration is inherently tragicomic: no less amusing than Potts's deliberate lies, Pip's involuntary mendacity panders to society's weaknesses, endorsing the kind of harmful fairy tales that Victorian England was gullibly telling itself—lies, for example, about the unlimited privileges of affluence. No one questions Miss Havisham's right to keep a coach indoors. In a country where Magwitch grows up "a thieving turnips" for a living (*GE* 344), she allegedly feeds her dogs veal cutlets.

Potts's temporary embarrassment in chapter 3 of *A Day's Ride* is rewritten as a formative experience for Pip in chapter 9 of *Great Expectations,* "a memorable day" that "made great changes" in him (73). It begins Pip's awareness of the world's fundamental "insufficiency."[11] Only eight, he already suspects that neither facing facts nor inventing fictions is satisfying. One can never remove the "accidents" (Potts's word) of one's situation; nor can one transcend them through creative fantasy (i.e., lies). As Joe rightly warns, "lies is lies" (*GE* 71). Yet remaining on the "level" of "common doings" will not necessarily enable one to "live well and die happy" as Joe exhorts Pip to do (*GE* 72). Estella taunted Pip with his commonness; her insults, he realizes, "somehow" prompted the lies (*GE* 71).

When Potts's rambles ended, Dickens had reached installment 17. Chapter 27 revolves humorously around Pip and Joe (as did chapter 2), chapter 28 indirectly around Pip and Magwitch (as chapter 1 did directly). By this point, the tension between comedy and catastrophe can be found within each chapter, not just in the contrast of each with the other. Installment 17 will be used to illustrate Dickens' revaluation strategy throughout *Great Expectations.* In chapter 27, he reemphasized his appropriation of Lever's principal theme: snobbery's perils and pitfalls. In chapter 28, he exposed the thinness of Lever's plot, prolonging Pip's uncertainties to repudiate the all-too-convenient resolution of Potts's.

Breakfasting with Pip and Joe in Barnard's Inn, Joe performs the sort of bungling that Lever reserved for Potts. In chapter 27, Dickens condemns Pip's superior attitude through the false moves it elicits from Joe. He squirms in his Sunday clothes and calls his former playfellow "sir." Yet whether fumbling with his shirt collar or spilling his food, Pip's self-styled "infant companionation" retains "a simple dignity" (*GE* 225), whereas Pip sinks in our esteem (and his own) without actually playing the buffoon. Subtler psychologically than anything in Lever, the unsettling effects Pip has on his earliest friend and protector reveal the consequences of snobbery more incisively than Lever did by repeatedly disconcerting Potts.

The damage is self-inflicted and self-contained when Potts pretends to be a government messenger eagerly awaited at Constantinople, or when his self-importance leads Mrs. Keats to mistake him for "the young C. de P.," a count allegedly touring Germany in disguise (*ADR* 199).[12] One smiles when Potts extolls the "grand stuff" he is "made of" (*ADR* 405), or when the "mythical narrative," of his exploits proves to be "a card edifice of greatness" (*ADR* 82–83). But Pip's superior airs result in Joe's humiliation, which hastens his departure from London. Snobbery can be socially disruptive, Dickens lectured Lever, just like the class consciousness that causes it. Furthermore, a snobbish outlook is almost impossible to overcome: having discombobulated Joe, Pip becomes "impatient' and "out of temper," which upsets Joe even more. "If I had been easier with Joe," Pip decides in retrospect, "Joe would have been easier with me" (*GE* 223). The episode approaches tragicomedy in that an element of cruelty seeps into Joe's plight, making readers uneasy in their laughter even when Joe's hat, symbol of the commonness he cannot lay down in Pip's presence, keeps tumbling off the mantlepiece until its owner finally knocks it "into the slop-basin." Correcting Lever, Dickens discloses snobbery's pernicious side: not just an obstacle to the individual snob's maturation, it threatens human relationships generally.

In the second half of the installment that coincided with the resolution of *A Day's Ride,* Pip is returning to his village by coach. He recognizes one of the convicts seated behind him as the man who gave him two one-pound notes in the Three Jolly Bargemen (*GE* 75–76). As the convicts converse, it becomes clear that the money was a gift from Magwitch, whom Pip seems fated to meet again. This prospect undermined Lever's parting view of Potts's rosy future with Kate Herbert, whose fortuitous summons brings him to her family in Wales and concludes the novel with the hero's reward. Lever's chapter 48 is later parodied extensively in Pip's flight to Egypt, his eleven-year absence from Estella, and the lingering ambiguity—will they part or not—in the novel's last line.[13]

For two years Potts wanders aimlessly after locating Kate's missing father, about whom more later. In the final installment, he receives Kate's letter of invitation, which has been gathering dust in the Paris police department. In chapter 28, Pip reads an article in the Blue Boar's coffee-room from a "dirty old copy" of the local newspaper proclaiming Pumblechook "the founder" of his fortunes (*GE* 231). Its obvious falsity compromises the credibility of Lever's happy ending. From one document Potts learns that he has acquired a patroness whom he seems not to deserve; from another, Pip comes no closer to identifying his patron. Lever promoted Potts to wedded bliss with an ironmaster's daughter. In rebuttal, *Great Expectations* continued to build toward Magwitch's catastrophic return which terminates Pip's social ascent, including his dream of an early marriage to Estella.

Pip's vicissitudes in chapter 29 permitted readers to consign Potts to Wales without a pang. Pip has journeyed to Rochester (ch. 28) because Joe brought him a summons from Miss Havisham (ch. 27): having completed her education, Estella wishes to see her former playmate. At their first meeting since childhood (ch. 29), Pip beholds "an elegant lady," whom Miss Havisham christens a "queen"; he feels like a "coarse and common boy again" (*GE* 235) despite his improved manners and dress. The week after *A Day's Ride* concluded, Dickens continued to undercut its unrealistic ending: he pitted Pip's summons to Rochester against Potts's to Wales. When Pip reenacts his first humiliating visit to Satis House, Potts's rise from apothecary's son to an industrialist's prospective son-in-law forfeits any remaining plausibility.

Kate's letter informs Potts that her father "loves" him and her mother "longs to know" him (*ADR* 447). In Dickens' parody of Potts's euphoria, Pip rejoices that Estella "should be destined" for the former "blacksmith's boy" (*GE* 244). Despite an unsatisfactory interview with Estella at Satis House and no encouragement from Miss Havisham, Pip concludes chapter 29 with a "burst of gratitude." Such a destiny occurs only in fairy tales, Dickens implied, ironically conflating *Cinderella* and *Sleeping Beauty*: unlike Potts, who has found his princess, Pip wonders when his Cinderella-like rise in the world will "awaken" Estella's "mute and sleeping" heart (*GE* 244).

Joe's first London visit in chapter 27 looks back to the Christmas dinner in chapter 4 and forward to Pip's breakfast with Magwitch in chapter 40, the morning after the ex-convict's unexpected return. Adults in Mrs. Joe's kitchen observe Pip "with indignation and abhorrence" (*GE* 28), making him feel as out of place at the Christmas feast as Joe later seems in Barnard's Inn. In chapter 27, the comedy turns serious when one of nature's gentlemen, having been made ill at ease, starts to behave like a comic version of Frankenstein's monster. In chapter 40, one watches a snob forced to entertain a guest who resembles Frankenstein's creature but has actually created the snob, a tragic yet absurdly comic turn of events.

As Lever's picaresque novel ended, *Great Expectations* pointed backward and forward to show that Dickens could write about snobbery more coherently than his rival had. Readers were invited to compare varieties of snobbery, which is consistently seen as a social monstrosity: the "abhorrence" for Pip, as if all children were little monsters (ch. 4); Pip's disdain for an "utterly preposterous Joe" (*GE* 223); and the consummation eight weeks later: Pip's "aversion" to Magwitch (*GE* 329).

Pip's strange manner of wooing Biddy (ch. 17) should also be placed alongside his conduct toward Joe. In these scenes, snobbery takes its toll on the two people who care most about Pip. The episode is Dickens' redoing of the conversation between Potts and Kate in chapter 16 of *A Day's Ride*. Potts has been mistaken for an experienced government agent and is escorting Mrs. Keats and her companion out of the Duchy of Hesse-Kalbbratonstadt on their journey south. Having yet to divulge his real name, he tells Kate his plans to write "reviews, and histories, and stories, and short poems, and, last of all, the 'Confessions of Algernon Sydney Potts' '' (*ADR* 173). Kate immediately discerns that Potts, whom she treats as an imaginary character, should be "a creature of absurdity and folly, a pretender and a snob." He will always be "thrusting himself forward, twenty times a day, into positions he had no right to" (*ADR* 174). Thus she describes Potts's adventures under the very sort of false pretenses that his real-life namesake is exploiting. Potts's addresses hit an unexpected snag as he becomes "a butt and a dupe," but he refuses the self-knowledge in Kate's good-natured mockery and grows angry instead.

Biddy also sees through a young man's inflated self-image, but Pip's ego is cruelly at odds with itself. The psychology of the snob is more complex than Lever realized, Dickens argues, because snobs are both pain-inflictors and self-tormentors. Having bound Biddy "to secrecy," Pip confesses his dreams much as Potts confides in Kate: "I want to be a gentleman," he says (*GE* 126). "Oh, I wouldn't if I was you!" Biddy advises, "don't you think you are happier as you are?" Kate disarms a simple snob, but Biddy recognizes Pip as both criminal and victim—unfair to her and cruel to himself. Debunking Potts's harmless deceptions, Dickens has Pip unwittingly demonstrate snobbery's heartlessness: "If only I could get myself to fall in love with you," he complains, tantalizing Biddy, who also wishes it (*GE* 130). Conceived in contrast to Potts, Pip is the product of Dickens' determination to reveal the snob as he looks *from inside* (i.e., to himself): a bundle of guilt and insecurity, not merely a figure of fun to be lampooned.

When Orlick, yet another version of Frankenstein's monster, intrudes upon Pip's walk with Biddy, she stammers "I-I am afraid he likes me" and Pip interprets the journeyman's "daring to admire her" as a personal insult: "an outrage to myself" (*GE* 131). Dickens carries snobbery well beyond the one-pointed satire in Lever's chapter 16: although Orlick's aspiring to Biddy is as presumptuous as Pip's claim to Estella, Pip considers himself so far above Orlick that the latter's interest in a woman supposedly inferior to Pip nevertheless injures his self-esteem. Ironically, Pip behaves contemptuously toward a projection of his baser self even when it wisely prefers Biddy to Estella.

In *A Day's Ride*, Potts is the only case presented in detail, but in-depth studies of snobs abound in *Great Expectations*. According to Humphry House, "the snob problem was not acute before the forties" (H 153), so in 1860–61 Dickens was assessing twenty years of its ravages. He claimed to understand snobbery better than Lever did because *Great Expectations* sees the epidemic beginning in the late twenties, when the London stages of the novel transpire. Supplanting *A Day's Ride*, *Great Expectations* proclaimed itself a virtual primer on the subject of snobbery, hence the real textbook on "the great Snob world."[14]

Some form of snobbery taints nearly everyone in *Great Expectations*, including Joe, whose awkwardness in front of Pip and Herbert (ch. 27) is not unlike self-abasement before an alleged superior.[15] Characters in *Great Expectations* are either undeservedly pleased with themselves and contemptuous of others, or they become snobs from a sense of interfiority, having been slighted by the superior sort of snob or by an uncaring society. Snobbery afflicts a regal Estella who makes young Pip feel common; it prompts Pumblechook and Mrs. Joe to take credit for Pip's good fortune; and it drives Wopsle to disgrace himself on the London stage and Orlick to attempted murder twice. Jaggers scraping a case from under his nails with his penknife is like Pip dreading to be seen with the soot of the forge upon him. Wemmick believes that "Walworth sentiments" make him more humane than the Londoners in Little Britain. Herbert calls Pip "Handel" out of dislike for the name "Phillip," but the substitution is a highbrow allusion to the German-born composer's "The Harmonious Blacksmith" (*GE* 177). Herbert's mother pities herself for not having married "a title" (*GE* 188). The Pockets consider the loutish Bentley Drummle "one of the elect" because he is "the next heir but one to a baronetcy" (*GE* 191)—that is, next to being next in line.

Snobbery does not produce a new kind of fool in *A Day's Ride,* Dickens scoffed, but it creates a new sort of criminal in *Great Expectations.* Compeyson uses society's respect for outward respectability to break Miss Havisham's heart; later it allows him to shift the blame for money-laundering to the uncouth Magwitch. Using Compeyson to extend Lever, Dickens showed another of snobbery's darker sides: it compels those who have been made to feel inadequate to punish their so-called betters. Both Magwitch and Miss Havisham, arguably the story's most desperate snobs, prosecute vendettas against gentlemen. They crave recognition through retribution, Magwitch by seizing pleasure through Pip, Miss Havisham by disseminating pain through Estella. Caught in networks of snobbery that seem coterminous with society itself, Pip changes from the second variety of snob to the first—from an inferiority revealed by Estella to a false sense of superiority in patronizing Biddy and Joe.

Dickens presented himself, not Lever, as an expert on snobbery's punishment and cure. Twice Potts's snobbish conduct nearly involves him in a duel (chs. 38, 47). He narrowly escapes a beating from the jealous husband whose wife he pursues by mistake for Kate (ch. 11). In contrast, Mrs. Joe is clubbed almost to death by Orlick, who later attempts to strangle Pip. Estella's spirit is "bent and broken" by Drummle (*GE* 480), who meets a violent end. Wopsle is lambasted by London's theater-goers; Pumblechook is shamefully mishandled by Orlick's gang. Miss Havisham dies of burns after accidentally setting herself afire. Magwitch is condemned to hang but expires beforehand from injuries sustained in an escape attempt, during which Compeyson is drowned. The wages of snobbery, Dickens decreed, are higher than Lever's comic novel had admitted.

Denigrating "this boasted civilization of ours" as nothing but "snobbery," Potts resolves "to overthrow the mean and unjust prejudices, the miserable class distinctions," standing between an apothecary's son and greatness (*ADR* 127, 246). That the novel's primary example of snobbery rails against it did not impress Dickens as a blistering indictment; he presents snobbery as the product of social injustice, a consequence of life's basic unfairness. At the heart of *Great Expectations* lie four cases of snobbish exaltation of self—Miss Havisham, Magwitch, Pip, and Estella. She is Miss Havisham's adopted child; Pip is Magwitch's "dear boy" (*GE* 317) and Miss Havisham's protegé, which initially makes him more brother to Estella than suitor. To minimize Lever's single snob, Dickens shows snobbery infecting society's key roles and relationships.

Dickens consolidates in Magwitch all the individuals toward whom society has behaved unjustly, while Pip, the beneficiary of Magwitch's labors, personifies the faults of everyone in the system who profits from its fundamental unscrupulousness. For Pip, unlike Potts, there can be no redemption unless he atones for the snobbery of society-at-large. Pip rises above himself in the best sense—above Selfishness, not merely above his station; he rectifies the social injustice in class distinctions not by scrambling up the social ladder to marry a wealthy man's daughter, as Potts does, but by bending toward Magwitch with compassion instead of condescension.

Pip's gradual acceptance of Magwitch as a fellow creature effects a cure for the snobbery in them both. It reverses the self-serving affection with which Compeyson deceived Miss Havisham. In addition, Pip eventually seeks to make the convict's daughter his wife, even when she is no longer a fairy princess. These actions ameliorate the consequences of Compeyson's pseudo-genteel criminality. Potts is repeatedly humiliated, Dickens contended, but Pip learns humility by seeking and extending forgiveness—that is, absolving Miss Havisham, embracing Magwitch, asking pardon of Biddy and Joe. He breaks the cycle whereby the snubbed become revenge-seeking snobs.

Yet Pip's encounter with Trabb's boy is surely a humiliating experience, more devastating than Lever's updatings of Potts. Three chapters after Joe's visit to London, Dickens replays the blacksmith's embarrassment when another former equal pretends to be disoriented by Pip's new splendor. Trabb's boy, says Pip, "feigned to be in a paroxym of terror and contrition, occasioned by the dignity of my appearance" (*GE* 245). But humiliation, Dickens reminded Lever, is the risk that snobs run, not a cure for snobbery. Pip's subsequent humility, in contrast, is a virtue.

Trabb's boy atones for his effrontery when he helps Herbert and Startop save Pip from being murdered by Orlick (ch. 53). Recalling his humiliation in Rochester's High Street, Pip concedes that he would gladly have "taken the life of Trabb's boy on that occasion" (*GE* 245–46). When Pip recovers consciousness in the old sluice-house and realizes that he has not been killed, the first thing he recognizes with gratitude is "the face of Trabb's boy!" (*GE* 426) His participation in Pip's rescue is one of several turnabouts that make conspicuous the absence of similar cure scenes in *A Day's Ride*. Joe's nursing Pip back to health in chapter 57, for example, reverses the blacksmith's self-abasement in chapter 27 and neatly complements Pip's unselfish attendance on the dying Magwitch (ch. 56).

"Throughout this true history," Potts exclaims, "I have candidly revealed the inmost traits of my nature." He hopes to "make some compensation to the world by an honest exposure of his motives, his weaknesses, and his struggles" (*ADR* 329). Unfortunately, Potts is an insouciant faker willing to live on credit from deeds as yet undone. No matter how disastrously Potts is outwitted or discredited, his voice remains the picaro's. *A Day's Ride* derives little benefit from its hero's afterthoughts, but Pip wrests from Potts the idea of chronicling a young snob's doings from the perspective of his older, wiser self. Pip, not Potts, reexamines his youthful adventures with a mixture of self-deprecating irony and genuine remorse, of humorous recollection tinged with self-recrimination.

George Bernard Shaw attributed the failure of *A Day's Ride* to Lever's incisiveness: forever daydreaming, his self-deceived hero was allegedly too close to real life and smote readers "full in the conscience" (*CL* 243). Potts, however, is hardly a Browningesque case study. Shaw overrated the young Dubliner as an "utterly original contribution to the study of character," a compliment better suited to Dickens's revaluation of Lever's protagonist.[16] Grey Buller, a minor British diplomat who arranges Potts's release from the Ambras Schloss, describes the hero as "the most sublime snob I have ever met" (*ADR* 430). The charge exonerates not just Buller but anyone intelligent enough to credit his observation. Pip, Dickens countered, is both the epitome of snobbery and no exception to the rule; his attitude reflects and enlarges upon the community's failings. Snobbery furnishes clues to life in Pip's village and in London as well. Dickens contended that Father Dyke's epithet for Potts—a "great psychological phenomenon" (*ADR* 65)—was self-congratulatory on Lever's part; it was also more appropriate for a blacksmith's boy turned gentleman than for an Irish apothecary's shiftless son on vacation from university.

Chesterton viewed *Great Expectations* as a "Thackerayan" tale that showed "how easily a free lad of fresh and decent instincts can be made to care more for rank and pride and the degrees of our stratified society than for old affection and for honour." Dickens' novel, Chesterton concluded, added "an extra chapter to The Book of Snobs" (GKC 197). Actually, Dickens took deadlier aim at Thackeray's *Pendennis*; he urged readers to believe that Pip—not Pen or Potts—is the *locus classicus* for snobbery in the Victorian novel. Abusing Thackeray's urbane satire, which he considered too lenient, through a devaluation of Lever's even lighter touch, Dickens branded snobbism a tragicomic disease: a national calamity too widespread for his rivals merely to scoff at. Dickens put Snobbery on an equal footing with his conception of Selfishness in *Martin Chuzzlewit* or Pride in *Dombey and Son*: it was one of several interrelated deficiencies in human nature, especially virulent in the 1840s and '50s, that struck at the foundations of Victorian society. The era's snobbish pretensions, its self-delusions—twin prerequisites, Dickens maintained, for the all-out pursuit of wealth and position during the 1850s—were not a foolish throwback as were Potts's; presented accurately, they were extensive, continuing to spread, and as detrimental as Pip's.

In both *A Day's Ride* and *Great Expectations,* a social outcast holds the key to the protagonist's future. He crosses the hero's path several times before their climactic confrontation. In each case, the hero falls in love with a bewitching girl without suspecting that she is the daughter of the figure repeatedly crossing his path. Dickens refashioned Lever's main ingredients —outlawed father, beautiful daughter, unsuitable suitor—into a suspenseful anti-fairy tale. One of his letters criticized Lever for not devising a "needful strong thread of interest" on which to string his story (*L* 3:183–84), but that did not prevent Dickens from strengthening what "thread" there was for his own purposes.

Through the first eight chapters of *A Day's Ride,* Potts's efforts to recover his rental horse supply a pretext for his wanderings. He sets out on foot after Father Dyke, who has ridden off on Blondel (ch. 4); then he enjoys the company of Edward and Mary Crofton, brother and sister. They befriend him at their cottage until Dyke's letter to Crofton tells about winning a horse from a fool (chs. 5–7). Dyke also reports having sold Blondel to his former owner at a handsome price. Apparently, Blondel, named for King Richard the Lionhearted's favorite minstrel, is still fit to be the circus star he once was in *Timour the Tartar* (*ADR* 13); the owner, who trained the animal years ago, considers him a good luck charm. Ironically, Blondel will prove the making of everyone who rides him *except* Potts.

Embarrassed by Dyke's letter, Potts flees by boat to Wales (ch. 8) and to London by train, hoping to overtake Blondel, whose new owner has sailed for Ostend. In the train depot, Potts meets Kate Herbert and is instantly smitten. She, too is traveling to the continent, reduced circumstances having forced her to become a lady's companion. Although they travel in different compartments, the conversation in Potts's reveals two things: a fugitive named Samuel Whalley is at large and Kate is his younger daughter. When Pip overhears the two convicts discussing Magwitch, Dickens redoes more dramatically the discussion of Whalley that Potts overhears in chapter 9. Potts immediately associates Kate with Whalley's daughter because "Herbert," which Dickens reuses for Pip's roommate's Christian name, was Lady Whalley's maiden name. Presumably, Kate has adopted it to escape notoriety.

Dickens recasts the Potts-Whalley connection as the grotesquely pivotal Pip-Magwitch relationship. The latter's crucial irony—Pip's discovery that he has betrayed his better self and best friends for genteel privileges financed by an ex-convict whose reappearance, in effect, cancels them—reversed Lever, who overcompensates Potts for less-than-spectacular exertions on Whalley's behalf. When the convict tells about executing Magwitch's errand, Pip feels the speaker's breath "on the back of [his] head" and "all along [his] spine," unlike Potts who is half asleep when he hears the story of Sir Samuel Whalley's fall from ironmaster to bankrupt fugitive. Potts has yet to see Whalley, so Lever generates none of the suspense that Dickens derived from beginning with a face-to-face meeting between Pip and Magwitch, then rekindling the excitement when the "secret-looking man" appears in the Three Jolly Bargemen as Magwitch's agent nine chapters later (*GE* 75–76).

Whalley has been disowned by his partner-patron, Sir Elkanah Crofton, malevolent uncle of the kindly Croftons. A passenger in Potts's carriage remembers that Crofton "first established Whalley in the iron trade" when the latter entered Milford, his worldly possessions tied up in a handkerchief (*ADR* 93). Dickens revised this bland report: Magwitch was just out of Kingston Jail "on vagrancy committal" when Compeyson "took [him] on to be his man and pardner" (*GE* 346). The Crofton-Whalley partnership is reworked as a parable in which the better-educated live comfortably off the less fortunate. Crofton's unfairness to Whalley, a malignity insufficiently explained as a snobs' quarrel over Whalley's right to a knighthood (i.e., has Whalley or Crofton been more useful to the other; *ADR* 94–95), is replayed as Compeyson's exploitation of Magwitch, a criminal who is nonetheless a victim of snobbish prejudice against the lower orders.

Lever immediately discloses the pertinent facts about Whalley, including a hint that he has not committed suicide as rumored but will turn up again in some unlikely place—"smelting metals in Africa," cutting a canal through an isthmus, or being "prime minister" to an Indian rajah (*ADR* 93). Dickens withholds full particulars of Magwitch's criminal career for twenty-six weeks until the returned transport relates his life story to Pip and Herbert (ch. 42). In addition to increasing the suspense, Dickens indicated how difficult it was for someone like Magwitch to obtain a sympathetic hearing. He also replaced Whalley's exotic options with Magwitch's hard-earned success in Australia, a more believable location to readers of *All the Year Round*. For a moment, one suspects that the speaker prophesying Whalley's resurgence "in a tone of confidence" might be the missing person incognito. But another passenger describes him as an eyewitness to the quarrel between Whalley and Crofton.

So Potts's informant does not rival Dickens' ominous improvement: the stranger who stirs his rum-and-water "with a file" in chapter 10, then sits behind Pip on the stagecoach (ch. 28).

After escorting Kate and Mrs. Keats part way to Lake Como (chs. 13–27), Potts has several run-ins with his future father-in-law, never suspecting that "Harpar the Englishman" is Whalley in disguise. In chapter 33, Potts is taken to the police station following a brawl at the "Balance" hotel in Constance; Thomas Harpar is there, embroiled in passport problems. Having invited Potts to breakfast, Harpar offends him by attempting to borrow ten pounds. Surprisingly, Potts regrets quarreling and follows Harper to Lindau in Austria. When he comes upon Harpar experimenting with two model ships, causing each to sink slowly to the lake bottom, the latter "sneers" at Potts "for making nothing of the experiment" (ADR 333), calling him "just the stamp of man for an apothecary" (ADR 339). This random insult hits home, though not as subtly as the London rowing coach's observation that Pip has "the arm of a blacksmith" (GE 195). Nevertheless, in chapter 36, Potts invites Harpar to dine and loans him ten pounds. Their relationship remains cooler and more coincidental than Pip's with Magwitch: upon separating, Potts and Harpar shake hands "not very warmly or cordially either" (ADR 342).

Four chapters later, Potts is arrested by mistake for Harpar. Curiously, he allows himself to be incarcerated for what seems nearly a year, first at Innsbruck, then in the Ambras Schloss, so that Harpar can effect his escape. From his cell at Innsbruck, he sees Blondel performing in a circus in the center of town (ADR 392). The horse is being ridden by Catinka, one of two circus people who were Potts's traveling companions from the time he was dismissed by Mrs. Keats to his meeting with Harpar. Later, at Odessa, Potts will hear of a beautiful circus girl having eloped with a Bavarian prince who bought Blondel for 30,000 piasters (ch. 48). Thus the horse that Potts never regains transforms Catinka into a princess while enriching his owner.

Harpar has been accused of assaulting a certain Rigges, his former associate and traveling companion who ran off with their money. By chapter 41, the disguised bankrupt has been officially outlawed. Rigges constitutes one of Lever's missed opportunities: scheduled to identify Potts as Harpar (ch. 43), he never materializes. Then he drops all charges (ch. 44); finally, one learns that he has died (ch. 48). According to the warrant describing Rigges's tussle with Harpar, they fell into a stream and "both went down beneath the water" (ADR 388). This may have given Dickens a clue for Magwitch's final struggle with Compeyson, Rigges's more integral counterpart. Pulled from the Thames, Magwitch whispers to Pip that he and Compeyson went overboard together: "they had gone down, fiercely locked in each other's arms, and ... there had been a struggle under water" (GE 442).

At Lindau in Austria, the Croftons, also on Whalley's trail, inform Potts that their uncle died repentant; to compensate for mistreating his former partner, Sir Elkanah has named Whalley's alleged widow his legatee (ch. 35). In the next chapter, therefore, Potts dines with the object of the Croftons' search. In chapter 39, having joined the hunt for Whalley, Potts is traveling in the Upper Rhine valley with an explanatory letter for Kate from Mary Crofton; his arrest in chapter 40 curtails his activities. By going to prison in Harpar's stead, Potts liberates the person he should have had detained. After being released, Potts visits Kate on Malta (ch. 45) to divulge his humble origins and declare his love; he accepts Kate's commission to locate her father.

Surely Lever's original readers suspected that Harpar is Whalley sooner than Dickens' equated Magwitch with Pip's benefactor. Otherwise they would have missed the joke: Potts is seeking someone he has already found *twice*; he will continue to look for him for another three chapters without realizing that he has already met Whalley repeatedly as Harpar.

Whalley wanders in and out of the later chapters without supplying the kind of stitching that Dickens prized. According to Crofton, the fugitive has been spotted at Riga, a Latvian seaport (ch. 35), or on the Rhine (ch. 45) according to Kate, a sighting that Potts fails to connect with the assault on Rigges and his own arrest. Presumably, Whalley is the Englishman mentioned in the *Levant Herald* who has left Musted Pasha's service for employment in Russia (ch. 45). Nevertheless, Whalley appears to exert little direct influence on *A Day's Ride* between chapters 9 and 33. Dickens' convict is away much longer (after chapter 5 until chapter 39—that is, for about sixteen years), but he always seems close at hand. Whalley has vanished only recently in chapter 9, and the meeting between Potts and Harpar at the "Balance" probably occurs not too long thereafter. For more than twenty chapters, Potts never seriously contemplates how important his association with Whalley will be, whereas Magwitch is rarely absent form Pip's consciousness.

Magwitch's interventions are Dickens' redoing of Harpar/Whalley's less impressive reappearances. These interventions have greater impact because, paradoxically, they are clearer to Pip, although less direct than Harpar's to Potts and seem more ominous than literal recrossings of Pip's path would have been. Magwitch resurfaces more pointedly through emissaries than Whalley does as Harpar: the man with the file for example (ch. 10), or Jaggers announcing Pip's "great expectations" eight chapters later. Reminders of Magwitch include the discarded leg iron with which Orlick fells Mrs. Joe (ch. 15): "my convict's iron," says a guilty Pip (*GE* 120). A visit to Newgate reminds Pip of the novel's opening scene, convincing him that the "taint of prison" has "encompassed" him ever since his "childhood out on [the] lonely marshes" (*GE* 263). Magwitch thus intervenes in chapters 10, 15, 18, 28, and 32, before returning in 39. The novel's pivotal relationship provides much of its spine. Pip's coach ride with the convicts occurs just eleven chapters before the transported felon's reappearance; the visit to Newgate only seven chapters prior to it. Dickens not only made the Pip-Magwitch relationship more representative of social problems than the Potts-Whalley connection that it parodically revalues; the former also functions more efficaciously for unity and suspense.

Potts finally overtakes Kate's father, whom he still knows only as Harpar, in Sebastopol (ch. 48). He puts his know-how as an apothecary's son to use in repairing a seriously injured American contractor—Harpar's latest impersonation. The immediate result for Potts is seven weeks of fever, beginning just after Harpar, battered and feverish, passes the crisis point. While Potts is out of action, Harpar/Whalley recovers financially as well as physically; the former industrialist recoups his fortune by raising sunken ships, the project for which he was rehearsing with toy models (ch. 36). In addition, his English creditors, having been appeased, want him to "recommence business." News of his rehabilitation, he informs Potts, is "well known in England now" (*ADR* 443); ironically, the last person to learn of it is Whalley's designated rescuer. In Dickens' reworking, Magwitch is the only person never to learn that, as an illegally returned transport, he cannot keep his fortune, much less bestow it on Pip.

Anxious to give Potts the brush-off, Whalley calls him "not much of a doctor . . . nor . . . very remarkable as a man of genius" (*ADR* 444). Before departing, he offers Potts "a capital travelling-cloak," but no capital. Having posed as a man of leisure, Potts must decline a monetary reward, a decision Whalley hastens to accept but that Potts styles "the coup de grâce of my misery" (*ADR* 444). Permanent frustration of Potts's expectations is out of the question, however. Inasmuch as Kate's letter recalls Potts to her side, Whalley either only pretends to gruffness in order to test his daughter's admirer, or else he has revised his belittling assessment of Lever's hero and is willing to play fairygodfather after all. Whalley's transformation is never convincingly explained. Potts's good luck is the novel's ultimate non sequitur in a picaresque world predicated on discontinuity.

Once Pip reencounters Magwitch, everything goes awry. Dickens' revaluation unravels Lever's happily-ever-after conclusion and the cheerful view of expectancy it conveys. Pip can neither keep Magwitch alive nor retain the ex-convict's money. Unlike the exonerated Whalley, Magwitch returns to England uninvited, becoming a criminal again in doing so. No one is pleased to see him; his old nemesis is not only still alive but eager to testify against him. In addition, Pip's bout with fever, the result of Herculean efforts to save Magwitch, proves costlier than Potts's: Biddy marries Joe before Pip recovers sufficiently to propose.

To substitute a maturer tragicomic perspective for Lever's overly simple comic conception of things, Dickens reduced the latter to the unreality of a

Cinderella-like fairy tale. *Great Expectations* parodies stories in which the hero-suitor, having faithfully served the father-king, perhaps by releasing him from enchantment, is amply rewarded with the ruler's daughter for his bride. In Lever's father-daughter-suitor triangle, society reinstates Whalley, whose daughter then embraces Potts. In contrast, Magwitch's return disenchants Pip, opening his eyes to his real situation. Magwitch is incriminated over again because the outcast, Dickens maintained, can never be incorporated until society undergoes extensive transformation. Instead of Potts catching up with Whalley, Magwitch comes back to haunt Pip because, like Frankenstein's monster, the wrongs a society condones never go away.

Dickens pulverized the unexamined optimism inherent in the picaresque format. Potts's ability to rebound from every setback, not to mention his Cinderella-like elevation in the final chapter, posed no threat to society's conception of itself as a steadily improving phenomenon. Through Pip's inability to save Magwitch (i.e., obtain justice) and win Estella (i.e., earn love), Dickens combined a cheerless social prognosis with the suggestion that life itself, no matter how droll, is inevitably full of disappointment.

Magwitch's determination to clasp Pip is more upsetting than Whalley's eagerness to be rid of Potts. But the deceptive contrast between the latter's bad luck and the former's apparent good fortune adds a comic twist to Dickens' bitter ironies. Much to his regret, Pip acquires the benefactor that Potts wants. The ex-convict disconcerts Pip not with the revelation of himself as the father of the latter's beloved—which, of course, it will turn out that he is— but as the benefactor whom Whalley, having acknowledged himself Kate's father, refuses to become. When Potts perceives that Harpar is Whalley, he clutches his arm "with amazement" (*ADR* 443). When Magwitch kisses Pip's hand and prepares to "embrace" him, signs of gratitude that Potts would have welcomed, a horrified Pip cries "Keep off!" (*GE* 314)

Magwitch's consanguinary salutation is more chilling for Pip than Whalley's coldness is to Potts. "Look'ee here, Pip, I'm your second father. You're my son," Magwitch exclaims (*GE* 317), having filled Pip with "abhorrence" and "repugnance." "But didn't you never think it might be me?" Magwitch then asks (*GE* 318). Pip's reply is a multiple negative followed by a double disclaimer: "Oh, no, no, no, . . . Never, Never!" Pip cries. This painful outburst is also comically hyperbolic, more protest than denial. Pip's excessive rejection of Magwitch as his benefactor parodies Potts's belated discovery that Harpar is Whalley.[17] It is Lever's world view and his unrealistic final chapter that Dickens, through Pip, is repeatedly negating—not to mention that he is also ruling out the individual's ability to suppress the past or society's to exclude undesirables.

The recuperating industrialist tries to repay the £10 that Harpar borrowed from Potts. In Dickens' revision, Magwitch refuses to be reimbursed for the two one-pound notes he sent Pip, setting fire to them instead. Dickens connects repayment to his novel's revenge theme: Magwitch cannot be bought off cheaply. There is comedy in Pip's anxiety to cancel a debt that is only a fraction of what he actually owes, but one also detects a hint of menace when Pip describes how Magwitch "gave [the notes] a twist, set fire to them at the lamp, and dropped the ashes into the tray" (*GE* 315).

Magwitch's munificence is more problematic than Whalley's rudeness. The latter acts brusquely but is ultimately and inexplicably kind, a comic reversal that one finds confusing psychologically. Magwitch's ostensible generosity contains an insidious mixture of cruelty in that Pip has been groomed to be the ex-convict's instrument for revenge. Dickens rewrites Whalley's attempt at loan repayment more believably (and more frighteningly) as Magwitch's long-term project to force society to make restitution to him through Pip.

Lever's fugitive ironmaster would prefer not to have been rescued by an idler with a "dreamy mode of life," a boulevardier proud of his freedom from manual labor (*ADR* 442). Ironically, Potts would have been more acceptable as the son of an apothecary. Dickens complained that Lever, as usual, ignored the gravity of the situation to obtain an easy laugh. Whalley's desire for a blue-collar rescuer is a snobbishness so unreal that Dickens contested it twice: in Magwitch's desperation to fashion his protégé into a gentleman even other gentlemen will envy, and in Pip's refusal to be made genteel by someone he is ashamed to be seen with publicly. Nothing could illustrate the width of the gap between Haves and Have-Nots more poignantly, Dickens countered, than Magwitch's lifelong obsession with crossing it, even vicariously, and Pip's realization that, given his ties to Magwitch, he has not really crossed it after all.

Whalley's rehabilitation is depicted chiefly in financial terms; his ordeal seems not to have furthered his moral advancement or Potts's. Dickens' reworking emphasizes the intricate mutual improvement that Pip and Magwitch work upon each other despite the forfeiture of the latter's fortune. Having bound Pip to Magwitch, Dickens separates money from redemption. Potts's father dies offstage during the hero's wanderings after succoring Whalley, so Potts inherits enough to get by on; Pip must be rescued from debt by Joe. Dickens dramatically resolves Pip's relationships with *both* of his fathers. Despite this double reconciliation, however, Pip cannot have two any more than Potts can, but Pip's conduct during the loss of one father (Magwitch) entitles him to regain the other (Joe).

As to Potts's "reasons" for helping someone with whom, as a gentleman, he could not expect to "hit it off" (*ADR* 442), Whalley remains puzzled. This "piece of devotion," Potts says, "I really did not understand myself." The answer is all too simple: their class origin not dissimilar, identification is from like to like. More newsworthy, Magwitch and Pip get along because

Dickens insisted that differences in age, class, and outward appearance need not erect insuperable barriers. The Pip-Magwitch connection exudes an affirmative (i.e., comic) afterglow within a tragic framework in that, although society remains divided into Haves and Have-Nots, the bonds between one of each become like those between father and son.[18] From the Potts-Whalley encounter, Dickens charged, readers with a complacent view of themselves as a progressive society would learn nothing, but the Pip-Magwitch association offers an instructive paradigm.

Whalley conceals his interest when Potts recounts his search for Kate's father. But when Potts displays Kate's "old seal-ring," Whalley declares that he gave it to her when she was sixteen; "I am her father," the missing parent asserts (*ADR* 443). In Dickens' revision, Magwitch's disclosure—"I'm your second father. You're my son" (*GE* 317)—causes a bigger sensation and, one must repeat, has more social ramifications. Once Pip has figured out Estella's parentage, it is he who tells Magwitch about his daughter instead of being apprised of her by him. Dickens preserves the secret of Estella's parentage even longer than he withholds the identity of Pip's benefactor. Pip makes his discoveries about a benefactor and his daughter in reverse order to Potts, and in a manner that confirms life's tragicomic complexities.

Seventeen chapters after learning of Magwitch as his patron, Pip breaks the news to him about Estella. Dickens's timing gives each revelation its due. When Pip tells the ex-convict that his daughter is alive, "a lady and very beautiful" (*GE* 456), his kindness surpasses Potts's to Whalley. In Dickensian tragicomedy, simultaneously a refutation of Lever's outlook and an explanation of the nature of things, positive events never obliterate negatives; instead they tone down life's disappointments in a manner loosely parallel to the way an ex-convict and a snob soften as they draw closer together. The reader balances Pip's loss of expectations—he is literally penniless at Magwitch's death—against the latter's regaining of a daughter. After telling the expiring father about Estella, however, Pip loses his benefactor more decisively than Potts appears to when Kate's father tells him about her.

At roughly the midpoint of *A Day's Ride,* Potts confesses that he likes to build "castles in Spain"—"architectural extravaganzas" that he eagerly decorates and inhabits. "I built my castle to live in it," he claims; "from foundation to roof-tree, I planned every detail of it to suit my own taste, and all my study was to make it as habitable and comfortable as I could." Usually, Potts admits, his "tenure was a brief one," ending suddenly while he was "breaking" an egg "at breakfast" or putting on his gloves "to walk out." Yet "no terror of a short lease ever deterred" him "from finishing the edifice in the most expensive manner." He "gilded" his "architraves" and "frescoed" his ceilings as though they were to endure for centuries (*ADR* 194).

Pip likens the loss of his unearned gentility and the consequent breakdown of his plans to marry Estella to the collapse of Misnar's pavilion. He develops this comparison in the last two paragraphs of chapter 38, just before the novel's turning point. Constructed by Horam, the sultan's vizier, Misnar's pavilion is engineered to cave in upon usurpers. In the best-known story from *The Tales of the Genii,* Horam returns Misnar to power by directing him to sever the rope that releases a stone slab over the royal divan, crushing the two Enchanters who have seized control of his sultanate.[19] In chapter 39, Magwitch's disclosure of himself as Pip's secret benefactor deals Pip's prospects a blow similar to the one Misnar's axe dealt the usurpers.

Retelling "the Eastern story," Pip describes how "the heavy slab . . . was slowly wrought out of the quarry . . . and fitted in the roof," while the "rope was . . . slowly taken through the miles of hollow [tunnel] to the great iron ring." Then, "all being made ready with much labour, and the hour come," the rope was cut "and the ceiling fell. So, in my case," Pip asserts, "all the work, near and afar, that tended to the end had been accomplished, and in an instant . . . my stronghold dropped upon me" (*GE* 309–10). Instead of Potts's ephemeral "ceilings," built one after another as if "for centuries" but actually no more than harmless repetitions of human folly, Pip recounts a painstaking process of self-deception, after which, at the appointed time, only one "ceiling" falls, but it permanently destroys unwarranted expectations.

Dickens revalued Lever's architectural symbol: in its stead, Pip invokes a deadly version of Potts's Spanish castles: Misnar's pavilion. It signifies Dickens' recognition that the temporal order, unsatisfactory in so many ways, may yet be purposive, a place in which the life process achieves long-term objectives by twists and turns, dramatic surprises that seem logical in retrospect, perhaps even providential. Misnar's pavilion is also a stark reminder of the precariousness of self-serving schemes, a caution against selfish daydreaming per se; it reinstates a tragicomic idea of expectancy—not as wishful thinking, but in terms of a retributive universe wherein consequences can be traced to their causes and one expects accounts to be settled eventually.

By novel's end, Pip and Magwitch embody Dickens' ideal of true friendship (BH 65); through Pip's disappointments, Dickens expressed reservations about Cinderella stories, of which Potts's is a blatant example. Snubbed by Catinka, herself a Cinderella who rises from gypsy circus performer to Parisian lady, Potts is nevertheless summoned by Kate to marital bliss and financial security. Unlike the Potts-Whalley association or Potts's success with Kate, Pip's tragicomic connections to Magwitch, Miss Havisham, and Estella emerge the way Horam built his sultan's palace: with a remorselessness akin to fate. Contrary to Potts's comedic world, which promotes unaccountability, Pip's relationships intensify into patterns requiring not just hindsight to be understood, but moral interpretation.[20]

*A Day's Ride,* Dickens maintained, is built flimsily, like Potts's Spanish castles. The novel's specious symmetry results from a facile economy of characterization, an artificial compactness at odds with the hero's rambles. Catinka's Bavarian prince is presumably Max of Swabia, with whom Potts quarrels in the hotel at Constance. Grey Buller, who arranges Potts release from prison, is the minor diplomat whose despatches Potts carried off by mistake from the Dover train. George Buller, with whom Potts almost duels on Malta, is Grey's brother; George reads Grey's letter about a snob named Potts to their cousin, Kate. Bob Rogers, who captains Potts's ship from Malta to Odessa, is brother to the skipper who ferried Potts from Ireland to Wales. When the first Rogers gives Potts a letter of introduction to his brother (ch. 8), Lever either foresaw Bob's appearance in chapter 46 or resolved to implicate him later. Lever probably began with a general idea for the Harpar-Whalley interchange and some notion of how to resolve Potts's search for Blondel, but as was noted earlier, many of the intervening incidents, the novel's midsection, lack a sense of urgency and seem extemporized. In short, Lever did just enough planning to foster the impression that his picaresque comedy critiqued a world of whose interlockings its author had full knowledge and control.

Dickens parodied Lever's meretricious designs by underlining profounder coincidences that he considered truer to life's tragicomic texture. Compeyson not only deceives Miss Havisham but also foresakes Magwitch twice: when they are partners and by betraying the returned transport. Estella proves to be Pip's only legacy from both his false fairygodmother and would-be fairy godfather. Having annihilated Pip socially, Trabb's boy later rescues him from Orlick.

Instead of the Buller brothers, fraternal sea captains, and Whalley doubling as Harpar, Dickens fashioned Orlick as a projection of Pip's darker self. He reserved one side of Wemmick for Walworth, another for London; he paired the gentleman Magwitch creates (Pip) with the lady Miss Havisham has made (Estella). Magwitch's return is pivotal for Pip's life, but Dickens deemed Whalley's reappearances no thicker a storythread than Blondel's. Although Dickens reused Lever's structural devices—reappearances, doubling, and co-incidence—he probed them for psychological complexity and social relevance while exposing Lever's enslavement to comic convenience.

Lever's picaresque universe unfolds as a comedy of errors: Potts mistakes a married woman for Kate; he is mistaken for a government messenger, a nobleman in disguise, a gypsy. The German authorities imprison him by mistake for Harpar. Such mistakes, Dickens opined, resemble Potts's castles; they arise rapidly from the narrative, then dissolve without a trace. In *Great Expectations,* when Dickens rethinks Lever's overemphasis on the comic, mistakes darken into tragicomedy and have far-reaching consequences more indicative, Dickens contended, of what life is. Pip mistakes Miss Havisham for his benefactor; he pursues Estella instead of Biddy for his marriage partner. He confuses his lifestory with Cinderella's when the tale of Misnar's pavilion is a more accurate paradigm for his rise and fall.

Just as the crash of Pip's expectations recalls the collapse of Misnar's pavilion, Dickens's collapsing of Lever's novel has reverberations for Thackeray; his fiction is often under attack directly in *Great Expectations* and always by proxy whenever Dickens denigrates *A Day's Ride*. Whether or not Lever believed he was writing the kind of Thackerayan novel for which Chesterton mistook *Great Expectations* (see note 6), Dickens treats *A Day's Ride* as an unfortunate consequence of the Thackerayan mode. He accuses both of his rivals of a similar misconstruction of the human condition. His revaluation of Lever amounts to a clarification of his doubts about Thackeray. That neither had been vigorous enough in satirizing snobbery, Dickens argues, puts them ultimately on a par.

"I have no use for out and out comedy writing or out and out tragedy writing," Christopher Isherwood declared; "I think both pictures that they give of life are false in the most heartless way. I don't know which is worse—the triviality of the total comedian or the superficiality of the total tragedian" (DJ 154). Dickens' reaction to Lever and, by extension, to Thackeray anticipates Isherwood's sentiments.

Dickens rejected lever as the "total comedian," an oversimplified version of the early Dickens himself. Throughout *A Day's Ride,* Potts's misfortunes invariably have comic consequences as one Spanish castle after another collapses. Lever's world view deceives by ignoring the presence of pain and sorrow. Although hardly the work of a "total tragedian," Thackeray's Horatian satire was just as superficial, an alternative that the increasingly angry Dickens of the 1850s refused to countenance. Implicit in his world's *vanitas,* its fickleness or emptiness, Thackeray's resignation precludes a Juvenalian indignation in the face of life's deficiencies; it also tends toward melancholy, thus falling short of the tragicomedian's healthier response: an ability to accept such deficiencies humorously. To both reactions—indignation and comic acceptance, especially the latter, Dickens laid claim in 1860–61.

That both Lever and Thackeray are ultimately unreliable—"false" in heartless ways—could be demonstrated, Dickens believed, without denying the latter's superior skills. Their different but equally incomplete perspectives cause both to deal too kindly with snobs. Endlessly amusing, they are funny but harmless in Lever's comic world, absurd and pointless in Thackeray's fruitless one, but never as tragicomic as Pip is or a national disaster as in Dickens' overview, which he strove to keep both funny and grave.

Had Thackeray addressed snobbery adamantly in *The Book of Snobs* (1846–47), *Vanity Fair* (1848), and especially *Pendennis* (1850), he might have prevented the "out and out comedy" of *A Day's Ride,* no substitute, Dickens belatedly realized, for the scourge that Thackeray should have wielded. When "the snob problem" (H 153) approached crisis proportions in the 1840s, he neglected to quash it, the urbanity of his satire in effect paving the way for the innocuousness of Lever's.

Compared to Potts's castles in Spain, Misnar's pavilion is the more complex symbol, subtler and centralized. Besides connoting a tragicomic world, it furnishes the superior model for a well-constructed novel that crushes snobs and rival novelists simultaneously. Multifaceted, it stands for collapse as well as craft or craftiness. Misnar's pavilion is both a rejection of Potts's (and Lever's) airy fabrications and a stronger admonishment than Thackeray's for the individual's extravagant hopes and the nation's. Which edifice, Dickens asks, does a society's overestimate of its progress and potential resemble, Potts's castles or Pip's pavilion?

Dickens may have been reminded of the Misnar story from *The Tales of the Genii* when Lever's serial caused the circulation of *All the Year Round* to plummet. The collapse of Pip's plans—"my stronghold dropped upon me" (*GE* 310)—is latent in Dickens' complaint to Lever that sales of the new periodical "drop rapidly" due to *A Day's Ride* (*L* 3:83–84), one drop suggesting the other.

Dickens' letter to Lever for "Sixth October" 1860 supposedly "tried to break the news . . . gently" (J 2:965). But the editor's ominous opening must have caused Lever to gasp: "I have a business report to make, that I fear I can hardly render agreeable to you" (*L* 3:183–84): "We drop rapidly and continuously with The Day's Ride." If one compares this letter from the offices of *All the Year Round* with one written the same day to John Forster from Gad's Hill, conflicts appear. In the former, Dickens reluctantly discloses plans for intervention. He depicts himself waiting "week after week" for "the least sign" that *A Day's Ride* was about to "take hold." Reporting the plunge in sales was "disagreeable," he admitted, but he felt "no other uneasiness or regret" (*L* 3:183–84). In the latter, Dickens revealed his displeasure with the "considerable advance" of Lever's novel in hand; he foresaw "no vitality" in upcoming installments (*L* 3:183). Either Dickens's original estimate was euphoric, or he felt that the promise of the opening chapters had not been kept. An unflattering third possibility is that the editor had allowed the public's indifference to reverse his opinion.

Lest *All the Year Round* be "much endangered," Dickens told Forster, he had resolved on "dashing in now" with *Great Expectations* (*L* 3:183). On "Fourth October," Dickens had written Forster about a "council of war" at the offices of *All the Year Round*; during this meeting, it became "perfectly clear that the one thing to be done was, for me to strike in" (*L* 3:182–83).

So the letter for 6 October confirmed decisions already brewing several days earlier, decisions outlined to Forster on 4 October but not to Lever. Dickens also informed Forster of the "thousand pounds" he would receive "for early proofs" of *Great Expectations* to America (he had granted the transatlantic serial rights to *Harper's*).

"Dashing in now" was Dickens' flamboyant phrase for a business decision that he had mulled over for several days, then began to implement with characteristic thoroughness. This was hardly another charge of the Light Brigade. The editor carefully mapped out a course that he felt confident would enable the novelist to redeem *All the Year Round* before irreparable damage was done. Dickens' sureness in settling on a plan of action in the first week of October suggests that he may have given the situation considerable attention even earlier. His last step was to inform Lever. The letter of 6 October outlined a rescue mission for which the practical details had already been hammered out; in effect, Dickens notified Lever of a fait accompli. When the crestfallen contributor volunteered to conclude *A Day's Ride* quickly, Dickens' follow-up letter of 15 October appeared to leave such decisions to Lever's discretion (*L* 3:186–87). Once Dickens resolved to transform *Great Expectations* into a weekly serial, chose 1 December as its starting date, and arranged for American serialization, however, Lever's actions scarcely mattered; the fate of *All the Year Round* was out of his hands and back in Dickens'.

When the "business report" for 6 October insisted that "there is but one thing to be done," it ruled out alternatives. "One thing to be done" is a phrase carried over from the "council of war." In the second paragraph, only five sentences long, "must" is used four times to create the requisite sense of necessity: Dickens "must get into" the pages of *All the Year Round* "as soon as possible"; otherwise, the triple adverb in the final paragraph stresses, it will be "very, very, very difficult" to halt the journal's decline. Dickens clearly fostered an atmosphere of emergency to prevent additional deliberations and justify his proposal.

On 15 October, replying to a mea culpa letter from Lever that morning, the editor waxed hyperbolic in "most earnestly" professing to have "not the slightest atom of reservation" about *A Day's Ride*. Not only was it the "best" novel Lever "ever wrote," but Dickens was as "proud and glad to have it" now as he had been the previous June. Unfortunately, "it does not do what you and I would have it do," Dickens added, as though the work itself were delinquent independently of its author (*L* 3:186–87). The blame, Dickens decided, should fall on the serial format, which became a convenient scapegoat. *A Day's Ride* failed to catch on because "it does not lay some one strong ground of suspended interest." Many of "the best books ever written would not bear the [serial] mode of publication," Dickens continued, because—and this is "one of its most remarkable and aggravating features"—the serialist must "fix the people in the beginning," or else it is "almost impossible to fix them afterwards."

Dickens found a way to associate Lever's "best" book with "the best books ever written" without actually specifying it as one of them. He identified a strong opening and a suspenseful proposition as hallmarks of the weekly serial. These attributes are preeminent in *Great Expectations,* put there no doubt to correct Lever's oversights while demonstrating Dickens' mastery of serialization's peculiar demands. To elevate Lever's spirits, Dickens sent him an essay on the serialist's art. Describing it as "a strange knack," he laid bare serious weaknesses in Lever's composition which he then turned into his own serial's major strengths. Dickens pretended that the veteran serialist was a victim of serial publication when even George Eliot, as yet a non-serialist, could readily identify its distinctive requirements.

"For as long as you continue afterwards," Dickens declared on 6 October with reference to the starting date for *Great Expectations,* "we must go on together" (*L* 3:183–84). This mixture of resolution with regret suggests that he felt yoked to his less talented contributor. Having finally separated from his wife in 1858, he saw himself trapped in a bad marriage of another sort. The letter-writer deserves some sympathy: his daunting assignment was to exculpate a novel that the editor had lauded initially but now considered a liability.

Circulation of *All the Year Round* allegedly rose quickly due to *Great Expectations,* but clearcut evidence of dramatic recovery is difficult to find. "No sooner had [Dickens] stepped in with his new story," Anny Sadrin asserted, "than the sales of *All the Year Round* rose gratifyingly" (AS 14). Her authority for this statement, Robert L. Patten, estimated the eventual readership of *Great Expectations* at 100,000 weekly. Nevertheless, Patten's chart of Dickens' income from *All the Year Round* indicates no immediate rebound in early 1861.[21] On 31 October 1859, Dickens realized £469 in profits from the periodical's first six months; by 30 April 1860, his income from the new venture had risen dramatically to £1,246 and rose again to £1,365 by 31 October 1860. At that time, *A Day's Ride* had been running for two and a half months and Dickens had already written Lever the two letters. The next six-month dividend on 30 April 1861, at which point *Great Expectations* had just passed weekly installment 22 with 14 to go, dropped to £509, not much higher than the figure for the journal's first six months; the dividend of £310 for 31 October 1861, nearly three months after *Great Expectations* had concluded, hit an all-time low. A full recovery did not take place until 30 April 1862, when Bulwer Lytton's *A Strange Story* had completed its run; Dickens netted £1,320, almost exactly his earnings a year and a half earlier for the six months ending 31 October 1860.

Small balances for 1861 presumably reflect the fall-off in sales caused by Lever's unpopularity, a decline already evident in September 1860 but not

felt in the pocketbook for several months—that is, not until booksellers returned unsold copies of *All the Year Round* and began reducing their orders.
The 31 October 1860 balance included the early Lever issues but profits
remained high due to record sales for installments 24–40 of *The Woman in
White*. Sales were in fact dropping despite the high balance. Contrary to
appearances, they were steadily rising between then and 31 October 1861,
when the consequences of Lever's failure showed up as low profits for that
April and October. The £856 decline in Dickens' earnings between 31 October
1860 and 30 April 1861 was nearly twice as large as his profits from *All the
Year Round* during the journal's first six months. Had Lever done his duty
by simply maintaining the circulation of *All the Year Round,* Dickens stood
to realize another £2,000 between 31 October 1860 and the same date a
year later.

If not exactly a financial disaster, inclusion of *A Day's Ride* was expensive.
Dickens sold the American serial rights to *Great Expectations* for £1,000,
half the price tag for Lever's debacle. Two thousand pounds was equivalent
to the profit Dickens could expect from twenty-five public readings in England.[22] If the fall from £1,365 to £509 to £310 had continued for another
period, Dickens' journal would have fizzled into the red. On 1 February,
Dickens told William de Cerjat that although Lever's story "had been a
deadweight," things were better now.[23] Yet it took from 31 October 1860
until 30 April 1862 before Dickens' account books confirmed that his *dash*
into *All the Year Round* had been in time to rally his journal.

Dickens paid Lever £750 for the serial version of *A Day's Ride,* a princely
sum for a circulation depressant (J 2:966). It brought the overall cost of
dealing with Lever to £2,750. What cannot be calculated, however, is Lever's
target value. Without stimulus from *A Day's Ride,* would *Great Expectations*
be as incisive a social satire, as compact a masterpiece of shock and suspense?
Would it be as grotesquely funny, as tragicomic? Would it ponder the definition of gentility so deeply or the problem of snobbery so extensively?

After 1860, Dickens the editor planned further ahead, relying on proven
crowd-pleasers instead of courting reluctant serialists such as George Eliot.
To Forster on 6 October Dickens announced that Charles Reade and Wilkie
Collins would follow *Great Expectations*. "Our course," Dickens boasted,
"will be shaped out handsomely and hopefully for between two and three
years" (*L* 3:183). As things turned out, Bulwer Lytton's *A Strange Story*
preceded Collins's *No Name* and Reade's *Hard Cash.* Dickens abolished the
overlap policy: *Great Expectations* ended on 3 August 1861 and *A Strange
Story* began on 10 August; although it concluded on 8 March 1862, *No Name*
did not start until 15 March. When Dickens accepted Bulwer's story on 23
January 1861, he envisioned prosperity ahead for thirty-six months—all the
way to 26 December 1863 when Reade's novel concluded. Dickens's *dash*

into the pages of *All the Year Round* was actually the first leg of a four-serial run, an impressive marathon.

"The difficulties and discouragements" of serial publication "are enormous," Dickens consoled Lever (6 October 1860); "the man who surmounts them today may be beaten by them tomorrow" (*L* 3:183–84). Dickens, however would not be "beaten" again. The invincible lineup of Bulwer, Collins, and Reade, sensational realists all, would see to that. For Lever, tomorrow never came. "It was clear to both men," Fred Kaplan has stated, that Lever "would not have a second chance" (K 432).[24] Despite avowals on 15 October that Lever continue to regard him as his "other self" (*L* 3:186–87), Dickens had done all he could—as editor of *All the Year Round* and parodic revaluator of *A Day's Ride*—to liberate himself from a burdensome contribution. In his remaining nine years as the journal's conductor, he never asked Lever for another serial.[25]

# NOTES

1. *All the Year Round* was not invariably "a writing workshop" in which Dickens collaborated with fellow novelists in a friendly manner (JAS 177–78).
2. Ada Nisbet observed that "discussion of Dickens' relationships with other contemporary novelists such as *Charles Lever,* Elizabeth Gaskell, George Eliot, Poe, Thackeray, and Trollope have in general been of more biographical than critical interest" (italics added, AN 111). In George Ford's update, *Victorian Fiction: A Second Guide to Research,* only Ruth apRoberts mentions "the early Lever" as an analogue for Trollope's Irish novels (GF 159).
3. Lever was sufficiently famous to be one of only five writers burlesqued in William Makepeace Thackeray's *Mr. Punch's Prize Novelists* (1847).
4. For most of his fictions, beginning with *Dombey and Son* (1846–48), Dickens outlined each installment; he also jotted down things to be done in future chapters. *Harry Lorrequer* established the pattern for Lever's novels: throughout most of the story, this officer on leave simply roams about Ireland. Lever tried to improvise a more coherent plot in *The O'Donohue* (1845) and actually planned *The Knight of Gwynne* (1846–47) in advance. Critics consider novels such as *Sir Joseph Carew* (1855) and *The Fortunes of Glencore* (1857) better constructed than Lever's earlier serials, but improvements seem negligible.
5. For a chapter-by-chapter synopsis of *A Day's Ride,* see Appendix A. I follow the one-volume Roberts Brothers edition (1898) instead of the two-volume Chapman and Hall edition (1863) in which, as with their *Great Expectations,* chapter numbering begins over again in the second volume. Chapters 1–23 in volume one are followed by chapters 1–25 in volume two.
6. In Fitzpatrick's opinion, *A Day's Ride* "displayed less humour and more irony than [Lever's] previous books": "Just as Thackeray meant 'Barry Lindon' [sic]

as the autobiography of a knave," Fitzpatrick commented, Lever's design was to do likewise for a "fool" (WJF 2:186).

7. In choosing a name, Lever may have been thinking of Pott, cantankerous editor of the *Eatanswill Gazette* in *Pickwick Papers*. There is also Wilkie Collins's parody of a pretentious painter's autobiography: "A Passage in the Life of Mr. Perugino Potts" in *Bentley's Miscellany* (February, 1852), but Collins's source could be the same as Lever's.

8. When Dickens edited *Bentley's Miscellany* in the late 1830s, he required new serials to follow those that were nearing completion. *Oliver Twist* had to wait to move into the lead-off spot. In a monthly magazine, however, positioning may not have been as vital to a new serial's success. The final four installments of *Oliver Twist* surrendered pride of place to William Harrison Ainsworth's *Jack Sheppard* (1839); by then, Ainsworth had assumed the editorship.

9. Johnson stated that "the protraction of Lever's story . . . reduced Dickens's readers . . . to desperation" (J 2:966).

10. "Of all first chapters," Swinburne rightly asked, "is there any comparable for impression and for fusion of humour and terror and pity and fancy and truth to that which confronts the child with the convict on the marshes in the twilight?" (S 31)

11. Robert Garis emphasized a "melancholy, mildly humorous acceptance of the world's insufficiency" as the tragicomic core of *Great Expectations* (RG 212).

12. That an uncritical Lever took "unalloyed delight" in this sort of misunderstanding was Lionel Stevenson's verdict in *The English Novel: A Panorama* (LS 252).

13. For a fuller discussion of Dickens' revised ending as a parodic corrective to Lever's, see JM 47–50.

14. This was Thackeray's epithet for Victorian England (*BS* 45).

15. Joe behaves almost as badly when he accompanies Pip to Miss Havisham's (ch. 13).

16. Michael Cotsell hails Pip as "one of the great achievements of Western literature" (MC 7).

17. In Philip Marcus's opinion, Pip's reaction was not supposed to be shared by readers of *All the Year Round,* to whom Dickens had given "anticipatory clues" (PM 65–67). Surely Dickens had things both ways: surprise for readers who did not expect Magwitch, confirmation of their worst fears for those who did.

18. Edward Said's reading of the Pip-Magwitch association as a parable in which England's wealth is owed to slavery and exploitation in other countries seems farfetched (ES 13–14).

19. See "The Enchanters, or, Misnar the Sultan of India," in *The Tales of the Genii: or, the Delightful Lessons of Horam, the Son of Asmar* (London: Henry G. Bohn, 1861; first pub. 1764). Supposedly a translation from the Persian, this was actually the work of the Rev. James Ridley, a native of Stepney, as Dickens probably knew.

20. Cf. Harry Stone's remarks apropos of *David Copperfield* (HS 197).

21. Robert L. Patten has discussed the circulation of *All the Year Round* (RLP 292); the chart showing Dickens' earnings from the journal appears on p. 464.

22. In fall 1868, Dickens began a tour of readings from his own works for Chappell's: 100 performances for £8,000.
23. MS in the Free Library of Philadelphia.
24. On the other hand, Dickens persuaded his publishers, Chapman and Hall, to issue hardcover editions of both *A Day's Ride* and Lever's next novel, *The Barringtons,* which was dedicated to Dickens. According to Stevenson, Lever made the dedication because he had heard "rumours" that he was "jealous" of Dickens and thought it politic to defuse them (*CL* 249).
25. Lever continued to publish articles in *All the Year Round,* but these were paid for upon acceptance, not commissioned (J 2:966). In addition, Lever kept Dickens under surveillance in letters to John Blackwood. He branded *Our Mutual Friend* "disagreeable reading," its characters "more or less repugnant" (7 March 1865; ED 2:91). He envied the "hatfulls of money" Dickens made in America (January 1868; ED 2:210). On 15 April 1870, he asked if Blackwood had read *Drood* (ED 2:277). Lever's letter, dated 9 July 1870, contained a spiteful eulogy: Dickens "was a man of genius and a loyal, warm-hearted, good fellow; but he was not Shakespeare" (ED 2:284–85).

# WORKS CITED

*ADR* Lever, Charles. *A Day's Ride: A Life's Romance.* Boston: Roberts Brothers, 1898; volume 28 in the Copyright Edition.

*AN* Nisbet, Ada. "Charles Dickens." *Victorian Fiction: A Guide to Research.* Lionel Stevenson, ed. Cambridge: Harvard UP, 1964.

*AS* Sadrin, Anny. *Great Expectations.* London: Unwin Hyman, 1988.

*BH* Hornback, Bert G. *Great Expectations: A Novel of Friendship.* Boston: Twayne, 1987.

*BS* Thackeray, William Makepeace. *The Book of Snobs.* John Sutherland, ed. New York: St. Martin's, 1978.

*CL* Stevenson, Lionel. *Doctor Quicksilver: The Life of Charles Lever.* London: Chapman and Hall, 1939; rpt. New York: Russell and Russell, 1969.

*ED* Downey, Edward. *Charles Lever: His Life in His Letters.* Edinburgh: William Blackwood & Sons, 1906.

*ES* Said, Edward. *Culture and Imperialism.* New York: Vintage, 1994.

*GE* Dickens, Charles. *Great Expectations.* Margaret Cardwell, ed. Oxford: Clarendon, 1993, but with chapters numbered 1–59.

*GF* Ford, George, ed. *Victorian Fiction: A Second Guide to Research.* New York: MLA, 1978.

GKC Chesterton, G. K. *Criticisms and Appreciations of the Works of Charles Dickens.* London: J. M.Dent & Sons, 1992; first pub. 1911.

H House, Hymphry. *The Dickens World.* London: Oxford UP, 1961; first pub. 1941.

HS Stone, Harry. *Dickens and the Invisible World.* Bloomington, Indiana: Indiana UP, 1979.

J Johnson, Edgar. *Charles Dickens: His Tragedy and Triumph.* 2 vols. New York: Simon & Schuster, 1952.

JAS Sutherland, J. A. *Victorian Novelists and Publishers.* Chicago: U of Chicago P, 1976.

JM Meckier, Jerome. "Charles Dickens's *Great Expectations*: A Defense of the Second Ending." *Studies in the Novel,* 25 (Spring, 1993), 28–58.

K Kaplan, Fred. *Dickens: A Biography.* New York: William Morrow, 1988.

L Dexter, Walter, ed. *Letters of Charles Dickens.* Bloomsubry: Nonesuch, 1938. All quotations are from volume 3.

LS Stevenson, Lionel. *The English Novel: A Panorama.* Boston: Houghton Mifflin, 1960.

MC Cotsell, Michael, ed. *Literary Essays on Dickens's Great Expectations.* Boston: G. K. Hall, 1990.

PM Marcus, Philip. "Theme and Suspense in the Plot of *Great Expectations.*" *Dickens Studies,* 2 (May, 1966), 57–73.

RG Garis, Robert. *The Dickens Theatre.* Oxford: Clarendon, 1965.

RLP Patten, Robert L. *Dickens and His Publishers.* Oxford: Clarendon, 1978.

S Swinburne, Algernon. "Charles Dickens." *The Quarterly Review,* (1902), 20–39.

WJF Fitzpatrick, W. J. *Life of Charles Lever.* London: Chapman and Hall, 1879.

# Appendix A: Chapter-by-Chapter Summary of *A Day's Ride*

1. After an undistinguished first year, Potts resolves to spend the long vacation from Trinity College, Dublin, traveling about Ireland on horseback, thanks to a legacy of £100 from an uncle.
2. He concludes the first day's ride at the "Lamb" in Ashford, where he joins a group composed of Lord Keldrum, Father Dyke, Oxley, and Hammond, all of whom easily see through his pretensions to be a person "of some note" (*ADR* 17).
3. Inebriated, boastful, Potts loses Blondel, his rental horse, to Father Dyke at backgammon.
4. Next morning, hung over, Potts sets out on foot after Father Dyke.
5. Potts is befriended by Edward Crofton and his sister, Mary, at their cottage, "the Rosary."
6. Their cousin, Rose, overhears Potts eulogizing himself.
7. Potts intercepts Dyke's letter about winning a horse that he has sold to its former owner for a hefty sum.
8. Potts flees to Wales by boat. Its garrulous captain gives him a letter of introduction to Bob Rogers, his brother, a skipper based at Malta.
9. In a farewell note to Crofton, Potts invents "great expectations" (*ADR* 86) from an uncle who is allegedly dying. At the train station in Milford, he assists Kate Herbert. She is journeying to London, then to Brussels to become companion to a widow. They travel to London in different carriages. Potts overhears the story of Sir Samuel Whalley's disappearance; Kate, he realizes, is the disgraced industrialist's younger daughter.
10. Having been misdirected, Potts follows a lady in mourning by mistake for Kate; he goes to Dover by train and across to Ostend.
11. The captain of the channel packet rescues Potts from the lady in mourning's irate husband, "the most jealous man in Europe" (*ADR* 124).
12. Potts reaches Hesse-Kalbbratonstadt in Northern Germany; he bears Grey Buller's despatches, which got mixed in with his luggage on the Dover train.
13. Calling at the British legation, Potts meets Miss Herbert again, who remembers him from Milford. Mistaken for a diplomatic courier, Potts is invited to dine by Sir Shalley Doubleton.
14. Potts dines with the Ambassador.
15. Sir Shalley instructs Potts to escort Mrs. Keats and Kate to Lake Como.
16. Dressed as a courier, Potts undertakes his mission. Kate deflates his literary ambitions.
17. Potts takes a dislike to Mrs. Keats.

18. He tells Kate that he is an important messenger eagerly expected at Constantinople.
19. Mrs. Keats suspects that Potts may be of consequence.
20. Potts describes his method of building "castles in Spain" (*ADR* 194). Mrs. Keats mistakes him for a nobleman in disguise.
21. Kate does not share Mrs. Keats's delusions.
22. The journey continues.
23. At a German inn, Potts behaves absurdly when a real nobleman compliments Kate.
24. The journey proceeds.
25. Potts meets Vaterchen, a German clown, and young Tintefleck, a pretty Moorish circus rider, both vagabonds.
26. Potts converses with his new friends.
27. Mrs. Keats, a snob, is insulted when Potts presents them.
28. She leaves Potts behind. He sends half the money he has left back to Dublin to pay for Blondel.
29. Potts joins Vaterchen and Tintefleck on their rambles.
30. Vaterchen tells his lifestory.
31. Potts continues with Vaterchen and Tintefleck.
32. Potts flirts with Tintefleck, now called Catinka.
33. Mistaken for gypsies, Potts and his friends cause a disturbance in the hotel at Constance, a lake between Germany, Austria, and Switzerland. Potts meets Harpar the Englishman at the police station. He takes Potts and his friends to breakfast, then attempts to borrow £10 from Potts, who declines. Potts follows Harpar to Lindau, Austria.
34. Having outpaced Vaterchen and Catinka, Potts nevertheless fails to overtake Harpar. At Lindau, an unidentified guest pays for his dinner.
35. The guest, Crofton, and his sister are searching for Whalley, whom their late uncle repented of ruining financially. Sir Elkanah named Whalley's alleged widow his legatee. Potts reveals that he knows Kate Whalley's story and has been her fellow-traveler. He is to search for Whalley in Savoy and Upper Italy, then rejoin the Croftons in Rome. Surmising Potts's feelings for Kate, Mary hopes that he will persuade her to accept Sir Elkanah's reparations. Miss Crofton brings Potts £100 from his father, who has remarried.
36. Still at Lindau, Potts reencounters Harpar conducting an experiment lakeside with two model ships, causing each to sink to the bottom. Potts invites Harpar to dine and loans him £10.
37. Potts overhears the count from chapter 23 telling of additional conversations with Miss Herbert; his story includes disparaging references to Potts, who challenges him.

38. Vaterchen and Catinka intervene to save Potts from Prince Max of Swabia. Potts snubs Catinka and they separate; she has been given a brooch, presumably by Prince Max.

39. Potts travels the Upper Rhine valley as it descends to the German plains.

40. He is arrested by two horsemen.

41. Potts is imprisoned at Feldkirch by mistake for Harpar, who has been outlawed for assaulting Rigges, his former associate and traveling companion.

42. From his cell at Innsbruck, Austria, Potts sees a circus performing in the center of town; a "pretty Moorish girl" rides Blondel (*ADR* 396).

43. Potts is jailed in the Ambras Schloss until he can be identified by Rigges, who never appears.

44. Potts is interrogated by a young Englishman who secures his release, Rigges having dropped charges. Potts confesses that he is neither Harpar nor "Pottinger," the name he assumed in chapter nine—simply Potts. The English official is Grey Buller, whose despatches Potts carried off.

45. Having located Kate with Mrs. Keats on Malta, Potts admits to being a druggist's son and professes his love. Daughter of a self-made man, Kate is receptive. He delivers a note from Miss Crofton. Kate has already heard from Whalley; she reports several possible sightings of him. Potts promises to find her father.

46. Potts overhears George Buller, Kate's cousin, reading her a letter from Grey, his brother, who describes Potts as a "sublime snob" (*ADR* 430); Kate defends him. Bob Rogers, who is to transport Potts to Russia, challenges George on Potts's behalf.

47. Rogers informs Potts of his appointment to duel with Buller. Potts escapes to Constantinople by ship.

48. At Odessa, Potts hears of a circus girl who eloped with the prince who paid 30,000 piastres to buy her a horse (i.e., Blondel). Potts finds Harpar at Sebastopol: posing as an American contractor, he had been badly injured yet cannot communicate with Russian doctors. Passing for a surgeon, Potts tends Harpar with directions from a German-speaking Russian physician. Harpar survives but Potts is stricken with seven weeks of fever. When Harpar and Potts finally compare notes, the latter tells of being imprisoned as the former. Harpar reveals that Rigges has died. Potts outlines his efforts to find Whalley. Harpar identifies himself as Whalley. By raising sunken liners, he has regained wealth and reputation. Whalley departs for home, leaving Potts unrewarded and in tears. Potts wanders Europe on a legacy from his late father. In Paris he is snubbed in excellent French by a stuck-up Catinka.

She refuses to recall their former association but has provided Blondel a splendid retirement. Potts receives Kate's letter of invitation; he leaves to join her permanently in Wales, his starting point in chapter seven. He has parlayed a day's ride into a life's romance.

Serial divisions for *A Day's Ride,* including overlap with *Great Expectations*: 18 August: 1–2; 25: 3–4; 1 September: 5; 8:6; 15:7; 22:8; 29:9; 6 October: 10; 13:11; 20:12; 27:13–14; 3 November: 15; 10:16–17; 17:18–19; 24:20–21; 1 December: 22–23 (*GE,* 1–2); 8:24–25 (3–4); 15:26–27 (5); 22:28–29 (6–7); 29:30–31 (8); 5 January: 32 (9–10); 12:33 (11); 19:34 (12–13); 26:35 (14–15); 2 February: 36 (16–17); 9:37 (18); 16:38–39 (19); 23:40–41 (20–21); 2 March: 42–43 (22); 9:44 (23–24); 16:45–46 (25–26); 23:47–48 (27–28).

# "John Rokesmith's Secret": Sensation, Detection, and the Policing of the Feminine in *Our Mutual Friend*

*Lisa Surridge*

In 1863, when Dickens began to write the first numbers of *Our Mutual Friend,* sensation fiction represented, in the words of the *Quarterly Review,* "a great fact in the literature of the day" (Mansel 512): *The Woman in White, East Lynne, Great Expectations, Lady Audley's Secret, Aurora Floyd* and *No Name* were all serialized between in 1859 and 1863. As *Fraser's Magazine* asserted in 1863, "[a] book without a murder, a divorce, a seduction, or a bigamy, is not apparently considered worth either writing or reading; and a mystery and a secret are the chief qualifications of the modern novel . . . " ("Popular Novels" 262). Among Dickens' own works, *A Tale of Two Cities* (1859) and *Great Expectations* (1860–61) are generally seen as being most closely associated with the sensation fiction genre. However, when *Our Mutual Friend* was published in 1864–65, its original critics perceived it as sensational in some significant respects. The *London Review,* for example, recognized in Bradley Headstone a character whom "a certain class of critics" might consider "sensational" (Collins, *Critical Heritage* 457). And *The Times* described *Our Mutual Friend* as a satisfying hybrid of sensational and domestic fiction: " . . . those readers who pant for what is called 'sensation' may feast . . . to their heart's content on sensation; and those who care more for quiet pictures and studies of character will also find that the author has provided for them" (Dallas 468).

As I will suggest, *Our Mutual Friend*—which features a *mort vivant,* together with such sensational devices such as investigation, reversal, discovery, marital imposture or anomaly, sudden surprises and sensational scenes—deliberately invites comparison to the sensation novel. Having thus inscribed itself, however, the text deliberately frustrates this generic expectation in its

265

reader by revealing its own secrets prematurely, refusing to solve its own mysteries, and foregrounding the anticlimactic nature of its anticipated discoveries. To quote the narrator, "the Harmon murder . . . [goes] up and down, and ebb[s] and flow[s], . . . until at last, after a long interval of slack water it [gets] out to sea and drift[s] away" (74). Having indulged in this self-conscious play with the reader's expectation of a murder investigation and mystery, however, *Our Mutual Friend* undergoes in its second half a fascinating and perhaps less self-conscious torsion. The focus of investigation and detection shifts from the problem of the Harmon murder to resolving and containing the "problem" of Bella Wilfer. In so doing, *Our Mutual Friend* reiterates and assuages many of the concerns surrounding femininity and domesticity articulated in the sensation novels of the early 1860s. As Lyn Pykett observes, sensation fiction "engaged in a general struggle about the definition of woman, and also about the nature, power, and function of the feminine within the culture" (10); texts such as *Basil, East Lynne, Lady Audley's Secret, Aurora Floyd* and *No Name* reflect and provoke anxiety concerning femininity, depicting the Victorian home as betrayed from within by the "devices and desires" (Chorley 147)[1] of the supposed "Angel in the House." In *Our Mutual Friend,* these anxieties focus on Bella's uneasy relationship with family obligation, domesticity, marriage ambitions, and marital trust. Such uneasiness is, however, assuaged through an inverted sensation plot, whereby the male householder's "pious" (841) deceit becomes a vehicle for containing and resolving two of the central anxieties of the sensation genre: the beleaguered home and the threat of an imperfect angel within it.

*Our Mutual Friend* follows the sensation genre[2] in its preoccupation with modernity, newspaper reporting, detection, criminality, and marital anomaly. Like sensation fiction, the novel insists on its own contemporaneity: it takes place in London, "[i]n these times of ours" (43). The novel also derives from the sensation genre its approximation of newspaper reportage. Like his character Sloppy, Dickens does "the Police in different voices" (*OMF* 246), imitating the jargon and shorthand of the Night Inspector and echoing journalistic style in his description of the Inquest (Robson 120–21). The novel features a detective (the Night Inspector) and, in Bradley Headstone, a powerful portrait of the criminal mind. Finally, although she does not commit actual bigamy, Bella is undeniably in an anomalous marital situation as "a kind of widow who never was married" (80). The marital intricacies typical of sensation fiction are exemplified by this unmarried "widow" who marries a man living under an alias who is in fact her destined husband, currently supposed dead. The novel's most significant parallels to sensation fiction, however, occur in its depiction of the *mort vivant* John Harmon/Rokesmith and the languid lawyer Eugene Wrayburn, its use of secrets and mystery plots, and its anxieties concerning femininity and the sanctity of the middle-class home.

The dead/alive John Harmon/Rokesmith has clear antecedents in sensation fiction, where the figure of the *mort vivant* was a veritable cliché. One thinks of *The Woman in White's* Laura Glyde, who confronts her lover over her own tombstone, or *Lady Audley's Secret's* Lucy Audley, who stages her death as Helen Talboys. At the beginning of *Our Mutual Friend,* John Rokesmith superficially resembles Lady Audley in his obvious concealment of a secret past. The "secret" of Rokesmith's identity is, however, swiftly revealed through circumstantial evidence: his taking up house with the Wilfers, working for the Boffins, and his resemblance to Julius Handford, the man who was overwhelmed by the sight of John Harmon's corpse. Readers' interest thus shifts from Rokesmith's mysterious past to the sensational double-take of his being at once alive and dead—able to identify his own corpse, and to be suspected of his own murder. But Dickens' central preoccupation was with the "singular view of life and character" attained by the *mort vivant*.[3] This is similar to *East Lynne*: both John Rokesmith and Madame Vine experience the loss of class identity which Loesberg identifies as fundamental to sensation fiction (117). In *East Lynne,* the (supposedly dead) wife's reappearance as governess to her own children (close to but not part of the family, caring for children but not as a mother) represents metaphorically the social exclusion of the adulteress. In *Our Mutual Friend,* the dead/alive John Harmon achieves a dynamic freedom through his "death" and social declassification. He removes himself from the patrilinear imperatives of his father's "will"; he also temporarily frees himself from the capitalist economy. In *Our Mutual Friend,* Dickens thus uses the sensational figure of the *mort vivant* less to excite suspense (as in *Lady Audley's Secret*), to create a sensation of the uncanny (as in *The Woman in White*), or to represent social exclusion (as in *East Lynne*), than to project a fantasy of life outside capitalism and patrilinear structures, outside the "will" of the father and the restrictions of social class.

Just as John Harmon represents a complex rendering of the *mort vivant,* the languid Eugene Wrayburn is a dark version of the sensation novel's lawyer/hero. Lawyers were a popular element of the sensation genre: *Great Expectations* features Mr. Jaggers, *East Lynne* Archibald Carlyle, *The Woman in White* Mr. Gilmore, *No Name* Mr. Pendril and *Lady Audley's Secret* Robert Audley. Eugene resembles Robert Audley in a number of key respects. Like Robert, Eugene is a reluctant barrister with no clients. Both men keep law chambers, but support themselves on independent incomes. Moreover, both share a homosocial bond—Robert with George Talboys and Eugene with Mortimer Lightwood; each novel moves its hero somewhat unconvincingly from strong male partnership to heterosexual marriage. The most striking difference between Eugene and Robert is that while Robert's listlessness is short-lived and comic, Eugene's is chronic and disturbing. In *Lady Audley's Secret,* detective work moves Robert quickly towards professional and sexual

maturity (56). He becomes "a Christian . . . fearful to swerve from the conscientious discharge of the strange task that had been forced upon him; and
reliant on a stronger hand than his own to point the way . . . " (157), embodying rational power as well as moral and religious certitude. In *Our Mutual
Friend,* Eugene's chronic weariness represents a complex and ironic maturity:
*any* resistance to the Veneerings' pursuit of money and prestige is a kind of
moral gesture. On the other hand, his detective-like activities (his near-stalking
of Lizzie and his cat-and-mouse game with Bradley Headstone) leave the
reader deeply uneasy. Hence whereas Robert Audley embodies the power of
reason and the knowability of truth, Eugene represents an ambivalent and
amoral figure to whom knowledge comes belatedly and unconvincingly—not
by inductive reasoning, but through a deathbed revelation achieved by the
mediation of a half-mad, crippled child/sage.

*Our Mutual Friend* thus establishes its relationship with the sensation novel
through its adaptation of a number of stock devices of the genre: its contemporaneity, its debt to sensational journalism and police reports, its preoccupation
with criminality, detection, and marital anomaly. It also features innovative
variations on stock sensational characters: the *mort vivant* and the lawyer/
detective. At the same time, however, the text frustrates some of the basic
plot expectations of the genre. Notably, while it features a murder mystery,
*Our Mutual Friend* conspicuously lacks a reliable detective. At the opening of
the novel, when the Harmon Murder is on everybody's lips, several plausible
detective figures present themselves. As lawyers, Mortimer and Eugene have
the reasoning skills for the task; the Inspector is an obvious candidate; even
Pleasant Riderhood shows detective skill when she observes the sailor's
smooth hands. Yet the Inspector fades away for much of the narrative and
Eugene never takes up the investigation. Instead, Eugene becomes darkly
confused with criminality as he and Bradley Headstone blur the identities of
hunter and hunted. Finally, as J. Fisher Solomon observes, various criminal
figures take up the novel's detective work: Wegg searches for the missing
will and Riderhood tracks down Bradley Headstone and decodes his red
neckerchief (42). Thus, with respect to the Harmon murder mystery, the
reader of *Our Mutual Friend* finds him or herself in the position of a Watson
without a Holmes, with no detective figure who will represent and offer order,
reason, and closure.

As many critics have pointed out, however, the novel is not much of a
mystery anyway. If this is a novel with a secret, the secret is badly kept: most
readers guess very quickly that Rokesmith is John Harmon. Dickens denied
that he had ever intended otherwise: "When I devised this story," he wrote
in the postscript, "I foresaw the likelihood that a class of readers and commen-
tators would suppose that I was at great pains to conceal exactly what I was
at great pains to suggest: namely, that Mr John Harmon was not slain, and

that Mr John Rokesmith was he'' (893). The notes for the novel confirm this: Dickens reminds himself to ''[w]ork on to possessing the reader with the fact that he [Rokesmith] is John Harmon'' (Boll 110). This technique of seemingly premature revelation parallels that of Collins's later sensation fiction. In *No Name* (1862–63), for example, the ''secret'' of the Vanstone daughters' illegitimacy is revealed in Chapter 8. In a preface which anticipates Dickens' postscript to *Our Mutual Friend,* Collins warns his readers not to expect a repetition of *The Woman in White*:

> . . . it will be seen that the narrative related in these pages has been constructed on a plan, which differs from the plan followed in my last novel, and in some other of my works published at an earlier date. The only Secret contained in this book, is revealed midway in the first volume. From that point, all the main events of the story are purposely foreshadowed, before they take place—my present design being to rouse the reader's interest in following the train of circumstances by which these foreseen events are brought about.     (5–6)

Yet Dickens' technique is more complex than Collins's, for while he too presents a secret which is no secret, he also presents a murder mystery (the Harmon Murder) which is at once (a) not a murder, since John Harmon is not dead, (b) prematurely solved, when the ''victim'' tells all halfway through the book, and (c) insoluble, since we may suspect, but never know, that Riderhood killed George Radfoot. Moreover, he presents the mystery of the lost or concealed will (*No Name* also relies on a concealed ''secret trust''), only to reveal it as a red herring: Boffin and Harmon find the real will only to ignore it and arrange matters as they please. The text thus inscribes itself in the sensation genre, only to frustrate many of the generic expectations that this sets up. *Our Mutual Friend* offers a plethora of metaphors for this literary play with the reader. For example, when Eugene, Mortimer, Riderhood and the inspector discuss how to exchange signals as they search for Hexam, Eugene remarks that ''to tip a whistle is to advertise mystery and invite speculation'' (216). This describes Dickens' own tactic in the novel, which is to ''advertise'' a sensational mystery (including a corpse, a *mort vivant,* a detective inspector, and a missing will) and invite—only to disappoint—speculation. Moreover, as Keily points out, Eugene's nightly luring of Bradley Headstone provides a geographical metaphor for Dickens' creation of literary dead ends to lure, trap, and frustrate the reader of *Our Mutual Friend* (278–79):

> One night I go east, another night north, in a few nights I go all round the compass. . . . I study and get up abstruse No Thoroughfares in the course of the day. With Venetian mystery I seek those No Thoroughfares at night, glide into them by means of dark courts, tempt [him] to follow, turn suddenly, and catch

him before he can retreat. (606)

In speculating on Dickens' reasons for proffering the non-mystery of the Harmon murder plot, Philip Collins argues that this constitutes "the obligatory 'mystery' element" for the novel (*Dickens and Crime* 284). This achieved, Hutter argues, Dickens can dispense with the "whodunit" element and concentrate on the psychological study of Bradley Headstone's criminal mind. While I see the Harmon murder plot as an act of self-reflexive play rather than as a sop thrown to readers demanding endless repetition of the same, I find convincing Hutter's perception that *Our Mutual Friend* moves from murder mystery to crime novel. I would suggest as well, however, that there exists between the Harmon murder plot and the Bella plot a corresponding movement whereby the narrative shifts from invoking and frustrating the paradigms of the sensation novel to confronting, through an inverted sensational plot, two of the central anxieties of the sensation genre: the instability of the middle-class home, and the moral unreliability of the woman at its center.

*Our Mutual Friend's* anxieties concerning the related issues of domesticity and femininity can be directly related to the fears raised by sensation fiction. As Pykett observes, "[t]he sensation novels of the 1860s were, at least implicitly and indirectly, produced by, and to some extent reproduced, the anxieties and tensions generated by contemporary ideological contestation of the nature of woman, and of women's social and familial roles" (7). Sensation writers, she argues, "explor[ed] the contradictions of the dominant ideology of the feminine, by charting the conflict between 'actual' female experience and the domestic, private, angelic feminine ideal" (6). Antithetical to the Angel in the House, the sensation heroine frequently embodied a misogynistic horror of femininity sundered from such an ideal, as she indulged in sexual transgressions, deceptions, bigamy, adultery, and even murder. Robert Audley's depiction of his uncle's marriage as a "diabolical delusion" represents the anxieties manifested in such plots:

> He thought of the beautiful blue eyes watching Sir Michael's slumbers; the soft white hands, tending on his waking wants; the low, musical voice soothing his loneliness; cheering and consoling his declining years ... [W]hat an arch mockery, what a diabolical delusion it seemed! (*Lady Audley's Secret* 231)

The *London Quarterly's* review of *Armadale* is similarly representative:

> In *Armadale* we have a Miss Gwilt, a portrait drawn with masterly art, but one from which every rightly constituted mind turns with loathing. Is she, we ask, a type of any class to be found in society, or is she simply a horrible monstrosity? Are we to believe that there are women, holding respectable positions, received into honest and even Christian circles, who are carrying on a system

of intrigue and wickedness which we have been accustomed to associate with
the name of Italy . . . ? (156)

As Trodd observes, "[t]here are of course male householders with secrets in
the crime fiction of the period, but they lack the representative force of the
criminal angel" (9).

Is it because *Our Mutual Friend* involves a man with a secret past deceiving
his wife instead of a woman with a secret past deceiving her husband that
critics have failed to perceive the sensational nature of its marriage plot? Like
Helen Talboys, John Harmon connives at staging his own death; like Lucy
Graham, he marries under an alias, concealing from his spouse all details of
his former life; like Lady Audley, he is suspected of murder. Indeed, Dickens'
notes for the novel even refer to this plot as "John Rokesmith's secret" (Boll
118), suggesting that he may have been conscious of these parallels with *Lady
Audley's Secret*. If, as the Archbishop of York argued, sensational characters
persuaded readers "that in almost every one of the well-ordered houses of
their neighbours there was a skeleton shut up in some cupboard; that their
comfortable and easy-looking neighbour had in his breast a secret story which
he was always going about trying to conceal" ("Archbishop" 9a), should
the figure of John/Julius Harmon/Handford/Rokesmith not arouse similar
anxieties?

While critics of *Lady Audley's Secret* have consistently focused on issues
of marital betrayal and deception, few critics of *Our Mutual Friend* have
expressed concern over Bella's deception by her husband. Commentary on
what John Harmon terms his "pious fraud" (841) is remarkably free of
sympathy for the deceived wife. J. Fisher Solomon, for example, sees Harmon
as "refus[ing] to submit to the system that oppresses him" and building "a
new family untainted by . . . 'evil' " (39). He celebrates the Harmon/Boffin
collaboration as a "deliberate rebellion by a group of people who refuse to
be manipulated by their world" (40). Nancy Aycock Metz sees Harmon as
embodying "the peace that can be gained through dispassionate self-questioning, patience, and discipline willingly entered into" (63). Richard T.
Gaughan acknowledges that Harmon's use of deception is "perilously close
to society's use of masks to manipulate and dominate others and, in particular,
to Bradley Headstone's use of disguise to stalk Lizzie Hexam and Eugene
Wrayburn" (233), yet he argues that Harmon's disguises are "a filter through
which he can clarify possible relations between himself and others" (233).
He celebrates Harmon's willingness to "[give] up the social power he could
have by laying claim to his father's legacy" and concludes that "[o]nly by
circumventing the power relationships on which society thrives in ways such
as this can Harmon make his relationship to others authentic" (234).

From a feminist perspective, however, Harmon's refusal to be manipulated
by others and his building of a new "untainted" family must be qualified by

the realization that Harmon does manipulate Bella, and that his new family is created in deceit. Moreover, while Harmon may undoubtedly give up wealth and class status to become John Rokesmith, no Victorian husband could be described as powerless—and Rokesmith makes full use of his power over Bella when he insists on her blind trust in him. Robert Kiely's discussion of John Harmon's loss of name and identity seems particularly significant in this light. Kiely analyses Harmon's near-drowning as representing "what it feels like to lose one's name, to feel it slipping away" (275). The same applies profoundly to Bella, who gives up her name and legal identity in exchange for an alias which signifies nothing but its own obfuscation. (To *roke* means "to give off smoke, mists and fogs" [David 114].)

However, while most readers seem unmoved by the trick played on Bella, many are angry when they discover that *they* have been tricked into believing in Boffin's degeneration. Critics from G.K. Chesterton on have speculated as to whether Dickens changed his plans for Boffin. As F. X. Shea's 1967 manuscript study demonstrates, there was no such change of plan—yet the attention to this issue suggests how deeply readers have resented this narrative deception. As Audrey Jaffe perceptively writes, "When Boffin reveals that his 'change' was feigned, . . . we glimpse the potential depth of our insecurity . . ." (97). Interestingly, however, only Margaret Flanders Darby and Dierdre David seem to have glimpsed the potential depth of Bella's insecurity. Darby questions the motive for testing Bella: "When is this trial no longer all for Bella's benefit, . . . and when does it become an exercise in power . . . ?" (27). Similarly, David reads the "happy ending" with a jaundiced eye:

> . . . Mrs Boffin goes off into her demented and oriental rocking because the strain has clearly become too much for her. . . . [It] makes us wonder how on earth she has borne her husband for so long. Bella, too, becomes hysterical . . . She manages to recover long enough to declare that she was becoming "grasping, calculating, insolent, insufferable," but these adjectives seem rather strong and self-lacerating for the confused responses of a lower-middle-class girl transported to the West End world of shops and parties.          (118–19)

As both David and Darby note, the testing of Bella seems excessive. Why does she arouse such uneasiness? Why must she be educated in such perfect passivity and blind trust? At what stage in the novel does the Harmon murder cease to be the center of anxiety and why should this anxiety be transferred to a relatively harmless, though mercenary, middle-class girl? Anthea Trodd's observation that the male householder with the secret lacks the symbolic power of the criminal angel (9) casts light on this transfer of anxiety and attention. The Rokesmith marriage contains two threats: the first (the threat of John Harmon's secret past, false identity, and suspected criminality) is a sensational plot which is known to the reader all along to be non-threatening. "John Rokesmith's secret" is not even a secret, as critics never tire of pointing out. The reader's attention and anxiety are thus directed away from the ostensible center of mystery and threat (the male householder with a secret) to a less obvious target: Bella. Despite John Harmon's superficial resemblance to criminal angels such as Lady Audley, Bella is the true focus of attention and anxiety; she, and not her husband, constitutes the real threat to the domestic ideal. Thus the second threat—anxiety concerning woman's power and woman's place in the home—comes center stage. Bella Wilfer's name, with its pun on "will", signals this transfer of attention from the non-plot of the Harmon will to the real issue of female wilfulness and its control.

If, as Collins argues, the Headstone plot moves *Our Mutual Friend* from "whodunit" to crime novel, then the Harmon/Bella plot moves from investigating Harmon as a threat to social order to investigating and "solving" the problem of Bella. In this respect, *Our Mutual Friend* resembles *Hard Times,* which shifts its attention from a consideration of utilitarian educational principles to the more vexed issue of Louisa's sexual status; it also parallels *Dombey and Son,* which "veer[s] from concern with the eponymous male hero to fascination with less reputable female characters" (Marsh 406). Just as *Dombey and Son,* in Miss Tox's famous words, turns out to be "a daughter after all" (225), *Our Mutual Friend* turns out to be a wife.

In Bella, Dickens avoids some of the most controversial aspects of the sensational heroine: she does not actually commit either adultery or bigamy, nor does she exhibit the undisciplined impulses or lack of sexual restraint that Ann Cvetkovich sees as primary sources of anxiety in sensation novels (47). Yet Bella does have significant points of resemblance to other sensation heroines. She parallels Lady Audley in her perception of marriage as a financial transaction. When Sir Michael Audley proposes to Lucy Graham, the governess tells him frankly she is in no position to refuse: "Remember what my life has been. . . . From my very babyhood I have never seen anything but poverty. . . . I *cannot* be disinterested . . . " (Braddon 10–11). Similarly, Bella tells her father, "I have made up my mind that I must have money, Pa. I feel that I can't beg it, borrow it, or steal it; and so I have resolved that I must marry it" (375). She resembles Estella Havisham (*Great Expectations*) in declaring that she "[has] no heart" (531). Most notably, she rebels at the thought of being "willed away, like a horse, or a dog, or a bird" (animal metaphors commonly used in Victorian texts to describe a wife's legal powerlessness) or being made the "property of strangers" (434).

Bella's disruptive female wilfulness is encapsulated in the childhood tantrum which prompts Old Harmon to will her to his son. Her father describes the encounter with Mr. Harmon as follows:

You were stamping your little foot, my dear, and screaming with your little voice, and laying into me with your little bonnet, which you had snatched off for the purpose . . . and you were doing this one Sunday morning when I took you out, because I didn't go the exact way you wanted, when the old gentleman [Mr Harmon], sitting on a seat near, said, "That's a nice girl; that's a *very* nice girl; a promising girl!" . . . Then he asked your name, my dear, and mine. . . .

(85–86)

The scene suggests that Harmon deliberately chooses for his son a girl whose disobedience to male authority will destroy her future marriage. To readers familiar with childhood tantrums, Bella's behavior may seem a poor predictor of adult behavior; however, the text returns obsessively to this scene. On Bella's wedding day, for example, she confesses to being a "vexatious, capricious, thankless, troublesome, Animal" (730) and recalls the tantrum in a disturbing moment of self-laceration:

Dear Pa, if you knew how much I think this morning . . . about the first time of our seeing old Mr Harmon, when I stamped and screamed and beat you with my detestable little bonnet! I feel as if I had been stamping and screaming and beating you with my hateful little bonnet ever since I was born, darling! (730)

Hence while it appears to be John Harmon who violates the sanctity of the home with his secret past, assumed name, and suspicion of murder, the real angst surrounds Bella. She must unlearn her wilfulness (which is framed as a childish trait) and "mature" into "adult" submission. Above all, she must learn duty to home and family: the obligation to show loyalty to her parents (however flawed and unattractive her home may have been); the obligation to demonstrate "perfect faith" (815) in her husband; and the manifestation of this familial and domestic focus through the home arts of cooking, housekeeping, and motherhood. Only through this redemptive process can she be, as Dickens wrote in his notes, "reclaim[ed]" as "the best and dearest of girls" (Boll 120). (Notably, *Our Mutual Friend* provides a number of foils who signal Bella's ultimate redeemability: the Lammle marriage, for example, provides a dark shadow of Bella's ambitions, and Bella's own mother, in her false submissiveness to her downtrodden husband, is a comic parallel of her wilful daughter.)

This scrutiny of Bella marks a shift in the very nature of investigation and policing in *Our Mutual Friend*. In the first half of the text, detection lies in official hands—those of the Night Inspector and the coroner. As Solomon has observed, in the second half of the text, the investigation of the Harmon murder dissipates from the official ranks of the detective police into the criminal underground. At the same time, the investigation of Bella follows the trajectory identified by D. A. Miller in his study of *Oliver Twist*: "the work of the police is superseded by the operations of another, informal, and extralegal principle of organization and control'' (3)—those of respectable middle-class characters who are not officially engaged in policing or detection. Miller terms this informal control the ''amateur supplement'' (8) of the law: that is, the policing apparatus of the community, which is inscribed in the ordinary practices of society (48). To use Michel Foucault's terms from *Discipline and Punish,* ''the individual [is] subjected to habits, rules, orders, an authority that is exercised continually around [her] and upon [her], and which [she] must allow to function automatically in [her]'' (128).

The disciplining of Bella is dealt with by those living with or closest to her, and through mechanisms of control which operate on a domestic and private level. The primary agent of this subtle control is Rokesmith, whose position first as lodger in her family home and then as live-in secretary in the Boffin's house enables him to scrutinize her behaviour almost continuously. He cast a ''covert glance at her face'' (254); he ''watch[es] her with another covert look'' (255); there is ''[a]lways a light in his office-room when [Bella comes] home from the play or Opera'' (363); and he is ''always at the carriage-door'' to hand her out (363). In a rare piece of free indirect discourse, the narrative renders Bella's impression of this relentless scrutiny: ''[i]n spite of his seemingly retiring manner, a very intrusive person, this Secretary and lodger . . . '' (363).

To some extent, Rokesmith's power is diminished by the reader's knowledge that his doting on Bella is unreciprocated, even scorned. Pity for him is ensured by the apparently insurmountable financial difference between him and Bella; indeed, Mrs. Boffin sees him as a forlorn child as he sits by himself mourning Bella's haughty refusal of his proposal:

> It was after a night when John had made an offer to a certain young lady, and the certain young lady had refused it. . . . I looked in, and saw him sitting lonely by his fire, brooding over it. . . . Too many a time had I seen him sitting lonely, when he was a poor child, to be pitied, heart and hand! Too many a time had I seen him in need of being brightened up with a comforting word! Too many and too many a time to be mistaken, when that glimpse of him come at last!
> (840–41)

Yet even at this early stage, Rokesmith's scrutiny combines erotic desire with moral judgement—and the measure of his power is that Bella swiftly internalizes this judgment. For example, he prompts her into self-scrutiny concerning her treatment of her family: ''he unquestionably left her with a penitent air upon her, and a penitent feeling in her heart'' (364). Bella herself is nonplussed by the power he attains over her: ''What can I mean by it, or what can he mean by it?'' she wonders. ''He has no right to any power over me, and how do I come to mind him when I don't care for him?'' (364). It is apparent to the reader, however, that her acceptance of his judgment, even at this early stage, anticipates the coverture of her future marriage. Rokesmith becomes her moral guide long before she accepts him as her husband. The second half of *Our Mutual Friend* traces this gradual escalation of Rokesmith's power over Bella, to the point when, as his wife, she directly asks that he test and judge her marital trust: "[T]ry me through some trial—and tell them after *that,* what you think of me" (746).

Rokesmith's scrutiny of Bella forms part of a pattern of almost relentless spying and following which occurs in *Our Mutual Friend*: Bradley Headstone and Charley are seen "spying eastward for Lizzie" (451); Eugene lurks around Lizzie "like a bailiff" (463); Mrs. Lammle tells Twemlow that she "may be watched" (474); Bradley follows Eugene; Eugene bribes Mr. Dolls to watch the correspondence between Jenny Wren and Lizzie; Riderhood watches Eugene; Headstone watches Eugene; and Riderhood watches Headstone watching Eugene watching Lizzie. In the context of this deeply threatening and in some cases murderous stalking, Rokesmith's scrutiny of Bella may seem comparatively benign. Yet it too has disturbing aspects. According to Foucault's analysis, this meticulous, apparently benignant, scrutiny of everyday activity functions to produce "subjected and practised bodies, 'docile' bodies" (138). Thus, to quote Wegg, Rokesmith's gazing on Bella has a "double look" (360). It embodies both hopeless unrequited love, and at the same time his disturbing power to scrutinize and police the most minute details of her conduct. The two sides to Rokesmith's scrutiny are represented in two illustrations (figures 1 and 2). In both, Rokesmith is positioned as the watcher of Bella. In "Pa's Lodger and Pa's Daughter," Bella's activity is benign, even if her expression is haughty; correspondingly, his gaze is depicted as non-threatening. But in "The Boofer Lady" there are deeply disturbing elements: Rokesmith lurks darkly in a shadowed doorway, a domestic version of the stalking Headstone. Meanwhile, Bella, ironically labelled the "Boofer Lady," is shown as a virtual phantasm of a misogynistic imagination—haughty and darkly self-obsessed, oblivious to the male look which seeks to subjugate her. The voyeuristic aspects of Rokesmith's scrutiny which are suggested by this illustration are implied in Bella's discovery that his room contains a print of a pretty woman who resembles herself. The darker implications of this gazing remain latent; however, readers of *Dombey and Son* would recall that Dickens used Carker's obsession with a similar portrait (one which resembled Edith Dombey) to suggest his predatory and voyeuristic relation with her.

Initially, Rokesmith's domestic surveillance involves him alone, and is directed, we discover, at both Bella and the Boffins. Where the Boffins are concerned, the erotic element of his scrutinizing gaze is missing, but it is clear that he observes meticulously how they behave under their new inheritance. His apparently humble position of secretary is thus combined with the powerful role of moral scrutineer and judge. In the chapter aptly entitled "Minders and Reminders," the narrator remarks that Rokesmith's mastery of the Boffins' affairs "might have been mistrusted by a man with better knowledge of men that the Golden Dustman had" (24). Indeed, the reader may come to feel uneasy about this apparently powerless figure whose relentless observation accrues him so much power. "If, in his limited sphere, [the Secretary] sought power," remarks the narrator, "it was the power of knowledge; the power derivable from a perfect comprehension of his business" (241). Certainly, Rokesmith seeks the power of knowledge—precisely the kind of policing power which Foucault sees as fundamental to the regulation of the liberal subject.

Having satisfied himself that the Boffins are deserving of the wealth they possess ("Dead, I have found the true friends of my lifetime still as true as tender and as faithful as when I was alive . . . "[(429]), Rokesmith joins with the Boffins in the "pious" (841) deceit and concurrent testing of Bella. This is perhaps the most relentless scrutiny of all in this novel so suffused with spying, as Bella is almost literally never out of the sight of one or other of her observers. Most interesting, however, is the way in which this plot produces the internalization of judgment on the part of the subject which Foucault sees as intrinsic to discipline. As Mr. Boffin pretends to become a miser and to mistreat his secretary, he does so ostensibly in order that he, his wife, and Rokesmith can observe Bella's reactions to his moral decline. Bella, in short, would appear to be the one who is being watched. But in fact the reverse is also true: Bella becomes the watcher, as she scrutinizes Boffin's moral conduct. The Boffin plot thus involves Bella in a circle of mutual observation and discipline, whereby she becomes an intrinsic part of the domestic policing mechanism. She is both observer and observed—and even invites and willingly submits to moral scrutiny when she asks Rokesmith to "try" her "through some trial" (746).

In terms of the relationship between *Our Mutual Friend* and sensation fiction, it is crucial that this key "trial" should test Bella's performance *as wife.* In order to succeed, this wilful girl who has rebelled against being "willed away" (586) must will away her will. In this respect, the novel turns its scrutiny and disciplinary force onto its true focus of anxiety; the role of the woman in marriage and the home. As Pykett argues, "[i]f the sensation heroine embodies anything, it is an uncertainty about the definition of the feminine, or of 'woman' " (81). *Our Mutual Friend* assuages this anxiety by testing and vindicating Bella's absolute compliance to a wifely role: to pass Rokesmith's test, she must display absolute obedience and loyalty to, as well as trust in, him. Specifically, Bella is tested when she discovers that her husband is hiding from Mortimer Lightwood, that he has been using an alias (Julius Handford), and that he is suspected of murdering John Harmon. Significantly, this incident incorporates the text's two levels of policing: the first is the official investigation of Harmon by the police. Both the reader and Harmon recognise this as an empty threat, a non-story, since he is clearly innocent of his own murder. But the second level, the discipline of Bella (which is carried on by the amateur supplement consisting of the Boffins and John Harmon), gains full narrative attention. In this plot, John Harmon triumphs when Bella refuses to demand explanations either for his actions or for the police investigation. As J. Hillis Miller observes, when Bella drives about on a winter night with a Police Inspector and with her husband apparently under suspicion of murder, her immersion in strangeness parallels the way in which both John Harmon and Eugene Wrayburn attain new selves through baptismal immersions in water (326):

> ... when [the Inspector] and she and John, at towards nine o'clock of a winter evening went to London, and began driving from London Bridge, among low-lying water-side wharves and docks and strange places, Bella was in the state of a dreamer; perfectly unable to account for her being there, perfectly unable to forecast what would happen next, or whither she was going, or why; certain of nothing in the immediate present, but that she confided in John....
>
> (*OMF* 833)

J. Hillis Miller describes Bella in this scene as "absent from the world and seeing it as the strange image of herself" (326). Surely, however, the image is not "of herself," but of her husband—hence its strangeness. What Bella experiences is perfect selflessness or absence of will; if this is self-discovery or self-attainment, it is a revelation of self predicated on the absolute moral authority of the male. In this light, Dickens' descriptions of Bella as "vanishing" in her fiancé's embraces (672) and being "swallowed up" by the church porch on her wedding day (732) can be seen to figure the absorption of the Victorian wife into her husband's legal and moral identity. (William Blackstone famously described this concept of legal incorporation as follows: "By marriage, the husband and wife are one person in law: that is, the very being of legal existence of the woman is suspended during the marriage, or at least is incorporated and consolidated into that of the husband . . . "[I:430]). The test, which commences in the Boffin home and continues until after the birth of Bella's first child, culminates when Bella achieves such perfect incorporation of herself with her husband.

*Our Mutual Friend* thus shifts its problem-solving energy from the non-plot of the Harmon murder mystery to the Bella plot, which centers on the investigation and resolution of female wilfulness by the amateur supplement in the novel. J. Fisher Solomon has made the fascinating observation that the culmination of Boffin's and Rokesmith's "pious fraud" reads like the dénouement of a detective story, where "Poirot makes his little speech and everything becomes clear" (42). Structurally, the classic mystery moves towards the moment of resolution and decoding, when order is restored and justice achieved. As a police investigation, *Our Mutual Friend* refuses such moments of certitude: we never really know who killed George Radfoot and Eugene Wrayburn refuses to punish Bradley Headstone. Yet insofar as it concerns Bella, the novel does—almost obsessively—seek order, resolution, and definite closure. The police may not solve the Harmon Murder, but the amateur supplement works to resolve the problem of Bella—and, by extension, seeks to assuage the anxiety over the false angel in the house which haunts its predecessors in sensation fiction.

Only the fantastic nature of the novel's conclusion suggests some doubt as to the stability of the newly redeemed angel in the house. Dierdre David has analyzed the implications of the conclusion's fairy-tale elements in class terms:

> Dickens . . . chooses to release Bella from her social misery through marriage to a fairy-tale prince about to inherit a kingdom founded upon dust. The combination of social realism and fantasy in Bella's experience suggests the impossibility . . . of Bella ever getting to the West End—she can, in fact, only do it in fantasy.                                                                 (119)

The same applies to the text's resolution of gender anxieties. The "pretty and . . . promising picter" (849) of Bella sitting by the hearth with her child in her arms, surrounded by tropical birds, flowers, water lilies, fountains, and gold and silver fish is more fantastic than believable and betrays a lingering anxiety as to the containment or resolution of the problem of female wilfulness which sensation fiction had raised and which *Our Mutual Friend* attempts to lay to rest.

*Our Mutual Friend* thus stands in complex relation to the sensation novels which preceded it in the early 1860s. The text presents itself as a sensation novel (with a missing will, *mort vivant,* detective police officer, murder mystery, and unknown man with a secret past), only to give away its own secrets and refuse to conform to the teleological nature of the classic mystery plot. At the same time, however, *Our Mutual Friend* returns obsessively to sensation fiction's central anxieties—the beleaguered home and the criminal angel in the house. While reproducing in the masculine plot ("John Rokesmith's secret") the classic ingredients of a sensation plot, the text centers its anxieties on the feminine, working to resolve "Bella Wilfer's Secret"—the wilful femininity which threatened the stability of Victorian gender roles and, by extension, the Victorian home.

Figure 1. *Pa's Lodger and Pa's Daughter*

Figure 2. *The Boofer Lady*

## NOTES

1. The quotation is from Chorley's review of *Armadale* in the *Athenaeum*: "This time the interest of [Collins's] tale centres upon one of the most hardened female villains whose *devices and desires* have ever blackened fiction . . . " (147; my emphasis). This in turn quotes the Anglican *Book of Common Prayer*: "We have followed too much the devices and desires of our own hearts."

2. On the principal features of sensation fiction, see Tillotson, Brantlinger, Hughes, Cvetkovich, Loesberg, and Pykett.

3. In 1862, Charles Dickens noted in his book of memoranda a "LEADING INCIDENT FOR A STORY": "A man—young and eccentric?—feigns to be dead, and *is* dead to all intents and purposes, and . . . for years retains that singular view of life and character" (Kaplan 467). Scholars now recognise this as the seminal idea for *Our Mutual Friend.*

## WORKS CITED

"The Archbishop of York on Works of Fiction." *The Times* (2 Nov. 1864): 9a.

Rev. of *Armadale. London Quarterly Review.* 27 (Oct. 1866): 107–09. Rpt. in *Wilkie Collins: The Critical Heritage.* Ed. Norman Page. London and Boston: Routledge and Kegan Paul, 1974. 156–57.

Boll, Ernest. "The Plotting of *Our Mutual Friend.*" *Modern Philology* 42 (1944):96–122.

Blackstone, William. *Commentaries on the Laws of England.* Oxford: Clarendon, 1765. London: Dawsons, 1966.

Braddon, Mary Elizabeth. *Lady Audley's Secret.* Ed. David Skilton. Oxford: Oxford UP, 1991.

Brantlinger, Patrick. "What is 'Sensational' about the 'Sensation Novel?'" *Nineteenth-Century Fiction* 37 (1982): 1–28.

[Chorley, H.F.] Rev. of *Armadale. Athenaeum* (2 June 1866): 732–33. Rpt. in *Wilkie Collins: The Critical Heritage.* Ed. Norman Page. London and Boston: Routledge and Kegan Paul, 1974. 146–48.

Collins, Phillip, ed. *Dickens: The Critical Heritage.* London: Routledge and Kegan Paul, 1971.

———. *Dickens and Crime.* London: MacMillan, 1962.

Collins, Wilkie. *The Woman in White.* Ed. Harvey Peter Sucksmith. Oxford: Oxford UP, 1991.

————.*No Name*. Ed. Virginia Blain. Oxford: Oxford UP, 1986.

Cvetkovich, Ann. *Mixed Feelings: Feminism, Mass Culture, and Victorian Sensationalism*. New Brunswick, New Jersey: Rutgers UP, 1992.

[Dallas, E. S. ] Rev. of *Our Mutual Friend. The Times* (29 Nov. 1865): 6. Rpt. in *Dickens: The Critical Heritage*. Ed. Philip Collins. London: Routledge and Kegan Paul, 1971. 464–68.

Darby, Margaret Flanders. "Four Women in *Our Mutual Friend.*" *The Dickensian* 83 (1987): 24–39.

David, Dierdre. *Fictions of Resolution in Three Victorian Novels: North and South, Our Mutual Friend, Daniel Deronda*. London: Macmillan, 1981.

Dickens, Charles. *Dombey and Son*. Ed. Alan Horsman. Oxford: Clarendon, 1974.

————.*Our Mutual Friend*. Ed. Stephen Gill. Harmondsworth, Middlesex: Penguin, 1985.

Foucault, Michel. *Discipline and Punish: The Birth of the Prison*. 1975. Trans. Alan Sheridan. New York: Vintage Books, 1995.

Gaughan, Richard T. "Prospecting for Meaning in *Our Mutual Friend.*" *Dickens Studies Annual* 19 (1990): 231–46.

Hughes, Winifred. *The Maniac in the Cellar: Sensation Novels of the 1860s*. Princeton: Princeton UP, 1980.

Hutter, Albert D. "Dismemberment and Articulation in *Our Mutual Friend.*" *Dickens Studies Annual* 11 (1983): 135–75.

Jaffe, Audrey. "Omniscience in *Our Mutual Friend*: On Taking the Reader by Surprise." *Journal of Narrative Technique* 17 (1987): 91–101.

Kaplan, Fred. *Dickens: A Biography*. New York: Avon Books, 1988.

Kiely, Robert. "Plotting and Scheming: The Design of Design in *Our Mutual Friend.*" *Dickens Studies Annual* 12 (1983): 267–83.

Loesberg, Jonathan. "The Ideology of Narrative Form in Sensation Fiction." *Representations* 13 (1986): 115–38.

[Mansel, Henry]. "Sensation Novels." *Quarterly Review* 113 (1863): 482–514.

Marsh, Joss Lutz. "Good Mrs. Brown's Connections: Sexuality and Story-Telling in *Dealings with the Firm of Dombey and Son.*" *ELH* 58 (1991): 405–26.

Metz, Nancy Aycock. "The Artistic Reclamation of Waste in *Our Mutual Friend.*" *Nineteenth-Century Fiction* 34 (1979): 59–72.

Miller, D.A. *The Novel and the Police*. Berkeley: U of California P, 1988.

Miller, J. Hillis. *Charles Dickens: The World of His Novels*. Cambridge: Harvard UP, 1958.

Pykett, Lyn. *The "Improper" Feminine: The Women's Sensation Novel and the New Woman Writing*. London: Routledge, 1992.

"The Popular Novels of the Year." *Fraser's Magazine* 68 (August 1863): 253–69.

Robson, John M. "Crime in *Our Mutual Friend.*" *Rough Justice*. Ed. Martin L. Friedland. Toronto: U of Toronto P, 1991. 114–40.

Shea, Fr. F.X. "No Change of Intention in *Our Mutual Friend.*" *The Dickensian* 63 (1967): 37–40.

Soloman, J. Fisher. "Realism, Rhetoric, and Reification: Or the Case of the Missing Detective in *Our Mutual Friend.*" *Modern Philology* 86 (1988): 34–45.

Tillotson, Kathleen. "The Lighter Reading of the Eighteen-Sixties." Introduction. *The Woman in White*. By Wilkie Collins. Boston: Houghton Mifflin, 1969. ix–xxvi.

Trodd, Anthea. *Domestic Crime in the Victorian Novel*. London: MacMillan, 1989.

# Wilkie Collins, Detection, and Deformity

## Teresa Mangum

" 'What do you think of that?' cried the detective, with the
air of a showman exhibiting his show."
—Arthur Conan Doyle, *A Study in Scarlet*

Encounters with Victorian sensation writers' obsessive attention to physical deformities embarrass, even shame twentieth-century readers. How, then, must they have affected nineteenth-century readers? Unlike Charles Dickens, who exploited physical eccentricity as a metonym for character, Wilkie Collins, particularly in *The Law and the Lady* (1875), exaggerates deformity into a linguistic, structural, and thematic staging of the differences on which gender and genre depend. Valeria Macallan, who occupies chief place in this early female detective novel—as first person narrator, as chief investigator, and as a potential victim of an unsolved crime—raises questions about the relationship between the categories gender and genre; Miserrimus Dexter, who is born without legs and, the novel coyly suggests, without genitals, and who is variously Valeria's associate, her antagonist, and her sensational counterpart, raises questions about the relationship between the broader categories, normal and formal.

Given the historical and literary contexts of Collins's novel, the character Miserrimus Dexter's flagrant, paradoxical display of all he lacks—legs and possibly his lower torso—poses ethical as well as formal problems for Collins's readers. By the 1870s, cultural and literary critics were as likely to groan with ennui as to rant of injustice in response to displays of deformity, as evidenced by the 1847 *Punch* sketch, "Deformito-mania." Walter Maclean of *The Academy,* in fact, dismissed Dexter as a poor parody of Punch, "He was born without legs; and so, at least in his earliest avatars, was Punch. He had a mania for homicide, a passion for disturbing domestic peace, a diabolic cunning, a faithful dumb attendant, and many other signs by which you may know him" (8). Algernon Swinburne similarly lamented that Collins's "remarkable genius" was limited by his repeated dependence upon "the help

285

of some physical or moral infirmity in some one of the leading agents or patients of the story'' (589–99). Why, then, Collins's persistent exhibit of what P.T. Barnum called "curiosities"?[1]

Despite our own well-intentioned attempts to rewrite social scripts and referential language for marks, limbs, absences, excesses, or other characteristics that code bodies as abnormal, a cultural preoccupation with anomalous bodies persists. Even more explicitly than Collins's novel, twentieth-century texts expose and exploit the scopophilia and the scopophobia which constitute the gaze upon and designation of a body as irregular. Both Tod Browning's film *Freaks* (1932) and Katherine Dunn's novel *Geek Love* (1983) inhabit the liminal worlds of the sideshow where "freaks" and "geeks" exhibit their bodies to paying audiences. Point of view, particularly in *Geek Love,* which is narrated by a bald, female, albino, hunch-backed dwarf who is also a proud member of a family of Geeks generated by the pregnant mother's chemical experiments, returns a cynical gaze at spectators (and readers) whom she and the other Geeks contemptuously label "norms."[2]

The reversal of point of view in *Freaks* and *Geek Love* and in the photographs of Diane Arbus worries assumptions that forms (and social relations as forms) are inherent, natural, appropriate, or constant. Susan Stewart astutely comments on the spectators' motivation during such an exchange: ''while the freak show may seem, at first glance, to be a display of the grotesque, the distance it invokes makes it instead an inverse display of perfection. Through the freak we derive an image of the normal; to know an age's typical freaks is, in fact, to know its points of standardization" (132–33). As Stewart's comments suggest, such reversals also flaunt the inevitable, uncomfortable, and therefore often ignored counterpart to voyeurism, exhibitionism. Repeatedly, *The Law and the Lady* asks who can look at whom (a function of social relations) under what circumstances (a function of plot). Because the detective must be free to look at anyone and anything, the middle-class detective female—like the middle-class emasculated, sexually ambiguous male—provokes anxiety when her behavior reveals how complicated "just looking" can be.

Working from the social and literary contexts which produced *The Law and the Lady,* I examine in this essay the biographical, spectatorial, and generic conditions that situate Misserrimus Dexter's body as well as ways in which representation of his body establishes correspondences between "a poor deformed wretch" (293) and a female detective. I argue that the physically anomalous masculine figure distracts attention from, yet shapes responses to, the formal aberrations produced when a masculinist plot, the emerging genre of detective fiction, re-forms itself around the socially anomalous body of the female detective. More abstractly, the body of the emasculated, yet libidinous male character and the unstable social identity of the female detective—struggling to learn whether her legal identity is Brinton or Woodville or Macallan and whether she is a woman or a wife or an ambiguously married single person or a mother—engage the formal paradoxes that characterize detective fiction. As critics of the genre are well aware, the detective plot depends upon the flagrant display of absences, secrets, and inexplicable fragments or clues which must be made to call attention to themselves in order to prompt a search for origins or causes.[3] The success of the detective plot thus turns on its exhibitionistic evocation of "curiosity," hardly a plot for a proper lady.

True to its character as a sensational novel about a woman's death by poisoning, *The Law and the Lady* first appeared in *The Illustrated Graphic Newspaper* between 1874 and March 1875. Collins's biographer, Catherine Peters, suggests that perhaps unconsciously Collins was borrowing from his brother Charles Allston Collins's novel *At the Bar* (1866), an earlier study of a woman's suicide by arsenic. Jenny Bourne Taylor and others cite Collins's fascination with the infamous 1857 trial in Scotland of Madeleine Smith, who was accused of killing a former lover with arsenic to clear the way for marriage to a more socially acceptable man.[4] I would argue that George Eliot's *Mill on the Floss* (1860), with its poignant and disastrous pairing of the physically impaired Philip Wakem and the socially misfit Maggie Tulliver, might also be an antecedent. Like Valeria, both Madeleine Smith and Maggie Tulliver struggle to reconcile "masculine" qualities of strength, intellect, and ambition with acceptable forms of femininity. In fact, Collins's interest in using a female as a potential detective surfaced two decades before his novel in a short story, "The Diary of Anne Rodway," published in *Household Words* in 1856, then reprinted in a collection of framed stories, *The Queen of Hearts* (1859). Here, a working-class woman investigates a crime in order to find the murderer of her best friend, another female servant. As in *The Law and the Lady,* Anne Rodway's detecting is motivated by love, hence justified by duty.

The narrative strategy of *The Law and the Lady* differs from Collins's better-known novels *The Woman in White* (1860) and *The Moonstone* (1868) in which various narrators offer accounts of the events. Here, the female character who takes on the detective role, Valeria, is the sole narrator; however, she pieces together her retrospective account of her marriage, the mystery that nearly destroys the marriage, her investigation of the mystery, and finally her salvaging of the marriage from fragments of many texts. The first person narrative not only intersperses memory with letters, diaries, court records and testimony, telegrams, and legal and religious contracts, but also reproduces visual texts (in language), including photographs, paintings, sculptures, and "curiosities." Moreover, the novel itself is accompanied by numerous illustrations, and the drawings of Miserrimus Dexter counteract characters' claims about his extraordinary appearance, portraying Dexter as a round-shouldered, sad-faced elderly gentleman in a wheelchair who peers intensely and somewhat anxiously at the reader.

To summarize briefly, the novel falls into three parts. The first words conclude the marriage service in the Book of Common Prayer on the ill-omened day of Valeria's private marriage to Eustace Woodville. Within days, Valeria begins to stumble upon clues which eventually reveal that Eustace Woodville is not who he seems. When Eustace refuses to explain his duplicity, Valeria turns to his sympathetic but uncooperative mother and to his womanizing elderly friend Major Fitz-David. The Major turns Valeria loose in his library, allowing her to find a published and bound Trial Report which reveals that her husband is, in fact, the infamous Eustace Macallan who three years earlier had been accused of poisoning his first wife, Sara Macallan, in a highly sensationalized trial that dominated the news for weeks. Humiliated, Eustace abandons Valeria.

Valeria's account of the Trial Report constitutes most of Part II. Her summary includes extracts from the Indictment, the prisoner's Declaration of Innocence, medical and police records, personal letters, Eustace's diary, and the testimony of various witnesses. Though the members of the jury cannot find sufficient evidence to declare Eustace guilty, they are so convinced that his plain wife repulsed him and his former lover Mrs. Beauly enticed him that, despite the pleas of his mother and his friend Miserrimus Dexter, they deliver the verdict "Not Proven." The legal system in Scotland did and does permit a jury to register suspicion when the evidence is insufficient for a guilty verdict. Exercising social rather than legal censure, the jury condemns Eustace to social purgatory; Valeria, as his legal appendage, is thus unwittingly sentenced to life as a social anomaly. The day after reading the trial proceedings, Valeria "awake[s]—a new woman, with a new mind" (182); the wife is transfigured into the detective. The last third of the novel recounts her desperate struggle to restore her husband's name, a search which brings her into contact with the aberrant, amorous, and increasingly deranged Miserrimus Dexter.

In the last chapters of the novel, Eustace is moved by Valeria's devotion to reunite with her, but only if she abandons her investigation. However, she surreptitiously continues her search through male agents whom she has involved in her "case." Her old family friend Benjamin and Eustace's solicitor Mr. Playmore painstakingly reconstruct fragments of Sara's letter from the Gleninch dust heap, which Jenny Bourne Taylor calls "the forgotten detritus of the household's past" (*In the Secret Theatre of Home*, 223), solving the mystery of Sara's death and thereby clearing Eustace of murder. While the letter is exhibited to the reader, those who have broken with formal conventions—Dexter as the literal and figurative exhibitor of secrets and Valeria as the curious, investigating spectator—are ultimately silenced.

The exhibition rather than repression of eccentricity is a characteristic shared by Wilkie Collins, his novels, and Miserrimus Dexter himself. Like freaks and freak shows, Collins and the sensation genre he helped to popularize occupied peculiar physical and imaginative spaces in Victorian culture. First of all, Collins perceived his own body as deformed. Friends reminisced that Collins commented on his delicate feet and hands (he often wore women's shoes), his small body and large head, and his misshapen forehead. His left temple was partially collapsed and his right temple bulged outward, which probably resulted from the use of forceps during a difficult birth.[5] Drawings and photographs suggest that these "deformities" may have figured far larger in his imagination than in fact. Nevertheless, Collins's self-image must have been magnified during the 1860s and 1870s when he suffered increasingly from what he called "gout" of the eyes. In *Memories of Charles Dickens,* Percy Fitzgerald quotes Charles Kent's memory of Collins's horrific appearance at times when his eyes "were literally *enormous bags of blood*" (262). Collins "treated" himself with goblet-sized doses of laudanum, inciting fantasies of ominous, green, gargoyle figures far more grotesque than even the most sensational of his characters.[6]

If Collins had inherited his physical anomalies, he himself was responsible for his social anomalousness. From 1859 until his death he lived with Caroline Graves and her daughter; in 1868 he also set up a household with Martha Rudd with whom he had two daughters and a son, a group he called his "morganatic" family. Thereafter, he maintained the two households within walking distance of one another. Letters and memoirs of friends cited by biographers Katherine Peters, William Clarke, and Kenneth Robinson document the uneasiness these irregular domestic arrangements caused Collins's friends.

Most importantly for the purposes of my argument, Collins's deformities participate in a long-established British tradition of exhibiting curiosities and of curiosity about human "exhibits." In *The Shows of London,* Richard Altick provides a sweeping study of the subject, noting that the Great Exhibition of 1851 instituted and legitimized "exhibitions" (507). Both before and after this edifying, nationalistic display of British technology, exhibitions, especially displays of the human body, were marketed as a form of social amusement that addressed innocuous, salacious, and/or scientific curiosity, whether the bodies were labeled monstrous births, freaks, prodigies, or curiosities. Collins was not the only writer to take note. In Book VII of *The Prelude,* William Wordsworth confers mutant nationhood upon exhibits at Bartholomew Fair:

All out-o-the-way, far-fetched, perverted things
All freaks of nature, all Promethean thoughts
Of man; his dullness, madness, and their feats

All jumbled up together to make up
This Parliament of Monsters (1805, 11:690–94)

Similarly, Charles Dickens picks out a dwarf and giant among other "natural curiosities" in his 1835 newspaper article "Greenwich Fair." Henry Morley's *Memoirs of Bartholomew Fair* (1859) also recalls similar exhibits in the countryside, and Thomas Frost's *The Old Showman and the Old London Fairs* (1881) lists a mulatto, fire eaters, Africans, dwarves, Siamese twins (301), giants, dwarves, and albinos (313) among the "living curiosities" (320) he witnessed. These sources suggest that through much of the century, humans with deformities along with other "curiosities" were routinely appearing in public houses, at street fairs, and in precursors to museums such as the Egyptian Hall or Saville House.

One of these "entertainers," the American Harvey Leach (sometimes spelled Leech), had only vestigial lower limbs and may have been a prototype for Collins's Miserrimus Dexter. In *The Shows of London* Altick details Leach's performances as "Man-Tiger," as the "missing link," as a boxer, and as an actor in plays such the Adelphi Theatre's *The Tale of Enchantment: or, The Gnome Fly* (1938) or the Olympic Theatre's *The Son of the Desert and the Demon Changeling* (1843) (Altick 265–67). Like Miserrimus Dexter, Leach's fame depended on his acrobatic feats and unpredictable temper. Leach died in 1846, after being exposed for pretending to be the "Wild Man of the Prairies" by a journalist from *The Illustrated London News* known as "Open-Eye" (September 5, 1846, 154). Another writer for *The Illustrated London News* smugly remonstrates a year later, "in these days, such tricks [imposture] are out of the question, and every wonder-monger must dread the detective police of enlightened public opinion." Ironically, even after Leach's death, Martin Howard notes that his skeleton was exhibited in the collection of University College Hospital (78).

Though city councilors and journalists alike presumed lower-class audiences funded the display of "freaks," the exhibitions also captivated the same kinds of well-educated, middle-class consumers who would have formed the readership for sensation fiction. In 1884 a surgeon, John Bland-Sutton, writes, "I often visited the Mile End Road, especially on Saturday nights, to see dwarfs, giants, fat-women, and monstrosities" at "freak-shows" and "freak-museum at a public house—The Bell and Mackerel" (139). Frederick Treves, the doctor who discovered and cared for John Merrick, known as the Elephant Man, first encountered his patient August 3, 1884 in an East End exhibition that was about to be closed by the city. Merrick's case suggests how easily human bodies could be rendered textual and thus begin circulating in discourses of the abnormal far beyond the venue in which they were physically seen. To earn a livelihood, Merrick exhibited his ravaged body first to pleasure-seekers and then to the medical community. In the first instance, his manager, Tom Norman, who had fourteen exhibition sites in London, supplemented their incomes by selling a pamphlet with a photographic frontispiece that purported to be *The Autobiography of Joseph Carey Merrick*. As Leslie Fiedler has pointed out, these pamphlets were a common feature of such exhibitions, rendering the body of the freak into language then into a sort of sensation fiction sub-genre.[7] In the second instance, Merrick was further translated into photographic and scientific texts as a medical exhibit. Even after the East End was incorporated into London in 1888 and the shows forbidden by city law, exhibits continued, then as now, to travel the countryside.

Perhaps the most telling evidence of popular fascination with deformity and the most blatant assimilation of the sensational and the scientific, even twenty years after the publication of Collins's novel, was the sale of an alleged medical text that was in fact a compendium of disfigurements, George M. Gould and Walter L. Pyle's *Anomalies and Curiosities of Medicine: Being an Encyclopedia Collection of Rare and Extraordinary Cases, and of the Most Striking Instances of Abnormality in all Branches of Medicine and Surgery. Derived from an Exhaustive Research of Medical Literature from Its Origin to the Present Day, Abstracted, Classified, Annotated, and Indexed* (1896). Gould and Pyle explained their object (and probably thereby assuaged the consciences of their readers) when they wrote: "it is often through the extraordinary that the philosopher gets the most searching glimpses into the heart of the mystery of the ordinary" (1). As Marie-Helene Huet has recently argued, science thus becomes "the normalization of the monster by the scientific gaze: its submission to rules, norms, and variations" (109). It seems no accident that Gould and Pyle called theirs a work of "medical jurisprudence," linking physical deformity to yet another system of rules, the endless legal perversities that so fascinated Collins. This medical text, like earlier studies of teratology, suggests that while side shows continued to exhibit freaks (and novels like *The Law and the Lady* continued to exploit characters like Miserrimus Dexter for sensational effect), medical studies had taken control of the forms of representation, the categorizations by which "monsters" could be known. Despite the medical community's claims to be objective, teratologists simply established a kind of "distance" that justified looking, comparable to the physical distance between spectator and "freak" in the context of the freak show that Susan Stewart calls "the pornography of distance" (110). The doctors' ethical tenuousness manifests itself in their fumbling attempts to name the subjects of their investigation. Medical journals like *The Lancet* continued to use terms like "monstrosity" throughout the period, words difficult to divest of their sensational connotations.[8]

The repetition and variation of similar terms associated with Miserrimus Dexter—curiosity, exhibit, exhibition, and eccentricity—constitute almost a meta-commentary on the problems of form posed in *The Law and the Lady*. Peter Caracciolo notes that Charles Dickens, along with "his young men," Collins and other writers for *All the Year Round*, took a "keen interest" in the etymology of words, as suggested by the interplay of these terms in his novel (400). Curiosity permeates boundaries between settings and among characters throughout the novel. During Eustace's trial, for example, the courtroom awaits evidence with "curiosity and interest" (141); Eustace's gardener, a witness, eavesdropped on his employer because his "curiosity was excited" (166); Miserrimus Dexter's court appearance is met with "suppressed exclamations of curiosity and surprise" (172). Despite Dexter's infirmities and ill temper, Valeria is riveted to him because "Curiosity made me as completely the obedient servant of his caprices as [his servant] herself" (234), and Dexter is enthralled by Valeria's investigation because he suffers from the "curse" of "insatiable curiosity" (293).

Provocatively, the *Oxford English Dictionary* notes that though "curiosity" originally meant carefulness, careful attention to detail, or a desire to learn, the term came to suggest a desire to know too much about matters best left alone. Such pejorative associations are often implicitly gendered; *scientific* curiosity (read masculine in Victorian terms) is admirable while curiosity about human affairs is faulted as a feminine weakness, an issue raised by both Valeria and her husband. Positioning Valeria with gossips and busybodies, Eustace uses emotional blackmail to forestall her investigation: " 'If you could control your curiosity . . . we might live happily enough. I thought I had married a woman who was superior to the vulgar failings of her sex" (54). Though Valeria coolly replies, "It is hard, Eustace, to accuse me of curiosity, because I cannot accept the unendurable position in which you have placed me" (54), soon after she confesses to Eustace's friend Major Fitz-David, "You know—everybody knows—that one of a woman's many weaknesses is curiosity" (72). She recognizes that curiosity stigmatizes her with immodesty, impurity, impropriety, and assertiveness.

By the 1870s "curiosities" are also defined by the *Oxford English Dictionary* as objects displayed in private collections, in street fairs, public houses, traveling shows, and in "museums," which were, in effect, indoor sideshows. As Valeria's investigation leads her from the Major's house to Miserrimus Dexter's house to Eustace's country house in Scotland where Sara Macallan died, she finds herself the spectator of one such display after another. The Major's library abounds with "costly curiosities" (86). Dexter's house, itself quite a curiosity (320), showcases his bizarre collection. After a quick look at "my host's taste in curiosities," explains Valeria, "I pursued my investigation [of the house] no farther" (248). Finally, at Gleninch, Valeria nervously examines Sara Macallan's "Indian cabinet, in which the crumpled paper with the grains of arsenic had been found" discovering it "still held its little collection of curiosities" (287). The sensational character of Victorian so-called museums informs Valeria's nervous voyeurism and suggests why "curiosities" also served as slang for erotic or pornographic materials.

The term "exhibition" provides one link between the staged display of the curiosity and the discursive domains of the psychologically and sexually perverse. Foucault claims that in France "exhibitionism," which he defines as "indecent exposure," becomes "a new category in the field of legal psychiatry" in 1876, just a year after the publication of *The Law and the Lady* (12). Exhibitionism is today defined as a disorder which depends on self-display and which is heightened when the viewer, usually either a woman or a child, expresses fear or shock at the visible. The same connections among gender, madness, and law that bind the deformed Dexter to the de-forming female detective tether the multiple connotations of the word "exhibit" since an exhibit can also be a law or a legal document. Moreover, like both a human "curiosity" and detection itself, an exhibit can be the producing of evidence or a submitting or exposing to view, a definition that draws attention to the shared characteristics of the sideshow and the courtroom (as the current example of the O. J. Simpson "show" makes painfully obvious).

Unlike such actual human beings as the Elephant Man, who was driven by terror and hunger to turn his disabilities into a meager livelihood, Collins's character Miserrimus Dexter possesses the wealth and status to buy sanctuary from callous, cruel, or even sympathetic voyeurs. Instead, the character repeatedly exhibits himself, in the courtroom, in his visit to Valeria's lodgings, and (most ostentatiously) in the gallery of his own home. He adorns his private mansion, itself described as one of his "freaks of fancy" (202), as a garish stage upon which he flagrantly displays his deformities so that even the compassionate Valeria frets during a visit, "What new piece of eccentricity was he about to exhibit?" (233). The house mirrors "museums" like the Egyptian Hall or the Saville House. The walls are lined with paintings of popular sensations dramatizing the "diseased and riotous delight of the painter in representing Horrors," the "Episodes in the Life of the Wandering Jew," the Flying Dutchman, and "Passion-pictures" portraying "Cruelty" and "Revenge" (229–30). Upstairs, Valeria finds the "same insatiable relish for horrors" (247). Her description smacks of another popular Victorian entertainment, a tour of Madame Tussaud's wax museum: photographs "represented the various forms of madness taken from the life. The plaster casts ranged on the shelf opposite, were casts (after death) of the heads of famous murderers. A frightful little skeleton of a woman hung in a cupboard, behind a glazed door" along with a leather shirt labeled "Skin of a French Marquis" (247). Most frightening of all, there is Dexter himself, "The fantastic and frightful apparition, man and machinery blended in one—the new Centaur, half man, half chair" (206):

the man in the chair sprang out of it with a shrill cry of horror.... For one moment we saw a head and body in the air, absolutely deprived to the lower limbs. The moment after, the terrible creature touched the floor as lightly as a monkey, on his hands. The grotesque horror of the scene culminated in his hopping away, on his hands, at a prodigious speed...                (207)

Dexter's exhibitionistic challenge to conventional categories and dichotomies is perhaps his only fixed characteristic. Valeria and others call him a centaur (critics today might substitute cyborg) because he uses his chair so dexterously and intimately. The court record reveals that at the murder scene when a policeman tries to push his chair aside, Dexter rages, "My chair is Me ... how dare you lay hands on Me?" (145). Later, more cruelly, Valeria's usually unimaginative family friend, Benjamin, calls Dexter "half monkey, half man" (347) in pseudo-scientific reference to popularizations of Darwin. This same public fascination with the evolutionary chain's missing link prompted a host of faked human exhibits, including one of Harvey Leach's more notorious performances (Altick, 266). The bestiality attributed to Dexter because he is literally less than a "normal" man and the tendency to characterize him as half one thing and half another suggest the fascination and fearfulness of the freakish, boundary defying body, a connection Sue Lonoff develops in *Wilkie Collins and His Readers*.

As these examples suggest, characters who attempt to categorize Dexter implicitly judge him. Authority figures like nurses and lawyers as well as humanitarian sympathizers describe him as a "cripple." When he throws off his lap rug and confronts characters with his body, we hear language that enacts what we would now call othering: he degenerates into the animal (a monkey [328, 347], a monstrous frog [260]), mutates into the grotesque ("horrible deformity" [292]), is exoticized into foreignness (a "Portent" or an "Indian idol" [292]), or fragments into madness. Perversely exhibitionistic, Dexter himself heightens confusion about who and what he is. In manic episodes, he speaks in the voices of great heroes—Napoleon, Nelson, Shakespeare, Shelley. Promethean, he revels in the lines of *Prometheus Unbound*. As Lonoff points out, he satirizes himself and his woman servant, calling the heavy-set, mindless, masculine near-slave "delicate Ariel" while alternating between the venomous plotting of a Caliban and story-telling wizardry of Prospero.

Most threateningly, Misserrimus Dexter transgresses the boundaries of gender though denied the biological markings of sex. From Valeria's first textual encounter with Miserrimus Dexter, when she reads about him in the Trial report, his unclear sexual status and complex gendering are presented as his greatest deformities, motivating the spectator's guilty gaze. According to Valeria's account of the trial, he glides into court in his chair "a strange and startling creature—literally the half of a man." His fallen coverlid "exposed to the public curiosity'' that he was "absolutely deprived of the lower limbs. To make this deformity all the more striking and all the more terrible, the victim of it was—as to his face and his body—an unusually handsome . . . man. . . . His large, clear blue eyes, and his long, delicate white hands, were like the eyes and hands of a beautiful woman. He would have looked effeminate, but for the manly proportions of his throat and chest.'' "Never" concludes Valeria "had Nature committed a more careless or a more cruel mistake than in the making of this man" (173). Valeria later realizes that her powerfully empathetic responses to Dexter have biased her supposedly objective summary of the trial. It is unclear whether her erotic characterization of Dexter depends most strongly on her attraction to the traits she herself marks as masculine and feminine or to his irregular union of the two.

Even after Valeria meets Dexter in person, his identity, in particular his gender identity, becomes more rather than less blurred, in no small measure because she is bent on straining gender codes. When she visits him to question him about her husband's trial, he nervously counters her investigation with performances that might be read as perverse, exaggerated displays of excessive femininity. Dexter takes on an oddly domestic persona, extravagantly proud of his bizarre interior decorating, his paintings, and curiosities. He embroiders to calm himself when Valeria's questions press upon him (236); he flaunts his skills as a gourmet to distract the detective from her quest (244–46). He delights in elegant, effete dress insisting that ''men have always worn precious stuffs and beautiful colours as well as women'' and bemoaning ''the brutish contempt for beauty and the mean dread of expense which degrade a gentleman's costume to black cloth and limit a gentleman's ornaments to a finger ring, in the age I live in'' calling instead for ''brightness and beauty'' (232). His unnerving, sudden performance of song, poetry, and recitation are his personal rebellion against rigid ''will'' of Victorian masculinity and an assertion of the mutable ''visionary'' (202). He even claims he can imaginatively shape-shift and slip ''into Mrs. Beauly's skin'' to help Valeria with her investigation (297). Readers, like Dexter's fellow characters, fear him because his changeability and formlessness defy categorization. Taylor argues that he ''overturns all rational and coherent ways of making sense of him, and thus acts out the investigation of the boundaries of consciousness at work in the novel in his continual transformations'' (Introduction xxii). I would argue that his behavior also intensifies readers' anxious preoccupation with the reconciliation of gender with sex and of sex with artificial, but implacable norms. Dexter's transgression of boundaries—between pleasure and guilt, ''normal'' and monstrous, sanity and madness, wholeness and fragmentation—becomes simultaneously a constant reminder of and distraction from the failure of those crucial boundaries between male and female, masculine and feminine.

Though most characters find Dexter repellent, Valeria's responses are mixed. At least twice she describes his physical features with erotic attention, his "lustrous waving hair . . . ; the long delicate white hands, and the magnificent throat and chest" (213); she also lingers over and exoticizes the "deformity which degraded and destroyed the manly beauty of his head and breast . . . hidden from view by an Oriental robe of many colours" (213). Moreover, she projects her own attraction to Dexter onto a fantasized other woman: "a young girl, ignorant of what the Oriental robe hid from view, would have said to herself the instant she looked at him, 'Here is the hero of my dreams!' " (214). Valeria's chief sentiment, however, is compassion, and compassion that argues for some level of identification. Even after Dexter covers her hand with burning kisses and clutches her waist in a scene *The Graphic* editor considered so lascivious, calling it an "attempted violation," that he infuriated Collins by expurgating it, Valeria continues her relationship with him against everyone's advice (a contretemps Taylor details in her introduction, [xi–xii]). Valeria alone recognizes and sympathizes with his hopeless love for the former Mrs. Macallan. She, like both his servants, at times sees him as a child who needs love and comfort. She empathizes with his behavior most, however, when she finds it feminine. When Dexter self-pityingly pleas that he is only a "poor solitary creature, cursed with a frightful deformity" (232), Valeria humorously recognizes a version of her own repeated complaint deployed as strategy and turns it back upon him: "I am only a friendless woman . . . who has lost all that she loved and prized" (241). After he has insulted her, demonstrating the depths of cruelty to which his mental instability can carry him, she marvels at her sympathy:

> Is there a common fund of wickedness in us all? Is the suppression or the development of that wickedness a mere question of training and temptation? And is there something in our deeper sympathies which mutely acknowledges this, when we feel for the wicked; when we crowd to a criminal trial; when we shake hands at parting (if we happen to be present officially) with the vilest monster that ever swung on a gallows? It is not for me to decide.     (329–30)

Valeria alone makes these connections between the monster and the criminal, the exhibit and the voyeur because once she defies her husband and embarks upon detection, challenging the norms of gender and genre, she, like Dexter, faces the prospect of being positioned as an exhibition of criminality, madness, or monstrosity.

If readers fear Dexter lacks a penis, the novel's transformation also insinuate that the character Valeria may possess the phallus, a psychological, cultural, and in the detective plot, fictional deformity. Because attention is focused upon the sensational display of Miserrimus Dexter's freakishness, readers are diverted from the social and fictional freak of the novel's title—the female detective. While beauty, breasts, even a uterus might be the unstated but accepted constituents of Victorian femininity, they are decidedly alien to the figure of the Victorian detective, whose plotted course lies down darkened alleys that would quickly become dead ends in the feminized marriage plot of middle-class female protagonists.

Mary Russo's poignant childhood memory in her recent book *The Female Grotesque* evokes the always already present gender differences that contextualize how we look at others and how we act in response to the ways we assume they are looking at us:

> There is a phrase that still resonates from childhood. Who says it? The mother's voice—not my own mother's, perhaps, but the voice of an aunt, an older sister, or the mother of a friend. It is a harsh, matronizing phrase, directed towards the behavior of other women:
> "She [the other woman] is making a spectacle out of herself."          (53)

Whereas a man in a similar position would be "exposing himself," Russo realizes that "anyone, any *woman,* could make a spectacle out of herself if she was not careful" (53). The moment Valeria's curiosity beguiles her to pry into her husband's secrets and then to investigate the evidence that secured the "Scotch verdict," she threatens to make a spectacle of herself.

The connections between the deformed man and the deforming female character reside in the same social and etymological history of exhibitions and curiosities that I have been discussing. Tracing changes in cultural interpretations of the monster and the monstrous body, Marie-Helènene Huet cites Aristotle's claims that "The monster and the woman thus find themselves on the same side, the side of *dissimilarity*" from the "normal" man (3). Huet then outlines the continuing attention to the monstrous generative powers of the mother, over centuries, from folk tales that attribute a baby's appearance to things its mother sees during pregnancy to the nineteenth-century French and English teratologists' experiments with embryos. The body of the woman and the monster remain inextricably entangled. Huet also notes that the degree of deviation from the "norm" mattered less than the fact of difference. An 1877 treatise by a leading French teratogenist Camille Dareste (who manufactured thousands of deformed embryos in his laboratory) argues that "The most extreme form of monstrosity and the slightest anomaly are essentially phenomena of the same order" (Huet 118). While Dexter's body makes his difference visible, Valeria's differences from conventional femininity and from the body belonging to the detective function as similarly disruptive phenomena. The fascination with transgressions against the "normal" sexed body and its correlative "normal" gendered behavior may explain why teratologists and showmen alike keenly sought human bodies that literally fused the freakish and the feminine. In effect, the hermaphrodite could be seen as the physical embodiment of the textual relations between Miserrimus Dexter and Valeria Macallan.

Though Kathleen Klein traces a fictional female detective back to the 1864 narrative *The Female Detective* and to W. Stephen Hayward's *The Experiences of a Lady Detective* (either 1861 or 1864), the emerging genre was heavily influenced by "police procedurals." Consequently, like London's police detectives, first appointed in 1842, "the detective" as a type was generally figured male. Charles Dickens' Mr. Bucket in *Bleak House* (1852–53) and Wilkie Collins's Sergeant Cuff in *The Moonstone* (1868), early male detectives, were professionals, police*men*, lower to lower-middle class, and oddly marginal to the secrets of middle-class citizens they were called upon to investigate.[9] Sherlock Holmes's appearance in *A Study in Scarlet* (1887), a decade after *The Law and the Lady,* substantially altered the class and character of the fictional detective. Nevertheless, the gender remains unchanged, and I would argue that despite the substantial number of female detectives who appeared in Victorian short stories and novels, as documented by historians of the genre, then (and even now) the word detective would most likely summon a masculine figure, an ancestor of the "gumshoe," "the flatfoot," "the nose," and most tellingly, the "private dick," before the popular mind.[10]

The first problem Valeria faces, then, when she undertakes detective work, is how to "look," the chief method of the detective, when by merely looking, in both senses of the word, she, like the woman of Russo's memory, makes a spectacle of herself. Her attempts, failures, and successes reveal the obstruction the female detective faces: problems of identity, of method, of the irreconcilability of gender and role characteristics, and, most importantly but most amorphously, of pre-existing assumptions about social spaces which determine how the female will be looked at when she enters spaces like the street, the court room, or even a profession.

The reason why the female body draws such attention to itself when it takes on the character of the detective in 1875 is that, in a sense, it appears on the wrong stage in the wrong show. Even in the sensation novels of the 1860s and 1870s, the lurid sideshow to the respectable feature exhibit of femininity, the marriage plot, the only "normal" role available to a middle-class Victorian heroine was that of wife. Valeria attempts to de-form that role by constantly struggling to justify her investigative impulses and her detective work as a wifely "duty."

Repeatedly, Valeria is berated by her husband, her mother-in-law, her family friend Benjamin, and her own conscience for her curiosity, which is labeled a perversely "feminine" flaw, even an "eccentricity"—a label often applied to Miserrimus Dexter's vagaries of body and behavior. Eustace makes this clear in the passage I mention earlier: "If you could control your curiosity . . . we might live happily enough" (54). Similarly, Valeria's mother-in-law argues, "If you value your peace of mind, and the happiness of your life to come, abstain from attempting to know more than you know now" (43). Major Fitz-David, Benjamin, and Mr. Playmore all urge her to be satisfied with ignorance and her husband's affection. Marriage, apparently, rests upon a wife's blind obedience and willing ignorance, both antithetical to the mindset of the detective. However, Valeria answers other characters by asking "what was my duty to my husband and my duty to myself" and deciding that "My tranquility as a woman—perhaps my dearest interests as a wife—depended absolutely on penetrating the mystery of my mother-in-law's conduct, and on discovering the true meaning of the wild words of penitence and self-reproach which my husband had addressed to me" (37). As Valeria assimilates detection into the role of "wife," curiosity turns Valeria into a curiosity.

In the context of the 1870s, as both Klein and Andrea Trodd's work on the connection between the fictional detective and the police force would suggest, Valeria's more abstract social and legal identities trouble the functions permitted and forbidden to the police detective for reasons relative to her gender. To begin with, her detective activity is motivated by her realization that she has no legal identity. As Jenny Bourne Taylor points out, Valeria must prove her "position as [Eustace's] legitimate wife—to provide herself with a full selfhood within a given set of symbolic meanings and social conventions—in other words, within the Law" (Introduction xiv). Valeria's "case" reveals that under Victorian law, a female is defined and positioned not as a distinct entity, but rather as a deformed male.

This problem determines the consequences when Valeria learns of her husband's former marriage and alleged murder: her humiliated husband abandons her, motivating her to clear his name. Most simply, the detective is motivated by a desire to solve an unresolved crime. However, given Valeria's legal status as the property of her husband, the female detective is in a certain sense both detective and client; she is the very property she seeks to recover when she investigates her husband's crime.[11] As her malicious landlady points out, "You are neither maid, wife, nor widow. You are worse than nothing madam" (40). Necessarily, therefore, Valeria's first act of detection is to investigate her own legal identity: she seeks a lawyer to be sure she is married according to the law because without Eustace Macallan's true rather than assumed name, she has no legal identity. She soon realizes, however, that without his innocence, she has no social identity.

Valeria's precarious social position intrudes at the first suspicion that the marriage may be irregular. Her landlady threatens to evict Valeria at the mere hint of her husband's impropriety: " 'I receive only the most respectable persons into my house. There must be no mystery about the positions of *my* lodgers. Mystery in the position of a lodger carries with it—what shall I say? I don't wish to offend you—I will say, a certain Taint" (38). Punitive possibilities grow when the female detective discovers she is pregnant. Unless she can produce evidence of her husband's innocence, she will herself become a visible freak—as the wife of a murderer, as the carrier of a murderer's blood line, as another potential murder victim of her husband, and, certainly, as a detective.

The male detective is defined as a professional in part because he has a place within the myriad institutions of law. By contrast, middle-class female identity depends, in part, on women's exclusion from public institutions. In particular, the middle-class woman must be free from labor; leisure is her labor. Tamar Heller argues in *Dead Secrets* that in novels by Collins female figures often threaten the profession of the male artist, hence writer, by taking on his professional role. The dismissive charges of male characters such as Valeria's uncle, who rants against "lawyers in petticoats" (121), suggest Valeria similarly teeters upon impropriety when she encroaches on the professional property of the policeman, the lawyer, the detective.

Deprived of the conventional methods as well as identity of the detective, Valeria alters the conventions, often exploiting her female/feminine difference from the detective to accomplish her ends. Well aware of the vulnerability of male vanity, she contemplates her investigative strategy: "Good or bad, compassionate or cruel, the Major was a man" (50). Before interviewing him, she allows a chambermaid to disguise her: "She came back with a box of paints and powders; and I said nothing to check her. I saw, in the glass, my skin take a false fairness, my cheeks a false colour, my eyes a false brightness-and I never shrank from it. No! I let the odious deceit go on" (57). Masked by "beauty" and armed by what her sidekick Mr. Playmore calls "rash" behavior and "extraordinary imprudence," Valeria tricks men into confession inaccessible to "the whole machinery of the Law" (277). Unfortunately, triumph as a detective spells disaster as a decorous woman. Whereas male detective figures, Sherlock Holmes preeminently among them, win praise for their clever disguises, the woman who manipulates disguise opens herself to charges of deceit, dishonesty, and fraudulent femininity.

Despite Michel Foucault's argument for the diffusive, inescapable permeations of criminality into nineteenth-century lives and institutions, police detectives and even the male private detectives can behave criminally, deceitfully disguising themselves and consorting with criminals, without suffering final, irrevocable social expulsion.[12] Certainly, male detectives negotiate within an arena of crime and an aura of criminality in excess of the particular crime they investigate as vividly argued in D. A. Miller's Foucauldian analysis of the relation of the police detective to the literal and ideological surveillance systems of the nineteenth century and Ron Thomas's positioning of detection as a correlative to the work of Cesare Lombroso and other self-styled criminal anthropologists. Still, the middle-class private male detective seems oddly protected from the world he infiltrates.

The Baudelairean figure of the late nineteenth-century flaneur has emerged in criticism of detective fiction as one antecedent for the middle- or upper-class male detective that helps to explain this figure's gender and class inoculations against the criminal world to which he exposes himself, as in the work of Dana Brand. Idling in the crush of Paris streets, Baudelaire's flaneur almost invisibly espies all before him, including urban crime. Feminist critics like Janet Wolff and Anne Friedberg have debated whether he could have had a female counterpart, the flaneuse. Wolff argues that the separation of space into gendered public and private spheres negates the possibility while Friedberg counters that late nineteenth-century activities, "Shopping, like other itineran-cies of the late nineteenth century—museum- and exhibition-going, packaged tourism and, of course, the cinema—" (37), rendered public spaces accessible to women. Indeed, Valeria describes herself as "not at all the sort of person who attracts attention in the street" (10) when she is merely a wife. Things change when she proposes to pursue her quarry "openly, through the streets" (108) in proper detective fashion: the Major and Benjamin "opposed this hasty resolution," appealing to Valeria's "own sense of self-respect" (108). Thus, despite the persuasiveness of Friedberg's argument, the phrase "a woman of the streets" implicitly charges any woman in the streets with sexual misconduct, even with actual prostitution. To enter "the streets" with her own version of criminal intent, that is to find a criminal, further taints the social identity of the female detective.

In *The Law and the Lady* this problem surfaces in the hostility of friends and family to Valeria's intent and actions as a detective; more obliquely, the tainting effect of criminality is represented through the intertextual omnipres-ence of the infamous Madeleine Smith, a far more potent and monstrous feminine freak than the character Valeria. As Jeanne Fahnstock points out, the pseudo-science of physiognomy powerfully affected literary characterization. Duncan Smith's 1905 account of Smith's trial includes a phrenologist's report and selections from newspaper accounts of the trial. Smith, whose guilt seems patent despite the peculiar verdict "Not Proven," reads like a prototype for Valeria, who is supposed to be the detective rather than the criminal. Smith has a "prominent straight nose and a strong under-jaw, indicating strength of character and strong will" (9) while Valeria is described as having a nose with an "aquiline bent" (10). Smith's spectators are taken aback by the fixed, penetrating glance of her large black eye" (14): Valeria's eyes are "of so dark a blue that they are generally mistaken for black. Her eyebrows are well enough in form, but they are too dark, and too strongly marked" (10). Pres-enting Smith as having more in common with the fearfulness of the hermaph-rodite than the promise of the androgyne, the phrenologist concludes that

Smith "possesses both the masculine and feminine qualities, more especially the former" but that her "drawback" is her "warm, sanguine temperament" and her tendency to "flirt" (292). Valeria's gender-crossing behavior coupled with her "curiosity" position her with Smith while her jealousy of, yet parallel position with the flirtatious Mrs. Beauly structurally "taints" her as well as her husband's former lover, an analogy Valeria acknowledges: "Were we, by any chance, the least in the world like one another?" (183). The novel also disperses Madeleine Smith's story among its characters, for it is Eustace Macallan who, like Smith before him, is publicly humiliated by the reading in court of his scandalous letters to his lover. Because Valeria is Eustace's property in a legalistic if unjust extension of the marriage contract, his guilt is her guilt. The immeasurable reach of Victorian domestic ideology is perhaps suggested best by the conclusion to the phrenologist's report. Despite his concerns that Smith acts too aggressively and would be best suited to be an "architect" or "engineer," he closes: "she will make a treasure of a wife to a worthy husband" (292), the same prescription offered to Valeria as a cure for what a character in Collins's earlier novel, *The Moonstone,* called "detective fever."

By the end of the novel, anomalies are repressed and the aberrant, deformed, monstrous bodies and desires of Dexter and Valeria are "managed" as Taylor would say, "disciplined" as Miller and other Foucauldians would say, "iced" as over-identified detective fans would say. Dexter is silenced and literally buried; Valeria succumbs to her body in pregnancy and to her domestic duties to husband and child in a partial restoration of her social identity. However, the novel once again uses repetition via analogous plotting to intensify the ambivalence of this seemingly conventional ending. When Valeria offers her husband the choice between reading his first wife's letter and thus learning the truth or allowing her to suppress the truth and thereby living in happy ignorance, he damns himself yet again from most readers' point of view by choosing the weaker path, the path Valeria had rejected when she refused to accept the mystery of his true identity and therefore hers. Such a conclusion exposes the deforming constraints of domesticity. Valeria's closing plea on Eustace's behalf chillingly identifies her with the most pathetic female character in the novel, Dexter's cousin and servant, the masculine, leaden Ariel. Just as Ariel had doggedly begged Valeria to beat and abuse her rather than punish Miserrimus Dexter, Valeria now appeals to her readers:

> Must I shut up the paper? Yes. There is nothing more for you to read, or for me to say.
>
> Except this—as a postscript. Don't bear hardly, good people, on the follies and the errors of my husband's life. Abuse *me* as much as you please. But pray think kindly of Eustace, for my sake.                (413)

Given that Valeria herself had imperiously forbidden Dexter to beat Ariel for his idle amusement, this echo sounds a dire prophecy for the future Valeria has accepted.

It is also significant that Valeria agrees to suppress the letter as much as a consequence of her newfound compassion for her predecessor, Sara Macallan, as of her love for Eustace. Sara's letter explicitly links "abnormal" womanhood with monstrosity. Denying Eustace's charge of prejudice against Dexter "on account of his deformity," Sara writes, "No other feeling than compassion for deformed persons has ever entered my mind. I have, indeed, almost a fellow-feeling-for them; being that next worst thing myself to a deformity—a plain woman" (387–88). If the conclusion conforms to gender conventions, it also reiterates the arbitrariness and cruelty of "norms."

Finally, Valeria, like Sara, commits suicide, if only social suicide, when she sets aside the letter now owned by both Mrs. Macallans. "English" law tolerates no ambiguity. However the Scotch verdict presumes a complicated world ridden with doubt, and not just "reasonable doubt." The Scottish jury judges against the defendant's reputation rather than his legal status. In this sense, the verdict is vindicated, not because the characters admit its justice but because the novel constructs a universe of anomalies and ambiguities which render the normalizing dichotomies of English law null and void.[13] While critics often judge the novel's conclusion inadequate, Valeria's suppression of the evidence she has collected plays out the structural logic of incompletion that governs both the story and plot from the ambiguous Scotch verdict to the repeated disruptions of her marriage to Miserrimus Dexter's fragmented body and mind to Valeria's retreat from detection. The judge in Eustace's trial pronounces a verdict that refuses closure to a marriage plot; the detective-wife, Valeria Macallan, carries out the sentence.

# NOTES

Thanks to Catherine Peters, Corey Creekmur, Tamar Heller, Martha Stoddart Holmes, Margaret Loose, and especially Kathleen Diffley.

1. Critics kept complaining. Nuel Pharr Davis says that to appreciate Dexter, the reader "must have sympathies that can extend to a legless, lustful lunatic in a wheelchair" (282), and Kenneth Robinson refers to a "half-human monster" and "this legless maniac" (277). Lonoff surmises that "He seems designed to evoke a mixed reaction in the reader, a sub-conscious aversion to the freak or the monster, mingled with fascination" (164). To the contrary, Jenny Bourne Taylor sensibly points out in her 1992 Introduction: "He is weird but never monstrous, never completely 'other,' even if he is made so by others' ignorance and fear" (xxii). She characterizes Dexter as "a figure who works on different registers

directly analogous to both the dreaming and the creative process'' (xxiii). Her book *In the Secret Theatre of Home* locates Collins's novels in nineteenth-century theories of psychology and sensation.

Collins's fiction does circle back repeatedly to physical disfigurements or disabilities. For example, Catherine Peters notes that while Collins had gout ''in both eyes'' in 1876, he was writing *The Two Destinies* in which a veiled woman who suffers from a disfiguring disease is one of the characters (Peters, 380). Martha Stoddart Holmes has written a dissertation on characters who have less sensationalized conditions such as blindness and deafness, as in *The Dead Secret.*

2. The problem of naming those who professionally exhibit their bodies has its own history. In *Very Special People,* Frederick Drimmer claims that when one of P.T. Barnum's employers, the Bearded Lady, Annie Jones, led a protest against the label ''freaks,'' it may have been a deliberate publicity stunt. He says that by the 1970s carnivals were using the terms ''prodigies'' or ''strange people'' and recommends using ''special people.'' Robert Bogdan interrupts his social history, *Freak Show,* to meditate on a related ethical problem. After years of watching ''freak shows'' and interviewing people who exhibited themselves or their employees, he was startled into re-examining his relationship to his project when his young daughter asked if she could accompany him to the sideshows at a carnival. I willingly share Bogdan's self-questioning. Writing about this topic is one way I am trying to understand how Victorians used representations of people whose bodies do not conform to prevailing norms and to call to account my own feelings about body differences. I welcome correction and further discussion.

3. The most famous demonstration of this claim is Lacan's reading of Poe's ''The Purloined Letter.'' As Lacan reminds us, the letter is visible throughout the entire story. The detective provides meaning to the clue rather than ''discovering'' it. Dennis Porter characterizes this visible absence as a function of time wherein detection becomes the recovery and interpretation of a story in the past based on the presence of a secret and/or an effect (such as theft or death) in the present.

4. Taylor also suggests other less well-known cases involving female poisoners as potential influences in her introduction. See also D. MacEachen's essay ''Wilkie Collins and British Law'' and Virginia Morris's study of literary adaptations of the female poisoner in *Double Jeopardy: Women Who Kill in Victorian Fiction.*

5. Several biographers and writers have commented on Collins's sense of himself as deformed. Davis speculates about Collins's self-description (52), explaining that Collins's right temple projected due to congenital swelling that probably resulted from a forceps delivery at birth. Lonoff speculates that due to Collins's appearance, Dexter ''may thus project or symbolize Collins's anxieties about his waning health or his failing powers as a man and as a writer'' (166).

6. Most biographies of Collins discuss his laudanum addiction. See Peters (she discusses the green phantom on p. 336) and Robinson (330). Althea Hayter places Collins's drug use in a larger historical and literary context in *Opium and the Romantic Imagination* (68–70).

7. I draw my information about Merrick from several sources, including Frederick Treves's *The Elephant Man and Other Reminiscences,* Bland-Sutton's *The Story of a Surgeon,* and Graham and Oehlschlaeger's *Articulating the Elephant Man:*

*Joseph Merrick and His Interpreters.* In *The Illustrated True History of the Elephant Man,* Howell and Ford reprint Merrick's two-page "Autobiography," an article about Merrick from *The British Medical Journal,* medical and "show" drawings and photographs, and pictures of casts and of Merrick's skeleton. They also reproduce several fascinating photographs of the spaces of exhibition, including a throng of people at the Stratford-Upon-Avon Mop Fair in the early 1900s. Fiedler, too, discusses the use of this and other pamphlets in *Freaks* (262).

8. Examples are easy to find, such as the report of a child with no limbs in *The Lancet* on April 25, 1857 under the heading "A Monstrosity" or Dr. John S. Beale's "Monstrosity and Maternal Impressions" in *The Lancet* on Nov. 3, 1860, or Dr. Meadow's "Case of Monstrosity" in *The Lancet* on January 10, 1863.

9. Though several of the major studies of the detective form that include an historical emphasis mention nineteenth-century fictional female detectives, most presume and base their arguments on novels by men and about male detectives, including Ian Ousby's *Bloodhounds of Heaven,* Audrey Peterson's *Victorian Masters of Mystery,* Dennis Porter's *The Pursuit of Crime,* Ernest Mandel's *Delightful Murder,* John Cawelti's *Adventure, Mystery, and Romance,* and D. A. Miller's *The Novel and the Police.*

10. My essay has certainly been enriched by the growing body of criticism counteracting the assumption that all nineteenth-century fictional detectives were male. Nevertheless, I still assume that the perception that "detection" is male (despite building evidence to the contrary) prevailed in the 1870s. The female sleuth is detected in Patricia Craig and Mary Cadogan's *The Lady Investigates: Women Detectives and Spies in Fiction,* Michelle Slung's introduction to *Crime on Her Mind,* Maureen Reddy's *Sisters and Crime: Feminism and the Crime Novel,* Kathleen Gregory Klein's *The Woman Detective: Gender and Genre,* and Fay Blake's essay "Lady Sleuths and Women Detectives." Studies of women criminals and the criminalization of women also helpfully contextualize the female detective. See, for example, Mary Hartman's *Victorian Murderesses,* Virginia Morris's *Double Jeopardy: Women Who Kill in Victorian Fiction,* and Anthea Trodd's study of sensation fiction, *Domestic Crime in the Victorian Novel* (as well as her article "The Police-man and the Lady: Significant Encounters in Mid-Victorian Fiction").

11. In his study of Collins's representations of women, Philip O'Neill sees Valeria as discovering "herself" as a subject when she considers her reflection in a mirror just after her marriage. His characterization of self-possession informs my own: "I want to extend the notion of propriety here to include our own most intimate sense of 'ownness' of owning ourselves, our own proper names and our own identity" (202).

12. Michel Foucault's *Discipline and Punish* and D. A. Miller's extension of the logic of surveillance to Victorian fiction, especially the detective novel, have dramatically shaped most recent discussions of the genre. Foucault's all-encompassing, constantly circulating discourses of crime, surveillance, and containment would leave no one untouched. I would argue, however, that various gradations must be factored in when we compare how middle-class men and women were

disciplined and punished. The social spaces, behaviors, acquaintances, entertainments, education, opinions, etc. allowed were, of course, far more limited for middle-class women than for men so that transgression was far easier and the consequences more severe. In part this is because when women were assumed to be less governed by reason and self-command than men, it would also be assumed that contact with undesirable others could have far more devastating consequences. Amanda Anderson explores this issue in *Tainted Souls and Painted Faces: The Rhetoric of Fallenness in Victorian Culture.*

13. Both Taylor and Lonoff come to this same conclusion that some kind of justice is served though each of us is following a different line of argument. The question of how to read Valeria's identification with a female suicide is helpfully complicated by Barbara Gates's work on attitudes toward suicide in *Victorian Suicide* and her article "Wilkie Collins' Suicides: 'Truth as It Is in Nature.'"

# Works Cited

Altick, Richard. *The Shows of London.* Cambridge: Harvard UP, 1978.

Anderson, Amanda. *Tainted Souls and Painted Faces: The Rhetoric of Fallenness in Victorian Culture.* Ithaca: Cornell UP, 1993.

Beale, Dr. John S. "Monstrosity and Maternal Impressions." *The Lancet* November 3, 1860.

Blake, Fay. "Lady Sleuths and Women Detectives." *Turn of the Century Women* 3 (1986): 29–42.

Bland-Sutton, Sir. John. *The Story of a Surgeon.* Boston: Houghton Mifflin, 1930.

Bogdan, Robert. *Freak Show: Presenting Human Oddities for Amusement and Profit.* Chicago: U of Chicago P, 1988.

Brand, Dana. "From the Flaneur to the Detective: Interpreting the City of Poe." In *Popular Fiction: Technology, Ideology, Production, Reading.* Ed. Tony Bennett. London: Routledge, 1990.

Browning, Tod (director). *Freaks.* MGM, 1932.

Caracciolo, Peter. "Wilkie Collins's 'Divine Comedy': The Use of Dante in *The Woman in White,*" *Nineteenth Century Fiction* 25 (March 1971): 383–404.

Cawelti, John G. *Adventure, Mystery, and Romance: Formula Stories as Art and Popular Culture.* Chicago: U of Chicago P, 1976.

Clarke, William M. *The Secret Life of Wilkie Collins.* London: Allison and Busby, 1989.

Collins, Wilkie. "The Diary of Anne Rodway." In *The Queen of Hearts*. 3 vols. London: Hurst and Blackett, 1859.

————.*The Law and the Lady*. 1875. New York: Oxford University Press, 1992.

————.Review of *The Law and the Lady. Athenaeum* 20 (February 20, 1875): 258.

————.Review of *The Law and the Lady. Saturday Review* 39 (March 13, 1875): 357.

Craig, Patricia and Mary Cadogan. *The Lady Investigates: Women Detectives and Spies in Fiction*. New York: St. Martin's, 1981.

Davis, Nuel Pharr. *The Life of Wilkie Collins* Urbana: U of Illinois P, 1956.

"The Deformito-mania." *Punch* September 4, 1847:90.

Dickens, Charles. "Greenwich Fair." Ed. Michael Slater. *Sketches by Boz and Other Early Papers, 1833–39*. Columbia: Ohio State UP, 1994. (First published in *The Evening Chronicle* 16 April 1835 as "Sketches of London, No. 9.")

Drimmer, Frederick. *Very Special People: The Struggles, Loves, and Triumphs of Human Oddities*. New York: Amjon, 1973.

Dunn, Katherine. *Geek Love*. New York: Knopf, 1989.

Fahnestock, Jeanne. "The Heroine of Irregular Features: Physiognomy and Conventions of Heroine Descripton." *Victorian Studies* 24 (1981): 325–50.

Fiedler, Leslie. *Freaks: Myths and Images of the Secret Self.* New York: Simon and Schuster, 1978.

Fitzgerald, Percy. *Memories of Charles Dickens*. Bristol, 1913; rpt. AMS P, 1973.

Foucault, Michel. "About the Concept of the 'Dangerous Individual' in Nineteenth-Century Legal Psychiatry." Trans. Alain Baudot and Jane Couchman. *International Journal of Law and Psychiatry* 1 (1978): 1–18.

————.*Discipline and Punish*. Trans. Alan Sheridan. New York: Pantheon, 1977.

Friedberg. *Window Shopping: Cinema and the Postmodern*. Berkeley: U of California P, 1993.

Frost, Thomas. *The Old Showmen and the Old London Fairs*. 1881. Ann Arbor: Gryphon, 1971.

Gates, Barbara. *Victorian Suicide: Mad Crimes and Sad Histories*. Princeton UP, 1988.

————. "Wilkie Collins's Suicides: 'Truth as It Is in Nature.' " *Dickens Studies Annual* 12 (1983): 303–18.

Gould, George M. and Walter L. Pyle. *Anomalies and Curiosities of Medicine: Being an Encyclopedic Collection of Rare and Extraordinary Cases, and of the Most Striking Instances of Abnormality in all Branches of Medicine and Surgery, Derived from an Exhaustive Research of Medical Literature from Its Origin to the Present Day, Abstracted, Classified, Annotated, and Indexed.* Philadelphia: W.B. Sanders, 1897.

Graham, Peter W. and Fritz H. Oehlshlaeger. *Articulating the Elephant Man: Joseph Merrick and His Interpreters.* Baltimore: Johns Hopkins UP, 1992.

Hartman, Mary. "Murder for Respectability: Madeleine Smith." *Victorian Studies* 16 (1973): 381–400.

———.*Victorian Murderesses.* London: Robson, 1985.

Hayter, Alethea A. *Opium and the Romantic Imagination.* London: Faber, 1968.

Heller, Tamar. *Dead Secrets: Wilkie Collins and the Female Gothic.* New Haven: Yale UP, 1992.

Holmes, Martha Stoddart. "Fictions of Affliction: Victorian Constructurions of Physical Disability." Dissertation in progress.

Howard, Martin. *Victorian Grotesque: An Illustrated Excursion into Medical Curiosities, Freaks, and Abnormalites.* London: Jupiter Books, 1977.

Howell, Michael and Peter Ford. *The True History of the Elephant Man.* London: Allison and Busby, 1983.

Huett, Marie-Helène. *Monstrous Imagination.* Cambridge: Harvard UP, 1993.

Klein, Kathleen Gregory. *The Woman Detective: Gender and Genre.* Urbana: U of Illinois P, 1994.

Lacan, Jacques. "Seminar on 'The Purloined Letter.' " Trans. Jeffrey Mehlman. *Yale French Studies* 48 (1972): 38–72.

Letter. *Illustrated London News.* April 3, 1847: 218.

Lonoff, Sue. *Wilkie Collins and His Victorian Readers: A Study in the Rhetoric of Authorship.* New York: AMS, 1982.

MacEachen, D. "Wilkie Collins and British Law." *Nineteenth Century Fiction* 5 (September 1950): 121–39.

Maclean, Walter. "New Novels." *Academy* 8 (July 3, 1875): 8.

Mandel, Ernest. *Delightful Murder: A Social History of the Crime Story.* London: Pluto P, 1984.

Mannix, Daniel P. *Freaks: We Who Are Not as Others.* San Francisco: Research Publications, 1976.

Meadows, Dr. "Case of Monstrosity." *The Lancet.* January 20, 1863.

Miller, D.A. *The Novel and the Police.* Berkeley: U of California P, 1988.

"A Monstrosity." *The Lancet.* April 25, 1857.

Morley, Henry. *Memoirs of Barholomew Fair,* London, 1859.

Morris, Virginia. *Double Jeopardy: Women Who Kill in Victorian Fiction.* Lexington: U of Kentucky P, 1990.

O'Neill, Philip. *Wilkie Collins: Women, Property and Propriety.* London: Macmillan P, 1988.

"Open-Eye." "Wild Man of the Prairies." *Illustrated London News.* September 5, 1846:154.

Ousby, Ian. *Bloodhounds of Heaven: The Detective in English Fiction From Godwin to Doyle.* Cambridge: Harvard UP, 1976.

Peters, Catherine. *The King of Inventors: A Life of Wilkie Collins.* London: Minerva, 1992.

Peterson, Audrey. *Victorian Masters of Mystery: From Wilkie Collins to Conan Doyle.* New York: Frederick Ungar, 1984.

Porter, Dennis. *The Pursuit of Crime: Art and Ideology in Detective Fiction.* New Haven: Yale UP, 1981.

Reddy, Maureen T. *Sisters in Crime: Feminism and the Crime Novel.* New York: Continuum, 1988.

Robinson, Kenneth. *Wilkie Collins: A Biography.* London: Bodley Head,1951. Rpt. London: Davis-Poynter, 1974.

Russo, Mary. *The Female Grotesque: Risk, Excess, and Modernity.* New York: Routledge, 1994.

Slung, Michele B. Introduction. *Crime on Her Mind: Fifteen Stories of Female Sleuths from the Victorian Era to the Forties.* New York: Random House, 1975: xv–xxx.

Smith, A. Duncan, ed. *The Trial of Madeleine Smith.* 1906; Edinburgh: William Hodge, 1929.

Stewart, Susan. *On Longing.* Durham: Duke University Press, 1993.

Swinburne, Algernon Charles. "Wilkie Collins." *The Fortnightly Review.* n.s. XLVI (November 1, 1889): 589–99.

Taylor, Jenny Bourne. *In the Secret Theatre of Home: Wilkie Collins, Sensation Narrative, and Nineteenth-Century Psychology.* London: Routledge, 1988.

———."Introduction." *The Law and the Lady.* Oxford: Oxford UP, 1992: vii–xxiv.

———."Psychology and Sensation: The Narrative of Moral Mangment in *The Woman in White. Critical Survey* 2 (1990): 49–56.

Thomas, Ronald. "Minding the Body Politic." *Victorian Literature and Culture* 19 (1991): 233–54.

Treves, Sir Frederick. *The Elephant Man and Other Reminiscences*. London: Cassell, 1923.

Trodd, Anthea. *Domestic Crime in the Victorian Novel*. New York: St. Martin's, 1989.

———. "The Police-man and the Lady: Significant Encounters in Mid-Victorian Fiction." *Victorian Studies* 27 (Summer 1984): 435–60.

Wolff, Janet. *Feminine Sentences: Essays on Women and Culture*. Berkeley: U of California P, 1990.

# Carlyle in Prison: Reading
## *Latter-Day Pamphlets*

### *Jeremy Tambling*

Carlyle's *Latter-Day Pamphlets* (1850) while they are not well known, are not ignorable and they are fascinating. Their tone is aggressive and abusive and often offensive, putting their author into what Emerson called "a pretty good minority of one," though he added that Carlyle was "enunciating with brilliant malice what shall be the universal opinion of the next edition of mankind" (Goldberg 231). While Emerson thought the "sanity" of the *Pamphlets* was "manifest," it is not necessary to argue whether Carlyle was right or wrong about most of the things he attacked: the very aggression and the uncontrolled nature of his writing invites a different kind of speculation about what is going on here in his thinking. Though the appearance of the *Pamphlets* made Carlyle "unpopular with at least one half of the kingdom," as David Masson put it—"Never before, probably, was there a publication so provocative of rage, hatred and personal malevolence" (Masson 337)—it did him no damage with others, such as Dickens, who in 1850 followed Carlyle specifically, in letters and in journalism and in *David Copperfield,* the novel then being serialised, and which I want to discuss later on in the paper.[1]

To look at the text as a revelation of Carlyle's character is too narrow: the work also gives some hint of conscious and unconscious states of mind in 1850, while the hatred he provoked may also require to be "read" critically, indicating that he had touched some unacknowledged feelings too nearly. Since the *Pamphlets* appeared in serial form, the degree of anger evoked was in any case calculated, and suggests both that Carlyle wished to be hated for what he wrote and that his public as it continued to read wished to hate him. That in itself is cause for giving *Latter-Day Pamphlets* attention, but I want to look at it for two other related reasons: because its very incoherence and hysteria illustrates a crisis of masculinity, which I want to relate to the conditions of modernity, which Carlyle felt in the 1840s and 1850s, and which

311

affects more than just Carlyle: it also reaches Dickens, Thackeray, and Tennyson, for example.[2] The second is for the attention it gives to the modern "model" prison.

It is time to rethink Carlyle in terms of his relationship to modernity. In 1968, Albert J. LaValley's study *Carlyle and the Idea of the Modern* began by discussing Carlyle in terms of Emerson's statement that "Carlyle's style is the first domestication of the modern system with its infinity of details, into style . . . the first emergence of all this wealth and labour with which the world has gone with child so long . . . " (LaValley 2). Emerson's Carlyle is excited by the variousness of modernity; LaValley's Carlyle is more ambiguous, finally hostile to its release of uncontainable energies, so that in *Latter-Day Pamphlets* LaValley writes that "the world becomes a divided camp: the separation between forces is now complete, and there can be no interaction. Ironically, Carlyle can now justify his rigidity, inflexibility and militarism . . . by what he feels is a prior commitment to a large, almost godlike, vision of freedom. But in this way the totalitarian, absolutist self is born, and applied to the present" (282–83). The modern as LaValley characterises it is authoritarian, "fascistic" (10). This applied as an assessment to much of *Latter-Day Pamphlets* is undeniable; the tone is racist, misanthropic, disgusted. Yet the tone is not single: it opens up a split in the subject who writes, for in November 1849, Carlyle pronounced that what he had written so far was "wrongish, every word of it." (Vanden Bossche 129). A melancholic sense of impotence runs through it, as in the last paragraph of "Stump Orator."

> Brave young friend, dear to me, and *known* too in a sense, though never seen, not to be seen by me,—you are what I am not, in the happy case to *be* something and to do something, instead of eloquently talking about what has been and what was done and may be!          (Carlyle 20:213)

The self-imposed project of righting England is recognised to be nostalgic and defeated. A reading of *Latter-Day Pamphlets* cannot salvage or rehabilitate a series of texts that defeated Carlyle himself, so much so that he abandoned them after only eight of the twelve had been completed, nor will it suggest the presence of artistic control when the texts themselves might be better described as almost paranoid-schizoid. It will need to respond to the notion that this psychic quality itself is a sign of the modern, in that Carlyle has truly, as Nietzsche puts it, in defining modernity and with Wagner in mind, "thrown off all shame." Modernity can be seen, following Nietzsche, in terms of a culture of demonstration and production, bringing everything of the subject into the open, since the modern state "conceals neither its good nor its evil" (Nietzsche 612).[3] It is not a condition of repression, but of the production of the heterogeneous, the heteroclite, which it also then represses in the name of order and (Weberian) rationalization. Such a split works through this text, only half-recognised, for though Carlyle may write about repression, and wish for it, as in his account of the prison, *Latter-Day Pamphlets* itself is hardly repressed. John D. Rosenberg comments that "reading the *Pamphlets,* with their obsessive repetitions, violence, tedium, and intermittent fascination, is strangely like reading pornography, only the sexuality has been transmuted into scatology and aggression, often directed against the reader" (Rosenberg 152). The absence of any repression of hatred also recalls a statement Adorno made about Wagner, when he defined disgust in Walter Benjamin's terms, as "the fear of being thought to be the same as that which is found disgusting" (Adorno 24). Disgust is wrapped up in questions of identification, what the subject identifies with, and therefore includes fascination with the object of loathing. It seems an important opening into a reading of David Copperfield's reactions to Uriah Heep, but staying with Carlyle, it should condition a reading of such a typical passage as the following, from "Model Prisons," which implicitly criticises John Howard (1726–90), the prison reformer and modernizer:

> Howard is to be regarded as the unlucky fountain of that tumultuous frothy ocean-tide of benevolent sentimentality, "abolition of punishment," all-absorbing "prison-discipline," and general morbid sympathy, instead of hearty hatred, for scoundrels; which is threatening to drown human society as in deluges, and leave, instead of an "edifice of society" fit for the habitation of men, a continent of fetid ooze inhabitable only by mudgods and creatures that walk upon their belly. Few things more distress a thinking soul at this time.    (65)

The fear is that those inside the prison will not be demarcated firmly enough from those outside: the benevolence towards prisoners will produce a regression where all distinctions will be lost. Fear of drowning, fear of being swamped, is fear of identity-loss, fear of the loss of borders or boundaries; it is important that Carlyle sees himself as "a thinking soul," positioned as far as possible (as *homo erectus*) from animals crawling in the mud. The thinking is declared to be as separate from the euphemistic "ooze" as possible—but the rhetoric gives Carlyle away, and the ooze with which he professes disgust is what this thinking soul produces in his text, as though he is fascinated by the idea of the dissolution of all borders and the loss of identity.

The "edifice of society" which would best preserve an inside/outside attitude to borders is the prison, and the context of visiting one modern "model prison" provides Carlyle with the opportunity to attack Howard and prison-reform. For the nineteenth century, the prison became an image of rational control and the power of discipline, and, in the "separate system," for self-discipline. In the form of the Panopticon, which was never literally built to Bentham's design, but influenced in its "rational" design much prison architecture and management, it represents a technology to produce model prisoners. The prison becomes the symbol of modernity's ability to control and produce the subject, but as such Carlyle hates it, perhaps because, as I shall argue, it threatens his own subjectivity as well. "Model Prisons" is his account of the short way he would make with criminals, in the face of such fictional creations as the wonderfully named "Mr Hesperus Fiddlestring" (70) preaching abolition of capital punishment. The "criminal question" for Carlyle is not to be settled by Utilitarian considerations whether capital punishment is a deterrent or not. Bentham was so much a modernizer, if not a post-modernist, that he was prepared to say "if hanging a man in effigy would produce the same salutary impression of terror upon the minds of the people, it would be folly or cruelty ever to hang a man *in person*" (Alain-Miller 12). This would be the triumph of the postmodern "simulacrum" indeed. In contrast, the author of *Latter-Day Pamphlets* wants to make the matter an absolute, a matter of revenge, and imagines saying to the "criminal":

We, not to be partakers in thy destructive adventure of **defying** God and all the Universe, dare not allow thee to continue longer among us. As a palpable deserter from the ranks where all men, at their eternal peril are bound to be: palpable deserter, taken with the red hand fighting thus against the whole Universe and its Laws, we—send thee back into the whole Universe, solemnly expel thee from our community, and will, in the name of God, not with joy and exultation, but with sorrow stern as thy own, hang thee on Wednesday next, and so end.                                                                    (77)

The desire for order is uttered in tones heady with violence: why such hatred, why such rhetoric, and why such desire to make clear-cut distinctions, to reify and to delimit the idea of the defiant criminal?

Gilles Deleuze and Felix Guattari, in *Anti-Oedipus,* their study of capitalism and schizophrenia, see the operations of modern capitalism as destabilizing, decoding and "deterritorializing" desire, (whether political, economic, or sexual) so that it overflows and has to be violently "reterritorialized" in a moment of crisis. *Latter-Day Pamphlets* works so much towards a violent reterritorialization because Carlyle has already seen the modern in terms of its opposite, as in *The French Revolution* (1837), or the first of the *Pamphlets,* "The Present Time," on the revolutions of 1848. But however much reterritorialization prevails, it can only be reactive against the overflow of desire, which in 1848 showed itself in the power of "Democracy" about which Carlyle wrote in the first *Pamphlet,* "The Present Time" that "the tramp of its million feet is on all streets and thoroughfares" (9). The railway-mania of the 1840s is an example of a literal deterritorializing: "railways are shifting all Towns of Britain into new places; no Town will stand where it did, and

nobody can tell for a long while yet where it will stand'' (266). This loss
of a secure place produces "private distress, uncertainty, discontent" and
"revolutionary movement" (267). Political revolutions, such as those of 1848
are the products of a modernity that Carlyle sees as discontented, but in
*The French Revolution* he read that earlier revolution as paradigmatic of the
deterritorializing energies of modernity. Early in *The French Revolution,* he
quotes from *Sartor Resartus*:

> But if "every man," as it has been written, "holds confined within him a *mad-
> man,*" what must every Society do;—Society which in its commonest state is
> called "the standing miracle of this world"! "Without such Earth-rind of
> Habit," continues our Author, . . . Society would not exist at all. . . . let but, by
> ill chance . . . your "thin Earthrind" be once broken! The fountains of the great
> deep boil forth, fire-fountains, enveloping, engulfing . . . " (Carlyle 2:40)

The unconscious comes into display, rises from below, like a display of
madness, and in the French Revolution it is incarnated in the Sansculottes
and asks "What think ye of me?" ((2) 222). The monstrosity that intrudes
here Carlyle attempts to give a name to and to domesticate in the epic question
of "The Present Time": "What *is* Democracy . . . which is everywhere the
portion of our Europe in these latter days?" (9). Sansculottism, as the return
of the repressed is called "the crowning Phenomenon of our Modern Time."
(2:222). In confronting the unconscious, we are looking at the crowd—that
new feature of nineteenth-century urban existence, and especially identified
by Carlyle with violent women, the "Menads." *The French Revolution* de-
centers the rational subject by suggesting the force of unconscious drives to
motivate individual actions:

> For a man, once committed headlong to republican or any other Transcendental-
> ism, and fighting and fanaticizing amid a Nation of his like, becomes as it were
> enveloped in an ambient atmosphere of Transcendentalism and Delirium: his
> individual self is lost in something that is not himself, but foreign though
> inseparable from him. (2:246)

The power and the content of the unconscious, forcing the subject and the
times into fuller self-consciousness, produces the material of *The French
Revolution,* and the terror it inspires prompts *Latter-Day Pamphlets.* One epic
form—that of *The French Revolution*—is to be replaced by another—the
projected twelve pamphlets: an epic form that failed, that remained as a
fragment, as though *ennui*—the final state diagnosed in the *Pamphlets*—caught Carlyle itself, or as if he was overwhelmed by the monstrosity
that everywhere appeared before him, disallowing the control of the essayistic
form. The importance of reading the *Pamphlets*—indeed, much of Carlyle—is

that these texts which discuss the unconscious in all but name point also to the unconscious that motivates them, and which Carlyle is at times just aware of. They repeat therefore the split processes of deterritorialization and reterritorialization. They both release the unconscious onto the page, and they repress it. *The French Revolution* records enthusiastically the fall of the Bastille; *Latter-Day Pamphlets* reinstates the prison as a wished-for seat of pre-revolutionary violence, but only to discover that the form of the prison has also changed since the Bastille.

It is time to re-read Carlyle on going to prison. Early into the second *Pamphlet*, "Model Prisons," Carlyle opens a narrative: "Several months ago, some friends took me with them to see one of the London prisons, a Prison of the exemplary or model kind" (52). In describing the prison, he begins with the architecture:

> An immense circuit of buildings; cut out, girt with a high ring-wall, from the lanes and streets of the quarter, which is a dim and crowded one. Gateway as to a fortified place; then a spacious court, like the square of a city; broad staircases, passages to interior courts; fronts of stately architecture all round.
>
> (52)

The building is separated from the city all around it, so that it has been architecturally produced *as* a prison. As an "edifice of society" it says what it is, and what it produces in its turn, announcing a difference between criminals inside and people outside. While it produces the borders and boundaries that Carlyle fears are in danger of dissolving, a hint of what Carlyle fears comes in the point that the prison's surface is by implication a deception: the architectural "fronts" belie the function of the prison; this is just surface, mere facade, disavowing the point that there are murderers/murderesses and thieves within the walls. Over two paragraphs, Carlyle describes the prison as "clean" (five times) and refers to it as completely furnished in every way, offering "substantial wholesome comfort" (a phrase repeated four lines later). There is an ambiguity here, which I note in passing but will return to: Carlyle seems disturbed by the cleanness, which he is very conscious of; and yet cleanness is the antithesis of the rhetoric of mud and filth that he uses (and quite repeatedly). The prisoners are working according to the fashionable "silent system' (they are "silent, or at least conversing only by secret signs"). They are distinguished from each other: thus the women include "some notable murderesses among them" who are referred to again in the next sentence:

> The notable murderesses were, with great precautions of privacy, pointed out to us; and we were requested not to look openly at them, or seem to notice them at all, as it was found to "cherish their vanity" when visitors looked at them.
>
> (53)

The detail is passed over by the text, but I want to hold onto it, as the marker of a sexual difference in the text, and as a pointer to something symptomatic in it.

Nothing is said about not looking at the men. Presumably "cherish their vanity" is a phrase taken from the guides to the prison. The women like to be looked at: such is the view of patriarchal authority. But the women's consciousness of being looked at suggests the importance of the sexual. Presumably the murders included infanticides: the last hanging for that took place in 1849 (Wiener 81). A more sensational double hanging, of a husband and wife together, took place on November 13, 1849, when the Belgian lady's maid, Maria Manning, together with her husband, was publicly hanged at Horsemonger Lane Gaol in Southwark for murder. At her execution she wore black satin and a black lace veil over her face as though still "cherishing her vanity," in circumstances that induced "heroine worship" from John Forster, who watched and described the proceedings in a letter to Bulwer.[4] "Model Prisons" later discusses Mrs. Manning:

> A Mrs Manning "dying game,"–alas, is not that the foiled potentiality of a kind of heroine too? Not a heroic Judith, not a mother of the Gracchi now, but a hideous murderess, fit to be the mother of hyaenas! To such extent can potentialities be foiled.                                    (65)

The reference to Judith recalls the "Menads" chapter of *The French Revolution,* where the insurrectionary women are repeatedly called "Judiths." The tone of this is quite dissimilar from the rhetoric Carlyle is prepared to address to the putative criminal to be hanged next Wednesday. A Bakhtinian dialogism enters the writing, as Carlyle quotes the phrase "dying game," which was used by victims about to be hanged: for instance, the last verse of a poem printed in *Punch* about the hanging of the Mannings, spoken as if by an onlooker, uses it:

> But after all, what is it? A tumble and a kick!
> And anyhow, 'tis seemingly all over precious quick,
> And shows that some, no matter for what they've done, dies game!
> Ho, Ho! if ever my time comes, I hope to do the same!     (Gatrell 607).

"Dying game" would destroy Carlyle's rhetoric of the criminal being turned off "with sorrow stern as thy own." The dialogic note entering this text that wishes for monologism, challenges Carlyle's stated attitudes, as does Mrs. Manning's gender. The text's ambivalence—even attraction—towards the violent woman, is a feature it holds in common with Forster, who hardly notices Frederic Manning hanging at the same time as his wife. Gender issues split Carlyle's text, and construct its anxieties.

Fascination with violent women, who must not be openly acknowledged in the prison, is also fascination with the crowd. The Mannings attracted a crowd of over 30,000 to their execution. Dickens and John Leech, who provided an illustration for *Punch* to go with the poem, attended the hanging, and Dickens wrote that morning to *The Times* to complain about the crowd's behavior and to advocate private executions. He complained about the crowd's levity. But as V. A. C. Gatrell puts it, in his study of nineteenth-century public hangings, "with his own axes to grind, who was Dickens to judge?" (75). Gatrell argues that the crowd was not simply enjoying a carnival at executions, but was frequently oppositional to capital punishment, seeing the process as state murder. In this opposition was a reason for the state instituting private executions (in 1868). The crowd, about which Carlyle is so excited in *The French Revolution,* and about which he writes so well, is analogous to the violent women in the prison whose reactions to being looked at he fears: both are a source of opposition to the calm practice of Carlylean (state) "justice." The quotation from Carlyle about taking revenge on the criminal fudges the issue as to who is to hang the prisoner, (and whether publicly or privately), by just saying "we," because the monological tone of the writing cannot allow for the idea of a crowd, acting as the voice of the repressed, contesting this justice. Dickens could not have expected any other behavior from the crowd (it was not the first hanging he had seen), so why did he go to see the woman and the man hanged? He says he went to observe the crowd's behavior, but this may well be a displacement of other repressed reasons, and a fascination with violence seems more likely, which requires a psychoanalytic explanation. In the same way, Carlyle's survey of the prison suggests a psychic investment in what he sees, which would be broken by the women reacting to his gaze. Neither Dickens nor Carlyle can tolerate the look of *the other*—the women, or the crowd—because their different ways of looking would destroy their own assumed position of a serene and controlled and controlling gaze.

This would align Carlyle—and Dickens—to the way of seeing inscribed in the Benthamite Panoptical system, premised on the dominance of the gaze which the prisoner is under but can neither escape nor return. While Carlyle hates the modern, model prison, he needs the prisoner to be model. The text tries to pass over the threat posed by the women knowing they were being looked at. Model prisons only questionably produce model prisoners. The women are sitting, Carlyle notices, "all in the like state of methodic composure." He is suspicious of such order; the women who have "all conceivable mechanical furtherances" are "not too arduously working"—they may be mimicking the order they submit to. And the murderesses are pleased to be noticed. Their vanity would disrupt their work, but the main danger might be that they would look back at the men looking at them. They might even laugh—as "hyaenas" do.

The paragraph finishes by taking the erotic out of the situation: "Schools too were there; intelligent teachers of both sexes, studiously instructing the still ignorant of these thieves." Class and gender-issues are implied in that sentence: presumably the women teach the working-class women. But despite the education, the impression remains: the women are dangerous because they are women, because they are likely to be activated into sexual behavior, which would certainly be an implication of their vanity being aroused, and they are, further, dangerous because they have no property share in this culture, which is the suppressed reason why Carlyle keeps reverting to the point that the provisions made for the prisoners are too good, that real property cannot compete: "probably no Duke in England lives in a mansion of such perfect and thorough cleanness" (52).

In Carlyle's text, despite the dialogism, and because of the anger, no one (except the conflicted Carlyle) answers back. But if no one answers back, the repressed fear is of someone *looking back*: the knowing woman, the woman who crosses gender-boundaries (murder being a metonymy for such transgression of borders). If the argument of *Latter-Day Pamphlets* tries to fix laws of nature which it also calls laws of right and wrong, and marshals these against the spirit of democracy and the revolutionary impulse that 1848 demonstrated, the danger represented by the women looking back at Carlyle is truly awful, since they subvert the whole idea of nature. On the next page of the description of the prison, Carlyle gives an account of the governor, "professionally and by nature zealous for cleanliness, punctuality, good order of every kind" (54).[5] Here again the ambivalence of Carlyle towards modernity may be noticed. He hates the place for being clean, as though the cleanliness were a fetish, a way of covering over some corruption; he later refers to "whitewashing the scoundrel-population" (69). Yet he admires the drive towards cleanliness in the prison governor. This man crosses the gender-divide in Carlyle's description, (and not just in his interest in cleanliness): "in the soft definite voice it was as if Nature herself were promulgating her orders, gentlest, mildest orders." The man is more "natural"—more like a "real" woman—than the women. The "Captain" is averse to what Michel Foucault in his study of "the birth of the prison," *Discipline and Punish,* calls "the gentle way in punishment"—it goes against his "natural instinct" as the next paragraph says; "nature and his inarticulate persuasion" teaches him the system of reform does not work. Some romantic, this non-modern Captain! But this persuasion is redolent of the feminine in remaining unspoken, unspeakable. Further, the Captain dislikes the recent loss of the treadwheel as a deterrent or threat against bad behavior. This leads in to the fifth reference to nature in relation to the prison-governor.

The "sympathy" of visitors, too, their "pity" for his interesting scoundrel-subjects, though he tried to like it, was evidently no joy to this practical mind.

Pity, yes—but pity for the scoundrel-species? For those who will not have pity
on themselves and will force the Universe and the Laws of Nature to have no
"pity" on them? Meseems I could discover fitter objects of pity!        (55)

In this free indirect discourse, where "he" becomes "I," with the foregrounding of "sympathy" and "pity," the voice of the Captain becomes the
voice of Carlyle. The last sentence could be spoken by either, the Captain
using the discourse of Carlyle, as in the choice of phrase "scoundrel-species."
There is an alignment here—of the voice of Nature as the voice of the Captain
and both as the voice of Carlyle, and involving a masculine protest, like that
of Macaulay in 1846, commenting on those who were against transportation
as punishment, that this reaction had led to "such a sort of effeminate feeling
in the country, that there was hardly a case of atrocity with respect to which
they [Members of Parliament] would not have thousands of persons petition-
ing for mercy, if the house gave any encouragement to the practice" (Gay
135). Philanthropy in Macaulay becomes effeminacy, just as, in Carlyle, philanthropists work by "charity and rose-water" (49), and pity for the criminal
in "Model Prisons" is "cowardly effeminacy" (83).

The investment in "nature" "notable murderesses" would laugh at, with
their vanity and their lack of nature. In this passage, where the Captain and
Carlyle are both made out to be more feminine than the women, that femininity is then exposed as empty or meaningless when the true violence of the
captain (a military man) comes out in what he would like to do—and what
Carlyle would also like to do—to the prisoners, those "sons of *in*docility"
(55). The constructed nature of gender (or the gender of nature) works
throughout Carlyle's visit to the prison. Nature which is feminine is what the
Captain possesses, but there is the secret dread that the women whose vanity
proclaims their femininity make apparent, as only modernity can in bringing
things into the open, the social and cultural construction of gender: there is
no nature, and no definition of what women should be like can hold. And
that might imply that between the violence of the women, the "notable murderesses," and the violence of the Captain, who wishes to impose order there
is also no difference: this would represent, for Carlyle, the return of anarchy,
but it would also be the source of general indifference, and so fit the melancholy that makes him conclude the *Pamphlets* with reflections on *ennui*.

Gender issues inflect "Model Prisons" consciously and unconsciously. As
he feminizes the philanthropists, he feminizes the two oppressed subjects of
"Model Prisons," the "Beautiful Black Peasantry"—the recently freed
slaves of the Caribbean—and the "interesting White Felonry" (66). The male
black is reduced so that the language of "And you, Quashee, my pump-
kin,–(not a bad fellow either, this poor Quashee, when tolerably guided!)–idle
Quashee . . . " (67) makes him no sexual threat. The black worker, non-
phallic, reduced to servility, is declared to toil no harder than the women in

the prison. And references to the phallic is not gratuitous, because a sexual urgency and anxiety, an obsession with the phallic, becomes explicit as "Model Prisons" works towards its conclusion with words put into the mouth of one of Carlyle's personae, "Crabbe, in his *Radiator,*" who talks of his fear of "the Worship of Human Nobleness" being abolished:

> and a *new* astonishing Phallus-worship, with universal Balzac-Sand melodies, and litanies in treble and in bass established in its stead, [but] what can I compute but that Nature, in horrible throes, will repugn against such substitution,—that, in short, the astonishing new Phallus-worship, with its finer sensibilities of the heart and "great satisfying loves," with its sacred kiss of peace for scoundrel and hero alike, with its all-embracing Brotherhood, and universal Sacrament of Divorce, will have to take itself away again!       (81–82)

How did Carlyle's essay get from fear of the women, which is fear of their sexuality, and which relates to his assertion of masculinity, to the concept of "phallus worship"? There is a fear of feminism here, apparent both in the wish for satisfying loves (presumably the woman's wish: the sexual referent is obvious) and in the desire for divorce, which is also fear, that he would like marriage to be analogous to a hard prison. It is as though he sees the Jane Eyre kind of heroine, for example, as phallicly empowered, or desiring the phallus.[6]

Carlyle writes as "Crabbe" when he denounces phallus-worship; he does not own the voice as his, but as that of a persona, and the name is obviously allegorical of an embittered mind. Nonetheless, it remains true that it is Carlyle who writes so angrily and explicitly about the phallus, implying his fear of it, and fascination. He had already left unfinished one article entitled "Phallus-Worship," (1848), which concludes "Unhappy generation of the world, which has no marching standards but these two: a Phallus and a moneybag" (Kaplan 133). Phallus-worship opens up Carlyle's anger in relation to the model prison and the term re-appears in a later *Pamphlet,* "Hudson's Statue" (1 July 1850). Again, the sentiments are attributed to Crabbe. In "this wild passage" as Carlyle puts it, distancing himself from "Crabbe" 's craziness, the clerisy and its hypocrisy are attacked, and it ends:

> Look round on a world all bristling with insurrectionary pikes; Kings and Papas flying like detected coiners; and in their stead Icaria, Red Republic, new religion of the anti-Virgin, Literature of Desperation curiously conjoined with Phallus-worship . . .       (289)

The passage associates the 1848 revolutions and socialism with sexual revolution. The "anti-Virgin" is George Sand, while the literature associated with sexual liberation includes Balzac, Geraldine Jewsbury, G. H. Lewes, and perhaps Charlotte Brontë. For Carlyle, political revolution seems the expression in the conscious of sexual drives:

> these universal suffrages, national workshops, reigns of fraternity and generally red or white republics in their fraternities and phenomena are to me very mainly a George Sand novel come forth from the land of dreams . . .    (Kaplan 2:22)

The region of desire spills over into the political. The diagnosis is Freudian in the place it gives to the unconscious, but the unconscious is gendered as feminine. The "notable murderesses" are the very surfacing of the unconscious, and they seem phallically empowered. In contrast to such destabilizations, the last essay of the *Pamphlets*, "Jesuitism," calls "Literature, Poetry and the other kindred arts" the place where "a certain manliness of temper and liberty to follow truth" (318) prevails. And the fourth of the Pamphlets, "The New Downing Street," concludes that Peel "has but to lift a finger in this enterprise, and whatever is wise and manful in England will rally round him." (169). The manful momentarily opposes the phallic: it protects order—reterritorializes the area of gender. Yet if Carlyle deals with the manly, he has the attraction of disgust towards the phallic. The O.E.D. gives *Latter-Day Pamphlets* for the first use of "phallus-worship," (giving only two references to the phallus and one to the word "phallic" before that: all in specialized contexts). The word can be linked to another which acquires general use in the nineteenth-century. In "Hudson's Statue" Carlyle refers to fetishes. He describes some epochs having

> along with their real worship an imaginary, and . . . [being] conscious only of the latter as worship. They keep a set of gods or fetishes, reckoned respectable, to which they mumble prayers, asking themselves and others triumphantly, "Are not these respectable gods?" and all the while their real worship . . . concentrates itself on quite other gods and fetishes,—on Hudsons and scrips, for instance. Thus is the miserable epoch rendered twice and tenfold miserable . . . having superadded to its stupid Idolatries and brutish forgettings of the true God . . . an immense Hypocrisy, which is the quintessence of all idolatries . . .                                                              (278)

The age's worship is fetishistic both in the sense of "idolatrous,"[7] (it forgets the "true God") but also because it involves a hypocritical refusal to acknowledge what it really worships—scrips (i.e., money), and more specifically, the "railway king" George Hudson, for whom a statue was nearly erected before his partial disgrace in 1849 (though questions were being asked about him as early as 1846). The worship is idolatrous and in addition fetishistic in Freud's sense of the term: that is, the worship acts as a screen by which the real worship (of the empty Hudson) is disavowed.

Freud would help to link phallus-worship and fetish-worship, since the fetish covers an absence that the male subject fears: the absence of the mother's phallus, which means in turn that the fetish is the means whereby the subject protects itself from castration-fears. The projected statue for Hudson is fetishistic for two reasons: firstly because it would disguise, in the monumentality of its statue-form, the ephemerality of Hudson and his near-criminality, secondly that the column—another edifice of society—would itself disguise its "real" worship—that is, that it is worship of the phallus. Hudson's projected statue is the object of Carlyle's satire; he refers to Nelson's column recently erected when he speaks of "Him you set on a high column, that all men, looking on it, may be continually apprised of the duty you expect from them" (258) and he suggests how contemporary town-planning organizes itself around such worship—"that extraordinary population of Brazen and other Images which at present dominate the market-places of towns" (261). It is as though monumental architecture is all concealed phallicism or fetishism.

But the worship of the phallus can only with difficulty be separated from Carlyle's "hero-worship." "Whatever gods or fetishes a man may have about him, and pay tithes to, and mumble prayers to, the real "religion" that is in him is his *practical Hero-worship*." (278) So Carlyle tries to distinguish fetishistic worship from something real, and so Oliver Cromwell, praised for his "noble manful simplicity" (quoted, Gray 102) is not, as far as Carlyle is concerned, to have a statue, though for Carlyle he is a hero. But the distinction is impossible. Any act of hero-worship would be open to the charge that it was no more than phallus-worship. The rhetoric of *Latter-Day Pamphlets* tries to distinguish what appears on the surface and what is underneath, what is apparent and what real, and this project is itself part of the project of modernity, since that is concerned with bringing to the surface, producing, what is in the depths of a subject's character. For Carlyle, the worship of Hudson (fetishism) conceals a deep principle of phallus worship. But the phallus is itself a fetish (Carlyle would agree), and phallus-worship reveals the emptiness of modernity, of modern life. Carlyle would like to turn to true hero-worship, but that also would turn by the same logic into fetishism, which would suggest that Carlyle was also a worshipper of the phallus and a fetishist.

Carlyle is caught by the unconscious of his own rhetoric. The prison-visitor confronted by the other must be a covert phallus-worshipper: it requires no underwriting of Freud to see the "notable murderess" as analogous to the castrating woman. When Jacques Lacan expands on Freud on the fetish, he discusses "the gaze," and the *object petit a*. The *object petit a* has to do with the fetishistic look that a subject gives to an object, a look or gaze that tries to preserve his own completeness. The subject is already threatened from the beginning with fear of loss (the castration fear) and responds by magnifying or giving some additional quality to what is seen in the object. This fantasy-looking which completes the object by giving it extra qualities, provides the basis whereby the subject confirms his own identity. Lacan gives several examples of the *object petit a,* noting that "these objects have one common feature in my elaboration of them—they have no specular image, or, in other words, no alterity" (Lacan 315). The fetishistic look requires that there be no return gaze, no differences or otherness (alterity) in the *object petit a* that would threaten the subject's identity by assuming a different character.

The Panoptical drive of Bentham and the vision of Carlyle have this in common, that they are both ways of managing the gaze, of controlling what is seen. The fear of being looked back at is avoided in the model prison, all of whose details—the facades, the cleanliness, the private court from which he watches the Chartist prisoners—help to stabilize Carlyle as the subject, to keep him in control, with the sense that nothing is out of order. The phallus worship his text fears would unman the male and his masculinity in a process of deterritorialization. The phallus worship his text protects devises strategies of control to try to hold on to its masculinity, and by its open hatred of everything that is other to the self. Historically, in fascism, modernity has done the same—which gives point to LaValley's comment—responding to a neurotic fear of the other, by its exploitation of possibilities of authoritarian control, carried out in terms of violence and disorder.

The cleanliness of the prison partakes of the fetish. The Captain's similarity to Carlyle may be focussed in the dual attitude to cleanliness and the treadwheel. The Captain hates the prisoners and in the indirect free discourse of his conversation with Carlyle his attitudes are discernible:

> You had but to look in the faces of these Twelve-hundred, and despair, for the most part, of ever "commanding" them at all. Miserable distorted blockheads, the generality; ape-faces, imp-faces, angry dog-faces, heavy sullen ox-faces, degraded underfoot perverse creatures . . .                                           (55).

This, in its unrepressed modernity, uses the antithesis of the language of cleanliness. But the Captain misses something of the rationalizations permitted in modernity, since he also resents the loss of the treadwheel, which represents useless labour. As far as Carlyle can see, everyone in the prison is working at useful occupations (including cleaning clothes). The pyschoanalyst Jacques Alain-Miller comments on the Panopticon that in it "Bentham has conceived a world without waste, a world in which anything left over is immediately reused, a surperusable world." (Alain-Miller 8) As one evidence, he cites and comments on Bentham talking to his editor, John Bowring: "Remember we do not exercise, or ought not to exercise, even a *besoin* ["need"—Bentham genteelly used the French word] in vain. It should serve for manure" (Alain-Miller 7, parenthesis in the text). Cleanliness—the exclusion of dirt—and useful labor go together: Carlyle as the only partially comprehending modern is ambivalent about both (his sarcasm about the labor in the prisons is suggestive). They suggest an economy which is modern in its making use of waste. Carlyle's fascination—and disgust—is with waste. He would hang the criminal, and he envisages a society which is returning to the primal mud, or to the "pig's trough."

Yet when discussing the pig's trough in "Jesuitism," it may be noticed how he distances himself: he attributes the words not to himself but to Sauerteig ("sour dough"):

> A singular piece of scribble, in Sauerteig's hand, bearing marks of haste and almost of rage (for the words, abbreviated to the bone, tumble about as if in battle on the paper), occurs to me at this moment, entitled *Schwein'sche Weltansicht*; and I will try to decipher and translate it.     (316)

The text contains its own self-criticism, and in referring to the "swine's-trough," it wittily declares itself to be a translation, as if it was an only partly effectual way of speaking. The negativity is accompanied by ambivalence: Carlyle is not wholly ready to sign up to the signature of Sauerteig. Hence the concern with cleanliness and usefulness is, I think seen as a fetishistic way of managing the prison's affairs; Carlyle's attraction towards the disgusting is part of his reaction from that. His commitment to "deciphering," too, is interesting: it could even suggest a desire to read the mind, the unconscious of Sauerteig. Can that fascination with disgust be "read" critically?

At this point, trying to decipher Carlyle, it should be asked again why his form of modernity, which throws off all shame, means he would rather see the prisoners as disgusting than as clean and potentially ready for reform (the other form of modernity). I have already argued that he sees them (like women, like crowds) as a threat to his own borders, his own ego, which can only be sustained with difficulty, but it is important to see that he is not alone in that perception. When Uriah Heep goes back into his cell in Pentonville Prison in *David Copperfield,*[8] from whence he has appeared to be displayed as a model prisoner, the hero, David, (henceforth to be called D.C.) experiences a "great relief." The ugly, the disgusting, the under-class, the phallic—Heep is all those things—has been excluded again. This is in chapter 61, "I Am Shown Two Interesting Penitents," which describes D.C. and Traddles being shown round a model prison by Mr. Creakle, and meeting Uriah Heep and Littimer, who are in adjacent cells and are on their way to transportation. "Interesting" I have already quoted twice as a description of the prisoners in "Model Prisons" and Number 27 (Uriah Heep) is called a "Model Prisoner." Many details in this chapter of wonderful comic drama, including the references to cocoa, show Dickens' attentive reading of Carlyle. It is easy to imagine how the scene in *David Copperfield* could be played in the theater; where it would be meta-theater, theater about the theater since Uriah Heep and Littimer, both hypocrites, are acting to a ready-made audience who have come to see them and are ready to be taken in. The appearance of Uriah Heep followed by Littimer from another door, as Number Twenty-Eight, is obviously theatrical, (and so played up by Phiz in his illustration) and this is suggestive, that the episode is a return to an earlier and simpler Dickens style.

The chapter title, however, suggests something else. It centers the "I" who is "shown" something; the "I" being the audience and the subject, the "interesting penitents" the object of the gaze. The "I" that speaks separates the narrative from being part of the theatrical show. The "I" of the narration, whose question all along has been whether he is the hero of his own life, is anxious to establish his subjectivity and his point of view, and from the beginning of the episode he plays up his commentary:

> I could not help thinking, as we approached the gate, what an uproar would have been made in the country, if any deluded man had proposed to spend one half of the money [the prison] had cost, on the erection of an industrial school for the young, or a house of refuge for the deserving old. (713)

> I wondered whether it occurred to anybody, that there was a striking contrasts between these plentiful repasts of choice quality, and the dinners, not to say of paupers, but of soldiers, sailors, labourers, the great bulk of the honest, working community . . . (713)

> It struck me . . . that there was a strong probability of the prisoners knowing a good deal about each other, and of their carrying on a pretty complete system of intercourse. This, at the time I write, has been proved, I believe, to be the case . . . (714)

The text proves self-confirming: D.C. says that what he thought then has been confirmed now "at the time I write." He writes, to give what he thought "then" more authority. Such a declaration of continuity between then and now guarantees the self-presence of the subject, makes D.C. a consistent subject.

This belief in self-consistency, performed in the text by the "I" directing the reader what to think before the revelation of the two interesting penitents, suggests a desire for control, the more necessary since the subject's being is disconfirmed, not by women, as potentially in "Model Prisons" but by men who recall D.C.'s rivalry over women, his hatred of Uriah with regard to Agnes and his quasi-homoerotic semi-aware connivance with Steerforth in seducing Em'ly. Uriah Heep tells D.C. "once you struck me a blow in the face, you know" (718), which, it is arguable, as a weakly violent and uncontrolled reaction to Heep feminises D.C.; and Littimer alludes to "having lived a thoughtless life in the service of young men; and . . . having allowed myself to be led by them into weaknesses'' (717). This in its wonderful inspecificity points up the veiled homoeroticism of ''Daisy'' and Steerforth, as well as implicating D.C. in Em'ly's seduction: Em'ly, whom D.C. had thought of as his own. D.C. as the subject must struggle to assert his voice as normal in the face of such a witty undercutting as it receives of his heterosexual manhood: D.C. has been guilty of phallus-worship with regard to Steerforth, and is punished for it through the mouth of Steerforth's servant, the real professional in matters of class- and gender-manipulation.

The desire for control takes place against a decoding performed by Heep and Creakle; Creakle and the others are taken in by the acting, roles are reversed, so that D.C. is put in the position of the accused—''Several indignant glances directed at me'' (718). The carnivalesque comedy of the criminals is a mimickry of respectability. D.C. refers to the *deserving* old, and Uriah speaks of bearing the consequences of his ''follies'' ''without repining'' (716), so that D.C.'s own terminology, his language of respectability, is now contaminated with the suspicion that it is no more than cant. And this mimickry leads to another point. Though the narrator ends by calling them ''hypocritical knaves'' (720), that is an attempt at closure, at shutting down the issues, for Heep and Littimer are not that: they are acting in response to the situation that is expected of them. Asked to perform in a particular way, they respond in kind. In a sense, they can do no other, for they are prisoners. The episode continues the fictionalising of a visit to prison that ''Model Prisons'' inaugurated, and involves the same looking back that Carlyle does not want and disconfirming of the bourgeois male subject. Uriah Heep's phallic ''writhing'' which he does plenty of in this chapter keeps him as the animal-like object of disgust to D.C., analogous to the disgust induced in the Captain; but how does the chapter relate to the hatred of the controlling devices of modernity that I have argued run through Carlyle?

The model prison D.C. goes to bears some relation to the Panopticon; it isolates the prisoners in conditions of cleanliness that are supposed to lead to self-discipline, and so it produces the subject, who has to speak in the way Heep and Littimer do: continuing a language of hypocrisy because that is what the dominant order wants to hear. Hypocrisy, which hides its shame and so is the opposite vice to Carlyle's in *Latter-Day Pamphlets,* uses the language of accommodation to dominant social interests; it pretends that there is no other language, no other way of seeing than the dominant order, and it is Carlyle's importance that he misses out on it. For Heep and Littimer to speak hypocritically scores no advantage to them: it confirms the dominant order in the way it sees things and manipulates them. Heep and Littimer score only local victories over the bourgeois subject who would like to be fully identified with the dominant order. It is hardly relevant to argue (as the criticisms of the reforming prisons did) that the separate system produced fake conversions and made no difference to the people so treated. Heep and Littimer are bound for transportation; they are ticketed as particular types of prisoners. They belong to a production of the subject, which works by its stress on cleanliness and by an assumed gentle way of punishment. The model prison, by not making prisoners animal-like and faceless, by making them different numbers (which personalises and degrades at the same time) is more of a technique for control and for discipline than Carlyle recognizes. Putting the point more sociologically, isolating some prisoners as "model" is a way to deal with the others who are not so labelled (and who are not represented in Dickens's text).

The novel in using the term "model prisoner" opens up several ironies: despite Carlyle's sarcasm about the way they are looked at, they are actually model *prisoners,* models of the way the state treats people in this new regime, models of its control which is the more real for seeming to be invisible. They are models in the sense that they perform like puppets for the prison-regime, and models in that they have been dehumanised, so that they fit the economy of the prison where there is no wastage, no loss: they come out of their cells and they go back there, they perform their circusturns and while they provide stand-up comedy for the reader, there is no sense that they will escape from the carceral regime, and the economy that produces them. As models they mimic bourgeois respectability, but as models their rebellion is contained.

David Masson, reviewing *Latter-Day Pamphlets* said with reference to "Model Prisons," "Hatred of scoundrels? True! but define your "scoundrel"!" Masson's decent sympathy leads him to argue that Carlyle's assessment of who is the scoundrel is merely conventional: he finds merit in "that classification of men which is determined . . . chiefly by their practical or success-bearing qualities." (Masson 356–357). Carlyle admires the prison-governor, but he treats the criminals in the mass, and though the modern prison-system makes distinctions between prisoner and prisoner, he does not. Dickens, though equally capable of a servile admiration of the same prison-governor that Carlyle discusses and equally able to be merely conventional in his judgements of worth, nonetheless in *David Copperfield* decentres judgements by making the prison-governor Mr. Creakle. To define the scoundrel in "I am shown two interesting penitents" is not easy. The nearest to a conventional figure is D.C. himself, and his disconfirmation takes place through a potential probing of the most intimate areas of his own sexual adequacy. In this scene, he is able to conceal neither his good nor his evil.

And despite the victory of the penal system, the two men coming out of their prison-cells still seem frightening, uncannily like the appearance of the unconscious. They appear to confront the subject's gaze with that Carlylean question, "What think ye of me?" If Carlyle thinks that the people in prison are mimicking order, and Dickens show hypocrites mimicking the language of respectable religion, the anxiety constructing both texts is that of the power of the unconscious—that it cannot be repressed. *Latter-Day Pamphlets* and *David Copperfield* both show their modernity as texts in wishing to deal with an unconscious which might or might not subvert an anxious masculinity. The Freud essay that really illuminates *David Copperfield* and to a lesser extent *Latter-Day Pamphlets* is "The Uncanny." One fear that recurs there is of the mechanical, which is implicit in repetition, where recurrence may indicate uncannily that everything, including the subject around whom things repeat, is no more than mechanical, certainly not humanly free, but puppet-like, no more than the model. Perhaps Dickens' interest in the inanimate which is also animate articulates with his sense of the Benthamite prison, which de-animates the animate, as much as capital punishment reduces the subject to a puppet on a string. So chapter 61 of *David Copperfield* shows a complete return of the repressed—where everything that D.C. had thought to have left behind him comes back with mechanical precision.

Carlyle and Dickens respond differently to the possibility of being looked back at, by that which is hauntingly both animate and sexual and de-animated and marionette-like. *David Copperfield* opens up everything to a panoptical gaze, even the subject who narrates. Everyone, including D.C. is, or could be, a subject for the police. While D.C.'s self-righteousness about the prison, and his imperception about its discipline and the purchase of its control make him analogous to aspects of Carlyle in *Latter-Day Pamphlets,* his reflections are contained in a text larger than he is, which questions his ability to make judgments. One difference between D.C. and Carlyle, however, is that the fictional hero, timid and and a phallus-worshipper, is anxious to protect himself against those people who might be mirrors for him, or who might disconcert his gaze—Uriah Heep outstandingly. He must keep himself as the single, centered subject. Whereas Carlyle, for all his anger, turns round also upon himself with equal ferocity, and *Latter-Day Pamphlets* in its rage and its fragmentation, shows the subject undoing himself as the centered subject, doing for himself the work that the notable murderesses would else have done for him. D.C. preserves himself from the drive within modernity towards self-exposure, and perhaps *David Copperfield's* popularity is a sign that the novel finally does the same, but *Latter-Day Pamphlets,* paying the price by remaining unpopular, throws off all shame while, conflicted to the last, it is obsessed with the apparent shamelessness of those women who do the same—whose victory is silently marked in the cessation of the writing of *Latter-Day Pamphlets.*

# NOTES

1. For example, take Dickens on Peel's death—(2 July 1850)—Peel "could ill be spared from among the great dust-heap of imbeciles and dandies that there **is**

no machinery for sifting, down in Westminster" — letter to Harriet Martineau, 3 July 1850. The editors of the Dickens *Letters* compare this with Carlyle on "Downing Street,"—"to clean-out the dead pedantries, unveracities, indolent somnolent impotencies, and accumulated dung-mountains there" (Dickens 6, 122). As a result of "Model Prisons," Dickens wrote "Pet Prisoners," *Household Words* 27 April 1850, on prisoners being pampered in comparison to paupers, shielded from temptation and encouraged by chaplains to feign conversion and repentance. Dickens shared Carlyle's estimate of Hudson, too, as early as 1846, calling him "that Great Humbug of England" (Dickens 5, 350).

2. For Thackeray, see the Preface to *Pendennis* (1850) on not being able to describe a MAN; for Tennyson, see James Eli Adams, discussing Tennyson in terms of a crisis in ways of seeing the feminine, and in relation to "the demonic woman as a motif of Victorian culture" (Adams 10). For male anxieties generally, see Neil Hertz, who in chapter 9, "Medusa's Head: Male Hysteria under Political Pressure," discusses the 1848 revolutions in Paris and the iconography of pictures produced then in terms of fear of castration. Revolutionary violence is emblematized "as a hideous and fierce but not exactly sexless woman." (Hertz 162)

3. I discuss this passage more fully in my essay on *Dombey and Son*; consideration of the prison in Dickens for me goes back to my essay on *Great Expectations*. For further connections between *Latter-Day Pamphlets* and *David Copperfield* see my edition of *David Copperfield* for Penguin, 1996.

4. Forster's letter is quoted in Dickens (5) 643n. I discuss it in more detail in *Dickens, Violence and the Modern State*, 145–6.

5. If the prison is Tothill Fields, the Governor would be Lieut. Augustus Tracey, a friend of Dickens, praised in a footnote to *American Notes*; see Dickens (4) 104n.,322n. On Tothill Fields (Westminster House of Correction) see Dickens (2) 270. Philip Collins (64) argues that the prison is Coldbath Fields.

6. For Charlotte Brontë's reputation as a dangerous writer, I have in mind Matthew Arnold on *Villette* in 1853: "the writer's mind contains nothing but hunger, rebellion and rage (Allott 201); see also Dickens' negative attitude towards her which I discuss in *Dickens, Violence and the Modern State*, 233.

7. "In the nineteenth century . . . [fetishism] frequently seems synonymous with *idolatry* in the polemical "protestant" vocabulary directed against the endowing of inanimate objects with values and powers which properly belong to human states of mind and feelings. As such, it takes on a much wider range of references outside the anthropological, and comes in fact to suggest itself as the word or concept most suited to describe the operations of a misguided and miscreating society" (Simpson 9).

8. The prison in *David Copperfield,* though not specified, is based on Pentonville, which opened in 1842 as an experiment in the "separate system." Only the most promising first offenders were sent to Pentonville, at a cost per prisoner of £50 per annum. "Model prisoners for the model prison" were required, according to William Hepworth Dixon, the journalist, whose book *The London Prisons* (December 1849) gave a title to Carlyle and encouragement to Dickens (Dixon, p. 156, quoted in Dickens 5, 688).

# Works Cited

Adams, James Eli. "Woman Red in Tooth and Claw: Nature and the Feminine in Tennyson and Darwin." *Victorian Studies* 33 (1989): 7–27.

Adorno, Theodor. *In Search of Wagner*. Trans. Rodney Livingstone. London: Verso Books, 1981.

Allott, Miriam. *The Brontës: The Critical Heritage*. London: Routledge and Kegan Paul, 1974.

Carlyle, Thomas. *Centenary Edition* ed. H.D. Traill, 37 vols, London: Chapman and Hall, 1872. *Latter-Day Pamphlets* vol.20.

———.*Latter-Day Pamphlets* ed. Michael K. Goldberg and Jules Seigel, Canada: Canadian Federation for the Humanities, 1983.

———.*The French Revolution,* ed. K.J. Fielding and David Sorensen, Oxford: Oxford UP.

Collins, Phillip. *Dickens and Crime*. London: Macmillan, 1962.

Deleuze, Gilles, and Félix Guattari. *Anti-Oedipus: Capitalism and Schizophrenia.* translated Robert J. Hurley, Mark Seem and Helen R. Lane. Minneapolis, U of Minnesota P, 1983.

Dickens, Charles. *David Copperfield.* ed. Jerome H. Buckley, New York: W.W. Norton, 1990.

———.(2) *The Letters of Charles Dickens*, vol. 2. ed. Madeline House and Graham Storey, 1969.

———. (4) *The Letters of Charles Dickens* vol. 4 ed. Madeline House and Graham Storey and Kathleen Tillotson, vol. 4, Oxford: Clarendon P, 1985.

———. (5) *The Letters of Charles Dickens* vol. 5 ed. Graham Storey and K.J. Fielding, Oxford: Clarendon P, 1981.

———. (6) *The Letters of Charles Dickens*, vol. 6, ed. Graham Storey, Kathleen Tillotson and Nina Burgis, Oxford: Clarendon P, 1988.

Foucault, Michel, *Discipline and Punish: The Birth of the Prison,* Harmondsworth: Penguin, 1979.

Freud, Sigmund. "Fetishism," *The Penguin Freud: vol. 7, On Sexuality.* Harmondsworth: Penguin, 1977.

———."The Uncanny," *The Penguin Freud: vol. 14, Art and Literature.* Harmondsworth: Penguin, 1985.

Gatrell, V.A.C. *The Hanging Tree: Execution and the English People 1770–1868.* Oxford: Oxford UP, 1994.

Gay, Peter. "The Cultivation of Hatred," *The Bourgeois Experience: Victoria to Freud vol. 3.* New York: W. W. Norton, 1993.

Goldberg, Michael. *Carlyle and Dickens.* Athens: U of Georgia P, 1972.

———."Carlyle, Dickens and the Revolution of 1848." *Dickens Studies Annual* 12, 1983.

Herz, Neil. *The End of the Line: Essays on Psychoanalysis and the Sublime.* New York: Columbia UP, 1985.

Kaplan, Fred. *Thomas Carlyle: A Biography.* Ithaca: Cornell UP, 1983.

———. (2) "Phallus-Worship," 1848; "Unpublished Manuscripts III—A Response to the Revolution of 1848." *Carlyle Newletter* 2, 1980.

———. "Carlyle's Marginalia and George Henry Lewes's Fiction." *Carlyle Newsletter* 5 (1984): 21–27.

Kaufmann, Walter. Preface to *The Case of Wagner, Basic Writing of Nietzsche,* New York: Modern Library, 1968.

Lacan, Jacques. *Écrits: A Selection.* Trans. Alan Sheridan, London: Tavistock Publications, 1977.

LaValley, Albert J. *Carlyle and the Idea of the Modern* (New Haven: Yale UP, 1968).

Masson, David. Review of *Latter-Day Pamphlets* in Jules P. Seigel, *Carlyle, The Critical Heritage.* London: Routledge and Kegan Paul, 1971.

Miller, Jacques Alain. "Jeremy Bentham's Panoptic Device," *October* 41 (1987).

Oddie, William. *Dickens and Carlyle: The Question of Influence,* London: Century P, 1972.

Rosenberg, John D. *Carlyle and the Burden of History, Oxford: Clarendon P, 1985.*

Seigel, Jules Paul. "Latter-Day Pamphlets: the Near Failure of Form and Vision," in K.J. Fielding and Rodger L. Tarr, *Carlyle Past and Present.* London: Vision, 1976.

Simpson, David. *Fetishism and Imagination: Dickens, Melville, Conrad.* Baltimore: Johns Hopkins UP, 1982.

Tambling, Jeremy. "Prison-Bound: Dickens and Foucault." *Essays in Criticism* 32 (1986): 11–31.

———. *Confession: Sexuality, Sin, the Subject.* Manchester: Manchester UP, 1990.

———. "Death and Modernity in "Dombey and Son." *Essays in Criticism* 43 (1993): 308–29.

————.*Dickens, Violence and the Modern State.* London: Macmillan, 1995.

Vanden Bossche, Chris. *Carlyle and the Search for Authority,* Columbus: Ohio State UP, 1991.

Weiner, Martin J. *Reconstructing the Criminal: Culture, Law and Policy in England, 1830–1914.* Cambridge: Cambridge UP, 1990.

# Recent Dickens Criticism: 1995

## Joseph W. Childers

One of the things that has always struck me about omnibus reviews of this sort is the obligatory self-consciousness of the reviewer, the way he or she remarks upon the difficulty of drawing together a coherent, or even merely a serial, statement about a disparate number of critical texts employing an equally diverse number of approaches. One would think that when the topic of the criticism is linked to a figure like Dickens that the job of summarizing and commenting upon a year's worth of criticism might become more manageable, if not easier. After all, the major commentaries will be on what have been designated the major works: *Bleak House, Dombey and Son, Our Mutual Friend, Little Dorrit,* and perhaps *Copperfield* and *Great Expectations.* There may be interesting work on *Hard Times, Oliver Twist,* even *Pickwick* or *Old Curiousity Shop,* but texts like *Nicholas Nickleby, Barnaby Rudge, Edwin Drood* or *A Tale of Two Cities* are nearly forgotten. And while the approaches used and the novels considered may be all over the Dickensian map, there is always the *figure* of Dickens as Victorian personality, effusive and prolific writer, public performer, providing a canopy under which to park all manner of critical vehicles.

Though most of the important essays of 1995 did deal with the major works, that canopy of Dickens as figure did not really materialize, which I must obligingly admit made my task a bit more difficult. Only two substantial critical monographs on Dickens were published in 1995, and even then the "inimitable one" shared the marquee with his contemporary and rival in John Reed's *Dickens and Thackeray: Punishment and Forgiveness* (Ohio). This paucity of single-author studies speaks volumes about the impact the new historical criticism has had on the study of Victorian literature as well as on the Dickens "industry." Dickens and his work almost always figure in some way in current examinations of the Victorian period, yet the suspicion of a dominant or originary authority seems always to inform the most complex and insightful of the criticism being produced. The imbrication of literary

335

texts and the issues of their age (and ours) have led Victorian literary scholarship into full-blown studies of Victorian culture. The subtitles of many of the best books that contributed to Dickens studies this past year bear witness to this phenomenon: "British Cultural Formation, 1830–1864"; "Women, Representation, and the City"; "Commodity Culture and Victorian Narrative"; "Social and Cultural Formations in Nineteenth-Century Literature"; "Women, Empire, and Victorian Writing," to name only a few. In the 1993 "Review of Dickens Criticism" in this journal, Barry Qualls remarks on the derivativeness of much of the work of this sort as well as its over-reliance on historical data at the expense of literary analysis. While this continues to be a problem with many studies that have succumbed to the historical imperative, a great deal of very good and important criticism has emerged from nuanced readings of the connections between the literary and the historical.

Mary Poovey's and Andrew Miller's very different but complementary essays on *Our Mutual Friend* are two premier examples of the rich yield that can result from such an approach. Poovey's piece, "Speculation and Virtue in *Our Mutual Friend*," appears in her *Making a Social Body: British Cultural Formation, 1830–1864* (U of Chicago P) and is essentially a reprint of the essay as it appeared in the 1993 volume, *Historical Criticism and the Challenge of Theory*, ed. Janet Levarie (U of Illinois P). This essay was the central focus of Qualls's 1993 review and needs little further summary or commentary here. It remains an exemplary model of a particular type of Foucauldian informed historical criticism and is especially good at suggesting a number of themes that have since been taken up in somewhat fuller measure by other critics. For instance, when Poovey remarks on the functions of Lizzie Hexam and Bella Wilfer as destabilizing "difference," especially gender difference, signalling it as "sheer metaphor, which reflects only male desire, not some nature beyond fantasy and language" (174), she points the way for the sort of work on masculinity that has recently been the focus of critics like Herbert Sussman, Richard Dellamora, Kaja Silverman, and James E. Adams. Further, by arguing that the effect of this destabilization is to "locate difference inside of man, hence to imperil both the guarantee of virtue and the integrity of male identity itself" (174), she suggests a further destabilization of commonly accepted critical conceptions of the ways identity functioned, both socially and psychologically, during the Victorian period. This is a very important argument, for it implies that the foundationalism that is usually assumed to structure mid to late nineteenth-century conceptions of identity was already being questioned, even as literary, medical, and social discourses were attempting to reassert it. What we see in Poovey's argument is that the collation of the material effects of these discourses leads to an ambivalence about the very assumptions upon which they operate; thus, while the essay asserts epistemological change, it also avoids easy, unilateral or correspondent explanations of the complex and mutual informing relations between the figure and bodies of women, the "morality" of speculation and business practices, and the manifestation of race and gender difference as necessary components of Englishness and masculinity.

Although there are one or two places where the reader is left desiring more elaboration of the argument—for instance the connections between woman as guarantor of truth on the one hand and as inextricably tied to the machinations of the market on the other, and the short but extremely compelling section on the links between woman and the racial other—this essay is easily one of the best of 1995. And while not strictly "new," its inclusion as a chapter in *Making a Social Body* should bring it even more of the attention it deserves. Another good contribution to the work on *Our Mutual Friend* is the chapter "Rearranging the Furniture of *Our Mutual Friend*" in Andrew Miller's book, *Novels Behind Glass: Commodity Culture and Victorian Narrative* (Cambridge UP). Miller argues that "among the dominant concerns motivating mid-Victorian novelists was a penetrating anxiety . . . that their social and moral world was being reduced to a warehouse of goods and commodities, a display window in which people, their actions and their convictions were exhibited for the economic appetites of others" (6). By taking the Marxian conception of the commodity as his point of departure, his concern is to suggest that "the Victorian novel provides us with the most graphic and enduring images of the power of commodities to affect the varied activities and attitudes of individual and social experience" (7). He contends that in *Our Mutual Friend* the

> home and, along with it, the space of writing, are presented as sanctuaries from the destructive energy of London's social and material environment. Represented by Dickens as effortless, writing and domesticity appear to be free from the mystification and emotional desiccation that attends the exchange of goods: this labor is not oppressive and its products are not occlusions. That these enclaves finally collapse means not only that writing and domestic life are subject to the routinization and commodication more characteristic of public spaces, but also that subjectivity itself can find no satisfying haven.      (10)

Although Miller is not interested in the gendering of that subjectivity or its detachment from foundations in quite the same way Poovey is, their conclusions about *Our Mutual Friend* complement each other nicely. For while Poovey is expanding her argument outward to include discourses of speculation and investment, the shifts in how that bourgeois domesticity operates, and the ways in which race is involved in issues of masculinity and national identity, Miller focuses on how the novel's narrative strategies structure enclaves that are heavily nostalgic. For him as for Poovey, Dickens is retreating from the fragmentation and reified relationships of the "modern" world. Miller's Dickens, however, constructs the domestic somewhat less nefariously than Poovey's. Miller reads Dickens' attempts at the construction of subjectivity as a means by which to exert control over a space, virtual or otherwise, that is ostensibly divorced from the exigencies of the market. But as Miller points out, this is at best a vexed effort for *Our Mutual Friend.* For instance, female subjectivity even when "domesticated" is also always informed by the very discourses which it seems to repudiate. Taking Eve Sedgwick's reading of Lizzie a step further, Miller argues for the predominance of exchange over sexuality via Luce Irigary's assertion that the libidinal economy between Eugene and Bradley is one based on the "circulation of women considered as goods." He goes on: "Erotic desire for Lizzie or between the two men is not absent in *Our Mutual Friend,* but the text presents Lizzie most fully as a symbol for qualities unrelated to sexuality: for Eugene, salvation; for Bradley, a danger to his status; for the pair of them an occasion for competition" (136). Thus, Miller argues, rather than signalling *merely* homoerotic desire between the two men, Lizzie comes to embody Dickens' attempts to manipulate an increasingly fragmented world. It is symptomatic of his own fetishizing as he attempts to ward off the effects of commodity fetishism. As Miller puts it

> Dickens' representation of women and the domestic provides a site for the volatile interplay between rationalization—the injunction to "keep things in their places," the desire to arrange women into a protecting home—and the "dissolution of the surrounding atmosphere. (138)

This sort of attempt at control is always being confronted by Dickens in his later work, for Miller contends that while the author attempted to see "writing as an imaginary space free from the capitalist exchange and the fragmentation of urban capitalism . . . fragmentation and reification" infiltrate not only "the body" but "the very substance and material of language itself" (151).

It is at this point that Miller's argument takes on the larger ramifications that apply to the thesis informing his entire book: commodity fetishism increasingly informs the act of Victorian novel writing even as that act attempts to expose the effects of commodification. In some ways, Miller falls victim to the incipient ethical humanism of his argument, and the essay almost longs for a time when the commodity did not hold sway over human relations or the production of literary texts. Despite seeming to place his own desires behind glass, however, Miller does a fine job detailing the important place *Our Mutual Friend* holds for what is often labeled the move toward "modernist" fiction. As Dickens' "domestic nature" struggles with the "surreality" of printing and circulation, their comingling inscribes the home "into a broad cultural discourse of moralizing domesticity, one that saw the organization of household objects as active elements in a narrative of improvement" (157).

It is this move toward regulating the fragmentation he cannot hold back that establishes *Our Mutual Friend* as unique of Dickens' work, a sort of last, only partially successful, attempt to assert authorial dominance and an enclave for the unified subject. "The creation of home," as Miller writes, "this imaginary space, must be rigorously defended, its order maintained so that the sovereign will residing within it can exercise its desires and picture things in their places" (158).

Another interesting, but less compelling, essay on *Our Mutual Friend* is Cathy Shuman's "Invigilating *Our Mutual Friend*: Gender and the Legitimation of Professional Authority." Shuman's argument runs a somewhat predictable Foucauldian route as well as takes up the issue of domesticity so important to Poovey's and Miller's essays. Shuman argues that this novel "provides a model of professional expertise, as valuable yet invaluable as domestic power, yet freed from its fragility" (154). Domesticity, in Shuman's account, is a failed discourse that gives way to professionalism. As the domestic is "demystified" it "plays a key role in mystifying and legitimating the professional's place in the Victorian economic system" (154). Professionalism in offering its own version of a doctrine of "separate spheres" makes "surprisingly unDickensian use of the growing Victorian state and its institutions" (154). She contends that it is through the examination "that paradigmatic form of interaction between the state and the intellectual worker" that this epistemic transformation is managed. And it is in the schoolroom and not the Victorian home that we find gender "reemerging as crucial" to the policing of these examinations. Finally, for Shuman, this "reemergence" helps to formulate a "borderland" between the economic and the extraeconomic that is also a space in which the division between the market and transcendence is blurred. And, it is the "testing of Bella—and Lizzie"—a knowledge, argues Shuman, not "easily subject to a valuation based on the labor theory of value."

While Shuman provides an interesting reading of this novel, some of her strategies seem suspect. For instance, in order for professionalism to establish itself over and against the domestic as the space of Victorian economic, and one must assume, political dominance, it first needs to write gender completely out of its functioning. Then it must take it up again as the *sine qua non* of its legitimation. This reinscription takes place in the schoolroom—a familiar Dickensian locale—and allows for a denigration of "masculine modes of transmitting knowledge" and for "granting women a special capability for blocking such transmissions. Femininity can then serve masculine professional authority by producing and containing a reified knowledge immune from the risks of exchange" (161). But are the risks of exchange ever minimized? And if so, does that minimization take place in the schoolroom, the courtroom, or any other "professional" sphere? Of course, this first question drives much of the recent criticism of this novel and cannot be resolved in this space. But suffice it to say that exchange and its attendant hazards inform nearly all of the relationships of this work, including the marriages. As Miller points out, in this novel no place seems truly outside the reification of relationships. Yet Shuman's argument that the "testing of Bella and Lizzie" provides an economics that "supplements the exchange of commodities with the finding and keeping of treasure" (169) assumes that these treasures "buried" in the women's hearts are somehow beyond either commodification or exchange. Here, through the gendered opposition of pedagogies the paradoxical "figuring of a reified knowledge that nevertheless escapes commodification" is somehow achieved (169). The question that obtains, however, is how? How is it that these activities are by definition extraeconomic? Mystifying and legitimating the professional by no means frees it from the rules of exchange. One of the most mystical aspects of Marxism is how commodities become fetishized, defining our intersubjectivity. Likewise, locating legitimating authority in the feminine does not extricate it from the market. After all, the marriage plot drives this novel, and as Miller points out, I think correctly, Lizzie is the *ne plus ultra* of commodities. The professional competition existing between Bradley and Eugene may be defined by gender and desire, but it is very difficult to imagine her as ever immune to the insistence of market valuation. Finally, while the commodification of knowledge may throw a monkey wrench into the concept of labor theories of value and may necessitate the sort of transcendental certainty that Lizzie represents for Shuman, that certainty itself is subject to exchange.

These theoretical difficulties are what makes Shuman's essay so interesting, and why I have given it so much attention here. It provides us with a reading between Poovey's and Miller's and investigates the connections between gender, the state, and the ubiquity of the effects of capitalism in a novel that has always been read as Dickens' attempt to establish a haven outside the market. Fascinating, then, that Shuman identifies that haven as the space which capitalism is having to come to immediate terms with.

Three notable books published in 1995—Deborah Nord's *Walking the Victorian Streets*, Elizabeth Langland's *Nobody's Angels,* and Dierdre David's *Rule Britannia* (all Cornell U.P.)— made important and distinct contributions to Dickens criticism. Although none of these books is "about" Dickens per se, each offers new readings of several of the works, and all read from the vantage point of gender studies. *Walking the Victorian Streets* provides one of the most provocative readings of *Sketches by Boz* in years. Concerned to examine the ways gender is used in the literary construction of the "middle-class city," Nord argues that not only did writers like the Dickens of *Sketches* begin to juxtapose a sense of distance from the lower orders with a new awareness of "possibilities for sympathizing, if not identifying with the poor,'' they also began to participate in the developing ''middle-class discourse about the presence on the city streets of the sexually tainted and victimized woman'' (51). Dickens' writerly involvement in the perception of the streets as a space of female licentiousness is particularly crucial to Nord's reading of the *Sketches,* for it buttresses her contention that gender acts as a kind of *cordon sanitaire* allowing the ''safe'' observation of the city's lower orders and their activities. According to Nord,

> Dickens deployed figures of female sexuality as a means to objectify, from an insulated point of view, urban pains that could be regarded as separate [from the experiences of the middle classes] but present. The female figure allows him simultaneously to isolate and to expose social misery: he quarantines that misery by sex and yet suggests the threat of contamination that women—particularly fallen women always represent. (51)

While Nord's observation about the fascination—revulsion of the middle classes with the lower urban orders is by no means a new argument—indeed it has been a critical pillar for commentary on early Dickens at least since *From Pickwick to Dombey*—her reading of the place of gender in this observational paradigm contributes importantly to our understanding of the complex ways that class, gender, and place combine to inform a representation of the early Victorian city. Unfortunately, despite the primary role gender plays in her argument, its discussion in the *Sketches* chapter is deferred longer than necessary. And while Nord's consideration of individual sketches is lucid and well informed, much of this seems very familiar ground. Another quibble I have with Nord's presentation is her elision of the difference between the visual and linguistic representations of the city that comprise the *Sketches.* Nord's discussion of the Cruikshank illustrations are instructive, but she seems too willing to consider them as nearly separate from Dickens' text.

Whatever the minor shortcomings of her discussions of *Sketches,* that chapter nicely sets up her argument about *Dombey and Son* and *Bleak House.* In these novels, contends Nord, the *cordon* has been breached by the very element that comprises it—women. The various threats of moral and physical contamination woven throughout *Dombey and Bleak House* are ''clustered around images of fallen female sexuality. . . . [T]he danger to middle-class survival and renewal is posed in the form of debased womanhood''; and ''the redemption of chaste reproductive female sexuality is prescribed as the antidote to middle-class barrenness and moral bankruptcy'' (84). As Nord points out, the suggestions of the connection between ''urban blight and sexual contamination'' that inform *Dombey's* narratives of Edith Granger and Alice Brown become ''the very machinery that drives *Bleak House*'' (96). As she astutely points out, female sexuality is not only ''central to representation of the dangers of the city, but also the nature of the relationship between the woman of the streets and the woman of the hearth became a social and symbolic question worth pondering'' (110). While both moral and physical contamination may be carried to "every quarter," it is through the "transformation of female sexuality itself" that the "social body may be restored to health" (111). Whether Esther's presence as "chaste daughter" whose sexuality is also ambiguous ultimately works to transform "female sexuality itself" and provide regeneration is a question that remains to be answered, however. Emphasizing the connection between the hearth and the streets through the sexuality of Lady Deadlock and Esther does allow the readers a useful insight into the novel's tracing of "the entire process from taint to purity, from a blighted female sexuality to the promise of nothing less than social regeneration" (111). But it is never entirely clear what form that regeneration takes. After all, Esther and Woodcourt retire to yet another "Bleak House," and there is little promise that the social body will be significantly transformed through the singular transformation of Esther. And while Woodcourt and Esther may indeed be able to produce and reproduce the middle-class haven that eludes Esther for most of the novel, there is no assurance that the forces of contamination that wreaked such havoc throughout the narrative can be successfully eradicated or even contained by the existence of a little island of bourgeois bliss.

Elizabeth Langland's *Nobody's Angels* discusses several of Dickens' later novels in terms of her thesis that the "angelic nature" of the heroines of *David Copperfield, Bleak House, Little Dorrit,* and *Our Mutual Friend* is informed by "a ready resourcefulness, energy, and efficiency" (81). And while these heroines' virtue first puts them "in possession" of the novels' heroes' love, it is only their "capacity for management that secures it permanently" (81). For Langland, Dickens "succinctly closes" the "gap between angel and manger" and links the success of domestic management with the hero's rise in the bourgeois world. Langland maps a sort of development of this trope in Dickens, beginning with the failure of domestic management in David's Dora—to be replaced by the much more capable Agnes Wickfield. In *Bleak House,* Esther's superior management skills are underscored even as the "nature of her work" is elided. For, argues Langland, "to reveal it is to introduce class issues prominently into the home-as-haven" (96). Instead, what we find is that Esther's skillful effacement of herself at the novel's end contributes to the "Victorian myth of the idle angel" (96). For Langland, this is immediately translatable into a class issue:

> The Victorian idealizations of home as outside of politics, as a refuge from strife, helped to facilitate its operation as a new base for struggle. Such idealizations, in which it is so easy for a public to participate because they feed into stereotypes of women, inevitably work to consolidate upper-middle-class centrality and power, separating the genteel both from the working classes who serve them, and the lower middle classes, who emulate them.          (97).

This is particularly well born out for Langland in her discussion of *Little Dorrit* and its eponymous heroine. Just as in *Copperfield* or *Bleak House,* when the alternative suitor is rejected in favor of the novel's hero, it is in large measure a choice between vulgarity—the lower middle class who emulates—(Heep, Guppy, Chivery) and the genteel—the solidly middle class (David, Woodcourt, Clennam). As Langland says, "of course the heroine is only following her heart; where she 'loves' she marries. . . . Fortunately, the heroine always 'falls in love' with an entrepreneurial individual of the gentrified middle class, a man of some delicacy and distinction, who must, nonetheless, make his own way in the world with the help of a pragmatic and experienced household manager" (97). Bella Wilfer represents a distinction in the development of this trope, however, for she must be taught both the importance of signifying status and skill at "managing a position." With her Harmon successfully undertakes the task that David Copperfield could not—the training of his mate in the intricacies of domestic management. Unlike Agnes, Esther, and Amy, Bella is not necessarily a "natural" domestic manager. Nor does she have the inherent grace with which to manage the social skills necessary to maintain her and her husband's place in "respectable society." She must be taught, and her resistance to learning must be overcome. It is in this teaching, and its effects, as well as in the representation of the "partnership" aspect of middle-class marriage that Langland identifies the importance of Dickens' contribution. His ability to "dramatize the clash between patriarchal ideology with its gender bifurcations and bourgeois ideology with its class bifurcations" give the reader "brilliant glimpses" into the "pragmatic side of middle-class marriage" (112). For Langland, the middle-class wife ultimately becomes "the figure whose mystifications protect patriarchal privilege with its rhetoric of dominance and subservience, while her disciplining presence at home and colonizing effect abroad secure England as a haven for the bourgeoisie" (112).

Dierdre David's new book, *Rule Britannia: Women, Empire, and Victorian Writing,* examines precisely those connections between English fiction of the Victorian period and that "colonizing" effect. In her chapter on *The Old Curiosity Shop* and *Dombey and Son,* David is concerned to show how these two novels,

> in order to shape some discursive insurance that Britain's heart continues to tick steadfastly, regularly, and in rhythm with the pulse of imperial expansion, appropriate[s] culturally available images of women as suffering salvational figures. Gender, in other words, conjoins with race in subordinating millions of indigenous peoples to Britannic rule and maintaining women in their private sphere (44).

Here David's argument is a bit at odds with Langland's, for while Langland identifies certain aspects of formative power, indeed agency, of class formation in the private sphere, David's concern is to read the power of the imperial project as an important contributor to the maintenance of domesticity. Read together, David's and Langland's books offer an interesting dialogue on the constitutive function of imperial discourse in regards to gender and the multiple possibilities available for reading the intersection of gender, the domestic sphere, and the masculinized sphere of public politics in the Victorian era.

Perhaps the most intriguing aspect of David's Dickens chapter is her choice of texts. While *Dombey and Son* is immediately recognizable in its imperialist trappings, *The Old Curiosity Shop* is another matter entirely. Yet, David's reading is not only persuasive, it is extremely subtle in its attentiveness to issues of race and colonization in a novel that, at least at first, and perhaps second, blush seems to have little to do with imperialism. David's reading of Quilp within the Victorian popular fascination with cannibals and exhibitions of indigenous peoples asserts him as a figure of the "authentic savage" by whom Dickens was nearly viscerally repelled. For David, "Quilp is a dark demonic force whose destruction allegorically requires the suffering and death of an English girl. . . . In *The Old Curiousity Shop,* eradication of male barbarism is accompanied by the forfeiture of female life, or to suggest how Victorian ideas of gender get affiliated with Victorian ideas of race, native savagery can be tamed only by the sacrifice of Englishwomen" (63). And just as Quilp is nightmarishly, imaginatively "present" at Little Nell's death, so too, argues David, does Dickens view the changes brought on by Britain's empire building as both inescapable and eventually ruinous. This metaphorical presence of the effect of empire is more directly asserted in *Dombey and Son,* and once again it devours women, body and soul. Florence Dombey's pain, like Nell's, is symbolic of the sacrificial place that the discourse of empire creates for the middle-class English woman. In order for the elder Dombey (and by extension, therefore, the House of Dombey) to flourish economically, he must be dependent on Florence domestically, to be sure, but must also repudiate her, if necessary by force and by striking her. For David this—and Nell's death—symbolize, in part, "the actual suffering demanded of women in the work of creating Britannic rule" (75).

Daniel Born's book, *The Birth of Liberal Guilt in the English Novel* (U of North Carolina P), offers an interesting, if not completely persuasive, reading of *Little Dorrit.* For Born, *Little Dorrit* (and *Daniel Deronda*) mark the "beginnings of guilty liberal awareness in the English novel" (35). It is in these, he argues, that we have an early example of how the "best novelists" turn "middle-class moralizing inward," forcing ethical "self-reflection." He goes on to assert that "the radical effect is to impose upon their audience the necessity of enlarging its sense of social breakdown to encompass social not merely individual terms of explanation'' (34). While I have no significant difficulties with Born's reading of the novel, he entangles himself in quite a mare's nest by claiming an ''originary'' place for liberal guilt in any particular novel or group of novels of the period. Claiming Arthur Clennam as the first novelistic hero to bear the heavy burden of liberal guilt, he essentially pinpoints the spot from which we can begin to read the English novel as invested not only in social change but as also accepting some of the responsibility for the opprobrium that existed as a result of the effects of industrialization and capitalism. While his argument for Clennam as a new sort of Dickens character is compelling, Born is not entirely persuasive in his insistence that he also marks the beginning of the articulation of the self-consciousness of middle-class culpability for lower-class hardships in the nineteenth century. Born reads the ''sociological'' literature of the age, from Peter Gaskell and J. P. Kay-Shuttleworth onward, with a rather uncritical eye. Consequently, he is all too ready to offer a somewhat underdetermined evaluation of this work as wholly centered in an individualistic morality in which prostitution, crime, and poverty are completely linked to the failures of the individual. And while this hypothesis certainly held important interpretive sway, even among utilitarians new explanations, often based on material conditions of life, were emerging even in the early 1840s. The links between these Royal and Parliamentary investigative reports and the social problem novels has been discussed thoroughly in a number of places, and for Born to forego a more considered discussion of the social problem novel and its relation to liberal guilt seems a major omission. Another difficulty I had with Born's book is its lack of a consistent definition of his use of the concept of ''liberal guilt.'' Clennam, as the example of a character who takes on the responsibility of his class (and his family's) actions, works well enough, but it is difficult to extend that example beyond *Little Dorrit.* Consequently, Born's characterization of liberal guilt seems to function only at the level of the intellectual, and he does not consider in any detail how it might function in a broader, constitutive way: such as how Casby uses it to enforce his power or how it operates in Pancks exposure of that ''benevolent patriarch.''

*Bleak House* received a bit less attention this year than in the past, but three works that deal with that novel deserve to be mentioned here: Carolyn Dever's ''Broken Mirror, Broken Words: Autobiography, Prosopeia, and the Dead Mother in *Bleak House*,'' in *Studies in the Novel* 27.1; Peter Thoms' '' 'The Narrow Track of Blood': Detection and Storytelling in *Bleak House*, in *Nineteenth-Century Literature* 50.2 and the chapter on *Bleak House* in Ilinca Zarifopol-Johnston's *To Kill a Text: The Dialogic Fiction of Hugo, Dickens, and Zola* (U of Delaware P). Dever's essay, as the title implies, investigates the connections between Esther's first-person narration and her ''losses'' of her mother through the course of the novel. For Dever, these losses—of which there are three—confront Esther with her own implication in her abandonment. According to Dever, "the extent to which Esther consents to and even comes to desire loss is directly proportional to her ability to master the terms of the autobiographical narrative" (42). Her ability to "represent herself as a subject, as an agent, is dependent on her status as a mourner" (42). The theoretical implications of Esther as willing and even participant "victim" of abandonment invite further elaboration, but Dever is less interested in exploring Esther's not-so-latent masochism than she is with the rhetorical conventions that force the ambiguity of her subjectivity. Dever argues that rhetoric insistently precedes embodiment and that Esther's "autobiographical articulation signals a form of agency: if she is capable of articulation she is capable of existence" (48–49). This, as Dever points out, is especially important for a character whose narrative of subjectivity begins with the presumption that she had "never to [her] own mother's knowledge breathed—had been buried—had never been endowed with life—had never borne a name." And while Esther uses language to make "something of nothing," to affirm or at least assert her existence in the absence of the body of her mother, her subjectivity, as Dever states, remains ambiguous in the highest degree: "Esther is surely the uncanniest homemaker in Victorian fiction; every aspect of her identity, from name to face to family to motivation, remains unfixed and unlocatable." The consequence, she argues, is that "in his location in Esther of an ideal of domesticity, Dickens deconstructs a traditional ethic of stability and constancy" (51).

In comparison to Dever's description of Esther's creation of herself in terms of maternal lack and the constitutive primacy of rhetoric is Peter Thoms article, which focuses on a similar, yet divergent, effect of "storytelling" within the novel. If Esther, through her telling is trying to uncover the mystery of her subjectivity, a mystery which, as Dever tell us, is only contingently and ambiguously resolved, as well as to assert her own agency, then Inspector Bucket attempts a similar sort of narrative authority. Thoms argues that in Bucket's attempts to follow the "narrow track of blood" to the explanation of Tulkinghorn's, the detective also is establishing the narrative "boundaries" of that track. He "desires" to possess the entire story of the murder but also he "craves more localized authority over the individual"— exemplified in the case he builds against Hortense (148). For Thoms, the desire of the characters who ferret out secrets, whether Tulkinghorn, Bucket—and one might even assume, though Thoms does not consider it at any length, Esther—is a desire for narrative itself and the power narrative holds over other characters. Of course this places Esther in a somewhat unique position, for not only is she a detective, but she is also the object of interest, the ultimate clue, the one for whom there is most at stake narratively. Yet for those like Bucket, Tulkinghorn, and even Vholes, there is an almost perfidious—or at least amoral—aspect to their desire for narrative, as Thoms indicates when he cites Tulkinghorn's comment to Lady Dedlock that her "discovered past is 'my secret' and not 'your secret' " (149). Thoms reads this as a nearly cannibalistic desire, since the upshot of possessing such knowledge is also to possess power over the "private identity" of another (149), a kind of consumption of the other that is metaphorically signified through tropes of ingestion marking everyone from Bucket, Vholes, and Tulkinghorn to the reporters who scribble down the story of Krook's blazing demise with their "ravenous little pens." Some characters like Lady Dedlock and Nemo are aware of the connection between their identities and their narratives and seek to conceal (Thoms writes "censor") their own stories from public consumption. To own one's story, apparently is to own one's subjectivity. Thus Esther's attempt at autobiography. Yet, again, Esther runs the risk of revealing herself and giving herself up for public consumption. Her autobiography, then, is contradictory and must fall somewhat short of resolving her need for solidifying her status as subject. She may "write" her story, much as Bucket writes the crime, but she also exposes herself. She both asserts and abdicates agency and identity.

Ilinca Zarifopol-Johnston's book, *To Kill a Text: The Dialogic Fiction of Hugo, Dickens, and Zola* contains two chapters on *Bleak House* and each focuses on the work as an anomaly: a novelistic hybrid outside of traditional poetics, a text that insists upon its multivocity rather than on its continuity. Interestingly, while Zarifopol-Johnston suggests the potential productivity of a discussion of the status of the conflict and supplementation of *Bleak House*'s two main narratives, she seems more concerned to concentrate on Esther's narrative. She writes that "[h]ad narrative discourse in *Bleak House* not been dialogized, Esther's own discourse, her narration, would have been illegitimate, an ill-fitting element, which probably would have been dropped out of the novel after a few tries, just as the first-person narration is abandoned in *The Old Curiosity Shop*." She goes on to suggest that the third-person narrative, what she calls the "author's narration," functions negatively while Esther's has a positive function—offering access to the "Other" on its own terms and allowing Dickens to "go beyond subversion" (137). This theoretical movement back and forth between a seemingly strict formalism and authorial intent disrupts Zarifopol-Johnston's own discourse. She grants Esther a kind of uncanny intersubjectivity that is unavailable to the authorial, except through Esther. Yet, Zarifopol-Johnston fails either to expand that assertion toward a biographical critique of Dickens' relation to his characters or to contain her discussion within the realm of the text itself. It is always a tricky business when one dwells on the line between characters as functions of narrative discourse and sources of their own production. And while Thoms and Dever accomplish it with some aplomb, Zarifopol-Johnston's particular use of Bakhtin does not allow her the kind of flexibility she needs to move easily between how and what the text does.

A year-in-review of Dickens studies would be a rather threadbare one without something by J. Hillis Miller to consider. Fortunately, Miller offers up a fine contribution in his "Sam Weller's Valentine," which appears in *Literature in the Marketplace* (Cambridge UP), edited by John O. Jordan and Robert L. Patten. Taking the instance of Weller's valentine in *Pickwick Papers,* Miller asks a number of questions about the performative aspect of valentines, poetry, novels, and utterances such as "Chops and Tomata sauce." Miller leads the reader through a fascinating nutshell history of valentines, from the Middle Ages to their place in Victorian culture, including their involvement with patent and copyright laws, and placing them, appropriately, with other public performatives such as wedding vows and christenings. He points out, via Derrida and de Man, that "performatives always exceed the intentions of their performers. They do not depend on intention for their efficacy. A performative always makes something happen, but it by no means always makes happen what the one who utters it intends or expects" (112–13). Sam Weller is completely aware of this fact; consequently, he signs Pickwick's rather than his own name to the valentine. As he tells his father who counsels him to sign it "Veller," "Won't do. . . . Never sign a walentine with your own name." Nevertheless, Sam ends up getting married—"performing" the valentine—despite his attempts to shirk the responsibility of his utterance. Likewise, concludes Miller, *Pickwick Papers* as a whole is a performative, exceeding "Dickens's intentions. It was radically improvisatory. Dickens had no idea where the story would go when he began writing it" (119). And while it "represents a whole range of English institutions and forms of behavior" as well as the "the narrative, dramatic, and even poetic conventions available to Dickens," it also "brings into the open those elements' absurdity and their potential for causing harm," thereby putting "in question the repertoire of features making up English ideology at the moment of Victoria's accession to the throne" (119).

While all of the articles in the Jordan and Patten collection are worthwhile and will be of interest to Dickensians, Robert Patten's contribution "Serialized Retrospection in *The Pickwick Papers*" is especially noteworthy for its rethinking of the usual analysis of serialization. Although he gives the view that Victorian serials are "forward looking and time-specific" its due, Patten argues that "[p]aradoxically *Pickwick* gains propulsion as a story and a commercial venture from its suffusion of pastness, and it speaks to and about its contemporaries by articulating a nostalgia for previous modes of discursive practice, feeling, and social organization" (124). Patten's argument skillfully weaves publication history and close reading of the novel to make his case. For Patten, "developing an appetite for the past, in a sense battening on moldy graves like the ivy green, was one secret of the success of serial fiction" (138). And *Pickwick,* Patten concludes, is in many ways, "the first text to discover, play with, and anatomize the retrospective potential of serialization.''

Another collection that Dickens scholars will find of interest is *Victorian Literature and the Victorian Visual Imagination* (U of California P) edited by Carol T. Christ and John O. Jordan. Like the *Literature in the Marketplace* collection, these essays are longer versions of papers originally given at the annual conference sponsored by the University of California Dickens Project. And as in the "Marketplace" collection, Dickens often has a prominent place even in those essays that are not directly about him or his work. As the editors write, many of the essays "locate in Dickens the paradigmatic writer" for their argument. As they point out, in his "partnership with illustrators, in his pictorialization of narrative, in his fascination with optical gadgetry, and in his uncanny anticipation of twentieth-century cinema, Dickens more than any other nineteenth-century writer, provides insight into the multiple aspects of the Victorian visual imagination" (xxvii).

One of the essays that *is* specifically about a Dickens text is Audrey Jaffe's "Spectacular Sympathy: Visuality and Ideology in Dickens's *A Christmas Carol.*" In this fine essay, Jaffe argues for what she understands to be the "circular relation that obtains between, on the one hand, spectacular forms of cultural representation, and, on the other, persons objects, or scenes, invested with ideological value and thus already surrounded in their cultural contexts with an aura of spectacle" (328). As she points out in her reading of the story, Dickens' "representational frames" that he uses "to set fantasy apart from reality—the dynamics that give *A Christmas Carol* its mythic or fairy-tale quality—turn out to be fully operative in the 'real' world" (334). The world is a spectacle, a series of frames, not far different from those scenes that Scrooge observes. And not only is the world an image, but "it is an image in which spectators seek to see themselves" (334). Of course they do see themselves as subjects constituted in this "imaginary lived relation to the real," a relation that is defined by the commodity form. Yet Jaffe does not claim "that the commodity form dominates culture, but rather that commodity culture draws its power from its status as an exemplary form of culture—its identity with a culture as a system of representations" (343, n16). Jaffe implies that in participating in "spectacular sympathy," Scrooge becomes completely interpellated by commodity culture, for it is from this culture that he has been absent: "his failure to participate in human fellowship is signaled by his refusal of, and need to learn, a gift giving defined as the purchase and exchange of commodities" (338). The upshot, she remarks, is that in capturing "the commodity's potential for sympathy, the story constitutes itself as an endlessly sympathetic commodity." As such, *A Christmas Carol* "returns annually" with an "emphasis (and relentlessness) it has itself projected" (340).

John Sutherland also weighs in with a fascinating contribution in his *Victo-rian Fiction: Writers, Publishers, Readers* (St. Martin's). As usual, Sutherland mines an extraordinarily rich vein in his examination of the circumstances surrounding particular publication events during the Victorian period. In his chapter, "Dickens, Reade, *Hard Cash* and Manic Wives," he moves nicely through Dickens' wooing of Reade as a novelist for *All the Year Round* and the difficulties that attended successful courtship. Then, working on this very image of courting and wedding, he skillfully draws the links between the novel's plot, which deals with the treatment of the mentally ill in English lunatic asylums, and Bulwer-Lytton's, Thackeray's, and Dickens' marriages, all of which had very real encounters with Victorian "bedlams." Sutherland's treatment of the three novelists' marriages tacitly implies an equal culpability in their treatment of their wives, though he often must make these evaluations in the face of less than overwhelming corroboration. For instance, while it appears nearly irrefutable that Rosina Lytton's temporary confinement and Dickens' complaints of Catherine's "motherly indifference" and "mental disorder" were indeed instances of powerful men attempting to rid themselves of what they considered troublesome spouses, Thackeray was almost certainly not acting under the same impulse. Rather, there is evidence to suggest that Isabella Thackeray was indeed mentally ill and that her husband struggled with his decision to "remove Isabella from his life" (67). Yet despite my minor complaint, this chapter, like his "Dickens's Serializing Imitators" chapter, which chronicles the rise and fall of serial publication, offers wonder-ful starting points for further investigation of the "culture" of novel publish-ing during the Victorian period.

As I have already noted, 1995 saw a relative dearth of books on Dickens, though Robert Patten's magisterial biography of Cruikshank (Rutgers UP, 1996) deserves much attention from Dickens scholars. It is a fascinating read for anyone interested in the life of this compelling figure. It is exhaustively researched, a treasure of details, yet wonderfully and imaginatively written. This study is bound to bring Cruikshank the broader attention he deserves as well as to serve as the authoritative biography for years to come. Patten's knowledge of his subject is, at times, overwhelming in its scope. He seems to have read not only everything that Cruikshank ever wrote, but to have become completely familiar with everything that has been written about him. This is a welcome addition to Dickens scholarship and *George Cruikshank's Life, Times, and Art* will become a standard for all Dickensians.

John Reed also turns in a notable effort on Dickens with his *Dickens and Thackeray: Punishment and Forgiveness* (Ohio UP). Unfortunately, the thesis of this book is not particularly well stated, nor is it entirely clear why Dickens and Thackeray are studied together except that they were so often paired during their own times. Reed is attempting to examine "certain underlying assumptions affecting the creation of texts.'' Those assumptions, as they are set out in three introductory chapters on ''punishment and forgiveness in moral texts,'' ''education,'' and ''legal punishment'' fail to fix the immediacy of the issues that Reed is focusing on, though it does become apparent that Reed is concerned with examining these two contemporary authors together in light of secularized Christian attitudes toward the treatment of criminals and the social goal of ''justice tempered with mercy.'' Not surprisingly, he finds that Thackeray and Dickens treat their shadier characters and those characters' crimes quite differently. For Dickens, there seems to be a need to ''hunt down'' villains like Carker or Sykes or Headstone, whereas Thackeray's characters' sins are ''discovered.'' The relative success or failure of the secrecy of their perfidy serves as a kind of vindication, and they often escape the spectacular ends that Dickens' characters come to. Instead of the deus ex machina punishment visited on Dickens' wrongdoers, Thackeray's miscreants ''do not require a specific agent of justice to punish them for their folly, since folly begets its own consequences'' (341). Reed's book is divided into three sections—the early introductory sections that I have already mentioned, which are chock full of the kind of strong historical analysis that has marked Reed's career—a section on Dickens' novels with a chapter devoted to each, and another, less lengthy section on Thackeray's work. While this is a very straightforward and utilitarian way of organizing his material, Reed may have been better served to intersperse his discussion of the two authors. As it stands, this text reads like two books sutured together by a common, and very large, thematic. Further, the structure of the book often leads its argument into unnecessary repetition. Despite the book's weaknesses, however, there is much to recommend it. The readings of *Barnaby Rudge* and the Christmas books, texts often overlooked today, are refreshing and useful. And its scrupulous attention to the plot details of both Dickens' and Thackeray's works reminds one of how appealing good close reading can be.

Another book that takes up somewhat the same theme, but from a more overtly theorized position, is Jeremy Tambling's *Dickens, Violence and the Modern State:Dreams of the Scaffold* (St. Martin's). For Tambling,

> Dickens needs to be put alongside not those writers who have more allegiance than he to Victorian social order and attitudes—Thackeray, Trollope, Tennyson, Arnold, Mill, George Eliot—but with those more uncomfortable with it, such as the Brontës, and those outside that ideology altogether (13).

Obviously in many ways directly at odds with Reed, Tambling constructs a Dickens who has been recuperated—mostly by American criticism—both as resistant to what Tambling rather blithely refers to as Victorian ideology—and as emblematic of it. For those readers familiar with the works of Steven

Marcus, J. Hillis Miller, Lawrence Frank, and D. A. Miller, this does not come as particularly startling news. And Tambling is frank enough about his indebtedness to these critics' work. The book's first half deals with what Tambling calls Dickens' responses to "modernism." Reading *Great Expectations, Dombey and Son, Bleak House,* and *Little Dorrit,* Tambling contends that Dickens' reactions to "modernity" were ambiguous and often internally contradictory, but that at bottom Dickens' Britain is "a subject for an archaeology and anatomy, but is static, has no possibility of forward movement unless a 'password' can be found" (15). In the second half of his book, he is more concerned to examine what he calls Dickens' "complex reactionary stance towards the violence of the state," even as he colludes with those strategies in ways that Tambling describes as "repressive, violent, even proto-fascist." This is a fascinating thesis, though it hardly marks Dickens as unique. Many of the writers of the period struggled with exactly these issues, the consequence being not only the mishmash of Victorian political agenda that could see Utlitarians and Evangelicals forming coalitions to reach shared goals (for very different reasons), but also the contradictions articulated in modern and late-modern liberal politics. Tambling's book, placing Dickens as an important progenitor of modernism (despite literary modernism's fairly broad repudiation of him), dovetails nicely with earlier estimations of Dickens' ambivalence about the possibility and definition of social "progress." And though the readings of the novels sometimes strain to fit Tambling's thesis, they are substantial and well grounded enough to merit consideration.

Perhaps the major work on Dickens for 1995 is one that is not a critical text at all: George Newlin's three-volume *Everyone in Dickens* (Greenwood). This is truly an amazing and welcome compilation. Need a little brushing up on "The Seven Poor Travellers" or "The Perils of Certain English Prisoners?" Not quite clear on what a "German merchant" or "hoveller" is? You can find this information in Newlin's *Everyone.* Up-to-date and computer compiled, this concordance/index/glossary should be on the bookshelves of anyone who regularly reads or writes about Dickens (and who can afford the hefty price tag). Newlin covers plot lines, publication histories, character lists, taxonomies by occupations and vocations of characters, their relationships to other characters, their status (named or walk on, full names or only first or surnames). It really is a compendium of "everyone" in Dickens and is one of the most useful indexes I have ever worked with. If you can afford it, buy it; if you can't afford it, memorize the call number for you will certainly be using it.

## Other Works of Interest to Dickens Scholars

Adams, James Eli. "The Hero as Spectacle: Carlyle and the Persistance of Dandyism." *Victorian Literature and the Victorian Visual Imagination.* Ed. Carol T. Christ and John O. Jordan. Berkeley: U of California P, 1995. 213–32.

Bennett, Rachel. "Hajji and Mermaid in *Little Dorrit.*" *Review of English Studies: A Quarterly Journal of English Literature and the English Language* 46.182:174–90.

Bottum, Joseph. "The Gentleman's True Name: *David Copperfield* and the Philosophy of Naming." *Nineteenth-Century Literature.* 49.4:435–55.

Clayton, Jay. "Londublin: Dickens' London in Joyce's Dublin." *Novel: A Forum on Fiction.* 28.3:327–42.

Elfenbein, Andrew. "Managing the House in *Dombey and Son*: Dickens and the Uses of Analogy." *Studies in Philology.* 92.3:361–82.

Gervais, David. "Dickens's Comic Speech: Inventing the Self." *Yearbook of English Studies.* 25:128–40.

Hecimovich, Gregg A. "The Cup and the Lip and the Riddle of *Our Mutual Friend.*" ELH, 62.4:955–77.

Levy, Eric P. "Dickens' Pathology of Time in *Hard Times.*" *Philological Quarterly.* 74.2:189–207.

Mugglestone, Lynda. "Fictions of Speech: Literature and the Literate Speaker in the Nineteenth-Century Novel." *Yearbook of English Studies.* 25:114–27.

Stein, Richard L. "Street Figures: Victorian Urban Iconography." *Victorian Literature and the Victorian Visual Imagination.* Ed. Carol T. Christ and John O. Jordan. Berkeley: U of California P, 1995. 233–63.

Thomas, Ronald R. "Making Darkness Visible: Capturing the Criminal and Observing the Law in Victorian Photography and Detective Fiction." *Victorian Literature and the Victorian Visual Imagination.* Ed. Carol T. Christ and John O. Jordan, Berkeley, U of California P, 1995. 134–68.

Wolfreys, Julian. "Dickensian Architextures or, the City and the Ineffable." *Victorian Identities: Social and Cultural Formations in Nineteenth-Century Literature,* ed. Ruth Robbins and Julian Wolfreys. St. Martin's, 1995. 199–214.

# Index

## DATE DUE

| | | |
|---|---|---|
| | | |
| | | |
| | | |
| | | |
| | | |
| | | |
| | | |
| | | |
| | | |
| | | |
| | | |
| | | |
| | | |
| | | |
| | | |
| | | |
| | | |

GAYLORD     #3523PI     Printed in USA